The Rediscovery of the Highest Good

A Philosophical and Critical Ethic

Stuart C. Hackett

THE REDISCOVERY OF THE HIGHEST GOOD
A Philosophical and Critical Ethic

Copyright © 2009 Stuart C. Hackett. All rights reserved. Except for brief quotations in critical publications or reviews, no part of this book may be reproduced in any manner without prior written permission from the publisher. Write: Permissions, Wipf and Stock Publishers, 199 W. 8th Ave., Suite 3, Eugene, OR 97401.

Wipf & Stock
A Division of Wipf and Stock Publishers
199 W. 8th Ave., Suite 3
Eugene, OR 97401

www.wipfandstock.com

ISBN 13: 978-1-60608-155-6

Manufactured in the U.S.A.

Contents

I. Introduction: The Concept of Moral Philosophy:
   Its Meaning and Methodology 1
   The Nature and Importance of Moral Inquiry 1
   The General Philosophical Context of Ethics 5
   The Principal Aspects of Philosophical Ethics 8

Part I: Meta-Ethics: The Meaning, Logical Status, and Context of Moral Discourse

II. General Meta-Ethical Theories:
    Cognitivism vs. Non-Cognitivism 17
    The Principal Task of Meta-Ethical Analysis 17
    A Classification of the Principal Meta-Ethical Theories 21

III. Meta-Ethical Cognitivism 25
     Intuitionism: A Distinctionist Stance 42

IV. Meta-Ethical Non-Cognitivism 63
    Non-Cognitivism as a General Meta-Ethical Position 63
    David Hume: Descriptive Relativism 65
    A. J. Ayer and C. L. Stevenson:
       Meta-Ethical Emotivism or Attitudinalism 73
    Qualified Objectivist Non-Cognitivism:
       The 'Good Reasons' Approach and the Ideal Moral Observer 81
    Conclusion Concerning General Meta-Ethical Theories 103

V. Determinism, Personal Freedom, and Moral
   Responsibility: A Meta-Ethical Postscript 107
   Statement of the Problems 108
   A Proposed Resolution of the Problems Concerning Determinism,
      Personal Freedom, and Moral Responsibility 123
   Arguments in Support of the Agent Causality View of
      Personal Freedom 128
   Criticisms of the Agent Causality View of Personal Freedom
      (and Response to Those Criticisms) 145
   General Meta-Ethical Conclusions 164

Part II: Normative (Substantive) Ethics: Alternative Conceptions of the Ultimate Moral Ideal

VI. The Principal Classifications of Normative Ethical Theories 169
The Central Concerns of Normative Ethics 169
A Proposed Scheme of Classification for Normative Ethical Theories... 174

VII. Normative Ethical Naturalism 177
Hedonistic Naturalism 178
Humanistic Naturalism 202
Realistic Humanism: Aristotle 205
Pragmatic Humanism: John Dewey 220
Existential Humanism: Jean-Paul Sartre 236
Evolutionary Humanism: Friedrich Nietzsche 248
Religious Naturalism: Baruch (Benedict) Spinoza 262

VIII. Normative Ethical Idealism 279
The Metaphysical Orientation in Ethical Idealism:
  Plato's Essentialism 281
Absolute Idealism: G.W.F. Hegel and F.H. Bradley 297
The Postulational Orientation in Ethical Idealism: Immanuel Kant..... 314

IX. Normative Ethical Theism 339
The General Theistic Perspective in Ethics 339
Augustine on Goodness, Freedom, and Evil 342
Aquinas on Nature, Grace, and Moral Law 357
Kierkegaard on Subjectivity and Purity of Heart 370

X. In Retrospective Reflection: An Epilogue 383

Index 387

The Rediscovery of the Highest Good

Chapter I

Introduction: The Concept of Moral Philosophy: Its Meaning and Methodology

The Nature and Importance of Moral Inquiry

It is the destiny of every human person to decide. Whether our choices are genuinely free or inevitably determined, invariably trivial or occasionally momentous, carelessly settled or reflectively reasoned, at least in one sense all this makes no difference: for the one thing about which persons have no choice is that we unavoidably and necessarily must choose, and cannot therefore escape our responsibility to do so. That is not to say that an individual's scope for choice is all-encompassing: many of our choices are made for us by our natural environment, by our biological heritage, by our family context, by the authority of other persons, by the structure of our society, by the relentless pressure of our education and upbringing, and by incalculably extended other influences that hem us in on every side and tie us down in every situation. And yet, although our destiny of choice is in this way not all-encompassing, nevertheless it is all-pervasive in the sense that, just in proportion as we become reflectively self-conscious, we can decide how to respond to all these strictures on our freedom, what attitude to assume toward this vast web of limitation, and to what extent we can actually use its dependable framework as a ladder on which to ascend toward what at least appear to us to be significant

1.1) The human destiny of choice

1.1a) Significant choice cannot be avoided.

1.1b) But the scope of choice is not unlimited since it is restricted by both heredity and environment.

1.1c) Yet the self can exercise freedom in relation to these restraints:
1.1c1) by deciding what attitude to assume toward them, and
1.1c2) by using them as a framework within which to make free choices.

goals. And in this process, we may well discover that the chains which seem on every hand to confine us, provide rather an unimaginable extension for the scope of our decision and choice, precisely because the links of those chains can themselves exist only by providing an endless succession of spaces that proportionally enlarge the scope of our decisions and choice. It may even be reasonable to claim that without the provocation of limits there could be no occasion to choose, and, in that sense, no freedom; so that perhaps Hegel was right in saying that the truth of freedom is necessity (and vice versa), although I am not certain whether he would agree with the meaning I have suggested for the words. And it is probably also the case that most of us have no legitimate complaint against our constraining bonds, since we have barely begun to take advantage of the slack that those bonds provide us. It is indeed therefore our destiny to decide. Nor can we excuse ourselves by suggesting that, for all we know with the whole of science at our disposal, our decisions and choices make no substantive difference. There are indeed many choices that can be reasonably classified as trivial in the sense that none of the alternatives involved seem likely to produce any consequentially different effect as over against the other choices: an orange or a grapefruit for breakfast, a symphony or an opera for a relaxing musical interlude, paddle ball or tennis for some rigorous exercise; but other choices bid fair to make enormous consequential difference, as in the choice of a life vocation, a spouse, or some particular medical treatment or surgery. And sometimes these major choices are themselves conditioned by previous decisions that seem comparatively trivial. If I had not decided to be at a certain place in Elyria, Ohio, on a particular evening in 1945, I would not have met the woman who has now been my wife for more than forty years. So we can never be confident about the consequences of even the options that seem essentially trivial and indifferent at the time. But more importantly (because apparently more under our considered control), the claim that one's decisions and choices as a whole make no significant difference is not only descriptively false, but is itself a choice that generates virtually incalculable consequences drastically different from those that would conceivably follow from choosing to believe that one's options are, in fact,

1.1d) It may be that restraint is a necessary condition for the possibility of genuine choice.

1.1e) Even choices that appear trivial can turn out to be of great consequence in their results.

1.2) The claim that choices are of no ultimate consequence is itself an attitudinal decision of the very sort that the claim denies.

of great moment. A life guided by rationally directed choice will clearly be very different from one governed by the passive indifference generated by the assumption that no choice ever really makes any significant difference. Hence, the indifference view is self-contradictory by constituting a clear exception to its own claim.

Decision and choice are therefore inescapable; and an indeterminate number of them are of the highest importance because they involve drastically different life consequences. Many more than two roads diverge in the yellow woods of even an average person's lived experience; and however nobly we may strive to keep our options open, there is a sense in which each substantive choice leaves all of its alternatives behind forever. To become reflectively self-conscious about all this is *ipso facto* to raise the question whether and to what extent our substantive choices can be rationally self-directed by ourselves as personal agents; and it is at the same time to raise the immediately ensuing questions as to what end, principle, or standard should logically serve reason as a framework for this self-direction. But here an important distinction emerges between goals or ends that are relative to one's personal uniqueness, capacities, propensities, preferences, and other such individually variable factors, on the one hand; and goals or ends that (if I may employ a mode of language at which some may strain) pertain to our common human essence, to our status just as personal agents capable of rational self-reflection, to our mere humanness as such. The outworking and realization of our personal idiosyncrasies and distinctive qualities, capacities, and talents is also the work of rational self-direction; and the common ends of our humanness may involve principles and procedures that provide guidance in the actualization of our distinctive individual propensities, so that our common essence invades and pervades, as it were, the domain of our individuality. But the more fundamental question concerns the point, purpose, and direction of our sheer being as persons. What then is incumbent upon me, not being musically inclined or athletically gifted or mentally brilliant, but rather by dint of my mere being as a human person? It is, in my opinion, this general sort of question, together with all its elaborated details, with which moral philosophy or philosophical ethics is concerned. Decisions and choices

1.2a) Choices are therefore both inescapable and significantly consequential, especially since every choice closes off all its contemplated alternatives.

1.3) Can choice be rationally self-directed by means of a justifiable standard?

1.3a1) Reason is the agent for the pursuit of both as interacting with each other.
1.3a2) But the goals of personhood as such are more fundamental.

1.3b) Moral philosophy may be plausibly viewed as concerned primarily with our common status as persons.

1.3b1) As such, it is concerned with clarification and analysis, as well as direction and motivations, especially in relation to some envisioned supreme end.	generate consequences; among these consequences are significant ends or goals of choice and activity; and somewhere, it has long been reasoned, among these ends or goals, there must be the supreme or highest end, the chief point of what it is to be a human person as such. Moral philosophy is concerned not merely to identify and characterize this chief point, not merely to clarify its status as linguistically explained, not merely to subsume all lesser ends (I shall hereafter call them values or goods), but also, through the achievement of these purposes, to motivate persons to recognize and, so far as finitely possible, fulfill that chief good or (in Latin) *summum bonum* in the determinate circumstances of each individual's life situation—a motivation provided, not so much by preaching, goading, conditioning, or exhorting, as by clear analysis, reasoned argument, and balanced critical evaluation. All this, put in the most general
1.3b2) This is at least one way of significantly characterizing the nature of ethics or moral philosophy.	terms, is what philosophical ethics or moral philosophy is about. I do not claim that the nature of that intellectual discipline could not be otherwise clarified in a preliminary sense, as indeed it often has been historically; but I do claim that what I have said is one significant way of generally, and effectively, I trust, achieving that clarification.
	Now if moral philosophy or ethics is thus understood, its importance and relevance to every reflectively minded individual's lived experience cannot reasonably be challenged.
1.3b3) On such a view, lesser ends are subsumed under more general ones as directed toward the supreme point of human existence, although each person's actualization of that point will be an individually distinct expression of that point.	Lesser ends are subsumed under more general ones, and these under still higher values until, hopefully and perhaps, the supreme point of human existence is envisioned as the capstone of all the values that bestow on human life its meaning and purpose. I have no question but that each individual's life, carried through with reasoned moral guidance, will reflect the chief point of all human existence in a unique and distinctive focus of determinate meaning that, in its details, is peculiar to that person; yet that focal junction will only be possible as an actualization of the *summum bonum* common to all. Given some such understanding of the thrust of philosophical ethics, no thoughtful person could possibly be indifferent to the questions of ethics thus understood, since each individual, whether consciously or not, is moving toward some end or ends in life, and cannot be reasonably unconcerned as to his or her moral direction.

The General Philosophical Context of Ethics

Philosophy as such, though including moral philosophy as perhaps the most important one of its three main subdivisions, obviously extends far beyond this ethical aspect. Traditionally, philosophy (both oriental and occidental, though with very different emphases) has been concerned with three principal topics: knowledge, reality, and value. Concern with knowledge is generally designated as *logic* and *epistemology* (the comparative and critical study of the origin, nature, and limits of knowledge; the nature of methodology, and tests of truth; the relation between ideas and their objects or referents). The study of reality is commonly called *metaphysics* or (adopting the name of its most general subdivision) *ontology* (the comparative and critical study of different levels or types of reality, of their relation to one another, and of the question whether there is an ultimate or self-existent reality through whose being, activity, or aspects all other sorts of reality can be systematically explained). Questions or issues about values are subsumed under the designation of *axiology* or (taking the name of what is generally regarded as the most significant type of value, namely, moral value) *ethics* (the comparative and critical study of different types of value, and of their relations to one another—for example, logical value, aesthetic value, prudential value, moral value).

1.4) The relations of ethics or moral philosophy to philosophy as a whole in its main subdivisions
1.4a) General subdivisions
1.4a1) Epistemology: knowledge
1.4a2) Metaphysics: reality
1.4a3) Axiology: value

I cannot here be occupied in detail with either epistemology or metaphysics, except so far as they have a substantial effect on the problems of ethics, which is the inclusive focus of all that I have to say in this work. I have written elsewhere in some detail about both topics; and I recommend that the reader peruse what I have to say about them.[1] But since all the subdivisions of philosophy aim at knowledge and truth about the topics concerned, and since an adequately construed epistemology, centrally concerned as it is with the theory of knowledge and of truth, seems to be logically prior to conclusions and methodology in the other subdivisions, including ethics, it is important to indicate the general nature of the epistemological assumptions to which I am committed and which will form the conceptual basis

1.4b) The primacy of epistemology: a summary of the author's position

---

[1] *The Resurrection of Theism; The Reconstruction of the Christian Revelation Claim;* and *Oriental Philosophy: A Westerner's Guide to Eastern Thought.*

1.5) Rational empiricism or synthetic apriorism	of my analysis and criticism in philosophical ethics. In my previous writing, I have attempted to render plausible an epistemological theory which, following Kant's terminology, I have called *rational empiricism* or (singling out a widely disputed emphasis of that position) *synthetic apriorism*. The main thrust of this view is the claim that all genuinely informative propositions that express a truth claim involve two sorts of basic elements: principles of reason, characterized by direct or indirect or self-evidence, which are therefore *a priori* in the sense that these principles have a truth value that is logically prior to and thus independent of the data of empirical experience (for example, the law of contradiction and other logically necessary truths dependent upon it); and the data or facts, or fundamental elements of empirical experience (primarily sense data accessible through the various modes of sensory awareness—seeing, hearing, smelling, touching, tasting). This position involves the dual affirmative and complex claim that sense knowledge is possible for the knowing subject only through the exercise and application of *a priori* principles of reason (whether consciously or not) to the relevant sense data, and that only through the content of such sense data is it possible for the mind, structured through *a priori* principles of reason, to know truths about contingent matters of empirical fact. Or to put it in an approximation of the language of Kant: percepts without concepts are blind; concepts without percepts are empty. Or again, no knowledge of perceptual contents without the application of rational principles; no conceptual knowledge of contingent matters of fact without perceptual content. To further identify my epistemology: the viewpoint thus sketched involves a type of classical *foundationalism* (all genuine knowledge claims run logically back to starting points that are finally grounded in immediate apprehension either through reason as such, or through rationally discerned sense apprehension); a modern version of *moderate rationalistic apriorism* (the basic principles of reason are intrinsic to or characterize the operation of the knowing mind logically prior to and independently of any grounding in sense experience); and (what I will call) *objective approximationism* or the *neutral criterion view*.[2]
1.5a) Two basic elements:	
1.5a1) *a priori* principles of reason	
1.5a2) data of empirical experience	
1.5b) Genuine knowledge is a combination of these two factors.	
1.6) Further characterization of the theory as involving:	
1.6a) foundationalism	
1.6b) moderate rationalistic apriorism	
1.6c) objective approximationism	

---

[2] By this I mean that the basic criteria, principles, or standards of knowledge are objective in the sense not only that propositions expressing them are true

All this previous epistemological summarizing is intended, not to provide a defense of my position developed in my other writings, but rather to provide a brief disclosure of it. It is possible, furthermore, to state all this in a considerably less sophisticated fashion. In ethics, as elsewhere in philosophy, it is desirable that our positions approximate objective truth, as far as finite minds are capable of reflectively and sincerely aiming at that goal. If this task is to be attempted, it will be necessary to identify criteria or standards of assessment by means of which to evaluate alternative viewpoints on various issues. My epistemology claims that there are basically two such criteria: *rational coherence* (freedom from self-contradiction, or pervasive rational consistency and compatibility) and *experiential relevance* (accountability to all the factual data pertinent to the issue or problem concerned). The degree to which a systematic explanation conforms to these criteria is then the degree to which that explanation approximates objective truth. I take these criteria to be those actually used by rationally reflective persons in assessing truth claims at any level or in any field of insight (with the stipulation or qualification that pure or formal logic involves no dependence on experiential data). If that seems too strong a claim, even in light of my writings on epistemology and metaphysics, then I simply make an explicit disclosure that these are in fact the criteria I intend to use in dealing with the problems and alternate theories of philosophical ethics.

It is not necessary to say very much about the relevance and/or relation of metaphysics to ethics at this preliminary stage, since a large part of my concern in the work as a whole will focus on problems about the degree to which various worldview contexts provide a backdrop for alternative ethical theories and the problems they address. I think it entirely fair historically, however, to say that in the history of philosophy both western and eastern, ethical theories have, on the whole, followed the lead provided by the worldview perspectives. There certainly are exceptions to this thesis; but it

1.7) A less technical statement of this epistemological viewpoint

1.7a) rational coherence

1.7b) experiential relevance

1.8) The relevance of metaphysics to ethics will be a principal aspect of the entire subsequent analysis; but in general, ethical perspectives have followed or been correlated with metaphysical views.

---

independently of any finite knower's awareness of them or opinion about them, but also in the sense that these principles, properly formulated and understood, express truths about being as such, while at the same time their intrinsic reasonableness does not depend on any finite knower's prior volitional commitment to any particular metaphysical worldview or perspective.

seems at least true that thinkers who proposed developed ethical systems saw it as part of their task to argue the compatibility of what they claimed by way of moral philosophy with what they regarded as believable about reality. With this all but universal trend I find myself in total agreement, so much so that I have used metaphysical classifications to categorize the three main types of normative ethical theories: naturalistic, idealistic, and theistic. But more about that in its proper place. Certainly ethics has almost invariably been, and continues to be, a principal segment of some larger and more inclusive whole of thought.

The Principal Aspects of Philosophical Ethics

1.9) Approaches to the study of ethics

1.9a) Moral beliefs are the basic data of ethics.

1.9b) Three different methods of approach to moral beliefs

1.9b1) Descriptive: factual characterization, which is the proper concern of various empirical sciences

The subject matter from which moral philosophy takes its point of departure consists in the moral beliefs, commitments, and practices of various individual persons, cultural subsets or wholes, historical epochs, and so forth. That this subject matter exists in the annals of human history and present experience is indisputable; and were this not the case, philosophers and ordinary people would have nothing in this arena of ethics to theorize about. To suppose otherwise would be quite analogous to trying to dispose of astronomy by supposing that there were no astronomical bodies with which our science might engage, or even beliefs about those bodies that required reasoned assessment. But granted the reality of ethical data in the sense indicated, there are different ways of approaching the systematic study of these data: the descriptive, the analytic (or meta-ethical), and the normative (or substantive). The *descriptive* approach to moral beliefs would consist in characterizing the moral beliefs of some segment of humanity (an individual, a group, a culture, an epoch, etc.), developing explanatory hypotheses about the causes and effects of these beliefs, and depicting their psychological, sociological, and even economic and political implications; and then, in all these and other respects, comparisons might be made between various human segments as to the comprehensive role that moral beliefs exhibited in those segments. This descriptive approach, however, is really and properly the complex project of the several empirical sciences that are concerned with the explanation of the place of moral beliefs in human individual and social life and institutions; and therefore, although philosophical ethics builds extensively on this scientific description as providing a systematic explanation of moral data, the descriptive approach is not the primary focus or concern of philosophy *as* philosophy. Scientific description of moral beliefs therefore, while it certainly and importantly is an ally or colleague of philosophical ethics, is not part of that ethics itself. Still, confusion is possible here: if a reflective thinker concludes that the psychological and sociological function exhausts the entire significance of their meaning, or entails the realm of moral values or principles which are the objects of those beliefs; or if such a thinker claims that, from the relatively universal prevalence of certain general moral beliefs, it can be concluded that such beliefs express moral truths that are incumbent upon all rational, moral beings (or at least all the human members of that set) as objective duties, obligations, or ethical ends; then all of that is genuine philosophy precisely because it attempts to transform empirical description into trans-empirical moral theses and conclusions. Whether this can be done in any of the ways suggested, or in still others as well, is a serious and central concern of philosophical ethics.

1.9b2) But providing organized data for philosophical ethics

1.9b3) Yet some genuinely philosophical moral claims are closely related to empirical moral data and may be confused with them.

The *analytic* (or *meta-ethical*) approach to moral beliefs as data consists in taking the linguistic (verbal) units in which moral beliefs are characteristically expressed, and attempting to dissect those units in such a way as to unpack and exhibit the authentic meaning and logical status of ethical *terms* (right, wrong, ought, must, duty, obligation, moral responsibility, moral goodness, etc.), *judgments* ('Breaking a promise violates a moral obligation,' 'Misrepresenting the truth is [always, or usually, or, etc.] morally wrong.'), and *arguments* ('Breaking a promise violates a moral obligation; You broke a promise; Therefore, you violated a moral obligation.'). In providing this explication, a thinker is engaged in the linguistic analysis of the elements illustrated, and other elements as well. All this involves such questions as: what am I saying about an act or principle of conduct if I ascribe to it the predicate 'morally right'?, or, what sort of premises (in the sense of logical character) will reasonably support a moral conclusion?, or, are 'good' and 'evil,' when used as moral ascriptions, terms that stand for properties of the

1.10) Analytic or meta-ethical: concerned with meaning and logical status of ethical terms, judgments, and arguments

1.10a) Explanation of this approach

1.10b) Supplemental concerns with conditions that make moral discourse intelligible and humanly relevant	subjects they qualify? Yet such analysis does not exhaust the analytic approach but is also concerned to investigate and specify the assumptions and conditions that, in a general way, make the whole realm of moral discourse rationally intelligible. What, specifically, must be descriptively and/or essentially true about human beings, if moral discourse is to be relevant and applicable to their experience?
1.10b1) Determinism and free will	Is the applicability of propositions expressing duty or obligation conceivable if all human choices and acts are causally determined by non-rational, non-personal elements, or are the notions of duty and moral obligation relevant to human experience only on the condition that personal agents, though influenced and motivated by such factors, are at their highest level radically free from such determination?
1.10b2) Relation of moral claims to metaphysical claims	Or again, what must be true about the cosmos as a whole or about reality in general, if moral judgments are to be adequately grounded and therefore genuinely pertinent to human decision and choice? Must moral principles be finally based on the character of Nature, or of the Absolute Mind,
1.10b3) Moral relativism and moral objectivism	or of the Personal God of theistic religion? Is there then, at the ultimate and highest level, an indiscerptible identity between Being and Goodness? Or does all moral judgment turn in the end on such individually and culturally variable factors as opinion, preference, feeling, or human response?
1.10b4) Relation between rightness and goodness	Or still again, and finally, does the rightness or wrongness of an act or rule of procedure logically depend on the moral value of its consequences; or is it rather the case that the moral value of those consequences is in fact itself dependent upon the rightness (or wrongness) of the acts and rules from which such results ensue; or is it perhaps the case that rightness and goodness are each autonomous and logically independent in relation to the other? All this, and much more besides, is of crucial concern to the analytic approach to ethics, centrally involved, as it is, in questions about the meaning and contextual presuppositions that clarify the relevance and intelligibility of human moral discourse. And this concern is clearly a matter of genuine philosophical substance.
1.10c) But analytic and descriptive approaches are not concerned as such with making moral claims	But neither the descriptive approach nor the analytic approach as such is engaged in making any actual moral recommendations or in formulating and defending any theory as to what the ultimately good or right actually is. If there were no moral beliefs about right and wrong, good and

evil, duty and obligation, the descriptive and analytic approaches would have no data or subject matter to activate their logical machinery or operation; but it is not the business of either approach, as such, to produce such data or to make judgment calls about them. So far as philosophy is concerned with making or defending or even evaluating actual moral theses or principles, it is involved in what is often called the *normative* (or *substantive*) approach to moral beliefs. But of course it is scarcely conceivable that normative ethics, as a philosophical concern, would have originated unless, as with descriptive and analytic ethics, it took the moral beliefs of individuals and society as a basic given; and yet the normative approach clearly goes beyond the other two by attempting critically to assess, extend, and systematize that given basis with a view to arguing the rational plausibility of some particular normative ethical viewpoint. But generally there is a restriction, since it is not usually regarded as the business of philosophical ethics even in its normative role to give pieces of explicit and detailed moral advice about particular moral issues and problems (such as abortion, war and peace, sexual mores, business conduct, etc.). Although normative ethics may use examples or models that concern such issues (as is clearly the case with analytic ethics also), prolonged concern with such matters is rather the business of moral exhortation or applied ethics or even preaching (construed in a non-pejorative sense). It is instead the concern of normative ethics to develop general theories about the ultimately right and/or the ultimately good, and to derive general principles of moral choice from those general theories in such a way that this general theoretical structure is relevant and pertinent to applied ethics and moral exhortation. Yet because the ultimate point of developing an ethical theory (and of course critically defending it against alternatives) consists in its application to actual moral practice, instruction in philosophical ethics has often, and now perhaps even characteristically, been construed to include such detailed, or at least extended and exemplary, application to specific moral issues. As the development of the present work will clearly show, however, I intend no such extended involvement here and will refer to these issues, if at all, only to illustrate and/or argue general points of ethical theory.

1.11) Normative or substantive: concerned with making and arguing actual moral claims in a systematic fashion

1.11a) This does not involve (except illustratively) specific pieces of moral advice.

1.11b) It is rather directed to forming and assessing general theories about the good and the right; and deriving from them general moral principles.

1.12) Historically:	Historically, until the last hundred years or so in the West, the descriptive, analytic, and normative approaches to ethics have, in the work of most moral philosophers, been intricately and pervasively intertwined with one another with little effort consciously to develop them separately and comparatively. Certainly Plato and Aristotle, Augustine and Aquinas, Kant and Hegel, along with many others, have followed this pattern of mixing analytic concerns about meaning and logical status with normative concerns about virtue and goodness, and in doing so, they have incorporated extended elements of moral description. But eventually it seemed to become clear that this commingling led to more confusion than it did illumination, as well as to the neglect of issues about meaning and the distortion of problems about actual moral norms or standards. In the English-speaking philosophical world, this conceptual dawning led to two consequences of great moment: the sharp distinction between the analytic and normative concerns of philosophical ethics (an essentially clarifying move, in my opinion), and an extended and almost exclusive preoccupation with analytic or meta-ethical issues to the serious neglect of normative theories and problems (a most unfortunate consequence, as I view the matter). It is commendable, however, that the last thirty years or so have begun to restore the balance between these two concerns; but, again unfortunately, the balance has tended to counter the analytic extreme with a preoccupation about applied ethics, as if (mistakenly, I think) particular moral problems could be plausibly solved without the rational guidance of general ethical theory. Of course, all these historical developments are far more complex than my brief consideration would suggest, but it is simply not part of my present concern either to extend or elaborate this smattering of intellectual history.
1.12a) The three methods of approach have been combined into a single, complex project.	
1.12b) When a clear distinction was made around the turn of the century, the emphasis was first heavily on meta-ethics.	
1.12b1) More recently, applied ethics has been dominant. 1.12b2) But normative ethics has been neglected, on the whole.	
1.13) A brief forecast of the current project	More pertinently to my imminent purpose, I shall, in what ensues, assume without further discussion or argument, that meta-ethics (or analytic ethics) and normative (or substantive) ethics are the proper concern of moral philosophy or philosophical ethics in general, and that its appropriate business is therefore to develop alternative positions, arguments, and counter-arguments about both arenas of concern, supplementing that with a summary of plausible conclusions that emerge from the theories thus developed. Other

serious students of the subject may have different agendas; but having identified my own agenda, I shall now attempt to carry it through, beginning with meta-ethics, and climaxing hopefully in the goal set by the title of my work: the rediscovery of the highest Good.

Part I

*Meta-Ethics:
The Meaning, Logical Status,
and Context of Moral Discourse*

Chapter II

*General Meta-Ethical Theories:
Cognitivism vs. Non-Cognitivism*

The Principal Task of Meta-Ethical Analysis

If moral discourse is to be understood clearly and specimens of it are to be assessed critically, it is a necessary prerequisite that the meaning and logical status of ethical terms, judgments, and arguments be thoroughly and plausibly investigated. But prior even to this investigation, it must be possible to identify linguistic units of a certain sort as specimens of moral discourse. One might initially suppose that any reflective individual could identify these specimens just from that person's own linguistic practice, and that of other persons, entirely without instruction and without further ado. But that supposition turns out to be descriptively false: there are so many nonmoral uses of the key terms that provide the clues to moral discourse, so much confusion about these varied uses in actual practice, and so much disagreement about moral discourse even on the part of informed, specialized investigators, that it appears essential to begin with a brief account of at least one plausible method for identifying authentic specimens of moral discourse. Ethical terms, then, are part of a much larger class of linguistic designators which I will call *normative terms*; and a normative term is one that connotes a standard, criterion, ideal, or measure of evaluation relatively to some type of action,

2.1) While the ultimate goal of meta-ethics is linguistic and logical clarity, the basic and first concern is to develop a method of identifying specimens of moral discourse.

2.1a) Ethical terms are a species of normative terms that also have nonmoral uses in relation to criteria or rules:

characteristic, or procedure. Put differently, normative terms connote rules of some sort: whether formally or informally, directly or indirectly, as such or in conjunction with other terms. For our purposes, however, the most important distinction is between nonmoral and moral uses of these terms, and then, within the class of moral uses, between moral uses that are employed in a fundamentally evaluative sense to make an actual moral claim or recommendation and those moral uses which, for various reasons, employ such terms but without making any actual moral claims.

<small>moral uses, in turn, either make a moral claim or not.</small>

<small>2.1b) Beginning with a partial list of normative terms, we can illustrate:</small>

I do not know how to make a beginning with these distinctions except by referring to an incomplete list of normative terms (for example: *must, ought, duty, obligation, right, wrong, good, bad, evil, responsible, guilty, innocent,* etc.); furthermore, I do not know how one might, with complete logical confidence, go about making an exhaustive list of such terms, since many terms, used primarily in non-normative senses, can acquire a normative sense through usage, and many normative terms can come, for some set of linguistic users, to be used in a non-normative sense. But it is clear that there are many nonmoral uses of normative terms; for example, consider the following uses of the normative term *ought*:

<small>2.1b1) Nonmoral uses.</small>

1. If you want to buy a quality overcoat at a very low price, you *ought* to purchase it at the Burlington Coat Factory.
2. Anyone who adds 53 to 47 *ought* to get 100 for the answer.
3. She left for Scranton at least three hours ago, so barring any mishap, she *ought* to be there by now.
4. There *ought* to be a crescent wrench in the toolbox.
5. Watching the Cosby show on TV *ought* to be at least as much fun as a quick game of checkers.

All these uses of the normative term *ought* are standard English practice; yet none of them, though clearly normative, is a moral use of the term. Perhaps (though not with total precision) 1 and 5 are preferential or prudential uses, 2 and 3 logical uses, and 4 a criterial or anticipative use of the term *ought*. But each usage could, in context, be differently interpreted. Yet it would be difficult (though I do not say impossible) to think of any context in which these sentences would illustrate the moral use of the term *ought*.

Of course, it is very easy to cite examples of *ought* used in a moral sense, given the right context:

2.1b2) Moral uses:

1. If you voluntarily make a promise, you *ought*, under standard circumstances, to keep it.
2. A husband and father *ought* to provide for the economic needs of his wife and dependent children (no doubt for many other needs as well).
3. No one *ought* to extend courage to the point of inevitable self-destruction.
4. You *ought* to manage your total resources responsibly.

Clearly these examples can and would normally be interpreted as pieces of moral advice, although, in some identifiable context, they might be taken in a nonmoral sense. Abundant illustrations of other normative terms could be given to exemplify both moral and nonmoral uses.

But it is also the case that a normative term can be used in a moral sense without being used in a fundamentally evaluative way to make a moral claim. Consider the following:

2.1c) But some moral uses are non-evaluative.
2.1c1) Examples:

1. In western society, not everyone agrees that it is always morally *wrong* intentionally to misrepresent the truth.
2. Jeremy Bentham claimed that pleasure was the chief and only morally intrinsic *good*.
3. To say that an act is morally *right* or *wrong* is merely to express an attitude of approval or disapproval toward that act.

The italicized normative terms are clearly used in the moral sense (as the adverb *morally* emphasizes), but in the propositions as a whole, this moral sense is not employed in a fundamentally evaluative sense to make an actual claim. Rather, each statement propounds a thesis, nonmoral in character, about the moral claim to which, as a thesis, it refers. The first is a descriptive sociological generalization and can be assessed only on empirical grounds. The second is a piece of intellectual (philosophical) history about a well-known thinker of the late eighteenth and early nineteenth

2.1c2) Each is about a moral claim but does not make one.

centuries. The third is a much-discussed meta-ethical thesis about the meaning of the terms right and wrong when used in the moral sense.

2.1d) Problem: how to identify a moral use that makes a moral claim

All this raises the question about how we can single out with confidence those moral uses of normative terms that are, in the context in question, employed in a fundamentally evaluative sense to make an actual moral claim. I have earlier asserted that normative terms, used in their moral sense to make such a claim, have as their central thrust a reference to obligations that are incumbent on persons merely and essentially as human beings in a certain clarified context. But this claim, of course, depends on the viability of acknowledged examples of fundamental ethical or moral usage. Since I do not know how to go beyond this claim as supported by such examples I suggest that, as a practical guide, one might assume that unless the linguistic context makes it clear, either that the normative term is being used in a nonmoral sense, or that the moral sense employed is not being used to make a moral claim, it is plausible to suppose that the moral term is functioning to make an actual moral claim in the fundamentally evaluative sense. If there were no such basic moral sense, at least the descriptive and meta-ethical uses of normative terms would have no foundation in linguistic usage from which to begin. And, although the thesis is far more controversial, that might even be true of the wholly nonmoral uses of normative terms illustrated above. It is at least possible, if difficult decisively to defend, that the moral and fundamentally evaluative sense of moral terms is, logically speaking, their primordial usage, and that all the other uses of normative terms are grounded analogically in that basic moral sense. I certainly believe that to be the case, although I have no special reason to argue it out at length in the present context.

2.1d1) Since there logically must be some basic moral uses that make an actual moral claim (otherwise there could be no descriptive or meta-ethical uses),
2.1d2) it is plausible to assume initially that such a claim is being made unless the context indicates otherwise.

2.1d3) It is even possible that the fundamentally evaluative sense of normative terms is the logical foundation of all other uses of such terms.

2.2) The principal task of meta-ethical analysis is to clarify all these uses of normative terms, and to analyze the logical status of judgments and arguments containing them.

It is therefore the principal task of meta-ethical analysis to sort out all these various uses of terms that have, or may have, a normative sense, to distinguish between the moral and nonmoral uses of these terms, and to clarify their meaning in the context of the propositions and arguments in which they occur. This characteristically involves the development of various analogies and disanalogies between normative judgments and non-normative judgments, and between the logical status of arguments involving these types of judgments. The eventual outcome will be to formulate and defend (against alternative positions) a general meta-ethical theory that purports to account systematically for the whole realm of moral discourse, within the larger realm of normative discourse, and to exhibit in detail the relation between such discourse and all the other (non-moral, non-normative) realms of human discourse. And it is to that complex consideration that we now turn our focus of attention.

A Classification of the Principal Meta-Ethical Theories

Normative, and, more narrowly, moral discourse, stands in contrast to the non-normative realms of discourse. But normative discourse has, on the whole, a structural similarity to two other kinds of discourse, namely those of empirical description and logical form, in that the principal unit of expression for all three is a proposition or judgment or statement that affirms or denies some predicate or characteristic of some subject of discourse, with or without an implied or explicit condition. It is perhaps the case that what is stated as a proposition of either empirical description or logical form could be conveyed in other linguistic forms which, at least structurally, are not propositions; but it is widely agreed that at least a partial equivalent of any ethical proposition could be expressed in nonpropositional form—for example, as an imperative sentence, or as a subjunctive expression of a wish or desire, or (less plausibly) as an emotive expletive or ejaculation. It may, of course, be the case that any such translation would lose something of the connotative meaning of the original proposition; but the reverse seems also to be the case—the propositional expression of an imperative or command would certainly lose something of the meaning of its original as well. In any case, the structural analogy, between ethical propositions and either empirical or formal logical propositions, raises numerous questions about the logical status of all three in comparison to one another.

It is generally supposed that empirical and formal logical propositions express truth claims; that is, they assert something to be the case (or deny it to be the case), and are therefore either true or false, depending on whether what is

2.3) Normative, descriptive, and logical discourse are all typically expressed in propositional form,

2.3a) although other forms may be possible for all three types.

2.4) There may, of course, be a loss of meaning through translation into different linguistic modes.

2.4a) Since empirical and logically formal propositions express truth claims, by assigning or

	affirmed or denied is the case. On reflection, it appears that
withdrawing predicates, do fundamentally evaluative ethical propositions also express truth claims?	they are cognitively significant expressions of this sort (i.e., they are susceptible of either being true or false) because the predicates of these propositions are terms that stand for identifiable properties, characteristics, or attributes. To say of a surface that it is green, or to say of any proposition that it is logically incoherent, is in each case to affirm respectively, an empirical and a logical property to the subject referred to. The question then arises as to whether fundamentally evaluative ethical propositions are therefore also property statements in this logical sense, so that ethical propositions also are either true or false and are therefore cognitively significant propositions. It is clear that there are some disanalogies between ethical statements and empirical statements:
2.4a1) There are disanalogies between ethical statements and certain types of empirical and logically formal statements.	it makes sense to say that two tables are alike in every other respect, except that one of them is red, and the other is not red (perhaps white, or etc.); but it appears to make no sense at all to say that two acts are alike in every other respect, except that one is morally right and the other is morally wrong. To differ morally, two acts would have to possess some further identifiable difference, since otherwise the supposition of their moral difference would be unintelligible. It is worth noting that many formal logical propositions have consequential predicates of a precisely analogous sort.
2.4a2) But the disanalogies are not enough to entail as such that ethical statements are not cognitively significant (i.e., incapable of being either true or false).	It is logically incoherent to suppose that two propositions are alike in every other respect, except that one of them is true and the other is false. Perhaps more striking still is the fact that there are even certain empirical propositions that fit the consequential model: it makes no sense at all to say that two objects or entities are alike in every other respect, except that one of them occupies space while the other (say, a thought or a feeling) does not. So while these examples raise questions about the analogy between fundamentally evaluative moral propositions, on the one hand, and either empirical or logical propositions on the other, the examples provide no basis for questioning the cognitive status of moral propositions.
2.5) The two main meta-ethical theory types differ as to whether ethical statements make truth claims:	Yet the two main types of general meta-ethical theories differ precisely on this question. Meta-ethical *cognitivism* (or *descriptivism*) stresses the propositional form of ethical statements in general, regards such statements as cognitively significant in the sense of being either true or false,

and therefore views those statements as property statements. (The view that ethical terms, employed in their basic, ethical sense, stand for qualities or characteristics of the subjects they appropriately qualify, is commonly called the *property doctrine* and is shared by all meta-ethical cognitivists.) It is then incumbent on cognitivism to provide an analysis of ethical statements that clearly and plausibly identifies moral properties, relates them to both empirical and formal logical properties, and meets the intelligibility criteria for standard ethical usage (or, alternatively, argues that such standard usage is itself unclear or incoherent and should therefore be restructured). Meta-ethical *non-cognitivism* (or *non-descriptivism*), on the other hand, stresses the disanalogies between ethical expressions in contrast to either empirical or logical propositions, and therefore emphasizes the non-cognitive functions of those expressions; for example, their directive, commendatory, prescriptive, and emotively expressive and evocative roles (which clearly, ethical propositions do encompass). Non-cognitivists thus reject the property doctrine, in its baldly stated cognitivist form, and claim that ethical statements, in their basically and distinctively moral role, are therefore neither true nor false, but rather appropriate or inappropriate, relevant or irrelevant, commendable or non-commendable, effective or ineffective, etc. Yet non-cognitivism virtually always acknowledges that ethical statements, though not themselves cognitively significant in the straightforward sense, are always made in the context of (and, perhaps even in part, on the basis of) a cognitive apprehension of all the relevant factual circumstances and logical consequences, though at the same time it is denied (at least purportedly) that any conjunction of empirical and logical truths would logically entail a distinctively moral conclusion. It is in turn, then, incumbent on any given non-cognitivist to provide, as in the case of the cognitivist, an analysis of ethical expressions that clearly identifies the non-cognitive functions of moral assertions and at the same time both accounts for cognitive claims (and arguments) and either accords with, or proposes reforms for, standard ethical usage. As is perennially the case with philosophically substantive issues, it is a matter for both views of clarifying alternative positions, providing a range of supporting arguments for one's own position, and responding

2.5a) (a) Cognitivism:
2.5a1) views ethical statements as cognitive (either true or false)
2.5a2) and views such statements as assigning or withholding properties (the property doctrine).

2.5b) (b) Non-cognitivism:
2.5b1) stresses the non-cognitivist functions of ethical statements, and rejects the property doctrine;

2.5b2) but also emphasizes the factual and logical context and consequences connected with ethical expressions;

2.5b3) while denying that such factors ever entail a moral conclusion.

2.5c) But there are significant differences on both sides of this main contrast. to the counter-arguments of critics. But neither cognitivism nor non-cognitivism is, in itself, a monolithic theoretical structure: serious differences and disagreements divide both sides of this central and crucial contrast; and it is to those distinctions that we must now turn.

Chapter III

Meta-Ethical Cognitivism

If cognitivism is to propose and defend the property doctrine, it faces the task of clarifying the logical status of such properties and providing a defensible account of their relation to the non-ethical properties with which empirical description and formal logic are concerned. One way of accomplishing this objective is appropriately called *definism*: according to this general standpoint, moral or ethical language is a useful and convenient way of expressing what, in cognitive respects, could be expressed by non-ethical statements that contain no normative ethical terms used in their fundamentally evaluative sense: every such term could, in cognitive respects, be replaced by a conjunction of non-ethical or nonmoral terms that are logically equivalent in meaning and reference to the ethical terms thus eliminated. Distinct species of definism differ with each other about the proper nonmoral substitutes for the ethical terms: if the substitutes are terms that stand for descriptive empirical and in that sense natural properties, then the result is *naturalistic* definism of some sort (for example, 'To say of any act that it is morally right [or good] means the same thing as to say that it will maximize pleasurable consequences and minimize painful ones either for oneself or for all the human [or even sentient] beings likely to be affected by the act.'); or if the substitute term stands for some transcendent reli-

3.1) Definism in general regards normative ethical statements as logically equivalent in meaning with other non-ethical statements that thus contain no normative ethical terms used in the basic moral sense.

3.2) Distinct species of definism:

3.2a) Naturalistic

3.2b) Religious-metaphysical	gious-metaphysical property, then we have what I will call *religious-metaphysical* definism (for example, 'To say of any act that it is morally right [or good] means the same thing as to say that it has been commanded by God.'); or if the
3.2c) Formalistic or rationalistic	substitute term stands for some formal logical property, the consequence will be what I will call *formalistic* or *rationalistic* definism (for example, 'To say that any act is morally right [or good] means the same thing as to say that it follows as a prescription from a maxim or rule that could be universalized without generating a logical or existential inconsistency.'). The illustrations cited are obviously only samples of a much larger number of theories that would fall into one or the other of these three general types; and even other general types are conceivable—my classification is merely a tentative one that I have found convenient for systematizing various species of definism. Since most widely discussed contemporary definist views are naturalistic, the designation *meta-ethical naturalism* (or often merely the term *naturalism*) is sometimes used as referring to all types of definism.
3.3) Clarification of the definist thesis	It is of the utmost importance to realize that definism of any sort (as with any general meta-ethical theory) is a thesis about the meaning and logical status of ethical terms and judgments, and not at all (or at least not meta-ethically) a normative thesis about the content to which that meaning
3.3a) No reciprocal logical entailment holds between meta-ethical definism and any normative ethical content thesis.	is applicable. A thinker could certainly hold that pleasure (and the absence of pain) was the sole ultimate and intrinsic good (a normative content thesis) without holding that goodness as a term meant the same thing as maximizing pleasure and minimizing pain (apparently Jeremy Bentham, for example, held both the normative and the meta-ethical doctrines indicated), and so analogously with other types
3.3b) Yet less rigorous logical associations are often urged between the two, so that the logical and argumentative connections are very complex.	of theories in this context. On the other hand, as Bentham also illustrates, the normative thesis is often argued partly on the basis of the meta-ethical doctrine: 'Why of course pleasure is the chief good—the very meaning of the term supposes as much!' Furthermore, it goes without saying that many aspects (arguably even all aspects) of meta-ethical doctrine are urged on the basis of normative ethical doctrines regarded as plausible or adequate. If, to extend our Bentham illustration, the good Jeremy did not already believe normatively that pleasure was the chief good, it would scarcely have occurred to him to claim that the very meaning of

the term 'good' supposed as much. The relations, logically and argumentatively, between meta-ethical and normative ethical doctrines are exceedingly intricate and complex; so that we may not blithely slide from one side to the other without carefully and thoroughly laying the groundwork for the move.

The intent of the definist is clear enough: to establish the thesis that ethical terms can always be replaced by non-ethical terms without cognitive loss; and then that ethical propositions can be similarly replaced with non-ethical propositions; finally, that arguments containing ethical premises can, again without cognitive loss, be replaced with arguments devoid of such premises. In a way, this complex move, if successful, renders moral discourse as such unnecessary, except as a convenient and sometimes shorthand way of saying something else in nonmoral terms. It is an oft-debated question whether normative and especially ethical conclusions can be derived from premises that are solely non-ethical. Is it possible to derive an 'ought' sentence from an 'is' sentence, or an evaluative thesis from a factual thesis? Clearly, a consistent definist would not only answer in the affirmative, but would claim (and try to argue) that all evaluative theses are derived from non-evaluative premises, since for any such thesis there is a logically equivalent non-evaluative proposition which is thus in some broad sense factual, though not necessarily descriptive in the empirical sense (a limitation restricted to naturalistic definists). On the other hand, it does not follow that, if a given thinker holds some ethical thesis or other to be derivable from nonmoral premises, the thinker must also be some sort of definist (though this may be the case): the thinker may merely be talking about a restricted class of ethical statements, or may merely be claiming that factual truths provide a plausible basis for ethical claims without supposing that the relation is one of analytic equivalence of cognitive meaning. There is therefore no need to attempt to unearth definists from graves in which they are not contained, to be exhumed (or ex-Hume-d?). It is still the case, however, that a definist can claim, as support of some sort at least, any attempted derivation of a moral claim (an 'ought' statement) from a nonmoral basis: at least it may serve as a paradigm for his or her universalized thesis.

3.3c) The definist intent is to show that ethical terms, judgments, and arguments can be replaced with no cognitive loss by non-ethical equivalents.

3.3c1) Hence, a definist would hold that all 'ought' statements are logically derivable from 'is' statements.

3.3c2) Yet the is/ought thesis does not in turn and as such entail definism.

3.3d) In principle at least, definism provides a strategic epistemological advantage by identifying a method of assessing moral claims on purely descriptive or factual grounds, especially in the case of naturalistic definism.

3.3d1) The empirical method of assessing truth claims is straightforward and relatively uncontroversial,

3.3d2) while the untranslated ethical originals are not.

If definism is a reasonably arguable position in any formulation, and if, for the nonmoral equivalents of moral declarations, there is a generally recognized standard method of assessing the truth claims of these nonmoral propositions, that will provide an enormous epistemological advantage for the definist in his or her presumed additional task (at least as a human person, if not as a philosopher) of assessing normative ethical truth claims, assuming, as definists do, the property doctrine. While it may be difficult to resolve moral claims cast in religious-metaphysical terms (Is there a standard method for identifying, for instance, God's commands?) or even in terms of rationalistic formalism (Is there any standard way of deciding uncontroversially whether the rule under which an act may be subsumed can be universalized without contradiction?), nevertheless there is a standard empirical method, however difficult in practice, for deciding such factual matters as to whether a certain act will maximize pleasurable consequences and minimize painful ones—it will be a straightforward question of empirical description and future anticipation grounded in the doctrine of natural uniformity. The general method of assessing the truth claim of empirical statements is widely and uncontroversially agreed upon by virtually all serious investigators of such propositions. It involves such processes as collecting empirical data, formulating anticipative hypotheses about these data as models for future expectation, deducing the probable consequences of the truth of such hypotheses, and verifying (or not) the adequacy of the hypotheses for handling the data as samples. If we accept some version of naturalistic definism, the non-ethical translation statements can be tested, therefore, by standard empirical procedures. By contrast, the ethical originals are typically engulfed in controversy for want of such a method. Hence, moral issues that otherwise seem insusceptible of resolution become resolvable, at least in principle if not in practice, if naturalistic definism is, in any version of it, correct. Nor is the case different in essence for religious-metaphysical or rationalistic-formalistic versions of definism. While there may be more disagreement here about God's commands or about the universalization of rules, still the tests, whatever they are, will be of a logical and empirical sort (barring sheer authoritarianism) and will therefore not involve highly controversial or purportedly intuited ethical premises. The testing of moral claims will be, at least in principle, a possible cognitive procedure for any version of definism; and this methodological gain is perhaps its strongest supporting argument. For we would, on this account, have an approximatively objective method of assessing moral claims, resolving ethical disagreements or disputes, relating ethical issues to all the other varied factors of our experience, and assimilating moral truths into a single framework of thought in systematic connection with all the other parts of our knowledge.

But there are other, though still logically related, arguments for definism. A thinker like Ralph Barton Perry, for example, argues that his version of definism (called the interest theory of value, according to which saying that an act is morally right [or good] means the same thing as saying that some individual or group has a favorable attitude toward it, and so on analogously for other ethical terms and judgments), if it is systematically developed, provides a more coherent total account of ethical data and standard ethical usage in language for all cultures than any alternative schematism. Of course, any reflective student of ethics would be prone to claim this for the positions he or she develops and defends, whether the student is a definist or not; and in the end I shall attempt to show this, with certain qualifications, for the positions I myself defend in meta-ethical and normative ethical theory. Hence, a judgment about such an all-encompassing argument must be suspended for the time being.

Meanwhile, a further line of argument can be developed in support of definism, especially in its empirical, naturalistic form. If we assume that typical ethical claims can be appropriately expressed as property statements that are either true or false, it is reasonable to believe that there should be a plausible objective methodology for deciding which they are. But no such methodology has been (or perhaps *can be*) reasonably formulated and defended except in connection with the nonmoral factual statements, empirical or otherwise, which provide the contextual circumstances for making ethical judgments relevant to our total experience and which make some ethical claims more reasonable than others, which differ from them, on the basis of these circumstances. No rationally reflective person will regard the nonmoral factual context of a moral act (whether considered or committed)

3.3d3) This methodological advantage is a strong argument for definism as such.

3.4) Arguments for definism:

3.4a) that an adequately stated definism provides a more coherent account of ethical data and usage than any other alternative meta-ethical perspective;

3.4b) that the relevance of nonmoral facts to the propriety of moral judgments in general is best explained by supposing

3.4b1) that those facts provide the sole rational judgments in question,

as totally irrelevant to the assessment of the moral propriety of the act and of the rule or maxim from which it would follow. To suppose otherwise would be to reduce moral discourse to irrelevant gibberish or emotional volatility. The relevant factual circumstances of a moral choice or act provide, for virtually any reflective thinker, a part of the rational basis for that choice or act. Not just anything at all can be counted or commended as good, or right, if moral judgment is to have any reasoned and objective basis at all. And if the propriety of a moral judgment is at least partly and necessarily dependent upon empirical circumstances (or logical principles, or even metaphysical worldview perspectives), then it is reasonable to suppose, with a high degree of plausibility, that such contextual circumstances provide, in the end, the whole rational basis for the truth claim of such a judgment, purporting as it does, to be assessing in moral terms what is nonmorally the case. And if, finally, that is true, then it is plausible to conclude that the nonmoral propositions concerned entail the moral propositions which are therefore reducible to expression in nonmoral terms. That, however, is precisely the essence of meta-ethical definism. With that issue settled, in general, the question, as to just which facts, metaphysical insights, or logical principles *are* morally relevant, and how they function in that role, will be a mere matter of detail. The only final (as distinguished from any provisional and intermediary) alternative would be to cut decisively the tie that binds moral judgment to its total nonmoral context; and perhaps that alternative would itself be both logically and morally irresponsible.

3.4b2) and that the nonmoral facts, propositionally stated, therefore entail the corresponding moral judgments—which is essentially meta-ethical definism.

3.5) Arguments against definism:

However, meta-ethical definism has, in the [twentieth] century, also been subjected to extensive negative criticism, not only from those who reject the property doctrine altogether (and are thus non-cognitivists), but also from those who accept that property doctrine in a different form. Understandably, the criticisms of definism, from these two markedly contrasting quarters (cognitivism and non-cognitivism), are strikingly different. The non-cognitivist criticism is based on the thesis that ethical sentences of the fundamentally evaluative sort are not property statements at all, since such sentences are not cognitively significant statements, but should rather be construed as performing a non-cognitive function such as commending, approving, or directing.

3.5a) Non-cognitivist criticisms are postponed until all forms of cognitivism are dismissed.

For my purposes it will be strategically more appropriate to discuss such criticisms after I have analyzed all the main forms of cognitivism; I shall, therefore, in this section, consider only cognitivist objections which agree that definism is correct in claiming that ethical sentences, *qua* ethical, are property statements and therefore also cognitively significant statements which make a truth claim that is itself either true or false. The error of definism, according to such critics, consists rather in mistakenly identifying the nature and context of the properties to which ethical terms, and the statements containing them, refer.

Definism, it will be recalled, regards ethical terms as equivalent in cognitive meaning to some non-ethical terms or conjunctions thereof. The question will then arise, assuming this claim is accepted as provisionally plausible, as to whether there is any objective and non-controversial (or at least generally agreed upon) method of identifying the nonmoral terms (or facts) with which ethical terms are thus equivalent in meaning. On this issue, I think it is descriptively correct to claim in criticism that there is no such general agreement among definists or rationalistic formalists. More generally, there appears to be no non-controversial or objective method at all for making the identification. If we knew that the proper equivalents were terms that stood for desires or aversions, pleasures or pains, preferences or non-preferences, divine commands or merely human directives, etc., then there might (just *might*) be an objective method of deciding the truth-values of the equivalent nonmoral statements containing the nonmoral terms. But there appears to be no such objectively plausible method of reaching the equivalent terms or translations themselves. On the contrary, there appear to be reasonable grounds for questioning any and all of the translations that have been proposed by definists. Every such translation can be met with counter-examples from standard ethical usage which challenge the propriety of the translation. If, for instance, *good* just meant the same thing as maximizing pleasure, then it would be (not just false but) logically absurd to challenge the moral propriety of an act that did maximize pleasure; or if *right* just meant the same thing as being commanded by God, it would be logically meaningless to say that God would not command an act if it were not the morally right

3.5b) Cognitivist criticisms agree in accepting the property doctrine, but claim that the nature and content of these properties are misinterpreted by definism.

3.5c) No objective and non-controversial method of identifying the nonmoral equivalents of moral terms can be reasonably identified, since:

3.5c1) There is serious disagreement about the propriety of all proposed candidates.

3.5c2) Every such candidate can be met with counter-examples from standard ethical usage.

3.6) Illustrations

thing to do; or if right just meant being subsumable under a universalizable rule or maxim, then it would be (again not just false but) logically absurd to claim that an act was morally right under the circumstances even though it could not logically be subsumed under such a universalizable rule or maxim. But the problem is that none of these implied absurdities are genuine logical conundrums, since, whether correct or not, they all make logical sense. Thus it can be reasonably claimed, on the basis of such examples, that, for any proposed translation, there are clear and consistent cases of standard ethical usage which the translation cannot accommodate. If, in response, it is claimed that standard usage is itself muddled and logically incoherent, that, even if it is true, will merely add support to the critical claim that the nonmoral equivalents and translations are controversial, arbitrary, and without objective support of the relevant sort. And hence it will follow that the purported epistemological advantage of definism, in being able to decide objectively the truth or falsity of the translation statements, will simply dissolve, since the translations themselves are invariably disputable without logical absurdity.

3.6b) If standard usage is itself challenged, that will show how arbitrary the proposed translated equivalents are.

3.6c) In view of this difficulty, the claimed epistemological advantage of definism dissolves.

3.6d) For many forms of naturalistic definism, the non-moral translation equivalents of moral terms are subjectively relational terms that refer to the responses of the person making the judgment rather than to the acts, character states, etc., being judged about in the original ethical statements.

A further difficulty that applies to many (but not all) forms of naturalistic definism concerns the fact that for those forms the translation equivalents are terms which have a subjectively relational meaning that depends for its propriety on the subject or person making the assertion containing the term, so that the actual reference of the term is to the subjective state of the person rather than to the objective property of the thing qualified. To take a nonmoral example of such subjectively relational meaning: if I say, 'The banana I ate this morning was delicious,' the term *delicious* is a subjectively relational term, since it refers primarily to my taste preference rather than to any property of the banana, however true descriptively it might be to claim that if the banana had different properties, I would not have claimed that it was delicious (at least not in the same way). It is a logical property of statements containing subjectively relational terms that their truth value is relatively dependent upon the identity of the person making the claim about the purported subject to which the predicate is attached. Thus my original banana example means the same thing as: 'I enjoyed (or liked) the taste of the banana I ate this morning.'

3.7) But this would mean that properly formulated judgments, which appear to contradict each other, would not really be doing so,

Meta-Ethical Cognitivism

32

The truth of the original statement is therefore relative to (in this case) the gustatory preference of the person making it; the translation suggested is a straightforward empirical statement. While the empirical translation makes an objective claim, the claim is not about the banana but about subjectively relative taste preference. It follows that, for such subjectively relational sentences, if, for example, I gave part of my banana to my wife, and she claimed that it was not delicious, while I claimed that it was delicious, we would not really be contradicting each other even though linguistically we appeared to be doing so. The reason: *delicious* does not have the same reference in the two claims, since one is about my wife's taste preference and the other about mine.

But now suppose all this is put in an ethical context where the nonmoral translation equivalents of ethical terms are themselves subjectively relational terms. It is clearly the case that the translation equivalents of numerous forms of naturalistic definism are of this sort: if, for example, these equivalents are terms that stand for such subjectively relational states as desires (even ideal desires), pleasures, pains, preferences, or aspirations, then it is clear that theories appealing to such nonmoral predicates as logical equivalents of moral terms are all proposing to reduce moral judgments to subjectively relative and variable judgments about the psychological states and preferences of the persons making the moral judgments rather than to judgments about the acts, states of character, choices, etc., that, from the form of the judgment, it would be supposed the judgment was about. On such terms, to say that, for instance, a certain act is morally wrong, would not be to assign a property to the act as such, but would instead be to make a judgment expressing (or perhaps even asserting) something about the psychological or preferential states of the person making the claim. But in that case, a moral judgment would no longer be an objective property statement about the moral act (or whatever), but a subjectively relative statement about the propounder of the statement. The analogy with the banana example is obvious. Here also, in the ethical case, if one person said that a certain act was morally right, and another said it was morally wrong, they would not really be contradicting each other, since the terms would have a subjectively relative dependence that varied with the person making the judgment

since the term would vary in relation to persons making the judgment.

3.7a) This is true in a nonmoral case about appetite preferences.

3.7b) But it also holds for many forms of naturalistic definism:

3.7b1) A summary of results for moral judgments thus interpreted: moral judgments would no longer be objective property statements about the things originally judged about.

3.7b2) Here again moral judgments, which appeared logically opposed, would not really be contradicting each other.	precisely because such subjectively variable terms are different in referential meaning for each different person relative to his or her psychological state. It is possible, of course, in a certain sense, to regard all judgments, expressing psychological states with such variable preference in a person-relative way, as objectively determinate empirical judgments about each distinct person making such a declaration. In that case, standard empirical methods for determining truth or falsity would be applicable; but it would be highly questionable to claim that such individually distinct empirical judgments were equivalent in meaning to the original moral judgments of which they purported to be a translation. While it seems plausible to claim that persons need only consult their own gustatory preferences to decide whether a banana they have tasted or eaten was delicious, it makes little sense (logically) to claim that persons need only consult their own attitudinal preferences to decide whether an act (theirs or anyone else's) is morally right or wrong. The question therefore now becomes the issue as to whether it is logically reasonable to accept all these consequences of any form of naturalistic definism that identifies the meaning of ethical terms with that of subjectively relational nonmoral predicates of any sort whatever.
3.7b3) All this raises questions about the supposed equivalence of meaning between moral and nonmoral terms.	
3.8) Are these consequences logically acceptable?	
3.8a) Questions that lead to a decision	To decide this issue, consider the following relevant questions:
3.8a1) The questions posed	1) When a person makes a moral claim, does that person intend to be making a claim which, though accepted by his or her own self, is either true or false independently of the fact that that person made the claim? Or does the individual intend that claim to be radically relative to, and dependent upon, his or her own identity as the person making the claim? 2) When a person makes a moral claim, does that person intend that claim to be *about* the act, decision, state of moral character, etc., which the claim purports to evaluate morally? Or, does that person intend the claim to be *about* his or her own individually idiosyncratic psychological attitudes, desires, or preferences? 3) If two persons make opposing moral claims, the

one claiming that a given act is morally right and the other that it is morally wrong (i.e., not morally right), are they making claims about the act that are logically opposed and therefore contradictory? Or, do their opposing claims merely express (or perhaps assert) contrasting but logically compatible attitudinal or preferential differences?

If one opts for the first alternative by answering yes to the first question in each of the three pairs, one is understanding the logic of moral judgments in a way that involves the rejection of subjectively relational forms of naturalistic definism; but if one opts for the second alternative in each of the three pairs, one is understanding the logic of moral judgments in such a way as to accept the reasonableness of some possible form of subjectively relational naturalistic definism. In my opinion, it seems plausible to argue that standard moral usage accords with the first alternative in each case, and that all forms of subjectively relational naturalistic definism are logically (perhaps also morally) unacceptable. If persons untarnished by philosophical sophistication reflectively consult what they themselves intend when they make a serious moral claim, I am confident that they will find the first alternative in each of the three cases to be far more in accord with their practical, moral intention than the second. Indeed, if any form of subjectively relational naturalistic definism were correct, it would, in my opinion, be extremely difficult to explain why every developed human civilization has found it necessary to concoct and employ moral discourse, when, given such a subjectively relational view, the language of psychological attitude and preference would have more than sufficed for the purpose. At the very least, we might conclude that if any form of definism provides a logically adequate account of moral discourse, it will not be any version of such subjectively relational definism. And if this conclusion is correct, then it would further follow that the fundamental defect of subjectively relational definism would be that it fails to realize that fundamentally evaluative moral judgments purport to make an objective claim the reasonableness of which is not logically dependent upon subjectively variable states of individual opinion, preference, feeling, or response. This

3.8a2) The logical consequences of the alternatives

3.8b) In general, the intention of a reflectively mature person, in making a moral judgment, cannot be viewed as compatible with the implications of subjectively relational naturalistic definism.

3.8b1) Otherwise, it is hard to explain why there should be any distinctively moral discourse at all.

3.8b2) The basic defect of all such definisms is that they fail to account for the fact that moral judgments purport to make an objective claim to reasonableness.

3.8c) This same difficulty applies in general to all forms of radical ethical relativism.	defect in all forms of subjectively relational definism is one of the most crucial negative criticisms of radical ethical relativism in general which claims that the propriety (or, even the truth value) of a moral judgment is relative to and dependent upon just such subjectively variable states of individuals and/or social groups. But whether that criticism spells the demise of radical ethical relativism, without further ado, will be considered in a later context.
3.9) Other forms of definism may not rest on subjectively relational ground;	However, there are other forms of meta-ethical definism, so it is generally conceded, that do *not* regard the nonmoral equivalents of ethical terms as subjectively relational terms of the sort analyzed above. Instead, these nonmoral equivalent terms stand for purportedly objective properties in some
3.9a) But it is hard to think of an example of naturalistic definism that does not involve this relational basis.	way or another. This would certainly be the case with both formalistic rationalistic definism and religious-metaphysical definism. It might even be the case with certain forms of naturalistic definism, though here such examples are more difficult to identify, since most of the empirical, descriptive forms of definism seem, on analysis, to rest on subjectively relational grounds. A possible non-relational example would
3.9b) Even an ideal cognitive observer theory may involve such a basis.	perhaps be some kind of ideal cognitive observer theory that identifies the meaning of moral terms with nonmoral predicates that describe what a fully informed, emotionally stable, disinterested judge would or would not approve morally. But aside from the difficulty of attaining such knowledge (since all human judges fail to meet the suggested criteria), the question would remain as to whether such an ideal cognitive observer would have objective rational grounds for a moral judgment in a particular case, or would, on the contrary, merely be expressing a subjectively relative opinion of his or her own. In the latter case, we would be back to subjectively relational definism; and in the former case, it would be those objective grounds to which moral terms referred and in which they found their application (or even their meaning), so that the moral terms could not be plausibly defined as equivalent in meaning to terms designating the approval or disapproval of even an omniscient judge.
3.9c) The definist fallacy and open questions arguments	But no matter: it has been claimed by G.E. Moore and C.D. Broad, among others, that there is a crucial logical aspect in *all* forms of definism, whether objective or subjective, an irremediable defect which at one stroke renders all those forms implausible as meta-ethical theories. In the

Principia Ethica, Moore was concerned primarily to criticize naturalistic definisms (though he referred briefly to other versions), and he therefore designated this purportedly devastating criticism the *naturalistic fallacy* argument, though in our terminology here we can use the phrase *definist fallacy* to cover all forms of definism. A generalized version of the same argument can be called the *open question* argument. For any nonmoral property, empirical or otherwise, the supposition that it is logically equivalent in meaning to some moral property (good, right, etc.) is linguistically and logically absurd, or so runs the definist or naturalistic fallacy argument. For in that case, the statement—that a thing or subject possessing that nonmoral property was good, right, or any appropriate moral predicate—would be merely the tautological statement that a thing or subject possessing that nonmoral property was a thing or subject possessing that nonmoral property. This would be the result if goodness, rightness, etc., simply means the same thing as some nonmoral property term. For example, if 'goodness,' as ascribed to any subject in the moral sense, means the same thing as the nonmoral phrase 'maximizing pleasurable consequences and minimizing painful ones,' then the statement that a given act, for instance, which maximized pleasure and minimized pain was morally good, would simply be the same as the statement that a given act which maximized pleasure and minimized pain was an act which maximized pleasure and minimized pain. And as a pointless tautological assertion, that statement would be linguistically and logically absurd. Yet the original claim, that such an act was morally good, would not be thus either linguistically or logically absurd, but a perfectly sensible cognitive claim, even if false. But from this fact it follows that goodness simply does not and logically cannot mean the same thing as any nonmoral term whatsoever. The same argument, in a different guise, urges that, given any nonmoral property, it always makes logical sense to ask whether a thing or subject possessing that property is morally good, or right, etc.; but if such a moral term simply meant the same thing as a term standing for that nonmoral property, then the same question as before would make no linguistic or logical sense at all, since it would be merely the question whether a thing or subject possessing that nonmoral property was a thing or subject

3.9c1) Statement of the definist fallacy: no nonmoral property can be equivalent in meaning to any moral property, since if that were so, the claim to that effect would be a tautological claim that a thing possessing that nonmoral property was a thing possessing that nonmoral property.

3.9c2) For example, take the claim that the term 'good' means the same thing as the term 'pleasure': the result would be an absurdity, although the original claim containing the ethical term would not be thus absurd.

3.9c3) Hence, the proposed equivalence is itself absurd.

3.10) Statement of the open question argument: the claim, that a thing possesses any nonmoral property, leaves open the question whether that thing possesses any given moral property, while that would not be the

possessing that nonmoral property. And that question, literally speaking, would be patent nonsense, even though it is not mere gibberish. In this form, the argument is therefore appropriately called the *open question argument*, since the statement that a thing or subject possesses any nonmoral property always appears to leave open (i.e., undecided) the question whether such a thing or subject possesses any given moral property.

> case if the two properties (moral and nonmoral) meant the same thing.

In formulating what I have called the definist fallacy argument, I have not bound myself to expressing that argument precisely in the way that would be approved by G.E. Moore, nor have I involved myself in the several different ways in which Moore himself, in various contexts, tried to characterize that argument. Instead, borrowing heavily from insights contained in Moore's *Principia*, I have tried to state the argument in what appears to me to be its most plausible form for my own expository purposes; and I do not know whether Moore would have accepted my version of the argument as even approximately representing his position. I have, for instance, deliberately avoided any reference to Moore's claim that the basic ethical term *good* is indefinable because it stands for a simple property which, if known at all, is understood by immediate apprehension rather than by definition of the sort that is possible only for complex terms. Whether basic ethical terms stand for simple or complex properties, if indeed, as we are in this context assuming, they stand for properties at all, is a crucial issue indeed; and so is the question whether those basic terms symbolize meanings that must be grasped by immediate apprehension through rational intuition. But though these claims, if accepted, comport well with the mindset of the definist fallacy argument, they are not relevant, in my opinion, to the main thrust of that argument as I have explained it.

> 3.11) In my statement of the argument, I have given it in what I regard as its most plausible general form without introducing other aspects of Moore's exposition, which I view as logically unrelated to the argument.

More pertinent to the critical evaluation of the definist fallacy argument is the question whether it is possible to derive normative ethical conclusions from non-ethical premises; whether, that is, it is possible, with logical propriety, to derive an 'ought' conclusion from an 'is' premise. Any definist would doubtless be logically bound to claim that such a transition would be logically appropriate, since, on my definition, definism is precisely the view that ethical terms are equivalent in meaning to some non-ethical

> 3.12) The relevance of the question whether 'ought' can be derived from 'is'
> 3.12a) Any form of definism implies the propriety of this derivation.

terms or conjunction of such terms; and that position would clearly entail the conclusion that ethical propositions are logically derivable from the non-ethical propositions that result from replacing the ethical terms in the original propositions with the logically equivalent non-ethical terms. However, it surely does not follow from the claim, that all definists believe that 'ought' can be derived from 'is,' that therefore all those who accept such a derivation are definists. It is widely held that the propriety of any ethical proposition is partly dependent logically on the truth or falsity of various non-ethical propositions that provide a relevant context for any given ethical judgment—propositions, for example, about the capacity and knowledge of a given moral agent, or about the consequences of certain acts or rules of procedure for the persons likely to be affected by the implementation of such an act or rule. And it might even be held that such non-ethical propositions provide the whole basis for the reasonableness of certain moral claims in the only sense in which such claims *can* be rendered reasonable. But neither of these views would constitute by themselves the position of definism, since neither view would be bound to hold that ethical terms were equivalent in meaning to non-ethical terms, but merely that ethical claims were partly (or wholly) supported in their reasonableness by contextually relevant non-ethical truths. All that I wish to conclude in this present context about the 'is-ought' debate is that the claim, that 'ought' propositions follow (in part or in whole) from 'is' propositions, does not logically entail definism; although the claim, that 'ought' propositions cannot logically follow from 'is' propositions alone, does appear to involve the denial of any form of definism.

3.12b) But not all positions that accept the derivation of 'ought' from 'is' are logically committed to definism.

3.12c) However, the rejection of the derivation of 'ought' from 'is' necessarily involves the denial of definism.

With these qualifications about my version of the definist fallacy argument, I now return to the question of the plausibility of the argument itself. Criticisms of the argument are indeed legion, and understandably so since so much philosophical substance hinges on its acceptance or rejection. An unprejudiced and respectable scholar like William Frankena, for example, in his widely read article entitled 'The Naturalistic Fallacy,' is generally thought to have 'delivered the death blow' to the naturalistic or definist fallacy argument. Aside from his reasonable claim that Moore's various comments about the argument do not present an

3.13) Criticisms of the definist fallacy argument

3.13a) Frankena argues that:

entirely clear account, Frankena offers the following criticisms. First, he holds that the term *fallacy* is misplaced here because definist views, while they may be mistaken, commit no formal logical invalidity, since it is always possible to construct a formally valid argument for any definist thesis. The real issue with such arguments will concern, not their validity, but the truth (or falsity) of their premises. And this issue cannot be resolved on formal logical grounds, so that the term *fallacy* is out of place here. Secondly, Frankena maintains that Moore's claim to the effect that all definisms involve confusing two different properties, can be rebutted by pointing out that the definists are not claiming that two different properties are the same property, but rather that two different words (for example, 'good' and 'pleasant') stand for the same property. Since it appears that Moore's arguments against definism simply assume, rather than arguing, that this last claim is false, it would also appear that his arguments beg the main question at issue between himself and the definists. Finally, Frankena argues that if Moore's definist fallacy argument rules out any definitions of terms (those of the definist, for example), then it would rule out all definitions of any term whatever, unless Moore again begs the question by assuming that moral goodness (or rightness, or both) should be construed as indefinable and therefore apprehensible only by immediate insight or intuition as an unanalyzable, simple property. But this again is merely to assume, not to argue, the basic issue at stake between Moore and the definists.

What I shall claim myself is that, whatever the virtues or vices of Moore's version of the argument, my own version of the definist fallacy argument is either not subject to the sort of criticisms Frankena urges, or is subject to these criticisms only in a sense that is innocuous and provides no substantive difficulty for the definist fallacy argument as I understand and defend it. To start with, the claim that the term *fallacy* is inappropriate, in the name of the argument in question, is a merely verbal point about the scope of the word itself: if it is insisted that the reference of the term should only be to instances of formal logical invalidity (such as undistributed middle term, four terms, contradiction, and the like), then Frankena's point is correct. But it would be difficult to claim that the word *fallacy* has no other appropriate use; that, for instance, it could not be used to designate a

3.13a1) definism need not involve any formal logical fallacy;

3.13a2) definists do not really confuse two distinct properties, but merely claim that two different words stand for the same property;

3.13a3) the definist fallacy argument would, if accepted, rule out all definitions of terms, unless Moore's conclusion is assumed at the outset.
3.13b) But Frankena's criticisms do not apply significantly to my version of the definist fallacy argument.

3.13b1) The objection to the term *fallacy* is a merely verbal issue: the term can have other meanings besides formal logical invalidity.

linguistic middle, impropriety, or unintelligibility (which is what the definist fallacy argument claims). But no substantive philosophical point is at stake here: were it not for the widely understood reference of the phrase *definist* (or *naturalistic*) *fallacy argument*, we would simply replace the word with some other less rigorously construable term (such as *mistake*, *ambiguity*, or *incoherence*). But precisely for convenience of reference I will retain the term *fallacy* with the explanation that it should not be understood in the sense of formal logical invalidity.

Frankena's second criticism, to the effect that definists do not, as Moore claimed, confuse two different properties, but merely hold that two different words or terms stand for the same property, this criticism, I repeat, simply does not apply to my version of the definist fallacy argument, whether or not it applies to Moore's version. For what my argument claims is precisely that a moral term, used in its fundamentally evaluative sense, logically (in the linguistic sense) cannot stand for the same property as any nonmoral term, since, if that were the case, the statement, that a thing or subject possessing the non-ethical property in question was morally good (or right, etc.), would be both pointless and nonsensical—which clearly it is not, in a typical case. The point is that, if moral terms stand for properties at all, they cannot stand for the same properties as any conjunction of nonmoral terms. That is not to say, however, that it could not be the case that a thing or subject possessing certain nonmoral properties always also (or even for that reason) possesses some moral property; it is merely to say that moral terms and nonmoral terms cannot, as such, stand for the same properties. If it should be objected that the linguistic improprieties with which I charge definism are merely the results of the ambiguity and imprecision of moral terms in standard usage, then that also could be interpreted as question begging. And if *all* appeals to standard usage are called into question, on what ground will the definist base his or her own equivalency claim between moral and nonmoral terms? If the identification is merely stipulative and reformatory in nature, then no substantive issue about the meaning of moral terms will have been settled by that ploy: the mere fact that someone decides to use a certain term in a certain way may raise the question whether the term

3.13b2) My version claims that a moral term, as such, cannot stand for the same property as any nonmoral term, since that would reduce perfectly intelligible sentences to nonsense.

3.13b3) If my appeal here to standard usage is itself challenged, then that will make the definist view itself merely a verbal stipulation.

3.13b4) Hence, no substantive issue on the point will be settled.

logically ought to be used in that way; it certainly does not settle that question.

3.14) The definist fallacy argument need not make all definition impossible.

Nor do I see, finally, that the logic of the definist fallacy argument, if accepted in my version of it or in some logically similar version, would imply the impossibility of defining any term whatsoever through the use of synonymously equivalent terms. What does follow is instead that terms which stand for nonmoral properties cannot by themselves constitute the definition of terms which stand for moral properties. Perhaps it also follows, on pain of infinite regress, that the basic elements of all definitions cannot themselves be apprehended by definition and so on without logical limit; so that the basic elements of ethical definition as well, therefore, cannot be apprehended by further definition either, but must be grasped by immediate rational insight or intuition.

3.14a) It merely implies that moral terms cannot be defined solely by nonmoral terms.

3.14b) But it may imply also that the basic elements of definition must be understood by immediate apprehension.

3.14c) The argument does therefore raise serious questions about definism.

I therefore conclude, in particular, that the definist fallacy argument, whether inappropriately named or not, does in fact throw all versions of definism into serious question, even if that same argument does not decisively eliminate definism with finality. More generally, I conclude that the various difficulties connected with alternative forms of definism are of such a magnitude that they make any version of definism theoretically implausible. If, therefore, moral terms stand for properties at all, they do not stand for properties that can be wholly defined in nonmoral terms, however relevant nonmoral truths may be to settling the truth value of moral or ethical claims.

3.15) In conclusion, definism is, in general, theoretically implausible, unless the property doctrine is itself rejected.

Intuitionism: A Distinctionist Stance

3.16) Summary of meta-ethical intuitionism

But all this does not dispense with what I have called the property doctrine, if that doctrine can be plausibly cast in non-definist terms. The meta-ethical theory generally designated as *intuitionism* claims that this feat can be accomplished. This position, held by ethical theorists otherwise as diverse as Richard Price, G.E. Moore, C.D. Broad, W.D. Ross, H.A. Prichard, A.C. Ewing, and even (in a qualified sense) by Henry Sidgwick[1] himself: this position in general, I repeat, while accepting the property doctrine, maintains

---
[1] Sidgwick's work, *The Methods of Ethics*, is the finest treatise on philosophical ethics I have ever laid my eyes on, though I disagree with his normative ethical position.

that ethical terms stand precisely for unique moral properties which cannot be defined wholly (or perhaps at all) in nonmoral terms and are therefore not empirically descriptive properties. It is further maintained that the meaning of basic ethical terms, used in their fundamentally evaluative sense, must therefore be apprehended by immediate rational insight or intuition in such a way that, although nonmoral truths may and do provide a context for such intuitions and even put the ethical judge in the proper position to make such intuitive judgments, the apprehension of the truth or falsity of those nonmoral judgments does not and cannot of itself constitute the whole meaning of the moral predicates assigned in a moral judgment, much less the moral propriety of the judgment assigning any given moral-predicate to a subject in a given instance. It is a corollary of this position that *at least one* basic ethical term ('good,' 'right,' 'ought,' or 'duty,' for example) must be indefinable in the sense of being unanalyzable into more logically simple elements, although other ethical terms would be definable in terms of the immediately intuited meaning of that one basic term, either by itself or in conjunction with other nonmoral psychological or generally descriptive terms. This is not to say, however, that the content, to which that basic ethical term would be appropriately applied, is either indefinable or unanalyzable. If, for example, 'good' is plausibly identifiable as the basic ethical term, then, although its meaning as a predicate could not be defined (analyzed into simpler elements), nevertheless '*the* good,' or 'that which *is* good' in the moral sense could clearly be identified and in that sense defined. It is therefore merely goodness *as a predicate* that is indefinable, not the subject matter to which that predicate could be appropriately applied. The hedonistic claim (in normative ethics), that pleasure is the one intrinsic good in the moral sense, would be one such content identification proposal, even if the claim turned out to be false while still quite intelligible. For various types of subjects or things being morally judged (for example, acts, rules, or even persons), there may even be criteria of applicability, peculiar to each type, that would determine the limits of propriety in assigning the moral predicate 'good' in a given case. Thus while intuitive rational insight is indispensable, it is not the whole ethical package, so to speak: much analysis and rele-

3.16a) Ethical terms stand for unique moral properties that cannot be wholly defined by nonmoral concepts.

3.16b) The meaning of basic ethical terms must be apprehended by immediate rational insight, although nonmoral truths may provide a relevant and essential context for such insight.

3.16c) Hence, at least one (perhaps more) basic ethical term must be analytically indefinable.

3.16c1) But the content to which such a term applies is not indefinable.

3.16c2) That which *is* good can therefore be defined (identified), even though the predicate *good* cannot be defined.

3.16d) For any one sort of thing being morally judged, there may be criteria of applicability for the relevant ethical term.

vant nonmoral understanding is typically involved, not to mention much analysis involving other ethical terms that are definable or analyzable primarily through the single unanalyzable basic ethical term.

Defenders of intuitionism (I myself will eventually defend a variety of modified meta-ethical intuitionism) maintain that any mature judge of moral matters whose judgmental capacity has been developed and trained by serious disciplined practice, either is or can become clearly aware of unique ethical judgment and decision, although such a person might not, of course, verbalize this moral awareness in the theoretical terms of moral philosophy. If any person claims not to be aware of such irreducible (i.e., in nonmoral terms) moral properties, then the logically proper response, from the intuitionist point of view, is that such a person has not analyzed his or her moral situation clearly and correctly, that this person has become confused by theoretical squabbles, that this person lacks sufficient practice in making moral judgments, or even, in untypical and hopefully rare instances, that this person's capacity for intuitive moral discernment has become perverted by the defective state of his or her own moral character. But self-conscious ethical intuitionists do not agree among themselves about which moral term or terms are morally basic, about how such basic terms are logically related to each other and to derivative moral terms, or about whether moral acts or moral rules are the basic elements of moral judgment. Of course, it is also trivially clear that, like all the rest of us moral judges (whether honed in our moral practice by theoretical philosophy or not), ethical intuitionists are often widely disagreed on particular judgments in applied normative ethics (for example, whether it is right or wrong to misrepresent the truth in a particular case, etc.).

The most striking disagreement here in the sphere of theoretical ethics is that between the teleological and the deontological approaches. The *teleological* view basically maintains that the moral rightness of an act is a function of the goodness or value (whether moral or nonmoral) of the consequences that performing the act would produce; or, more briefly, rightness logically depends upon 'goodness.' A proponent of this view might hold either the strong position that this dependency implies that rightness is definable

---

3.17) The elaboration of meta-ethical intuitionism
3.17a) Any mature moral judge can become clearly aware of unique moral properties through disciplined practice.

3.17a1) If anyone claims the contrary, there are always plausible reasons for his or her disagreement.

3.17a2) But even intuitionists often disagree on theoretical detail and practical application.

3.17b) The disagreement between the teleological and deontological approaches.
3.18) The positions defined.

3.18a) Teleological: rightness logically dependent on goodness, either in

in terms of the goodness of consequences, or the logically weaker and more moderate position that, as a matter of fact, it is always the case that the right act is *ipso facto* the act productive of the most good consequences; of course, it would be logically possible to hold both these views in conjunction, as G.E. Moore originally did, although he later surrendered the first and retained only the second. The *deontological* view, on the other hand, maintains that the moral rightness of an act is, at least in certain crucial instances, logically independent of the goodness or value (whether moral or non-moral) of the consequences that performing the act would produce, so that the rightness of that act is a function of certain other characteristics of the act (for example, the immediate discernment of the act as a duty, or the conformity of the act to a formal rule or principle of duty and/or reason); or, more briefly, 'rightness' is (in certain crucial instances, or perhaps even unqualifiedly) logically independent of 'goodness.' Both teleological and deontological positions occur in both 'act' or 'rule' versions, depending on whether it is held that each act is to be individually evaluated in its moral status without the guidance of general rules (except as practical 'rules of thumb'), or that any particular act is to be evaluated in its moral status through its conformity (or not) to a general rule or principle which is, as such, judged to be morally sound.

    For my purposes, I shall make no issue about either act or rule versions of either general position, except to say that, given the intelligibility of moral claims as property statements, it seems plausible to argue that, whenever a person judges an act to be morally right or wrong, that person is making an objective claim to the effect that any other person, in relevantly similar circumstances, logically ought (and morally ought) to make the same judgment, so that from the very nature of an objective and moral claim of this sort, the act is being brought under a general rule. The only immediately discernible alternative to this position, in the context assumed, would be to radically relativize the judgment to the individual making the claim and thus to deprive the claim of both objectivity and universality, and in this latter case it is questionable whether any genuine moral claim is being made. More succinctly, to make the moral claim that an act is right or wrong is *ipso facto* to imply its conformity

---

meaning or in content or in both.

3.18b) Deontological: rightness logically independent of goodness, either wholly or in part.

3.19) Act and rule versions of both views.

3.19a) My view would defend the rule versions, since the objectivity and universality of any moral claim would entail its subsumption under a general rule.

3.19b) Otherwise it is questionable whether any genuine moral claim is being made.

3.20) As to the general theories, it is essential to clarify what sorts of consequences are being regarded as relevant or otherwise.

3.21) The nonmoral consequence view bases moral worth on such consequences alone.
3.22) But this view is confusing, since it is very difficult to distinguish unprejudicially between moral and nonmoral consequences:

3.22a) Any morally relevant consequence would appear to be a moral consequence just for that reason.

to a general rule and, in that sense, to subsume it under that rule, whether consciously or not.[2] If this general argument is, as I believe, correct, then rule versions, of either the teleological or deontological views, would be logically preferable, although I will build no substantial philosophical conclusion on this claim.

But the issue at stake between the general teleological and deontological positions is a different matter and one of considerable significance. A preliminary clarification will be important to lay the groundwork for an analysis of these competing claims. If we are to consider the relation between the moral worth of an act and the value or goodness of its consequences, it seems necessary to specify what sort of consequences are involved. Some ethical theorists take the position that a properly and clearly stated teleological position would make the *moral* worth of an act logically dependent upon its *nonmoral* consequences and would not therefore take its moral consequences into consideration. But I myself find this claim confusing, since I doubt that a clear criterion for the distinction between moral and nonmoral consequences can be given in a fashion that is both morally relevant and non-prejudicial. For any proposed type of so-called nonmoral consequence, it will be possible to argue that there is a normative ethical theory which identifies the content of the intrinsically good or right with precisely that sort of consequence. Suppose, for instance, that 'maximizing pleasure and minimizing pain' is taken as a nonmoral consequence: but that would be prejudicial, since ethical hedonism identifies the intrinsically good with precisely that type of consequence, and virtually no ethical theorist would claim that such a consequence is morally irrelevant. If, on the other hand, we seem able to suggest at last a truly non-prejudicial consequence that is nonmoral, it will be morally irrelevant to the rightness or wrongness of an act, and it will be absurd to claim that the moral worth of an act is a function of such consequences. It appears, therefore, that any consequence that is relevant to judging the moral worth of an act will for that very reason be a *moral* consequence, not a *non*moral consequence; otherwise, it will be impertinent to judging the moral value of the act. However, I am not

---

[2] F.H. Bradley referred to this characteristic of moral judgments and termed the process, for most moral judges, intuitive subsumption.

sure that there are absolutely no consequences of an act of moral significance that are at the same time nonmoral (relevant to judging the moral worth of the act) and non-prejudicial; although I doubt seriously that there are. So I will simply say that a properly formulated teleological position would claim that the moral worth of an act is a function of the value or goodness of *both* its moral and (if there are any) its relevant nonmoral consequences. If my logical point is correct here, then numerous criticisms of the teleological view, criticisms that turn on a clear identification of non-morally good consequences, will be largely deprived of their argumentative force and will scarcely be worth discussing.

One might suppose at the outset that the teleological claim, to the effect that no act could be morally right unless its performance would either increase or (at least) leave undisturbed the total amount of moral good in the world, would, as a claim, be so intuitively obvious that any counter-claim would be scarcely intelligible. Would not such a counter-claim imply that an act could be morally right even if consequentially it either would reduce, or appeared on the whole likely to reduce, the total amount of moral (and nonmoral) good in the universe? And is not this implication clearly absurd? So argues G.E. Moore, for example. If the range of consequences considered is sufficiently broad, then perhaps every person, in the depth of his or her being, whether consciously or not, profoundly believes that moral duty and consequential expediency could never be opposed in the end. But however surprising, arguments to support such a counter-claim have been so legion as to constitute a veritable deluge of logical reasoning in support of the opposing deontological position and against the teleological view.

Perhaps the most striking deontological argument to this effect has been produced by H.A. Prichard in his notoriously debated article entitled, 'Does Moral Philosophy Rest on a Mistake?' Here it is argued that, if what we mean by moral philosophy is the systematic attempt to justify the rightness of an act by showing (or attempting to show) that the act will be instrumental in producing something either as good as the object of desire (for example, happiness or pleasure for oneself and/or others) or good in itself (for example, the act itself, or some state of virtuous character), then moral philosophy, so construed, involves a

3.22b) It is at least an open question whether there are any morally relevant nonmoral consequences.
3.23) So the most plausible teleological view would appeal to both moral and (if there are any) nonmoral consequences: and that inclusion would eliminate many criticisms of the teleological view.
3.23a) While the denial of the teleological view seems counter-intuitive by implying that a morally right act could make the world worse, nevertheless such a denial has been widely defended by the deontologists.

3.24) Prichard argues that moral rightness is, logically speaking, absolutely underivative, immediate, and self-evident, so that the rightness of an act cannot depend on its being a means to something good, whether moral or nonmoral.

basic mistake; and the mistake consists, so Prichard claims, in supposing that moral rightness, which is, if present at all, absolutely underivative, immediate, and self-evident, can nevertheless be shown to be derivative, mediate, and evident precisely through its dependence on something else, namely, a good or a good consequence. This can be clearly seen by noting several logical relationships: first, that there is no way of showing that a good desire ought to be fulfilled or a good consequence produced morally except by arguing from, and therefore presupposing, the rightness, morally, of the act or acts by which such results would ensue; second, that from the presence of a desire or motive, no moral obligation follows, although there may certainly be moral obligation without the presence of any such desire or motive (Is a person absolved from an obligation merely by lacking a given motive or desire?); third, that since desire and/or motive often oppose recognized obligation, it is clear that they are always logically distinct and that therefore an obligation cannot be justified by a desire or motive (unless, of course, we construe the immediate recognition of an obligation as itself a motive); and finally, that if the recognition of an obligation to act rested on some further motive, then it would be impossible to explain how a person could be morally motivated to the act itself as such in the morally obligatory sense—to be moved toward a morally obligatory act from some motive, would be to be moved toward being moved, and then to be moved toward being moved toward being moved, and so on indefinitely. From all this, Prichard reasons, it follows that the moral rightness of an act, though often conjoined with morally good motivation and often productive of morally good consequences, is nevertheless logically independent of these considerations. All this is not to say that the factual context and the consequences of a proposed action are not necessary preliminaries to its being immediately apprehended as morally obligatory; it is merely to claim that, in the context of such relevant considerations which spell out the proposed act in detail, the recognition of the act as morally obligatory is underivative and, in that sense, self-evident. Of course, it is a preliminary that the act be completely stated or described. If it be objected that obligations cannot be self-evident, since moral judges often disagree about them, then the answer is that the capacity for

3.25) The goodness of a consequence is rather itself dependent on the rightness of the act.

3.25a) Moral obligation is essentially independent of either desire or motive.

3.25b) Moral obligation can oppose desire or motive and is thus logically independent of it.

3.25c) The dependence of rightness on a motive would entail an infinite regress.

3.25d) The factual context and consequences of an act are part of the complete description of the act, but are not a justification of its rightness.

moral judgment is susceptible of different degrees of development in different persons, that in such cases the act has not been described in complete detail, and that, even for a mature moral judge, lack of thoughtfulness can blind him to his moral obligations. If, again, it is objected that moral obligations sometimes conflict and cannot therefore all be self-evident, the answer is that one must then decide which is the greater or greatest obligation, since their joint fulfillment is not possible. If these responses are plausible, and if Prichard's basic claim is correct, then the teleological claim, that 'rightness' logically depends upon 'goodness,' is indeed a serious and basic error.

3.25e) Nor does moral disagreement undermine the intuitive character of moral insight, since some persons are more experienced moral judges than others.

There are, however, numerous other arguments that have been and can be urged against the teleological view. Given any motive or desire as a consequential basis for purportedly justifying the moral rightness of an act, it is always possible to envision cases where our duty or obligation opposes that motive or desire (unless we take the recognition of moral obligatoriness itself as the motive in question); or conversely put, there are duties that are incumbent on us in certain circumstances, even if they have, in their fulfillment, consequences that do not maximize the good, however (i.e., morally and/or nonmorally) construed. Again, if the moral rightness (or otherwise) of an act were a function of the goodness (or otherwise) of its consequences, there would be no way of rationally choosing between alternatives in which the value of the consequences was equally balanced; but in fact we often clearly make valid moral decisions in such cases on non-consequentialist grounds.[3]

3.26) Additional arguments against the teleological view
3.26a) Given any motive, it is always possible to construe cases in which duty would oppose following that motive.

3.26b) How do we decide when consequences are equally balanced?

Again, if moral worth were totally a function of consequential value, there would be no way reasonably to decide between maximizing average good consequences and maximizing total good consequences for all the persons (or even sentient beings) likely to be affected by the act chosen in the relevant moral sense. Yet most moral judges would have little difficulty in deciding between an alternative in which the total relevant consequences would be greater, while one

3.26c) How do we decide between average and totally good consequences?

---

[3] For example, if two alternatives of moral choice are judged to have indistinguishably the same degree of consequential worth, while one involves breaking a promise (or telling a lie) and the other does not, most moral judges would opt for that alternative, as morally right, which does not involve a broken promise or a lie, precisely on the ground that these breaches are morally wrong as such.

person affected would accrue an enormous tally of good consequences (e.g., in realized desire) but the large group of remaining affected persons would each accrue only a moderate amount of good consequences, on the one hand, and an alternative in which the total consequences were less, but all those affected would individually accrue more good consequences than each of the members of the large group would in the first alternative. It follows, clearly, that the rightness of such a choice cannot be totally a function of the worth of the consequences of performing it, so that at least to that extent the teleological view is morally implausible.

3.26d) Total consequences are often uncertain and always practically incalculable.

A further argument against teleologism in ethics urges that if the moral rightness of an act depended crucially on the worth of its consequences, then, since such consequences are often uncertain and inaccessible to our knowledge and always incalculable (practically) in their extent, there would be no way of deciding with moral propriety whether or not to perform a given morally significant act. Nevertheless, we characteristically do decide such cases with firm confidence in the moral correctness of our choice, though of course errors in moral judgment are possible even in the face of such confidence.

3.26e) Since motives and intentions are an aspect of the moral worth of an act, the worth of the consequences cannot be the sole basis of the rightness of the act.

On the whole, most moral judges would also agree with Immanuel Kant that the nature of an agent's motive is relevant to estimating the moral worth of the action; and they might also agree that an otherwise morally right choice done purely out of a sense of duty or moral obligation has greater moral worth than the same choice done out of greed or the fear of painful consequences to the agent. But the motive or intention of a moral agent is quite independent of the objectively considered consequences of following that motive or intention, since morally distinguishable motives (for example, duty vs. fear) can lead to the same choice in action and therefore the same consequences. Hence, it follows, on the assumptions granted, that those objective consequences do not provide a total ground for the moral worth of the act.

3.27) If motives are regarded as aiming at certain consequences, then, since one cannot voluntarily produce any given motive, moral obligation must be

This argument about motives can be stood upon its head, as it were, by claiming, as has been done by David Ross, that, however commendable motives may be in the agent in certain cases, nevertheless it can never be the moral obligation of an agent to perform an act out of a good motive, since, again following Kant to his own detriment, it cannot be the case that I ought to do anything that I cannot do; and it is clear that I cannot, by choice, produce a certain motive or intention, much less make it effective in deciding a moral issue. I can only act from a certain motive if I have it, but it cannot be my unqualified duty to act from that motive, since I cannot by sheer choice produce it. I may, on the other hand, have a duty to cultivate a certain motive by thinking and acting in certain relevant ways; but that is a different issue. Since it cannot be my moral duty to act out of a certain motive, and since motives, when acted upon, are oriented by intention to produce certain consequences of an objective sort, it follows that my moral duty is always merely to act in certain ways (which I *can* do by choice) and never to act in those ways out of a certain motive (which I *cannot* do by choice); and hence it further follows that the rightness of an act cannot be logically contingent on the worth of the consequences of following a certain motive. Thus, whether I emphasize the distinction between a motive as a subjective intent and the consequences of performing an act under the guidance of that motive (as in the earlier part of this argument), or, alternatively, I emphasize the relation of a motive to its objective consequences (as in the inverted latter part of this argument), it appears that the rightness of an act is, at least partly, logically independent of the worth or goodness of the consequences of performing it.

the duty to perform a certain act, irrespective of intended results.

Now while the cumulative effect of all these deontological arguments may seem all but overwhelming, nevertheless the defenders of the teleological position have scarcely been reduced to silence by that effect. Such a teleologist might begin a defense against the deontological critics by pointing out that at best these criticisms show no more than that the moral rightness of an act is not *totally* a function of the worth or goodness of the consequences of performing it: but one way or another, all the deontologists, with the possible exception of Kant, recognize that the consequences of an act are logically relevant to, and therefore partly determinative of, the moral rightness (or otherwise) of the act. Some deontologists acknowledge this forthrightly, while others, like Prichard, include clearly consequential details in the complete description of the act whose moral worth is to be judged in its rightness or wrongness by immediate apprehension. But either way, the consequences of performing an

3.28) The teleological view in response

3.28a) At most, the deontological criticisms show that the consequences of an act are not the sole basis of its worth.
3.28a1) In general, deontologists recognize consequences as partly relevant to the determination of moral worth.
3.28a2) This is especially true if both moral and nonmoral consequences are considered.

act are recognized as one important basis for determining its rightness. If the consequences considered are sufficiently broad in their range, so as to include not merely such elements as realized desire or pleasure or preference, but also effects on the character and personal well-being of those individuals affected by a given act, it will be plausible to argue that the rightness of an act is at least partly a function of such consequences. It would certainly be arbitrary to make a sharp distinction between moral and nonmoral consequences, and therefore argue, in various ways, the irrelevance of such consequences to the rightness or wrongness of a morally significant act. Certainly the value of moral consequences must be factored in as well; as a matter of fact, in the end it is the moral effect of an act that is crucially relevant to the determination of its moral rightness or wrongness for any plausibly formulated teleological position. If that claim is correct, it takes much of the bite out of many of the deontological criticisms.

3.29) A well-phrased teleology would not claim that all moral worth is consequential, since that would involve an infinite regress in arguing any moral point.

It is of course quite incorrect, in my opinion, to argue that the justification of any moral claim without exception, whether of rightness or goodness, is a function of the value of the consequences that ensue from acting on the claim. That would be to contend that all moral value is a derivative of the worth of the consequences of putting that value into practical operation, and the worth of those consequences themselves a derivative of still further consequences, and so on without assignable logical limit; and thus a critically objectionable infinite regress (admittedly of a peculiar sort) would ensue.

3.29a) Unless some moral goodness or rightness is intrinsic or self-contained, nothing at all could be consequentially good or right: the ultimately good or right must be good or right as such and in itself.

Unless there is some moral value the worth of which is intrinsic and self-contained, rather than instrumental and derivative, it would follow that nothing could even be instrumentally and derivatively valuable either, since, by virtue of the infinite regress, there would be no ultimate foundation for such a claim. Something must be good in itself or right in itself, if anything at all is to be good or right through something else. The *ultimately* good or right is therefore not itself good consequentially; it is rather good or right as such, in the moral sense, and itself the intrinsically valuable basis of the worth of whatever is correctly regarded as consequentially good or right. Such ultimate good or right is therefore the indispensable deontological capstone of every teleologically justifiable moral claim. If this analysis is correct, there can be neither deontology without teleology, nor teleology without deontology: the former would be an ideal without relevance or application, and the latter would be an instrument or means without basis or end.

Thus Prichard's arguments for the claim that rightness is logically independent of consequential (or instrumental) goodness are both sound (in one sense) and unsound (in another sense). His arguments are sound if they are meant to show that behind every consequentially good effect there is an intrinsically right (or good) foundation; or if they are intended to show that nonmoral values (if, as I question, they can be non-prejudicially and relevantly identified) are of moral significance only through what is morally good or right, and that without such a basis no moral obligation can be claimed; or if they are designed to show that nonmoral desires or motives often oppose recognized moral obligation and cannot therefore provide a basis for it; or if they are supposed to indicate that a moral obligation can be incumbent upon a person, whatever the contingent state of that person's motives, desires, inclinations, or aspirations, so that moral rightness, though it may be reinforced by such psychological states, cannot be morally grounded in them. But on the other hand, Prichard's arguments are unsound if anyone supposes them to show that an act could not be derivatively right or wrong by reason of the morally good consequences of performing it; or that moral goodness is of no relevance in judging the moral rightness of an act; or that moral desires or motives, correctly understood, provide no part of the basis for assessing the moral quality of an act; or that a moral obligation can be incumbent on a person wholly apart from any capacity or controllable disposition of that person to respond to such a moral claim. Of course, no person could be moved toward the performance of a certain act on the basis of some further motive (such as desire, a sense of duty, fear of consequences, etc.), unless that person could be moved toward the performance of the act itself as such; but that any person can be thus moved itself involves a motive (that which inclines the person toward an end), and sustaining any and all such motives is the moral subject or agent who, I shall later attempt to show, possesses the transcendental freedom to choose between systems of inclining motives

3.29b) There must therefore be a deontological basis for every teleologically argued moral claim.

3.30) Prichard's arguments:

3.30a) are sound if they are intended to show that every teleology has a deontological starting point in self-contained or intrinsic moral worth;

3.30b) But they are unsound, if they are intended to show that rightness is wholly independent of either intrinsic or consequential goodness.

3.30c) It is, of course, possible to be moved toward an act as such, rather than on the basis of some motive: but behind every motive stands the free moral agent who decides between alternative motives.

and to direct his or her subsequent actions according to the motives thus chosen.

3.31) The criticism of teleology will be greatly relaxed in its effect, if it is admitted that an act can be subjectively right in relation to an agent's intention and knowledge, while at the same time being objectively wrong on the basis of consequential worth, and vice versa: here again deontology and teleology supplement each other.

A further distinction will help to defuse the otherwise explosive effect of deontological criticisms against teleologism (of a qualified sort). It seems plausible to distinguish between the rightness of an act objectively in terms of its morally relevant consequences, and the rightness of an act subjectively in terms of the agent's motive or intention together with his rationally grounded belief as to the morally relevant consequences of performing the act. If the distinction is made, then it will not be a paradox for an act to be right (or wrong) for the agent to perform, given his motives, intentions, and knowledge, while at the same time it has the opposite moral quality in its morally relevant consequences objectively construed. It is possible for an agent to do the right thing for the wrong reason or the wrong thing for the right (i.e., correct and individually justifiable) reason; and not merely or even characteristically the case that wrong acts always proceed from morally wrong reasons, and right acts from morally right ones. If this distinction between subjectively right or commendable and objectively right or consequentially good is accepted as qualifiedly correct, then of course it will be the case both that the objective consequential rightness of an act will indeed be a function of the moral worth or goodness of those consequences, and that the subjective rightness or moral propriety of an act, as morally commendable on the part of the agent, will be independent of those objective consequences, so that once again deontology and teleology will be conjoined in the total explanation of the moral worth of a morally significant act. An act done out of morally commendable motives will be a morally better act than one done out of purportedly nonmoral emotional or prudential motives, while at the same time the objective consequential rightness or wrongness of such an act will be logically independent of such subjectively contingent motivational considerations. If this analysis is logically and morally sound, all objections to a properly qualified teleology, on the supposition that such a view ignores the moral character and personal virtue of the agent, will appear to be vacuous. If, on the other hand, one takes a consequential view of motives themselves (where a motive is viewed as the disposition to act in order to produce certain purportedly valuable consequences), then it will be clear that nonmoral motives (for example, the propensity to realize a desire) will be morally relevant only if the consequences of conforming to them are themselves morally good, while moral motives will be, if commendable, an important part of the total moral significance of a given act as chosen by the agent.

As for the claim that teleologism would, as such, be incapable of deciding between maximizing average good consequences and maximizing total good consequences, this criticism too can be seen to be of little consequence: for the intrinsic worth of a person as a moral agent is clearly the most significant moral good to be considered in such cases. If maximizing *total* good consequences would have the effect of failing to give equality of consideration or treatment to all the persons affected (of course it is clear that this result is not inevitable in every relevant case), then it is also clear that maximizing *average* good consequences would be morally preferable, and that the factoring in of the intrinsic worth of the persons involved would, on the whole, virtually if not totally erase the distinction between total and average good consequences. Hence, the original criticism would become impertinent.

3.32) Deciding between average and total good consequences is possible if the intrinsic worth of the persons involved is taken as basic.

The argument based on the incalculability of the consequences of morally significant acts (on the ground that such consequences, as contingent probabilities, are uncertain in their occurrence, as well as indefinitely extended and thus beyond the reach of knowledge by a finite moral judge) is hardly a greater difficulty for any plausible teleological approach than it is for any reasonably grounded deontologism, since any plausible version of the latter would regard the consequences of such an act as relevant to the complete description of the act itself which is to be judged right or wrong. If, therefore, there is any insuperable difficulty here, it will rest with approximately equal weight on both positions. But in my opinion, no such difficulty is a serious problem for either view. Finite moral agents at their best can be held responsible morally only for the consequences which, under their limiting circumstances and inevitably limited knowledge, they can reasonably be expected to understand and anticipate; and they can make moral judgments, for either deontology or teleology, only under the same restrictions. This means

3.33) As for the incalculability of consequences:

3.33a) This presses equally hard on both views.
3.33b) In either case, a moral agent is only responsible morally for the consequences which he or she could reasonably understand and expect:

| | that moral judgments are in principle subject to fallibility
3.33b1) So we are | and error: none of us, as finite persons, are in principle and
practically fallible in | unexceptionably inerrant in our moral judgments about par-
the moral judgments | ticular moral cases, even if we are sometimes clearly correct in
we make. | our judgment and very nearly certain about the logical pro-

priety of the general principles that guide us in making such
judgments. So we always make our moral decisions with incomplete knowledge of all the conceivably relevant circumstances; yet we cannot, for this reason, persistently refuse to make such decisions—it is enough if we make them with an open sincerity under the guidance of plausible general rules and instructed by all the relevant knowledge that the circumstances make possible for us. Who would want us to decide on any lesser basis, and who could reasonably blame us morally for the fact that we are not omniscient moral judges or absolutely ideal moral observers? And it may be that the problem of incomplete knowledge can be even further alleviated, if certain students of moral philosophy are correct: just as the ripples on a pond, caused by dropping a stone into it, tend very quickly to approximate zero, so, it is suggested, the remote and therefore inaccessible consequences of acts occasioned by moral choice are less relevant to our moral decisions than the immediate and accessible consequences for the knowledge of which we can be held morally obligated. No one could reasonably claim this principle to hold for all moral choices; and perhaps no one can with solid confidence draw a clear and unmistakable line between the remote and the immediate. But it is nonetheless true on the whole that it is the clearly apprehensible consequences with whose relevance we are primarily concerned in making responsible moral choices.

3.33b2) And it may even be that, on the whole, the remote and inaccessible consequences are less relevant to moral decision than the immediate and accessible.

3.33b3) In general, an adequate view will have both deontological and teleological elements.

If, now, we review the arguments and issues at stake between deontological and teleological approaches to making decisions concerning moral rightness and goodness, it would seem plausible to conclude that an adequate perspective would include elements of both views, as I have already suggested in an earlier context: moral rightness and moral goodness are, it appears, inseparable, so that neither can account for the logical status of moral judgment without the support of the other. Any cognitivist theory that is intuitionist, and that thus denies any form of definism in meta-ethics, will need to be a mixed theory here: a teleological view qualified by a deontological basis, or a deontological view qualified by a teleological context and application.

At this point it is appropriate to ask how meta-ethical intuitionism in general supports its basic claim by argument, and how critics of this perspective argue against it and its supporting arguments in response. Much of the work of supporting arguments for intuitionism is already in place from our previous analysis. If ethical terms stand for properties of the subjects that they appropriately qualify, and if ethical propositions express cognitively significant truth claims, and if no form of meta-ethical definism provides an adequate account of the logic of moral discourse, then, since a plausibly formulated intuitionism is the only alternative cognitivist account of that logic, it follows that some such form of meta-ethical intuitionism would be, on the assumptions made, a reasonable position to adopt here. To put it another way, if we assume the property doctrine and the cognitivism it entails, all the critical defects of the various forms of definism are so many persuasive arguments in support of intuitionism. In the previous context of argument against definism, I have already stated many of these arguments for intuitionism in both negative and positive forms, and I will not restate these arguments in the present context, although they are all crucially and directly relevant as an important part of the case for an intuitionist perspective.

A general positive argument is, however, clearly important. The rejection of definism, or the critical defectiveness of the claim that the meanings of ethical terms can all be defined as logically equivalent in meaning to some conjunction of non-ethical terms, suggests that moral knowledge is a unique and distinct area of cognitive awareness in its own right, provided it is assumed, as previously noted, that some version of cognitivism and the property doctrine is true. If, in addition, some version of modern foundationalism in epistemology is regarded as plausible (i.e., if it is assumed that all properly based knowledge claims run, as it were, logically backward through a series of intervening premises to starting points that are true as such or in themselves rather than through still further logically prior premises), then it will follow that, as in every other distinct field of knowledge, so also in ethics, the basic and ultimate concepts and principles of moral philosophy will be true as such (principles)

3.34) The general arguments for meta-ethical intuitionism

3.34a) The previous arguments against definism are already supporting arguments for intuitionism, if cognitivism and the property doctrine are assumed.

3.34b) If it is assumed that moral knowledge is a unique area of awareness, and if moderate foundationalism in epistemology is adopted, then it will follow that the basic concepts and principles of ethics are meaningful and true as such, so that they must be apprehended by direct and immediate insight.

or meaningful as such (concepts), and will therefore be apprehensible by a knower only through direct and immediate rational insight or intuition. Thus ethical truth claims, if true, will, at least at their foundations, be characterized by a self-evident character that parallels that of the basic presuppositions of all knowledge. It is true that, in general epistemology as I construe it, there are some immediately evident empirical truths; but the rejection of naturalistic definism entails the conclusion that the immediately evident character of ethical concepts and principles is clearly non-empirical. Hence, those basic insights are apprehensions of our rational faculty rather than of our sensory capacity, even if the uniqueness of ethics means that the foundations of ethical reasoning are not merely grounded in pure logic; after all, rationalistic or formalistic definism is as implausible as naturalistic definism. Thus the rationally self-evident character of the logical starting points of moral reasoning clearly supports the central claim of meta-ethical intuitionism to the effect that the meaning and truth of the basic concepts and principles of ethics are apprehensible only by immediate insight or intuition.

3.34b1) Such basic ethical concepts are not empirically evident.

3.34b2) Instead they are rationally self-evident, although not merely a matter of pure logic.

3.34c) As to how the rational self-evidence of basic moral truth is compatible with the obvious commission of judgmental errors, and the resultant conflict of moral intuitions:

Yet this argument, however plausible, raises a number of critical issues. If ethics is a matter of immediately evident rational insight at its foundations, then how, critics ask, can we account for the fact that errors of moral judgment are possible both at the level of principles and at the level of practice or application? And still more crucially for this 'self-evidence' argument in support of intuitionism, how will it be possible, within the parameters of an intuitionist view, to resolve a genuine conflict of moral intuitions between or among equally sincere and serious moral judges? Yet, on any meta-ethical view obvious improprieties in moral judgment are possible, and evident oppositions of moral judgment among different moral judges are all but chronically recurrent. But these purportedly insuperable difficulties, urged by such a 'conflict of intuitions' argument, may not be as obstructive as they seem. Errors of rational judgment occur in every field of knowledge; but we are not, for that reason, on the verge of jettisoning all knowledge claims in favor of a self-paralyzing and self-contradictory skepticism. The capacity of effective judgment, though present in principle in all knowers, is not equally developed by practice in all of

3.34c1) Such problems occur in every meta-ethical view, and in every field of knowledge.

them; so that some are more accurate judges than others, even if we cannot develop infallible criteria for classifying individuals into these categories. Furthermore, moral judges of cases involving practical application of moral principles to particular instances of moral choice may not all have the same, much less complete, relevant factual information in the particular issue at hand; and they can be inadvertently guilty of inattention as well. As Aristotle once wisely noted: there are many ways to miss the mark in our decision and judgment, but only one way, in a given set of circumstances, to hit it. But that does not mean that there is anything logically (or morally) perverse about recognizing this limit and attempting to come as close to the mark as we can. Errors, therefore, are in principle correctable, even if they persist; and conflicts of judgment, at whatever level, are in principle resolvable, even if they never cease. None of our substantive judgments about anything are, as judgments on our part, in principle infallible, so that it is no special problem of ethical judgments, no matter how they are construed or apprehended basically, if they share the fate of all our substantive judgments without exception. And that is all that a meta-ethical intuitionist needs to claim (within the parameters of cognitivism) to answer the 'conflict of intuitions' criticism, since it is obvious that error and disagreement leave our moral decisions fallible on any meta-ethical presuppositions whatsoever.

On the other hand, it may be possible to argue, with Henry Sidgwick, that while certain basic principles of ethics have a formal logical character that renders them intuitively self-evident (he opts for the principles of reciprocal justice, rational self-love or prudence, and rational benevolence), nevertheless such principles, precisely because of their requisite formal character, lack any intuited, specific, and determinate content of goodness through which such intuitively self-evident principles may be put into application in particular moral decisions. That all persons have a moral right to equal considerations, that it is morally appropriate for every person to further proportionately his or her own well-being as possessing intrinsic worth, and that every responsible moral agent has a moral obligation to further the well-being of other persons on similar grounds and so far as his or her actions are reasonably judged to be relevant

3.34c2) Variations in practice, relevant factual knowledge, and even attention, tend to moderate these problems.

3.34c3) Thus errors and conflicts are, in principle, correctable and resolvable, even if they persist in practice: and the problems are, in general, the same in all fields of knowledge.

3.34d) Still, the basic self-evident moral concepts and principles may need supplementation by definite content, as a requisite to practical application.

3.34d1) Thus intuitionism seems plausible in principle, as a meta-ethical theory, but the basic content of the moral ultimate must be determined by normative ethics.	to that well-being—all this, though perhaps intuitively self-evident, leaves open the question as to precisely in what the well-being of persons consists, and the question as to what sorts of actions would further the realization of that goal. What this criticism claims is, not that intuitionism is implausible in principle, but that it is, in its basic insights, incomplete in its range, since it lacks a content which must therefore be supplied on some non-intuited basis. However, that is hardly a serious criticism of intuitionism as a meta-ethical theory, since the identification of the ultimately good or right in terms of content is in fact the principle concern of normative ethics; so that the criticism reduces to the question, 'What normative ethical theory (for example, ethical hedonism, ethical humanism, ethical idealism, etc.) has the most plausible claim to adequacy?' And that question will
3.34d2) Yet the intrinsic worth or rightness of ultimate moral content will itself have to be rationally intuited.	be dealt with in its turn at the proper place. But one thing seems clear: whatever content the ultimately good or right possesses, the intrinsic worth or rightness of that content, if a claim about it is not to be logically arbitrary and radically relative to variable personal opinion, will have to be discerned as immediately evident and in that sense intuited. It is the logical character of intrinsic worth or rightness that it contains the whole ground of its worth or rightness in itself and therefore, if apprehended at all, must be apprehended as such by direct insight at a crucial point. If its worth or rightness could be grounded in anything but itself, it would simply not actualize ultimate intrinsic value. And if, to avoid this, one simply denies that there is anything that possesses such ultimate intrinsic moral authority, that would be the death not of intuitionism, but of objective ethical truth itself.
3.35) Conclusion:	I conclude therefore that, within the scope of cognitivist theories (if, that is, fundamentally evaluative judgments are objective cognitive claims) some version of meta-ethical intuitionism, which combines deontological and teleological elements as previously suggested in my analysis,
3.35a) Given a cognitive meta-ethic, an intuitionism that combines both deontological and teleological elements is a highly plausible view.	is a highly plausible and comprehensively adequate theory about the nature and logical status of ethical terms, judgments, and arguments. The definist alternatives to intuitionism, though in some cases possessed of limited merit, are so beset with critical difficulties that any reasonable case for cognitivism will best be cast in intuitionist terms. But this

provisional conclusion by no means settles the central issues of meta-ethics. What if cognitivism and its conjoined property doctrine are fundamentally mistaken? What if, that is, fundamentally evaluative ethical statements are not cognitive claims at all, are not therefore either true or false in any objective and non-metaphorical sense, and thus perform a function that is primarily non-cognitive and hence yet to be analyzed? These questions embody our next object of concern.

3.35b) But cognitivism itself may be challenged.

Chapter IV

Meta-Ethical Non-Cognitivism

Non-Cognitivism as a General Meta-Ethical Position

Non-cognitivism in meta-ethics is fundamentally the claim that ethical terms are misunderstood if they are regarded as standing primarily for either moral or nonmoral properties of the subjects they are appropriately ascribed to in moral sentences, and that those sentences themselves are misconstrued if they are regarded as asserting truth claims in the straightforward sense in which such claims are asserted by empirical statements and by the propositions of a well-formed system of formal logic (the negative claim of non-cognitivism). And it is further the claim that ethical terms, and the propositions containing them as used in their fundamentally evaluative sense, perform a function which is essentially that of expressing some commendation, approval, attitudinal slant, relevant emotive feeling, or suggestion for the guidance of choice and/or activity. Thus the function of moral discourse is essentially both practical in its role as guiding behavior, and person- or group-relative in its role as involving the response of individuals and social groups to relevant situations involving moral decision and choice. However, it would be a mistake, from the non-cognitivist standpoint, to regard ethical statements in their fundamen-

4.1) Non-cognitivism involves:
4.2) negatively:
4.3) the rejection of the property doctrine;
4.4) the denial that ethical sentences make truth-claims in an unambiguous sense.

4.5) Positively:
4.6) ethical sentences fulfill attitudinal, emotive, and rational functions;
4.7) ethical discourse is thus both practical and person—or group—relative.

4.8) Though related to empirical claims about such functions, ethical sentences

Meta-Ethical Non-Cognitivism

do not themselves assert such claims.

tally evaluative sense as equivalent in meaning to some conjunction of empirical statements to the effect that such and such a person or group has a given attitude, or is making a commendation, or is approving some choice or action, or is providing guidance for behavior. These latter statements are, as ordinary empirical truth claims, the proper concern of various descriptive sciences (psychology, sociology, anthropology, etc.) and are not at all the same as the acts of expressing an attitude, or making a commendation, or approving something, or providing guidance. It is one thing for a person to commit these acts in moral discourse, and quite another thing for that person or anyone else to make the descriptive claim that he or she is committing or has committed those acts. Ethical sentences (again, of course, in their fundamentally evaluative sense) are the acts themselves in the form of moral speech or discourse, not empirical claims to the effect that the acts have been, or are being, committed. Ethical sentences, more briefly, *express* something (an attitude, etc.), but they do not *assert* anything, even though the correlative empirical assertion may be characteristically or even invariably true.

4.9) But evaluative terms can come to have a descriptive and therefore cognitive aspect of significance.
4.10) This is true in both ethical and nonethical uses of evaluative terms.
4.11) This use involves a set of generally understood but socially relative criteria.

On the other hand, evaluative terms (like 'good,' 'splendid,' 'excellent,' 'poor,' 'ordinary,' or 'average') can and do frequently come to have a secondary, descriptive, nonmoral, and therefore cognitive component. This is clearly true in cases unrelated to ethics: if we speak of an automobile as either excellent or ordinary, most listeners would regard us as assessing the vehicle in terms of a set of generally accepted criteria for automobiles in a certain segment of society. But even relevant ethical uses become descriptive in a parallel sense: in our society, to speak of a man as a 'good' husband and father would be to appeal to generally understood and accepted criteria for assessing a man in those roles. And the more descriptive an evaluative term becomes, the more it loses what I will term as its moral force, so that persons using such terms in this primarily descriptive sense need not be, and quite generally are not, understood as expressing any relevant attitude, appraisal, or feeling themselves. This would even be true of persons who say, for example, that polygamy is morally wrong in the United States (and many other places); it is, after all and in this same descriptive sense, not morally wrong in Saudi Arabia. In actual practice, it is often very difficult to tell whether moral discourse is being used in its fundamentally evaluative and non-cognitive sense, or in its primarily descriptive and empirical-cognitive sense.

Again, it is important to point out that non-cognitivism does not entail the conclusion that nonmoral circumstances and factual data are irrelevant to the propriety and plausibility of sentences in evaluative moral discourse. Attitude, approval, feeling, guidance, etc., are unintelligible apart from a descriptive factual context (whether actual, remembered, or anticipated) with respect to which such an expression is being made, although the same sort of expression is often appropriate toward a merely imagined but possible context. It might even be said, on the whole, that the factual context provides a basis for the rational and objective propriety of a given moral expression, although different non-cognitivists may disagree about the extent to which this is the case. But the knowledge of the conditions and consequences of morally significant acts is certainly, for non-cognitivists, relevant to their moral evaluation.

4.12) It is often difficult to distinguish the evaluative and descriptive senses of such terms.
4.13) Nonmoral circumstances and factual data provide a context and even a basis of propriety for ethical expressions.

Beyond this general description of non-cognitivism, it is both possible and appropriate to recognize distinguishable trends, types, or even (to some extent) schools of non-cognitivism, even though there is still much disagreement among individual thinkers within a given type. Since David Hume was, in an important sense, the instigator of the non-cognitivist ethical tradition in the ethical thought of western civilization, it seems fitting to begin with an analysis of his *descriptive relativism* as a starting point from which all subsequent varieties of non-cognitivism have taken their point of departure. I will then proceed to analyze what I take to be the two main contemporary types of non-cognitivism: the meta-ethical *emotivism* or *attitudinalism* of such thinkers as A.J. Ayer (in his early period) and C.L. Stevenson, and the so-called '*good reasons*' *approach* of scholars like R.M. Hare, S.E. Toulmin, and even (with some stretching) the '*ideal observer*' *theory* in the form expressed by R.B. Brandt, if not also by William Frankena as well.

4.14) Identification of the main varieties of non-cognitivism to be discussed:

4.15) Descriptive Relativism

4.16) Emotivism or Attitudinalism

4.17) 'Good Reasons' Approach

4.18) 'Ideal Observer' Theory

David Hume: Descriptive Relativism

From Hume's point of view as a classical modern empiricist in epistemology, there is no question about the reality

4.19) Hume recognizes the empirically objective reality

of moral distinctions between right and wrong, virtue and vice, since, with 'virtual' universality, human beings make such distinctions in every organized society and the moral discourse in which they do so is therefore an undeniable dimension of the response of human beings to one another in society. But there is a serious and frequently disputed issue about the basis or foundation of these distinctions: do they arise from reason in its legitimate cognitive function so that propositions expressing them are either true or false as descriptive of the subjects to which, for example, moral praise and blame are assigned? Or do they rather arise as a response of sentiment or feeling to persons and actions that have a certain descriptive or factual character? Those who support what I will call the rationalist thesis here, to the effect that moral distinctions are discernible by pure reason, commonly argue that moral judgments are asserted in the form of truth claims and can be logically opposed or disputed. In this respect, such judgments are formally the same as propositions expressing matters of fact or relations of ideas. Sentiments or feelings, on the other hand, while they can be descriptively characterized in logically disputable propositions, cannot themselves be logically disputed or opposed, but only approved or disapproved, praised or blamed. Hence, the claim that sentiment or feeling provides the basis or ground of the moral distinctions is highly questionable, since such a view cannot explain how moral opinions can be significantly opposed or disputed, and it is further the case that a moral claim cannot reasonably be registered except in the context provided by its relevant facts and logical relations; and since these are based on reason, it seems plausible to suppose that moral distinctions made with respect to them are based on reason as well.

But Hume strongly contests any such rationalist view of the ground of moral distinctions. Reason involves judgment concerning truth or falsehood expressed in propositions; and these in turn are true or false on the basis of their agreement or disagreement either with relations of ideas or with matters of fact. Moral distinctions and the claims or rules embodying them, on the other hand, are practical in the sense that they influence and motivate behavior, while judgments based on reason are impotent to provide such motivation except in conjunction with sentiment, feeling,

---

of moral distinctions, but raises the question whether they are founded on reason or sentiment.

4.20) The rationalist thesis:
4.21) Moral judgments express truth claims and can be rationally opposed;

4.22) but sentiments or feelings cannot be logically opposed and are therefore inadequate as a basis for moral distinctions.

4.23) The relevance of facts and logical relations to moral claims suggests that all are grounded in reason.

4.24) Hume's sentimentalist thesis:
4.25) Reason, as expressing truth claims, can never motivate behavior except in conjunction with sentiment, feeling, or preference, and hence reason cannot be the ultimate basis of moral distinctions.

or taste (i.e., preference). Such sentiments, passions, or volitions, as well as the actions furthering them in relation to objects and the moral principles guiding them in their application, are neither true nor false (though they can, as noted, be described by propositions which are either true or false about them); while conclusions based on reasoning are invariably either true or false, depending on their agreement or disagreement with relations of ideas or matters of fact. Hence, since moral claims are never made apart from sentimental response, it seems clear that such claims are not truth claims but rather expressions of response that evince approval or disapproval, desire or aversion.

But of course reason has a role in the operation of moral distinctions, since it provides relevant information about the relations of ideas and matters of fact with respect to which those moral instincts are drawn and those moral claims are expressed. Yet it is clear that moral insight cannot be entirely based on such rationally apprehended truths. This is so, in the first place, because truth or error about such matters is never itself the proper subject of moral evaluation; it is rather the sentimental or preferential response to what is perceived as true or false, and the person that expresses that response, which are the proper subjects of moral evaluation. The rational discernment of relations could not be the sole or even the primary basis of moral distinctions for a number of reasons: first, because the same relations, rationally discerned, can exist in two different cases without their being viewed as having the same moral character—as in the case of incest being judged morally wrong among human beings, but not among animals (nor is the difference based on the fact that human beings have the rational discernment requisite to apprehending the turpitude involved, for that moral turpitude would have to *be* there to be discerned in the relation itself, and no descriptive aspect of the relation could be so discerned differently in the two cases); again, the same conclusion follows because, if moral worth or turpitude were a characteristic of acts as relations, then that character would attach to the act irrespective of the rational will or rational discernment of the agent so that animals too, and not merely human beings, would be appropriately assessed as virtuous and/or vicious in the commission of such acts—and both these results are clearly at variance with our

4.26) Reason provides a context, not a basis, for moral judgment:
4.27) because matters of fact and relations of ideas are not, as such, ever the proper subject of moral evaluation;

4.28) because there can be a sameness of facts and relations with a difference of moral evaluation;

moral sense in making moral distinctions. If, on the other hand, the distinction is based on a difference of sentimental preference or response, the problems involved in the rationalist theory simply dissolve.

4.29) because it is impossible to identify any factual character of a given object of moral assessment with its moral properties;

Nor is it any different in the case of the rational discernment of matters of fact. Consider any person or action as an object of possible moral assessment, and try to identify any factual character of such an object as its moral property. Such an attempt will simply not disclose any such identity in the object of moral judgment, but will merely reveal certain facts about the motives and consequences of actions *about* which it will then be possible to make a moral claim. No, the basis of the assessment lies in the sentiment or feeling of the moral judge. Furthermore, moral judgment assigns, for example, praise or blame, virtue or vice, in view of an adequate understanding of all the relevant facts (and relations), so that it cannot itself be an additional fact (or relation) of the same sort. But a speculative judgment of reason, by analyzing discerned facts (or relations) that are thus known, derives from the unknown facts and relations still others that are not known. Finally, and perhaps most significantly, according to Hume, it is never possible logically (i.e., without a logical gap or flaw) to move from any rational knowledge of relations or facts to any moral or ethical conclusion on such rational grounds alone; to move logically, that is, from an 'is' to an 'ought.' It is the office of reason to apprehend that which *is*; but the apprehension of what *ought* to be is the office of sentimental preference.

4.30) because moral judgment assigns praise or blame in view of all relevant facts and relations;

4.31) because there is no valid inference to any moral conclusion on rational grounds alone (no derivation of 'ought' from 'is').

4.32) Moral distinctions are thus based on sentimental response, to which virtue and vice are relative.

Moral distinctions therefore, although made with respect to the objects of rational discernment, are based on the sentimental response of the moral judge, so that the assignment of virtue and vice, praise and blame, are relative to such sentiments or feelings of pleasure (or approval) and uneasiness/pain (or disapproval). It is with moral distinctions as it is with the discernment of aesthetic beauty: the beauty is in the eye of the beholder, not in the descriptive qualities of the object viewed; and the moral character is in the breast or sentiment of the moral judge, not in the rationally discerned relations and facts. It is therefore appropriate, I think, to characterize Hume's position as *descriptive relativism*: it is *relativism* because it denies that moral qualities are properties of the object judged—they are rather expressions of, and

4.33) Hume's view is thus a descriptive relativism.

therefore logically relative to and dependent upon, the sentiment, feeling, or preference of a moral judge; yet it is *descriptive* in the sense that this sentimentally relative response is made toward relations and facts that are rationally discernible by empirical apprehension at one level or another. Yet I do not wish to be unfair to Hume; his ethical theory in its total compass is much broader than the arguments I have explained: the sentimental basis of morality, for Hume, is not radically individualistic and idiosyncratic—it is rather a universal human sentiment; and it is not a view of self-preference or ethical egoism that Hume defends—it is rather a morality grounded in benevolent sympathy and sentimental assessment that are quite independent of any merely prudential self-interest. But I have said enough fairly to depict Hume's position as a prototype and variety of meta-ethical non-cognitivism.

4.34) But the sentimental basis is not radically individualistic; it is rather common to humanity as such.

In critical response to Hume's outlook from a meta-ethical (rather than a normative ethical) standpoint, I would first like to raise the question whether, in all his analysis, Hume is really subscribing to the objective reality of moral distinctions (between right and wrong, virtuous and vicious, good and evil) in the sense in which that subscription would be relevant to moral judgments in their fundamentally evaluative sense. He seems to recognize (and claim) that moral distinctions are objective in the sense that moral judges make these distinctions as a matter of descriptive fact—rather like arguing that of course there is such an objective reality as infant baptism, since it is indisputable that the rite is practiced by Roman Catholics, Episcopalians, Presbyterians, and others. But what is at stake in the latter case is not whether certain religious bodies perform a ceremony they *call* infant baptism, but rather whether the rite practiced can be correctly and objectively described as baptism in the proper Christian sense. Analogously, those who believe in the reality of moral distinctions in the logically relevant sense are not merely affirming the truism that human beings make what they call moral distinctions, but they are rather affirming that if there were no such thing as moral distinctions objectively and in themselves, no one would be correct in claiming that he or she had made such a distinction in that intrinsically objective sense. In a way, Hume seems to admit the thrust of this criticism by claiming that moral

4.35) Critical response to Hume:

4.36) It is questionable whether Hume really subscribes to the objective reality of moral distinctions in the fundamentally evaluative sense:

4.37) The question is not whether persons make moral distinctions, but rather whether the moral distinctions are objectively there to be recognized by persons.

4.38) Perhaps Hume's sentimentalism admits this critical point.

4.39) In any relevant sense, however, the objects of moral criticism are always independent of the sentiments of the moral judge: and for moral criticism itself to be objective as such, it must have a basis in those same objects.

distinctions are based on sentiment or feeling which are clearly subjective and relative, not to mention variable and transitory. But of course moral judgments, while motivated by such subjective factors, are not directed toward them as objects, except in the obviously impertinent sense that we sometimes morally criticize a person for having acted out of a certain motive (perhaps greed or sexual lust or the desire for fame)—and here it is certainly not the motives of the person thus criticized that is the basis of the judgment, but rather the motivation of the person offering the criticism, to whatever extent sentimental motivation provides the basis. Hence, the objects of moral criticism are invariably independent of the sentiments of the moral judge and are in that sense objective. But if the moral criticism itself is to be significantly objective, it must have some basis in the nature of the object judged, even if, psychologically, the judgment is, in part, sentimentally motivated. Thus I think it fair to say that Hume does not admit the objective reality of moral distinctions in the logically relevant sense, so that in that same relevant sense Hume's overall position involves the denial of objective moral distinctions.

4.40) If, as Hume seems to admit, not all sentiments are equally appropriate morally, the singling out of certain sentiments, as more or less worthy, would imply a non-sentimental criterion to make the distinction, and hence the inadequacy of Hume's general theory.

At the same time, a serious question can be raised about Hume's claim that moral distinctions are grounded in sentiment, even if that claim is understood descriptively in Hume's own terms. Clearly not all sentimental states are on logically equal moral ground: many sentimentally motivated acts are themselves the objects of negative moral criticism and judged to be morally unworthy. But if that is a plausible sort of judgment, then it cannot be sentiment or feeling as such that are the basis of moral distinctions, but only certain types of sentiment or feeling that themselves meet some criterion of moral propriety. But then that criterion could not itself be grounded in sentiment, since any claim to that effect would be reasoning in an objectionable circle by dividing between sentiments that were morally appropriate and those that were not. Whatever the criterion for this distinction is, therefore, it will involve a moral distinction that is either question-begging and arbitrary or else non-sentimental in its basis. And either way Hume's view will appear in a questionable light. Even if Hume is correct, for example, in urging the universality of the feeling of benevolent sympathy, how can the moral propriety of that feeling be vindicated in Hume's terms? Perhaps prudent self-interest and fear of exposure or punishment are also universal; but that does not make them morally appropriate motives, as, I should think, Hume himself would agree. Nor will the fact (if it is a fact) that benevolent sympathy is universally esteemed while those other motives are universally disapproved, do anything to remove this objectionable logical circle, since universality, as a criterion, is clearly not itself sentimentally based. Hence, either all sentimental motivations are on an equal basis logically (which would involve the abolition of moral distinctions) or else there is some non-sentimental criterion that justifies the moral propriety of certain limited sentimental motivations as over against others. How, it might be asked, consistently with Hume's sentimentalist theory, are we to know if the requisite sentimental motives are themselves morally good or the principles based upon them morally right?

Hume claims that it is logically fallacious to derive a moral 'ought' from a descriptive, factual 'is,' since that would involve a logical gap between the descriptive and the morally normative. Yet the sentiments, on which he claims to base moral distinctions, are admittedly matters of descriptive fact in motivational psychology. If we propose with Hume, then, to base genuinely normative moral distinctions on such descriptive psychological facts, we are making precisely the very logical jump that Hume castigates in his philosophical opponents. If, to avoid this difficulty, we claim that no normative moral claims are actually made here (a move which, to my knowledge at least, Hume did not make), then there will be no genuine moral distinctions about the logic of which to dispute, but only descriptions of the way human beings make what they mistakenly designate as moral distinctions. So Hume's dilemma here is either to surrender the 'is-ought' fallacy claim, or to emasculate it by contending that there is after all no genuine moral ought to be derived. To point out Hume's confusion about this matter is not, of course, to determine the final fate of the claim that no ethical conclusion can be derived from logical and descriptive premises alone. But it is to show that the issue can hardly be settled on Hume's turf.

A further criticism lies in the fact that Hume seems to define the objects of reason (logical relations of ideas and

4.41) If no 'ought' can be derived from an 'is' (no moral claim from a descriptive fact), then how can Hume base moral claims on descriptive facts about sentiment?

4.42) Either there is no genuine moral 'ought' involved,

4.43) or there is, on Hume's ground, no 'is-ought' fallacy.

4.44) Hume defines facts and relations in such a way as to

arbitrarily exclude the concept of moral facts and relations.

descriptive matters of fact) in such a way as arbitrarily to exclude what might be called objective moral facts and relations. If facts and relations are nonmoral by stipulative definition, it will of course be impossible to derive from them, as thus restricted, any moral conclusions. But if the question is not arbitrarily begged in this way, then it will be an open question whether the proper objects of reason may include both moral and nonmoral facts and relations. A stipulated and therefore arbitrary presupposition can provide no fair basis for an objective and substantial philosophical conclusion. This point becomes especially clear in Hume's argument to the effect that, since moral judgment assigns praise or blame in the light of all the relevant facts and relations, the judgment itself cannot be the statement of an additional fact or relation of the same kind, but must be wholly based instead upon sentimental preference or response. That conclusion could only follow (if at all) provided we assume that the facts and relations we begin with are by definition nonmoral; but if it is left open whether some relevant relations and facts might also be moral, then all that follows would be that moral conclusions cannot follow from nonmoral grounds alone, even if those nonmoral grounds are always also involved. What then seems to follow is not that moral distinctions are not the proper objects of rational insight, but rather (at least with equal propriety) that rational insight includes moral relations and facts among its proper objects. And if that is so, Hume's criticism here is either empty or impertinent.

4.45) But this decides no issue of real substance.

4.46) All that really follows is that moral conclusions cannot follow from nonmoral facts alone, and not that moral distinctions are not the proper objects of reason.

4.47) As to motives:
4.48) Sentimental motives need not exclude rational motives.

4.49) Moral worth cannot be wholly based on motives, but is also dependent on the value of the consequences of moral choices and acts.
4.50) Conclusion: Hume's meta-ethical

No doubt moral judgments are, as Hume claims and at least in part, motivated by sentiment, feeling, and even taste, but it would be arbitrary to claim that moral judgment had no identifiable rational motives as well, unless, as in the previous argument, we identify any effective and operative motive for moral judgment as therefore *ipso facto* sentimental in character. And it is further the case that the moral worth of an act or choice cannot be wholly based in the motive of the agent, whether sentimental or rational, since it is also a function of the moral goodness and/or rightness of the ensuing consequences. If there is no objective moral good or right to be aimed at, that character can hardly be bestowed by the motive of the agent, however construed. I therefore conclude that at least Hume's version of non-cognitivism in meta-ethics is implausible. Whether some other version can remedy this defect remains to be seen.

non-cognitivism is highly implausible.

A.J. Ayer and C.L. Stevenson: Meta-Ethical Emotivism or Attitudinalism

An equally strident version of meta-ethical non-cognitivism confronts us in radical form in the early work of A.J. (Alfred Jules) Ayer and in more moderate form in the principal ethical writings of C.L. (Charles Leslie) Stevenson. It is clear that the epistemological basis of Ayer's logical meta-ethical position (as reflected in his widely read book *Language, Truth, and Logic*) is to be found in the radical form of twentieth-century empiricism usually designated as *logical positivism* or (less frequently) *scientific empiricism*. Since my interest in the present work is primarily ethical and not epistemological, I will develop this epistemological orientation only to the extent necessary to provide an intelligible context for the meta-ethical perspective involved.[1] According to this epistemological point of view, it is of the utmost importance to distinguish sharply between the cognitive and non-cognitive uses of language. There are, accordingly, only two types of cognitively significant statements (i.e., statements that make an assertion which is either true or false): *logically* determinate statements of some formal logical system (such statements are true or false through their necessary logical relations to other such statements as grounded in a set of stipulated axioms or first principles which are simply posited as definitionally true by the author of the system), and *empirically* determinate statements (such statements are true or false on the basis of either direct empirical observation or indirect inference from such a direct empirical basis, although a statement may be cognitively significant in this sense even if it cannot be empirically verified in fact and practice, provided it is possible to conceive of observations that would tend either to verify or falsify the statement in principle on empirical grounds). The propositions of formal logical systems and those of the various empirical sciences,

4.51) Analysis of the Emotive or Attitudinal Theory:

4.52) This theory is based on the radical empiricism of logical positivism in epistemology.

4.53) Here cognitively significant statements are either logically determinate or empirically determinate.

---

[1] I have written at some length about this epistemological stance in several earlier writings: *The Resurrection of Theism*, *The Reconstruction of the Christian Revelation Claim*, and a journal article: 'Contemporary Philosophy and the Analytic–Synthetic Dichotomy.'

rightly construed, would exhaust in principle the whole class of cognitively significant statements. All other uses of language are, for this view, non-cognitive (i.e., they do not make assertions that are susceptible of being either true or false on logical and/or empirical grounds). Broadly speaking, non-cognitive uses of language can be conveniently characterized as *emotively expressive* (they *express* a feeling, wish, or desire, but do not *assert* it) or *emotively evocative* (they are intended to call forth or motivate emotional response in the listener). If therefore a given use of language is not cognitive in the stipulated sense, it is appropriately categorized as emotive in the sense indicated, and it is neither true nor false in any straightforward epistemological sense, even if the statement form is grammatically identical to that in which a cognitive assertion could be made. There are, however, other linguistic forms, aside from statements, which bear a more striking resemblance than statements to the logical function of ethical expressions, and that is especially true of imperatives, commands, or exhortations. Like ethical expressions, these forms also are intended to evoke a response in the listener either in emotional attitude or action. And while no responsible meta-ethical emotivist would claim that the whole meaning of ethical expressions is exhausted in these forms, the similarity is sufficiently impressive as to make it appropriate to use the term *imperativism* as a designation of at least some versions of meta-ethical emotivism. And it scarcely needs mentioning that imperatives, commands, or exhortations do not make assertions: they may be appropriate or inappropriate, effective or ineffective, even reasonable or unreasonable; but they are neither true nor false (a point that follows from the grammatical structures in which they are expressed).

Now consider ethical expressions (whatever their grammatical form—statement or otherwise): their partial parallelism with imperatives, as to function and intent, suggests that they too are neither true nor false, but rather appropriate or inappropriate, and so forth. And while the statement form in which ethical claims are expressed may incline us to interpret them as truth claims, yet it is clear that they are neither statements of empirical fact (they are 'ought' statements, not 'is' statements) nor statements of formal logical equivalence. If therefore cognitively significant statements

4.54) Non-cognitive uses of language are, in general, either emotively expressive or emotively evocative.

4.55) These uses may employ the statement form,

4.56) but their function is similar to that of imperatives, commands, or exhortations.

4.57) In any case, none of these linguistic uses are susceptible of being either true or false.

4.58) Ethical expressions are clearly non-cognitive: since they are neither empirically nor logically determinate.

are limited to these two types (empirically determinate and logically determinate), then it would clearly follow that ethical expressions are, for that reason, non-cognitive. Such expressions are therefore, as with non-cognitive expressions generally, emotively expressive (on the part of the speaker) and emotively evocative (from the standpoint of the listener). This is not to say that a third-party observer could not be reasonably led to believe or even properly to infer certain descriptive truths about both speaker and listener—about their desires, wishes, feelings, or intentions, for example. But the relevant ethical expressions are not assertions of such descriptive truths; their function is rather expressive, evocative, directive, commendatory, and so on. If this analysis is correct, then it would appear to follow that different persons can have different and contrasting moral (i.e., emotive) responses to what is factually the same situation or set of circumstances, but they logically cannot have logically incompatible moral opinions or moral judgments about that situation, since ethical expressions do not actually opine, logically judge, or assert anything whatsoever. At the same time it is clearly the case that ethical expressions are themselves describable in factual terms, and that they always occur in view of, and in reaction or response to, an understanding of some set of factual circumstances—so that for this view also nonmoral facts are relevant to the propriety of ethical expressions. All this is, of course, a kind of ethical relativism, since it interprets ethical expressions as having a basis in emotive states (wishes, desires, feelings, etc.); but it is not an ethical subjectivism which claims that those expressions are either true or false relative to such subjective psychological states—that would be to confuse an emotive response with some descriptive statement about it, which is quite different from the response itself.

A common (but allegedly mistaken) criticism of meta-ethical emotivism, of the sort we have been describing, is to the effect that, if this position about ethical expressions is itself a true and correct analysis of them, then it would follow (as admitted by the emotivist) that ethical statements or claims could not logically oppose or contradict each other, since they would be neither true nor false; whereas it seems clear that in practice moral judgments do so contradict each other. If I say that a certain act is morally right, and another

4.59) Hence such expressions are emotively expressive and evocative, although they may be a partial basis for inference.

4.60) Thus moral responses can be contrasting, but they cannot be logically opposed, since they assert nothing.

4.61) Ethical responses are a reaction to factual circumstances.

4.62) This view is ethical relativism, but *not* ethical subjectivism, which confuses emotive responses with their description.

4.63) Ethical statements may sometimes appear to be logically opposed:

person disagrees by saying that it is not, or that it is wrong, our statements appear to be logically opposed in precisely the way that they could not be, if the emotivist analysis were correct. The only recourse of the emotivist in response is to claim that the appearance is misleading, and that while there is an opposition of sorts, there is not a logical opposition or contradiction between statements in their fundamentally evaluative sense. Ayer's claim is that so-called moral arguments or disagreements are never about moral principles or ethical values as such. Instead, where there is genuine and logically resolvable disagreement, it reduces to a dispute either about a question of logical inference or about the relevance and character of pertinent empirical facts. Ayer even challenges his reader to try to construct even a single imaginary case in which the argument does not so reduce itself; and he is confident that no one can succeed in producing a single such example.

4.64) but the appearance is a misinterpretation.

4.65) In general, so-called moral disagreements are about relevant logical inferences and empirical facts.

4.66) Stevenson's moderate version:

C.L. Stevenson's emotivism is far more moderately and guardedly expressed than that of Ayer, although he is in substantial agreement with the latter about the non-cognitive and therefore emotive status of ethical expressions. His moderation shows clearly in the present context: he acknowledges that there is such a thing as substantial ethical disagreement (in his own obscure way, I suppose, so does Ayer), but he claims that the disagreement, if it is fundamentally evaluative, is never a disagreement in belief (about matters of fact or logic), but rather it is a disagreement in attitude or emotive response *about* the relevant facts or logic. He claims that two disputants can agree on every question of fact and logic and still disagree in attitude, or they can agree in attitude even if they disagree in belief (and when that happens, no further argument about the disagreement in belief is morally relevant from the standpoint of the disputants). Of course, it is possible for two persons to agree in both attitude and belief. Stevenson even entertains the heuristic assumption that if two erstwhile disputants really did agree about every question of fact or logic in a given moral case, they would very likely agree in attitude also. At least we can hope this is the case, since fact and logic are the only issues we can reasonably dispute about logically: we cannot argue out a disagreement in attitude or moral response on logical or factual grounds; we can only hope for a

4.67) Ethical disagreement is genuine, but it is a disagreement in attitude or response, rather than in belief.
4.68) These two types of disagreement (belief, attitude) can vary independently and are thus logically distinct.

change in attitude in our moral opponent if we can get him or her to view the logic and the facts differently. Stevenson even urges that there is a limited but non-cognitive sense in which ethical judgments may, with logical propriety, be said to be true or false, and that it is logically confusing to deny this. It is linguistically appropriate to express agreement or disagreement in attitude, in relation to an ethical judgment, by saying it is either true or false. But this propriety is the result of a generally accepted linguistic rule which accepts that propriety of utterance for any sentence in the declarative mood or statement form, so that the propriety relates only to grammatical structure and settles no issue about cognitive status. So in ethical contexts the epithets *true* and *false* serve only to repeat a remark of the speaker and express agreement or disagreement in attitude (though the same linguistic propriety can be used to express agreement or disagreement in belief quite apart from the sphere of moral discussion). If one were to deny this grammatical and structural propriety in moral discourse, one might indeed be led to adopt the mistaken belief that ethical claims cannot be argued, or even that their expression is practically irrelevant. If this analysis by Ayer and Stevenson can be maintained in the face of critical examination, one of the main objections to meta-ethical emotivism will have been so far forth eliminated.

4.69) Ethical statements may even be said to be true or false: but this is a linguistic device for expressing agreement or disagreement in attitude.

But can such analyses be reasonably maintained after all? The stipulative limitation of cognitively significant statements to logically and empirically determinate propositions rests, after all, on a decisional definition and is therefore arbitrary as grounded on the thinker's choice; and if that is the case, that limitation can settle no substantive philosophical issue. That is not to say in contrast that there is any serious epistemological question about the cognitive status of the well-formed propositions of formal logic or empirical description; it is rather to raise the question whether these two types of statements exhaust the whole class of cognitively significant statements which are capable of being assertions that are either true or false. Admittedly, and in agreement with the emotivist, ethical claims, in their fundamentally evaluative sense, are neither standard empirical descriptions nor formal logical equivalences. But that does not entail that such basic ethical claims are not cognitive assertions, unless

4.70) Critical Response to Emotivism:

4.71) The cognitivity doctrine (underlying emotivism) is a decisional definition.

4.72) As such, it does not establish the

claim that empirical and logical statements exhaust the scope of cognitivity.

4.73) The cognitivity doctrine:

4.74) appears itself to be neither an empirical nor a formal logical statement;

4.75) if then it is itself emotive, it is neither true nor false (by the positivistic doctrine itself), and cannot imply the non-cognitive status of ethical claims.

4.76) Nor is the claim reasonable that ethical statements cannot be logically opposed:
4.77) if the disagreement were merely about facts and logic, there would be no moral issue, to which

there is some reasonably argued basis for the logical positivist doctrine of cognitivity which the emotivist presupposes. Certainly ethical statements are generally understood as making some sort of objective truth claim, even if they also have non-cognitivist and emotive aspects as well. That the cognitivity doctrine of the logical positivist is seriously questionable can be clearly seen if we ask whether the propositions expressing that doctrine itself are either empirically determinate or logically determinate. It is certainly difficult to claim that the proposition, that all cognitively significant statements are either empirically determinate or logically determinate, is itself either empirically determinate or logically determinate in any way that would not be damaging (or perhaps even devastating) for the purported truth claim of the proposition itself. From what empirical data could this unqualifiedly universal and unexceptionable claim be derived? If, on the other hand, the doctrine expressed in the proposition is regarded as logically determinate, then, as with all logical truths for the logical positivist (for whom logical truths are based on conventional axioms selected arbitrarily by logicians), the doctrine will represent merely a convention chosen by the logical positivist. And if, by reason of such difficulties, the cognitivity doctrine of logical positivism is itself neither logically determinate nor empirically determinate, that doctrine will, by its own logical status, be a non-cognitive and therefore emotive expression which, as such, is neither true nor false and thus asserts nothing. But if it asserts nothing, then clearly it makes no epistemological claim and cannot be used as a basis for concluding the non-cognitive or emotive status of fundamentally evaluative ethical claims. Thus the claim of the logical positivist cognitivity doctrine clearly commits an existential self-contradiction by reason of the fact that it is itself a statement of the very sort that the doctrine itself claims cannot be cognitive.

It can certainly also be claimed, that the emotivist attempt to explain away the apparent relation of logical opposition or contradiction between ethical statements used in the fundamentally evaluative sense, is unsuccessful at the very least. Persons who disagree ethically (or appear to do so) sometimes do so partly because they disagree about the relevant facts and logic; but unless it was possible in principle to disagree logically about ethical claims (of right or wrong, for example), there would simply be no issue to which those facts and that logic would be relevant. If persons change their ethical position on a certain moral issue because they come to see the facts differently or to interpret the logical reasoning differently, there would have to be contrasting logical positions in substantive ethics itself for them to change their minds about. Otherwise there would be no disagreement to resolve by means of the facts and logic. Nor will it help to say that the disagreement is one of attitude rather than belief: if persons disagree (or differ) in attitude, it is because they have different beliefs about what is morally at issue—different beliefs not merely about facts and logic (though that is also relevant), but about the moral propriety or impropriety on which contextual facts and logical method have a bearing. It goes without saying that persons with logically opposed moral beliefs have also therefore different attitudes (of approval or disapproval, for example); but that is not the whole of the matter, since, if it were, there would be nothing objective at stake about which their attitudes could clash. Both Ayer and Stevenson, along with other emotivists and attitudinalists, agree that different persons can begin their moral reasoning from different value principles and therefore end up disagreeing about moral conclusions, even when they are in complete agreement about the relevant nonmoral facts and logic. But neither those principles nor those conclusions can be different merely in attitude in a wholly non-cognitive way, since then there would be nothing objective about which they morally disagreed at all, and with respect to which they differed in attitude. If this analysis is correct, it is also an open question—when an individual expresses moral agreement with someone else, by stating, of that other person's moral claim, that it is true—whether that individual is merely accepting the other person's attitudinal slant; that individual seems clearly also to be accepting the moral claim to which both are acceding in attitude.

There is also an equally serious question about the extensive parallelism, between imperatives or commands and ethical claims or expressions, a parallelism strongly emphasized by emotivists (and some other ethical theorists as well). There is no question but that a person making a genuine moral claim may be attempting, by so doing, to elicit

facts and logic would be relevant;

4.78) if the disagreement were purely attitudinal, there would be no objective issue about which attitudes could clash.

4.79) The parallelism between ethical claims and imperatives is overworked by emotivism:

	a behavioral response from some other person or persons; and that is clearly and primarily what is being done by a person issuing a serious imperative or command. But that similarity does not, of itself, establish the non-cognitive status of ethical claims, even if it is admittedly the case that imperatives are clearly non-cognitive themselves, unless there are no relevantly important differences here between the logic of imperatives and the logic of such ethical claims. However, there certainly are such differences, as many writers (such as W.D. Falk) have pointed out. Both imperatives and ethical claims are prescriptive (at least, in part for the latter): they designate some act to be performed, some policy to be carried out (or not, in both cases). But they are thus prescriptive in strikingly different ways: imperatives, for example, prescribe by goading or prodding the listener to act conformably to the speaker's desires, and are therefore *directly* prescriptive; while ethical claims are *indirectly* prescriptive by guiding the listener to act in ways that are reasonable quite apart from the speaker's desires as such. In fact, an ethical claim suggests (or contextually implies) that there are objectively plausible grounds for acting conformably to the prescription embodied in the claim—grounds that are proportionately pertinent to the well-being of both speaker and listener alike. Ethical claims do not (characteristically) constitute these objective reasons or grounds, but they are themselves, as ethical statements, the embodiment of the claim that there are such reasons which should appropriately guide the hearer in an objectively moral sense. If an ethical statement does purport to make an objective claim in the sense indicated, by the very form of its expression, then it is certainly misleading to classify such statements as largely assimilable to the logic of imperatives, and still more misleading to classify those statements as non-cognitive and emotive (terms that seem to connote the very 'essence' of non-objectivity or radical subjective relativity).
4.80) though similar in attempting to elicit behavioral response,	
4.80a) they do so in strikingly different ways:	
4.81) imperatives directly prescribe in conformity with the speaker's desires,	
4.82) while ethical claims indirectly prescribe by appealing to objectively reasonable grounds.	
4.83) Since ethical statements make an objective claim, it is misleading to designate them as non-cognitive and emotive.	
4.84) In conclusion: 4.85) Emotivism is meta-ethically inadequate by reason of its arbitrary category of non-cognitive usage.	In retrospect, these critical weaknesses of meta-ethical emotivism raise genuine doubts about the adequacy of such a meta-ethical perspective, since it sweeps all genuinely ethical uses of language into a common non-cognitivist closet along with every other use of language that cannot be reasonably regarded as either empirically or logically determinate. And perhaps this recognizable inadequacy paves the

way for a perspective that attempts to remain non-cognitivist while at the same time recognizing that ethical claims have an objective aspect that is logically commensurate with the attempt. The position I designate as qualified objectivist non-cognitivism is precisely this sort of approach.

4.86) What about a non-cognitivism that ascribes objectivity of a sort to moral claims?

Qualified Objectivist Non-Cognitivism: The 'Good Reasons' Approach and the Ideal Moral Observer

If previously analyzed forms of non-cognitivism in meta-ethics seem critically inadequate on the central ground that they fail to account for the implied objectivity of moral claims and their rational justifiability on non-prudential grounds, then the question arises whether one could develop a meta-ethical theory which was non-cognitivist in a broad sense but which could take full account of the plausible supposition that moral claims are indeed susceptible of rational evaluation, justification, and criticism. A principal trend in contemporary meta-ethical discussion clearly makes the claim that fundamentally evaluative moral judgments are of this sort. When a person sincerely makes a moral claim expressed in a moral judgment, the very form and thrust of the claim carries with it the implication (contextually or loosely construed) that there are rationally defensible grounds for accepting that claim and therefore acting upon it, although, of course, this character may be mistakenly claimed for any particular case of moral judgment. This last is only to say that not all moral judgments are sound, so that, while objectivity of some sort is clearly suggested by the form and context of a sincerely propounded moral judgment, still the moral correctness of a moral judgment is susceptible of critical challenge. To judge something in moral context or from the moral point of view is therefore to suggest that there are logically good reasons for accepting that moral claim; it is also to suggest that the only rationally plausible way of challenging such moral claims is to argue (whether correctly or not) that such good reasons cannot be provided for this or that particular moral claim.

The obvious further question asks for an account of the sort of reasons that are logically good ones in supporting moral claims. No definist answers will do—that would be cognitivism again; nor will an intuitionist account be the

4.87) Analysis of qualified objectivism:

4.88) The general thesis is that moral claims, by their linguistic form, imply that there are good and objective reasons for conforming to the claim.

4.89) The implied claim may be mistaken (or false) in a particular case;

4.90) to challenge such a claim is to argue that the objective grounds cannot be provided.

4.91) The question, as to what sorts of reasons are logically appropriate, involves normative ethics (and thus goes beyond meta-ethics).

proper response, since intuitions themselves must be critically assessed; and any emotivism, no matter how qualified, would be the surrender of rational objectivity in ethics altogether. So one must at this point introduce some general framework of *normative* or *substantive* ethics as a context for answering the question, what sort of reasons are logically good ones. Thinkers like R.M. Hare and S.E. Toulmin propose that there are two levels of consideration here: if the question is about the moral propriety of certain acts, motives, or character traits, then judgments at that level can only be well grounded logically in the context of the moral code or structure of a particular social order. To show that such an act, etc., conforms to the generally accepted moral practice is to provide a well-grounded justification at that level. But what if the question is about the moral propriety of the ethical principles themselves that constitute the structure of morality in a particular social context? There are, presumably, differing and even opposed structures of ethical principles in different social orders: are those differences themselves susceptible of rationally objective moral criticism? The answer, for the 'good reasons' moral theorists, is a qualified 'yes.' At this higher level, where the ethical principles of the whole social order are up for moral assessment, Toulmin, for example, does not hesitate to introduce a sort of utilitarianism of desire: if we find it appropriate to assess the principles of moral practice in a given society, we can ask of the principles to be evaluated whether their application and consequences would maximize the desires of the persons composing that society to a greater extent and compatibly with the harmony of the social order, than would be the case in any viable alternative system of social practice in the moral context. If so, then the principles are so far forth and to that extent rationally and morally justified; otherwise, they are not, and changes are morally called for. R.M. Hare, on the other hand, while approximately agreeing with Toulmin, at the level of acts, motives, and character traits, that at this intuitive level (as he calls it) the rightness of particular acts, etc., is derived from ethical principles grounded in moral training and upbringing (hence, socially accepted moral practices in one's culture or subculture), nevertheless finds difficulty with the concept of the maximization of desire to the extent compatible with social harmony. As an alternative, he introduces the notion

4.92) Hare and Toulmin distinguish two levels:
4.93) the subsumption of acts, motives, and traits under a given and accepted moral code of a particular social order;

4.94) the evaluation of accepted moral principles themselves:

4.95) Toulmin introduces a utilitarian standard of the maximum fulfillment of desire that is compatible with social harmony;

4.96) Hare appeals to preference:

of preference in two ways. First, he says that when it comes to decisions of principle (the structural principles that constitute the framework of this or that system of social practice), individuals have no recourse but to ask themselves which system of social practice they themselves would prefer to live in, all things considered, and then to opt, judge, and act accordingly. But on later reflection (see his book, *Moral Thinking*), Hare proposes that, instead of settling for such an individually idiosyncratic culmination of moral commitment, we aim at the highest conceivable level of judgment that would be occupied by an 'archangel' or ideal observer. Such a moral judge would know all the relevant facts and all the ensuing consequences pertinent to the adopting of moral principles and the making of moral choices on rational grounds. The morally right choice objectively would be what such an ideal judge would prefer and choose in a state thus fully informed and fully guided by that comprehensive insight. Of course, none of us is such an archangel or ideal observer; but we can at least, and at best, aim at being as fully informed as is finitely possible for us and as fully guided by such rational insight as the expanding stability of our character makes possible. And the decision we make under such circumstances comes as close to being objectively right in the moral sense as it is possible for finite moral agents to be. At the same time, when dealing with consequences for other persons who are not at this elevated height of archangelhood, nor are they even striving for the highest human approximation thereof, we can only act on what we properly believe to be the actual preferences of such persons or their likely preferences under the circumstances envisaged as probably following from this or that moral act or choice. So here Toulmin and Hare are both qualified utilitarians—the former defending a utilitarianism of desire, and the latter a utilitarianism of preference, both of which perhaps (how difficult it is to say in the end!) come to the same result.

 The 'ideal observer' theory extends well beyond the utilitarian versions of it elaborated by Toulmin, Hare, and other thinkers of note such as R.B. Brandt, however different even these versions are from each other in their details. One of the most balanced versions is propounded by W.K. Frankena, whose position, though still purportedly non-cognitivist, exhibits a sort of balanced compromise

4.97) the individual must opt for the system of social practice he or she would 'prefer' on the whole;

4.98) but a still higher standard logically involves appealing to the decision of an ideal observer or judge, who would be aware of all relevant facts and consequences:

4.99) The objectively right choice would be the one that best approximates that of such an ideal observer;

4.100) but when dealing with persons unguided by such a standard, our choices should be guided by the actual or likely preferences of such persons.

4.101) Thus Hare and Toulmin end up as similar utilitarians on the whole.

4.102) Frankena's non-cognitivist version of the 'ideal observer' theory

4.103) Other versions are not truly objective because they appeal to basic principles that are individually or culturally relative.

with the critical concerns of cognitivists in meta-ethics. He criticizes certain other versions of the 'good reasons' or the 'ideal observer' approach by claiming that, in the end, the basic evaluative principles, claimed by these theories as providing an objective foundation for moral claims, are actually grounded in commitments that are either individually or culturally relative, with the result that no true objectivity is provided and that logically conflicting basic value judgments may all in principle be susceptible of rational justification—a result that would appear to be contradictory in objective terms. If this sort of meta-ethical and normative ethical relativity and incoherence are to be avoided, then it must be possible to define an evaluative and, more narrowly, ethical or moral point of view that can claim rational universality. According to Frankena, such a moral point of view provides a context of judgment for a particular person if he or she fulfills certain conditions:

4.104) True objectivity involves a rational universality that defines a moral point of view or context.

4.105) The elements of such a moral context

1) the person must be making normative judgments about the logically proper objects of moral concern—namely, actions, desires, dispositions, intentions, motives, persons, or traits of character;

2) the person must be willing to universalize his or her judgment in relation to all moral agents in relevantly similar circumstances;

3) the reasons the person cites in support of his or her judgment must concern factual information about the consequences of what is judged for all the persons (or even sentient beings) likely to be affected by a given moral choice and its results, even in cases where what is being judged are the agent's own actions, dispositions, or character.

4.106) The basic principles for such moral choice are:

1. beneficence, 2. justice.

Here, of course, Frankena appeals to the basic principles of his own normative ethical position: beneficence (the *prima facie* obligation to do good and prevent harm for beings [personal and sentient] likely to be affected by one's moral choices and acts); and justice (the obligation to treat individuals with an equality or consideration in the distribution of goods and privileges relative to their needs and abilities. It is these principles which provide the norm or standard for estimating the worth of those consequences that result for persons affected by moral choices and actions. If one judges from such a moral point of view, if one is free, fully informed about all relevant facts, clearheaded, and impartial in judgment, then one can claim that he or she is justified in judging that a certain action, for example, is right, wrong, or obligatory, and one can also claim that the judgment to that effect is objectively valid. At the same time, a person who reaches a moral conclusion in this way is implicitly, if not explicitly, committed to the claim that all other judges who meet these required conditions will reach the same conclusion. If they do not, then it will be a function of the fact that no actual finite moral judge ever meets these 'ideal observer' conditions perfectly; and under such circumstances, the conflicting parties must be willing to reassess, while each claiming to be correct and yet knowing that both cannot be thus correct in the final analysis, so that what is required here is open-mindedness and tolerance. After all, no meta-ethical stance will free finite agents from their limitations of knowledge and insight; so we must be willing to settle for the closest approximation to ideal observerhood that is humanly and realistically possible. Hopefully, the consequence will be that moral judgment will escape the net of radical individual and cultural relativity, while at the same time it aims at a goal of universal objectivity.

4.107) A moral judgment made in this context can claim to be justified (logically) and objectively valid.

4.108) To judge in this way is to claim that, ideally, all other judges operating in the same context will reach the same result.

4.109) If disagreement persists (since no actual judge is an ideal observer),

4.110) it must be met with open-minded tolerance and persistence in aiming at universal objectivity.

That a *cognitivist* version of the 'ideal observer' theory is possible is illustrated in the meta-ethical perspective of Roderick Firth at a certain stage in the development of his ethical thought, in which he is aiming at a perspective that will reconcile certain types of so-called non-cognitivism, of the sort I have previously discussed, with a particular type of cognitivism. The basic formula of Firth's analysis of standard ethical statements is illustrated in the claim that '*x* is morally right' is equivalent in meaning to the claim that 'an ideal observer would approve *x* under certain precisely specified conditions.' The analysis does not require a decision as to whether such an ideal observer (who would have certain properties we ordinarily might ascribe to God) actually exists: it is enough that the existence of such a being is logically possible in the sense of being consistently

4.111) Firth's cognitivist version of the 'ideal observer' theory

4.112) Basic thesis: that *x* is morally right means that *x* would be approved by an ideal moral observer, whether or not such an observer actually exists.

conceivable; otherwise, all ethical statements would be false by definition, if their validity depended on the *actual* existence of a certain being while at the same time the being did not exist. An ethical analysis on this model has certain identifiable features: it is *absolutist* (rather than relativist), since the analysis does not contain any egocentric expression (such as 'I,' 'you,' 'this,' etc.) which varies in meaning and reference with any variation from one speaker to another; it is *dispositional*, since it regards ethical statements as asserting that a certain possible being is disposed to react in a certain way to certain specified conditions (for example, to the commission of a certain act); it is *objectivist* (rather than subjectivist), since it does not entail that ethical statements would be false by definition if a certain experiencing subject or subjects did not exist—and it has this feature because the ideal observer is merely a *possible* being whose actual existence or non-existence is logically irrelevant to the meaning of ethical statements; it is *relational*, since it regards ethical statements as equivalent in meaning to a relation of an ideal observer, by way of reaction, to any given proper object of ethical judgment (such as an act or character trait); and it is even *empirical*, in an extended sense, since the reactions of an ideal observer are in principle describable in terms of certain psychological traits and responses.

4.113) An analysis so based is:
4.114) absolutist,
4.115) dispositional,
4.116) objectivist,
4.117) relational,
4.118) empirical.

The further question arises as to the requisite characteristics that would define an ideal observer of the sort Firth envisages as possible: such an observer would have to be *omniscient* with respect to all relevant non-ethical facts, *omnipercipient* in being capable, in imagination, to visualize these facts and their consequences for different alternatives of action or choice; *disinterested* in the sense of being uninfluenced by any particular person-relative concern either of his or her own, or of some other person, in contrast to other individuals who do not receive the same consideration; *dispassionate* in the sense of never being unbalanced in judgment through the influence of emotion; and finally, as a derivative quality following from the previous characteristics, *consistent* in the sense that his or her ethically significant reactions to any particular envisaged act would always be exactly similar on different occasions of envisioning that act. Since no actual human judge possesses these qualities in any completed sense but can at best imperfectly approximate

4.119) Properties of an ideal observer:
4.120) omniscient,
4.121) omnipercipient,
4.122) disinterested,
4.123) dispassionate,
4.124) consistent.
4.125) Any actual human moral judge can at best only

them to a limited degree, our own ethical claims are always subject to challenge and reconsideration. But our moral judgment is likely to improve only to the extent that we are able to improve our approximation of an ideal observer as thus described.

Firth's type of analysis is certainly *cognitivist* since on its terms ethical judgments will be either true or false, and will thus be capable of logically opposing one another in judgments regarding the same (or any similar) object of moral concern. At the same time, the analysis recognizes the sort of objectivity in ethical claims that has been emphasized by thinkers like Hare, Toulmin, and especially Frankena, all of whom claim to be non-cognitivists. Undoubtedly, Firth's challenge to those thinkers would consist in raising the question whether genuine objectivity of the sort implied by moral claims can be plausibly maintained outside the limits of meta-ethical cognitivism.

In any case, I now turn my attention to the question whether the 'good reasons' or 'ideal observer' approach, however formulated, can constitute an adequate meta-ethical perspective. Toulmin provides an extensive argument in support of the 'good reasons' approach as he espouses it. On his view, the objective claim that ethical judgments imply by their linguistic form, need not and logically should not end up by supposing that ethical terms, used in their fundamentally evaluative sense, stand for properties of the subjects they appropriately qualify; but that is precisely what previous ethical theorists had held. If, however, ethical terms did stand for properties, they would have to be either descriptive qualities of the subject (or subjects) being judged about (Toulmin designates this as the objective [property] approach), or they would be subjectively relational terms and thus stand for a relation of response *to* the subject being judged about on the part of the person making the judgment or on the part of other persons whose reactions are being characterized (Toulmin designates this as the subjective [property] approach). But both of these views make the logical mistake that ethical terms must stand either for objective properties or for subjective relational properties; and then they argue for one alternative against the other. Yet the objective approach cannot be correct: for if goodness or rightness (etc.) were a property of this sort, it would

approximate these properties.

4.126) This view combines cognitivism with the objectivity that moral claims imply.

4.127) Critical evaluation of qualified objectivism

4.128) Toulmin's defense of this view:

4.129) The objective claim of ethical judgments need not imply that they are property statements, whether objective or subjective.

4.130) If they were objective property statements, the property should be either

simple and directly perceived, or complex and confirmed by a universal routine;
4.131) but there is no general agreement about the relevant perceptions or about the relevant routine,

4.132) and hence the issue reduces to a conflict of intuitions that cannot be objectively resolved.

4.133) That this does not happen with empirical statements (which are property statements) indicates that ethical statements are not objective property statements.

4.134) If ethical judgments were subjectively relational property statements,
4.135) they could not logically oppose each other, which they clearly can;

either have to be a simple, directly perceived property (the view of G.E. Moore) or a complex property whose presence was confirmable by a set of recognized criteria or an established procedural routine. But if it is claimed that goodness is a simple property, the decision as to its presence would depend on an arbitrary set of chosen instances and thus lack objectivity after all; and if goodness (etc.) were regarded as a complex property, then it should be possible to recognize and apply the relevant criteria or routine, whereas there is no such set of criteria or routine recognized universally by competent investigators (quite unlike the case of complex empirical properties—we all recognize, for example, what procedure to follow to find out whether a given polygon has or has not eight hundred sides). For either simple or complex properties we are driven back to an actual or possible conflict of intuitions for which there is no non-arbitrary method of resolution. In the case of nonmoral descriptive properties, apart from deception or organic defect (for example, color-blindness or tactual insensitivity), a disagreement about perceived properties logically cannot arise if both parties employ the same language, dialect, or usage, and are both apprised of all the relevant facts to the same degree; yet in the case of so-called moral properties, there can still be disagreement even if all these same conditions are met. Hence, for Toulmin, it is clear that ethical terms cannot stand for objective properties of the subjects they appropriately qualify.

The case is similar with subjectively relational properties (such as 'delicious,' 'enjoyable,' 'satisfying,' etc.). If ethical terms stood for such properties, there would be no way in which opposing answers to questions about them could contradict each other, since the meaning and reference of such terms vary with the identity of the person employing them with respect to himself or herself. In some sense, two persons who disagree as to whether a meal is delicious, etc., are opposing one another, but they are not logically contradicting one another, since it is possible for each to be telling the truth with respect to what each believes to be the case. But, according to Toulmin, it is characteristically possible for ethical claims by two individuals logically to contradict each other—which could not be the case if the ethical terms had the logical properties of subjective relations. It is further the case that it is perfectly intelligible to ask another person whether a given act is morally right or wrong relatively to oneself; but it would be absurd to ask such a question of another person in regard to subjectively relational properties. At best, for instance, it could only be a joke for me to ask you whether a beverage I had just consumed was thirst-quenching. Hence, for Toulmin, ethical terms logically cannot stand for subjectively relational properties, any more than they can stand for objective properties.

4.136) nor could they be person-transferable without alteration in reference, which they clearly are.

But if both objective and subjective views about ethical claims are rejected, and if, as is the case, Toulmin joins with these perspectives in rejecting the emotivist or attitudinalist view on the ground that such a view ignores the objective claim that is implied by the form of moral judgment, how is that objective reference to be logically defended? The answer is that the objectivity implied by moral language (used in its fundamentally evaluative sense) is situated in the good (i.e., logically appropriate) reasons that justify a moral claim on non-moral factual grounds and logical relations. Propositions expressing those reasons are indeed either descriptive empirical or formally logical property statements (or a combination of both). These reasons support (or, in a negative case, tend to reject or dismiss) the moral claim, although they do not logically entail that claim (hence, this is not a version of meta-ethical definism). In this way, the objective implication of moral claims is retained, while the property doctrine is not; and hence we have a qualified objectivism that is, strictly speaking, a variety of non-cognitivism.

4.137) Hence, it is plausible to ground the objectivity claim entailed by an ethical judgment on the logically appropriate reasons which support that claim or call it in question.

In critical response to such a qualified objectivism, I have no contest with the contention of all versions of this perspective (that I have discussed) to the effect that ethical statements, employed in their fundamentally evaluative sense, involve or imply an objective claim that the moral content of the judgment should be and can be supported by logically appropriate reasons; nor do I disagree with the rejection of either the subjective approach or the emotivist approach. I have already argued in an earlier context that not all disagreement in ethics can be merely about facts or logical relations—there are also substantial moral disagreements that logically oppose each other, as there could not be if either the subjectivist or emotivist approach were correct.

4.138) Critical difficulties of qualified objectivism

4.139) This perspective is clearly correct in supporting ethical objectivism, and in rejecting both subjectivism and emotivism in ethics.

4.140) But such views commonly revert to subjective elements such as preference or desire as the basis of the justifying reasons, and are thus themselves relativistic in nature.

But I also agree with Frankena that approaches like those of Toulmin or Hare ultimately appeal to individually or culturally relative elements as the foundation, in the end, of the 'good reasons' they regard as decisive—elements such as preference, desire, aversion, etc. Mere facts and logical relations do not, as these thinkers admit, entail ethical claims except in conjunction with normative ethical principles that provide the moral basis of these claims. And that is where these relativistic elements enter the picture. Yet surely preference or desire (or any other similarly relativistic basis) cannot provide the whole moral foundation of an ethical claim, unless we are willing to regard all preferences and/or desires as standing on an equal footing of moral worth. But that seems certainly not to be the case for most moral judges:

4.141) Preferences and desires cannot, as such, provide a basis for moral objectivity, since they are themselves subject to moral appraisal;

some preferences and desires are morally wrong; a given person often has to decide among alternative preferences or desires, and can only do so in terms of some non-preferential or non-desiderative criterion or basis, unless force or strength of psychological motivation is to settle the whole issue; and some preferences or desires are more worthy morally than others, even in cases where all possess some positive moral value, so that again there must be a non-preferential or non-desiderative criterion to determine the difference. It can also be claimed that, at best, as even John Dewey insisted, the fact that I prefer or desire something only raises the question whether it is morally desirable; it does not settle that question. In all these ways, it turns out that the 'objective reasons' needed to support moral claims are dispossessed of their objectivity just to the extent that such individually and culturally relativistic grounds are appealed to. Of course, these issues encroach on the territory of normative ethics and will come up again in that context. In the meantime, it is sufficient to observe that the standards of preference or desire are either themselves regarded as ultimate value criteria in the moral sense, or else the reference to them is merely a matter of descriptive psychological properties. In the former case, the question arises as to how it is possible to apprehend the ultimate value status of these (or any other) normative principles so regarded—could it be that these (or any other) ultimate normative principles are apprehended as such by immediate rational apprehension (that would be meta-ethical intuitionism at this ultimate level)? Certainly the value

4.142) and this appraisal in turn requires a non-preferential criterion of assessment.

4.143) Preference and desire would have to be regarded either as ultimate moral criteria (which is highly questionable), or else the reference to them would be merely descriptive and empirical;
4.144) the first alternative would lead to ethical intuition (which these thinkers reject),

of ultimate or basic normative ethical principles cannot in turn be justified by appropriate logical criteria, since such principles are themselves, if correctly identified, the criteria for justifying all lesser moral claims. If, on the other hand, we are dealing merely with descriptive psychological properties (x [an individual], or some group of x's, or even all x's prefer or desire item A as over against all alternatives), then several results follow: first, how does one move logically from such purely factual and empirical claims to any conclusion whatever about moral worth? Second, why select these psychological traits, rather than any others, as value criteria? And third, all such descriptive statements are clearly objective property claims and cannot, according to the 'good reasons' approach, have normative value status. Finally, for *either* alternative (ultimate value statements or descriptive psychological statements) we appear to find ourselves either without any justifiable basis for moral claims, or else with a basis that involves the property doctrine which theorists of this persuasion reject.

This sort of argument can be differently put in support of the same conclusion. The 'good reasons' approach claims that factual and logical reasons never, by themselves, entail moral conclusions, but are morally relevant merely in the sense of providing a context for drawing such conclusions. To think otherwise would at least involve a logical transition from 'is' to 'ought'; and it might even involve a disguised version of meta-ethical definism. But how then does one move with logical plausibility from factual and logical reasons to any moral conclusion whatsoever? Or more pointedly, how can such admittedly nonmoral considerations provide any logically justifying reasons for moral claims? It is certainly not unthinkable to argue that such moves involve fallacious reasoning; and that if there are any justifiable moral claims, they must, in their moral sense, be grounded in ultimate moral criteria that, although applicable to the interpretation of facts and logic, are logically independent of such facts and logic, so that they must, in the end, be apprehended through immediate rational apprehension. Given that definism is an unwarranted escape from these difficulties, they might at least be attenuated or softened by accepting the milder conclusion that at the ultimate moral level, there could be a transition from 'is' (facts and logic) to 'ought' (moral values)

4.145) while the second provides no plausible basis for moral objectivity,

4.146) and both alternatives lead to the property doctrine (which is again rejected by these thinkers).

4.147) If factual and logical reasons never entail, as such, moral conclusions, how can they provide a basis for such conclusions as objective, except in conjunction with a moral premise grounded in immediate rational insight or intuition?

that is not, after all, fallacious. Perhaps so; but this would be a drastic emasculation of the original 'good reasons' approach, and would leave unanswered the question whether any facts or logic could function in this role except in conjunction with some basic moral premise that would render the facts and logic relevant or pertinent.

4.148) As to the question whether these difficulties of qualified objectivism (the 'good reasons' approach) might be alleviated by the 'ideal observer' theory:

Is it conceivable that the 'ideal observer' thesis could provide a resolution to all these problems either in its non-cognitivist or cognitivist form? Except possibly in a strategic sense, I have no important complaint philosophically about the verbally distinguishable but substantially similar descriptions of such an ideal observer as provided by Hare, Frankena, and Firth, since all acknowledge that actual human judges of morality can at best remotely approximate the description of such an observer: here (in ethics) as elsewhere (in philosophy, science, etc.) rational objectivity in judgment is an ideal or goal, not a completely realized standard, although we have every reason to struggle for the closest possible approximation of that goal, and no plausible reason whatever to be lax about it. I cannot, how-

4.149) Firth's view

ever, accept Firth's clearly definist claim that 'x is right' (or substitute any other basic moral predicate, such as 'morally good or obligatory') means the same thing as the claim that 'an ideal observer would approve x under specified

4.150) involves definism and all its problems,

conditions.' Such an equivalence is subject to my previous criticism of definism, which I will not reiterate here. But more pertinently to the present context, if it is the function of an ideal moral observer to approve x as right

4.151) and involves the absurdity that there would be nothing objectively right for the observer to approve.

in itself when viewed in moral context, how could the observer's approval of x mean the same thing as the rightness of x, since in that case there would be nothing morally right for such an observer to approve, except perhaps his or her own act of approval, which would be nonsensical. I will therefore take it that Hare and Frankena do not intend the approval of the ideal observer to be identical with the meaning of any given moral predicate, but that they regard that approval as a guide to our own approving of what is morally good, right, etc. The question will then be whether the theory, thus interpreted, is a plausible solution to the

4.152) Frankena holds
4.153) (1) that moral judges who

problem of qualified objectivism. The general concept, as developed for example by Frankena, is that the more nearly various moral judges approximate the properties of an ideal observer, the more likely they are to reach substantial agreement about any moral issue with which they are concerned in common; and if all such judges *actually were* fully informed about all relevant nonmoral facts, calm and dispassionate, disinterested and unbiased, as well as judging from within the moral point of view, they *actually would* reach substantial agreement about any such moral issue. This heuristic or (as Kant might say) regulative thesis cannot be known by us to be certainly true, since the conditions are never perfectly fulfilled; it might even be the case that, while the thesis held for a large number of cases, there could still be moral disagreement for moral judges who meet the conditions as fully as it is possible for human judges to approximate them. We simply cannot be sure. But nevertheless accepting the thesis may be the best way to undergird our most urgent attempts to become the most adequate moral judges in the long run. The correct moral judgment then is the one that is ultimately fated or destined to be agreed upon by all competent moral investigators, a point that Charles Sanders Pierce had long since made about correct opinion in general, even (and especially) in empirical science.

With all this I have no particular quarrel. Of course, it means that moral judgment in particular cases can never be more than highly probable or approximative, simply because there are so many variables involved. With such a theory, as with most (perhaps all) others that I am aware of, it is extremely difficult to be fully confident about the adequacy of moral judgment in a particular case; but a problem that extends to all theoretical alternatives constitutes no special critical problem for any particular alternative. The really substantive critical issue for the 'ideal observer' theory is situated in a different dimension. Suppose I imagine myself as the closest approximation of an ideal moral observer that I am humanly capable of becoming; and suppose that you are in a similarly utopian condition. Then let us make the case even more remarkable by supposing that we agree in judging a particular moral act to be right (or wrong), and that we are therefore bolstered with confidence that our moral judgment in the case is objectively correct. A third party who was aware of our status as judges in the case but who lacked that status himself or herself could perhaps

approximate the properties of an ideal observer are more likely to agree on moral issues;

4.154) and (2) that the appropriate moral judgment is the one likely to be agreed on by such judges.

4.155) While this would make moral judgment never more than probable, that seems to be a feature of most ethical theories in judging particular issues.

4.156) The crucial difficulty of the 'ideal observer' theory can be stated as follows: The really substantive critical issue for the 'ideal observer' theory is situated in a different dimension. 4.157) Suppose a number of ideal observers are in agreement about the rightness or wrongness of a given act.

also reasonably judge the act in question as morally right (or wrong, as the case may be) on the ground that you and I agree in our judgment, and he or she knows that we are ideal observers. Unless our third party is a bonehead, however, he or she will not suppose that the act is right (or wrong) because you and I are agreed about it; there would have to be reasons or grounds that *we* had which *led* to our agreement. Those grounds could, of course, be that we found ourselves in agreement with still other ideal observers, and that they found themselves in agreement with still others. But this circularity could not continue *ad indefinitum* (much less *ad infinitum*): for then there would be nothing about which any of the observers agreed except that they agreed with each other. Somewhere the circle must be broken by an ideal (or actual) observer whose judgment of rightness or wrongness is based upon something other than agreement, something about the moral act itself in relation to its morally relevant context. The case is a species of the problem of knowledge by authority: it may be that I know (or claim to know), for example, that something like Newton's general theory of gravitational attraction, with appropriate reservations, is true because I take it on the authority of Newton and other physical scientists—most of what any given individual purports to know is grounded in this way. But unless Newton or some other 'ideal observer' has grounds other than authority, then there is no basis in physical reality itself for agreement among authorities or for the recognition of any particular authority. The case of moral judgment is wholly similar: agreement among moral authorities (ideal moral observers) cannot be the last word, so to speak. Objective moral claims cannot therefore have their ultimate ground or basis in the agreement of ideal observers: for such persons could only occupy their status as such observers by reason of their ability plausibly to identify independently objective grounds that provide the 'good reasons' which justify the moral claim being assessed; and that justification could logically not be found in the agreement of such observers, since, in that case, there would be nothing objective (independent of the observers as knowing subjects) about which they would be agreeing morally, and since, as previously argued, there would be nothing to stop the otherwise infinite regress of successive ideal observers.

4.158) there would have to be reasons that led to that agreement—reasons other than mere agreement, since otherwise there would be nothing about which the observers agreed.

4.159) It is a case of knowledge by authority;

4.160) but the agreement of authorities cannot provide an objective basis for any truth claim, 4.161) and therefore moral claims cannot be ultimately based on the agreement of ideal observers.

This conclusion could be avoided if defenders of the 'ideal observer' theory should surrender the claim to objectivity in moral judgment and resort to some individual or social variety of radical ethical relativism (such as ethical subjectivism or ethical emotivism); but these are the very positions that 'good reasons' theorists of the 'ideal observer' sort are attempting to avoid, since such positions would reduce differences in moral judgment to mere trivialities. And if that were the case, it would be difficult to explain why there is any such linguistic framework as moral discourse at all—as obviously there is.

If then objective moral claims must be assessable on grounds objectively independent of the psychological responses of qualified moral judges, what would those grounds be, and how would they be apprehended by correctly functioning moral observers? Clearly these grounds could not consist of any combination of nonmoral properties of the objects being morally judged: that would either involve some version of definism, or else it would terminate in the supposition that the 'is-ought' fallacy could be rejected, and that moral claims could be inferred from premises, none of which were themselves moral premises. But these views are typically rejected by defenders of the 'good reasons' approach, and I have myself already brought these views into serious critical question. Could it be after all that the objective grounds of moral claims are suspended upon unique moral properties that can be either directly or indirectly apprehended by rational insight? Some moral conclusions could be indirectly argued from more basic moral premises in conjunction with premises based on relevant nonmoral facts. But how would reason apprehend the ultimate moral premises that lie at the logical heart of every normative ethical theory? Here, as elsewhere with objective knowledge claims, the logically basic premises would have to be directly and immediately evident to rational apprehension on the part of a qualified or 'nearly ideal' observer: just as there are immediately apprehensible empirical truths and immediately apprehensible logical truths, there must also be immediately apprehensible moral truths which provide the objective and ultimate premises of all moral claims. If this analysis is correct, we are left with some version of meta-ethical intuitionism: either that or the claim to ethical objectivity must be surrendered.

4.162) This difficulty could be avoided if ethical objectivity were surrendered, but that is what the 'good reasons' approach wishes to avoid.

4.163) Moral objectivism:

4.164) cannot be preserved by any version of definism or by rejecting the 'is-ought' fallacy.

4.165) It would appear that it can be defended only by accepting the property doctrine, and by regarding the most basic moral properties as apprehensible only by immediate rational insight.

4.166) This would be meta-ethical intuitionism.

4.167) Moral objectivism *vs.* radical ethical relativism	If indeed we were to give up on the objective aspect of moral claims, we would be carried over the precipice to some version of radical ethical relativism: is this, after all, the morally and logically best that can be expected? The issue can be characterized as a choice between the *objectivist* (or, if a different term is preferred, *absolutist*) claim that there is at least one fixed and ultimate principle of moral value or moral obligation which has unconditional and unexceptionable authority over all rational, moral selves in all cases of moral choice, and which, as a principle, is intrinsically valid independently of individual, group, or cultural preference or opinion, on the one hand; and the *relativist* claim, on the other hand, that there is no such objective principle, and that the propriety or validity of any ethical judgment without exception is a function of its relation to subjectively and/or culturally variable states of opinion, preference, feeling, or response, with the result that there would be no logically appropriate method for providing, even in principle, an objective justification for any moral claim in its distinctively evaluative aspect. Such meta-ethical and normative ethical relativism is to be carefully distinguished both from *situational* relativism and from *descriptive* relativism: the former recognizes objective and ultimate moral truth but claims that its principles apply to particular cases of moral choice in a way that varies with the contextual factual situation; the latter argues that moral beliefs (as distinguished from moral truths) characteristically vary from individual to individual, group to group, and culture to culture. Both of these claims are logically compatible with ethical objectivism, as I have defined it, and the latter (descriptive relativism) is compatible with ethical relativism, as I have defined it. Nor do ethical objectivists or absolutists find themselves forced to claim that every moral rule has all the logical properties of an ultimate moral principle: some rules of this sort are applicable within certain limits, but not beyond those limits (in other words, they impose *prima facie* obligations but not absolute obligations—perhaps the moral prohibition against intentional misrepresentation of the truth is an example); but such examples are themselves to be justified by appeal to still more inclusive moral rules with broader applicability and finally by appeal to ultimate moral principles which
4.168) Definitions: 4.169) moral objectivism	
4.170) radical ethical relativism	
4.171) This involves the surrender of objective moral justification.	
4.172) It is contrasted with situational and descriptive relativism.	
4.173) Ethical objectivism need not entail that all moral rules are universal and unexceptionable.	

are unexceptionable.

With such clarifications clearly in mind, how have radical ethical relativists generally argued their case? In the main, two sorts of positive arguments have been offered in support. The first is a sociological argument which premises descriptive relativism from it: if moral beliefs do in fact vary, at every level of generality, from individual to individual, group to group, and culture to culture, and if there are no universally recognized criteria for resolving these disagreements objectively, it is reasonable to conclude that moral truths are as pervasively relative as the moral beliefs that purport to express them. However, in response to this argument, truths and tenets (beliefs) have clearly different logical properties: a belief, for example, can be false, while a truth cannot; or again, a belief is conceivable only in relation to persons who accept or reject it, but a truth has no such person-relative status. Radical variation in belief about a given subject is logically compatible with there being objectively true propositions about that subject: if, for example, Ptolemaic and Copernican theories of astronomy were both still serious options among scientists, it would be both absurd and bizarre to argue that this disagreement implied that there was no correct and true description of the motions of the heavenly bodies (much more so to conclude that there *were* no heavenly bodies to be described). Similarly, even the most radical disagreement about ethical issues would not logically entail that there were no objective moral truths, although, of course, such disagreement would be logically compatible with that claim. In short, variation in belief about any subject logically implies nothing about the truth or falsity of propositions about that subject, unless the subject is the description of those very beliefs as such (if it were true that beliefs of any sort do vary, then the claim that they did not vary would, of course, be false). Hence, the argument to ethical relativism from descriptive relativism establishes nothing: it is completely inconclusive.

The second positive argument for ethical relativism is the descriptive psychological claim that ethical beliefs (indeed, all beliefs), considered as psychological responses of individuals, are the product or effect of non-rational factors, such as environmental influences, biological dispositions, or emotive preferences, and cannot therefore be relied on

4.174) The case for radical ethical relativism

4.175) The sociological argument

4.176) Thesis: that descriptive relativism is true, and it implies radical ethical relativism as a reasonable belief.

4.177) But the descriptive relativism of moral beliefs does not logically entail the relativism of moral truths or principles.

4.178) Astronomy as an illustration

4.179) Ethical disagreement does not entail the non-objectivity of moral truths.

4.180) The psychological argument:
4.181) Thesis: that ethical beliefs are the product of non-rational causes that undermine their objectivity.

4.182) But:	as objectively true. This claim, however, fairly bristles with logical difficulties: first, it starts with ethical *beliefs*, as in the previous argument, and we have already shown that beliefs are logically distinct from truths, so that this argument also is inconclusive; second, it seems clear enough that beliefs are often grounded, at least in part, on the recognition of certain premises as true and as logically entailing a certain conclusion (in other words, some beliefs are based on rational factors), so that the universal thesis of the argument is clearly compromised; and third, this argument itself would be composed of certain beliefs of the psychological investigator and would therefore be subject to the very criticism which, as an argument, it directs toward ethical beliefs. If there is any way for the investigator to retain objectivity for the beliefs that compose his or her argument, that same way would be open in principle to the ethical objectivist. If therefore the psychological argument for relativism establishes anything to the point, it also establishes its own invalidity as an argument. So far, therefore, ethical objectivism appears to emerge unscathed.
4.183) This applies (if true) only to beliefs, not to truths.	
4.184) Even beliefs are often grounded on rational factors.	
4.185) The claim of the thesis would destroy its own objectivity.	
4.186) Arguments from defects of ethical objectivism:	Ethical relativists also offer indirect support for their position by appealing to negative criticisms of ethical objectivism. A.J. Ayer, for example, appeals to his radical empirical epistemology, and especially to the claim that all cognitively significant statements are either empirically determinate or logically determinate in order to classify ethical statements, used in their fundamentally evaluative sense, as purely emotive responses which therefore make no truth claims; but I have already critically dismissed this claim in an earlier context. Again, it is argued that even ethical objectivists cannot agree among themselves as to the identity of the ultimate moral principle or principles; but this argument is again to attempt to reason from disagreement in ethical belief to a conclusion about the truth-status of ethical propositions, a logical move already recognized by us as fallacious. It is further argued, by John Dewey, for example, that the most plausible candidates for ultimate moral principles are so excessively general and so extremely remote from moral problems that they provide no effective guidance for moral choice; but this is merely a question of strategy which is, in principle, correctable, not a serious theoretical difficulty— the same could be said of Dewey's own (or anyone else's)
4.187) that ethical statements are non-cognitive emotive responses;	
4.188) that objectivists cannot agree on ultimate moral principles;	
4.189) that so-called ultimate moral principles are too vague and remote to provide ethical guidance;	

general normative ethical theory. Finally, it is commonly argued that every proposed candidate for the status of ultimate moral principle admits (inconsistently) of exceptions in its application to particular cases of moral choice; but while this is true of many moral rules (as I have indicated previously myself), the only way to justify an exception is by appeal to a more inclusive moral rule and ultimately to an ultimate principle which is itself unexceptionable in its application. If any critic on this last point explains that it is merely a descriptive fact that, for any given rule, a person can be found who takes exception to its application in a particular case, that is simply the old 'belief-truth' fallacy (if I may call it that) all over again. In all these negative arguments, therefore, the case for ethical relativism and against ethical objectivism is once more inconclusive. At the same time, my critical analysis of both the positive and negative arguments in support of ethical relativism does not establish as either certain or probable that such relativism is false, but merely that the stated arguments in support of it do not establish as either certain or probable that ethical relativism is true.

What arguments, in turn, are characteristically offered in support of ethical objectivism (as I have previously defined it)? Here again it is appropriate to speak of both negative and positive arguments. On the negative side, which involves arguing the critical inadequacy of ethical relativism, the whole structure of our critique of that position, in the preceding analysis, yields the conclusion that none of the arguments for ethical relativism entail, either separately or in conjunction, the falsity of ethical objectivism, since none of those arguments entail the truth of ethical relativism. It is however possible to provide a stronger negative argument against ethical relativism and in support of ethical objectivism (since the two views, generally stated, contradict each other, it follows that one of them must be true and the other false, and that the falsity of either view would entail the truth of the other). By virtue of the nature of inductive logic, in which universal conclusions are inferred from a limited number of particular instances, there seems to be no way to argue with finality that ethical relativism is descriptively either true or false (our previous critical analysis illustrates that). But is it perhaps possible to show that ethical relativism is logically (or formally) false by showing that its claim

4.190) and that such principles always admit of exceptions in their application.

4.191) Conclusion: that the arguments for ethical relativism are inconclusive by failing to entail that relativism.

4.192) The case for ethical objectivism

4.192a) Negative arguments:

4.193) that ethical objectivism is rendered plausible by the inconclusiveness of the arguments for ethical relativism;
4.194) that while inductive arguments cannot show conclusively that ethical objectivism is descriptively either true or false,

4.195) it may however be possible to show that relativism

is, in some applicable sense, self-contradictory? Although I am not firmly confident about this issue, I am strongly inclined to believe that such a logical disproof of ethical relativism is indeed possible, subject to certain conditions. These conditions include the following: first, that the defender of ethical relativism claims that the doctrine is itself objectively true (rather than claiming more weakly that its truth is merely logically possible); second, that the defender also holds, as objectively true, that a proposition's being objectively true provides a reason why a person ought to believe it, since truth has an assignable value, by way of belief, that is greater than that of falsity; third, that ethical relativism is regarded as a species of a broader doctrine according to which there are no objective values of any sort, whether moral or nonmoral; and finally, that a proposition can be self-contradictory, not only in cases where its predicate is logically incompatible with its subject (for example, 'A triangle is not a plane figure.'), but also in cases where what is being asserted is incompatible with the fact that it is being asserted (for example, 'I cannot write a single word of English.').

Assuming these conditions, the self-contradictory character of ethical relativism can be expressed (in one of many ways) as follows: the ethical relativist regards as objectively true the claim that there are no objective value judgments, and he or she further claims that, precisely because it is true, persons ought to believe in this universal claim about values, since it is valuationally better to believe what is true rather than what is false. But in that case the relativist is making the very sort of objective value claim, about his or her relativist doctrine, which that same doctrine claims to be false. Hence, belief in the objective truth of relativism as better by way of belief than objectivism with respect to values, undermines (or entails the falsity *of*) its own assertion—which is existentially self-contradictory. If, as a response, the relativist retreats to the position that his or her arguments, and even the alleged truth of valuational relativism, provide no reason why anyone ought to believe his conclusions, then he or she is conceding that there is no objective reason why anyone should believe either this claim itself, or the doctrine of ethical or valuational relativism, or any other proposed proposition or set of propositions. Hence, the relativist's arguments

---

is self-contradictory, provided that certain conditions hold:

4.196) (a) that ethical relativism is regarded as itself objectively true,
4.197) (b) that being true provides a reason and an obligation to believe,

4.198) (c) that all objective values are denied,
4.199) and (d) that a proposition can be existentially self-contradictory.

4.200) Ethical relativism is existentially self-contradictory
4.201) for it claims to be true and that persons ought to believe it for that reason—which is itself an objective value judgment.

4.202) If the relativist surrenders such an objective claim, he or she acknowledges that there is no objective reason to believe in relativism other than preference.

make no epistemic (and certainly no moral) claim on the relativist or anyone else, so that whether a person believes a particular doctrine reduces, on the relativist view, to a question of preference. And of course there is no particular reason why any other person should be bound by the relativist's preference or by true propositions about such preferences. The final upshot is that the doctrine of valuational relativism, thus understood, deprives its own claim of any objective ground for believing it, and is, in this sense, again self-contradictory. It is perhaps not too much for critics of relativism to claim that the doctrine is therefore shown to be false, rather than true, in the only sense in which human beings can have a significantly important interest in truth and falsity. And if that conclusion is reasonable, it is also perhaps not too much to claim that ethical objectivism is, as the logical contradictory of relativism, objectively true in the same sense. Should the relativist respond that, if his or her doctrine is self-contradictory, then, since the two sides of a contradiction mutually cancel each other, the doctrine is neither true nor false, so that one cannot argue the truth of ethical objectivism from the falsity of ethical relativism; then my answer is twofold—first, that this admission dissolves any critical claim of ethical relativism against ethical objectivism, and second, that it is perfectly legitimate both logically and linguistically to extend the meaning of the concept of falsity to include the indisputable claim that self-contradictory assertions are necessarily false.

4.203) It appears to follow that:
4.204) (a) ethical relativism is false,

4.205) (b) ethical objectivism is true as its contradictory.

There are, of course, some positive arguments in support of ethical objectivism in addition to the negatively critical arguments previously considered, although none of these arguments have anything like the status of demonstrative clinchers. From an existential point of view, human beings have a variety of limited concerns about issues that matter to them—about health, peace of mind, economic assets, friendship, romance, parent-child relationships, etc. As stated, these concerns are limited in that, while they concern us deeply, they do not concern us absolutely or unconditionally. At the same time, we view such concerns as rationally and morally justified within such recognizable (though not always consciously formulated) limits. Yet how could any limited concern be justified in this way, if there were not something (some value or end) that concerned us absolutely

4.206) Positive arguments for ethical objectivism:

4.207) that limited concerns imply absolute and unconditional concern as a rational and criterial base, and unconditionally, and which, when formulated as a principle, could function as an ultimate ground for justifying other, though limited, concerns? That we take at least some of our concerns with unmitigated seriousness vaguely intimates that at the root of all such seriousness there is some self-evidently valuable end which itself possesses absolute seriousness for us: otherwise, all our lesser concerns would be reduced to triviality or even folly. Such ultimate and unconditional concern would be irrational, if there were not some ultimate principle of objective moral value. Of course, we cannot demonstrate decisively that our concerns at every level are *not* irrational. But that is not the relevant issue; the relevant issue is whether we are prepared to *regard* all of our concerns at every level as unjustifiable and utterly irrational; that would be equivalent to admitting that nothing really matters, that nothing makes any difference, that any state of circumstances is as satisfactory as any other, or that, in short, human life is objectively meaningless ('a tale told by an idiot, full of sound and fury, signifying nothing...' in Shakespeare's parlance). Apparently even committed ethical relativists believe that it matters whether other persons believe their views, and whether they themselves believe them.

4.208) and this, in turn, would be irrational without an ultimate principle of moral value as its ground;

This same argument can be stated in a variety of alternative ways that might illuminate its significance for our reflection. From a pragmatic point of view, while persons do not always act as if they believed they stood before the bar of ultimate and unconditional moral authority, they always expect others to treat them as if those others were thus situated morally. They may not be ready to *dispense* moral justice and fairness of consideration, but they are always ready to insist that they receive it, nevertheless. From a different existential standpoint, personal agents inevitably find themselves choosing among alternatives, making decisions. Many of them are trivial, of course, in the sense that it seems to make no difference which alternative is chosen. But no one seriously claims that all of his or her decisions, across the board, are trivial and inconsequential; some of them are of great importance and make a significant difference to our personal well-being and that of others. Either way, an objective standard of value is implied: that we recognize *some* decisions as trivial suggests a standard of justification for applying that designation; and if any of our decisions

4.209) that moral objectivity is assumed by the fact that persons always expect to be treated with impartiality and justice;

4.210) that the same conclusion is implied by the fact that no one regards all of his or her decisions as trivial in their consequences,

are really of great moment, that same standard confronts us again. From a directly moral point of view, if any human person ever has an unconditional moral responsibility, or even claims (as is characteristically the case) that other persons have such responsibilities toward him, he is accepting a relationship that contextually implies an objective value standard as the ultimate ground of such responsibility. Even ethical relativists seem to be transformed into believing ethical objectivists when their own rights are at issue. I have not fully stated any of these last alternative versions; but they all point to some variety of ethical objectivism as the only adequate ground for taking life seriously from the moral point of view.

4.211) and that there could be no genuine moral responsibility without moral objectivity.

Conclusion Concerning General Meta-Ethical Theories

While various perspectives of meta-ethical non-cognitivism have contributed significantly to the understanding of the functions of ethical language and the meaning of ethical discourse, none, in my opinion, is to be judged critically adequate: Descriptive Relativism (Hume) and Emotivism (Ayer and Stevenson) make the propriety of ethical judgments, in their fundamentally evaluative sense, relative to individually, culturally, or humanly relative states of opinion, preference, feeling, or response, and therefore fail to account for the evident fact that such ethical judgments make an objective claim; the combined 'Good Reasons'/'Ideal Observer' approach acknowledges the objective claim but fails to provide any base for it that is compatible with a consistent non-cognitivist perspective. In the end, we seem led back to some version of meta-ethical intuitionism that leaves radical ethical relativism as its only alternative; differently put, ethical objectivism implies ethical intuitionism as its only plausible contextual foundation. The objectivity of moral claims can, it seems, only be reasonably defended on cognitivist grounds, which regard ethical judgments, when expressed in adequate logical form, as making an evaluative claim that is either true or false. Of course, such judgments also have non-cognitive functions as well: they are emotively expressive and evocative, commendatory (they express approval or disapproval), directive, prohibitive, etc.; but these non-cognitive functions could not be tested in their propriety

4.212) Meta-ethical non-cognitivism falls short:

4.213) either in failing to account for the objective claim implied by ethical judgments,

4.214) or in failing to do so consistently with non-cognitivism.
4.215) Ethical objectivism appears to imply meta-ethical intuitionism, although this perspective can consistently acknowledge that ethical judgments have non-cognitive functions as well.

if ethical judgments did not make an objective claim and thus possess cognitive meaning. The cognitivist alternative to intuitionism would be some version of definism: but our conclusion about such views is that at least naturalistic definisms of whatever variety are critically inadequate; other versions of definism (theologically or metaphysically transcendent; rationalistic or formalistic) will be dealt with in the normative discussions of ethical idealism and ethical theism. In the meantime, since non-naturalistic versions of definism are rarely urged as serious alternatives in ethical theory, if we are to defend ethical objectivism, we are left to do so by appealing to some version of ethical intuitionism.

I shall therefore designate my own meta-ethical theory as *modified teleological intuitionism*; and although the various elements of this perspective have emerged in previous discussion, I will put them together in summary form here. According to this theory, ethical terms stand for unique moral properties and cannot be fully defined by means of (or logically equivalent in meaning to) any conjunction of non-ethical terms, when the original terms are used in judgments that employ these terms in a fundamentally evaluative sense (thus definism, in all its forms, is rejected). Furthermore, the meaning of basic ethical terms must be apprehended by immediate rational insight in a way that is analogous to the empirical apprehension of the meaning of basic descriptive terms, so that in both cases the elements of definition cannot themselves be defined but only identified by direct insight (in the case of basic descriptive terms, the insight is empirically evident; in the case of basic ethical terms, the insight is rationally evident). It is in this sense that the theory is appropriately called *intuitionism*. Finally, the theory is *teleological* in a *modified* sense: the moral rightness of an act or principle is a function of both the moral and the nonmoral worth, value, or goodness either of the act or principle itself, or alternatively of the worth, etc., of the consequences of performing the act or following the principle. Yet the ultimate content of moral worth (depending on the normative ethical theory in question) must itself be intrinsic and therefore also be apprehended by immediate rational insight; so that at this ultimate level there is a deontological capstone (hence, the *modification* of the teleological aspect of the theory). If, at intermediate levels, in contrast to the ultimate

---

4.216) Definism would be the only other cognitivist alternative;
4.217) but naturalistic definism has been argued to be implausible, while other versions are rarely appealed to in philosophy.

4.218) A summary of modified teleological intuitionism:

4.219) Ethical terms stand for unique moral properties.

4.220) The meaning of basic ethical terms is disclosed to immediate rational insight.

4.221) Moral rightness is a function (directly or indirectly) of moral goodness.

level, the rightness of an act or principle is a function of its instrumentality in producing valuable consequences, then the rightness or goodness of the ultimate principle of value would have to be both self-evident and self-contained (not instrumental), since otherwise we would be involved in an infinite regress of teleological means which were in principle devoid of even the possibility, in theory, of final justification. Hence our theory is a mixed (or modified) teleological/deontological one: deontological at the ultimate and intrinsic level, teleological at the intermediate and extrinsic levels. Basically, my argument is that, from a meta-ethical point of view, some such theory (this one or some similar one) is the only plausible perspective in meta-ethics for defending the intelligibility and plausibility of ethical objectivism over against any sort of radical ethical relativism (which I have claimed to be inadequate and incoherent in various ways). Yet the defense of this theory does not entail the overall falsity of other meta-ethical views; in fact, I have attempted to incorporate in this perspective what I regard as the valid and sound aspects of other views. The deontological aspect of my position will, I think, disclose itself as increasingly reasonable when we discover that every normative ethical theory, without serious exception, regards the ultimate of goodness or rightness as intrinsically self-evident in its value or worth, so that it could never be justified instrumentally but only through immediate rational insight. Still, this does not mean that the choice of normative ultimates is arbitrary or non-rational, since, as we shall see, there are certain formal conditions of adequacy that any ethical ultimate of value logically ought to exhibit as a foundation of its adequacy as an objective criterion of value. But more of that in the proper place (in the discussion of general theories of normative ethics). Meanwhile I turn my attention to one final meta-ethical issue which many sober thinkers regard as absolutely decisive for the relevance and meaningfulness of moral discourse itself as such, regardless of theoretical differences about its basis.

4.222) But the ultimate content and principle of moral goodness must be immediately apprehended as self-evident and self-contained,

4.223) so that the theory is a mixture of teleological and deontological elements.

4.224) The main supporting argument for such a view is that it is the only critically defensible alternative to radical ethical relativism.

4.225) The intrinsically self-evident character of the ultimate good does not mean that the choice among normative ultimates is logically arbitrary.

Chapter V

Determinism, Personal Freedom, and Moral Responsibility: A Meta-Ethical Postscript

Meta-ethics is, of course, interested in other issues aside from general meta-ethical theories: it is concerned with nonmoral factual (and even metaphysical) issues which bear on the relevance or even the intelligibility of moral discourse as a pervasive aspect of human experience. Some of these issues (like the immortality of the personal self, or the existence of an ultimate and transcendent reality such as the God of theism) I regard strategically as best reserved for consideration in the analysis of normative ethical theories, which disagree extensively about such issues and which make that disagreement a central part of normative ethical discussion. But one such issue (or cluster of issues, it seems better to say) is so decisive and crucial for the understanding of the meaning of moral discourse in general, that its consideration cannot be reasonably postponed: and that is the controversy about the logical relations among the concepts of metaphysical determinism, personal or individual freedom, and moral responsibility. The issues are so complex that it seems virtually impossible even to explain these issues without at least provisionally implying some theoretical solution to them in contrast to other perspectives. But I will try, at the outset in any case, to be as unprejudicial in my formulation of these issues as possible.

5.1) Some other meta-ethical issues can be discussed in connection with normative ethical theories.

5.2) But the problem of determinism, freedom, and moral responsibility is too crucial for meta-ethics to postpone.

Statement of the Problems

Perhaps the most appropriate way to start is with a series of questions:

5.3) Six basic questions:

5.3a) moral responsibilities;

1) Are mature human persons ever correctly held to be morally responsible for their moral choices, morally significant acts, moral rules or principles to which they purport to be committed, and/or moral character traits?

5.3b) whether moral responsibility is proportionate to the degree of personal freedom;

2) If they are thus responsible (in the sense of being regarded as morally praiseworthy or blameworthy for their causal role in originating these elements), does that ascription logically require that the degree of such responsibility is proportionate to the freedom of human persons in these respects?

5.3c) the morally relevant sense of freedom;

3) If so, in what does the morally relevant sense of freedom consist, in the case of finite moral agents like ourselves?

5.3d) whether determinism and freedom are logically compatible;

4) Is this morally relevant sense of freedom logically consistent (or compatible) with a deterministic view of reality?

5.3e) the proper and relevant sense of determinism;

5) If so, what sort of determinism is thus compatible, and why is it more plausible than other varieties of determinism?

5.3f) whether the relevant senses of freedom and determinism can be logically justified.

6) Are the morally relevant senses of freedom and/or determinism susceptible of being subject to testing, and either being justified as true or rejected as false with either logical probability or logical necessity?

A logically viable theory about these issues would need to take a stand on the answers to all of these questions, either directly or indirectly, and then it would need to provide arguments to defend that stand against major alternatives.

5.4) The major alternative theories

A plausible second step would be to name and characterize the major theoretical alternatives with respect to the issues formulated in the above questions. The major disjunction would appear to be the contrast between *compatibilism* and *incompatibilism*. *Compatibilism* holds that the relevant senses of freedom and determinism are logically consistent with each other (so that both could be true without logical contradiction). The position then goes on to divide into two further views which I will designate as *weak* compatibilism (human persons are free in the morally relevant sense, and it makes no logical difference whether the relevant sense [or perhaps any sense] of determinism is true or not, since either its truth or its falsity is consistent with the morally relevant sense of freedom), and *strong* compatibilism (the morally relevant senses of both freedom and determinism are both true, sometimes with the stipulation that if the relevant sense of determinism were not true, the relevant sense of freedom could not be true either). *Incompatibilism* holds that the morally relevant senses of freedom and determinism are contradictory, so that the truth of either implies the falsity of the other. Again the position divides into two viewpoints which, in this case, logically oppose each other, depending on which side of the contradiction is embraced as true and which is rejected as false. *Libertarianism* holds that the morally relevant sense of freedom is true and that therefore determinism (as its logical opposite) is false. In contrast, *rigorous* or *hard determinism* claims that some version of metaphysical determinism is true, that the morally relevant sense of freedom (as the logical opposite of determinism) is false, and that therefore, since the pertinent sense of freedom is a necessary condition of moral responsibility, human beings are not to be held morally responsible in any of the traditionally characteristic ways. Over against this hard or rigorous determinism, the strong version of compatibilism explained above is designated as *soft* determinism.

The next step would be to spell out the main perspectives regarding the meaning of both freedom and determinism in their (supposedly) morally relevant senses. In my opinion, there are four clearly distinguishable views concerning the morally relevant sense of personal freedom. The first position regards freedom as *indeterminateness* and is characteristically called *contra-causal* freedom: an act is free, for this view, if it is uncaused or if the choice leading to it is uncaused, so that the principle of causality is simply inapplicable to it.

5.5) Compatibilism: freedom and determinism are logically consistent.

5.6) Weak version: moral agents are free, but whether determinism is true or false is irrelevant.

5.7) Strong version: freedom and determinism are both true and required.

5.8) Incompatibilism: freedom and determinism inconsistent

5.9) Libertarianism: freedom true, determinism false

5.10) Hard determinism: determinism true, freedom false, and no moral responsibility

5.11) Soft determinism equals strong compatibilism.

5.12) Four Views of Freedom:

5.13) contra-causal indeterminateness:
5.14) act or choice uncaused;

5.15) Main supporting argument: being uncaused is a necessary condition for the moral responsibility of the agent.

The main argument for this view is that any act or choice for which there is a necessary and sufficient cause is an act or choice which, as causally determined, divests the agent of moral responsibility for the act, and that therefore, if persons are to be held morally responsible for any of their acts or choices, those acts or choices must be uncaused in the ordinary sense, since persons can be held morally responsible only if they could actually have acted otherwise than they did in the same identical circumstances (including effectively operative causes).

5.16) Main criticism: an uncaused act or choice, as random, would not be under the control of the agent who could not thus be morally responsible for it.

The main criticism of the contra-causal view of freedom is that the absence of operative causes, which explain the occurrence of an act or choice, renders that act or choice entirely random and therefore removes it from the causal control of the agent, so that the agent is still, on this view, divested of moral responsibility: a morally responsible act simply cannot be a random, wholly unpredictable, and indeterminate act. The theory, therefore, though purportedly making moral responsibility possible, fails to achieve its purpose. Obviously this view is a critically defective version of libertarian incompatibilism (but clearly not the only possible one).

5.17) Avoidability:

The second perspective holds that the morally relevant sense of freedom is simply *avoidability* or the *capacity to have acted otherwise*, where the word *act* is extended to cover the making of a choice and not merely its execution. On this view, an act or choice is free in the morally relevant sense if the agent, in morally similar circumstances, could, in some intelligible sense, have acted (or chosen) otherwise, had the agent decided to do so, irrespective of whether the act (or choice) the agent did make was causally determined. Here it is essential to clarify the meaning of the phrase 'could, in some intelligible sense, have acted otherwise.' All that is connoted by this phrase is that the act or choice would have been logically and empirically possible in the circumstances; that is, the concept of the different act or choice does not involve any logical contradiction, nor any contravention of empirically describable circumstances. It would not, for example, be a free choice for me to have decided not to square the circle this morning (since it would be logically impossible to do so in any case); nor would it have been a free choice for me to have decided not to hold my breath for ten minutes this morning (since it would be empirically

5.18) The agent could have acted or chosen otherwise had he or she chosen to do so, irrespective of whether the act was causally determined: that a different act or choice would have been logically and empirically possible in the circumstances;

impossible for me to do so in any case, given my biological characteristics). But it is important to add that the notion of 'empirically possible' also involves a person's not having been either constrained (to perform an act) or restrained (from performing an act) in the circumstances. It is obvious, in addition, that the notion of 'empirical possibility' includes the genuine probability of alternatives having occurred mentally to the agent in the circumstances. Acts or choices made under such conditions are free in the sense of having been performed voluntarily by the agent, and hence are acts for which the agent may be held morally responsible, whether the acts or choices were determined or not, or even if it is clear that they were determined in the relevant sense. The main arguments for this view are that this sense of freedom is all that is required for the moral relevance of ethical judgment and the assignment of moral responsibility, and that, since causal explanation of an act or choice remains an open question on this view, it makes it possible to enable and explain the generally reliable prediction of moral choices made by a given agent whose past propensities are known by an observer. The main argument against this view is that, although the conditions prescribed in the theory are *necessary* conditions of moral responsibility, they are *not sufficient* to justify the assignment of such responsibility, since they merely make it *theoretically* conceivable for the agent to have acted otherwise, whereas an agent can be reasonably judged morally responsible for an act or choice only if it were *actually* possible for the agent to have acted otherwise in the same morally relevant circumstances. Nor is it a plausible response to this criticism to argue that the only condition, under which an agent could not actually have acted otherwise, would be in a case in which the agent could not act voluntarily by reason of some external constraint or restraint; for if the act or choice were both voluntary and at the same time wholly determined by antecedent and contemporaneous circumstances to which the agent could not, for that reason, have responded differently, the agent would clearly have been incapable of acting otherwise in the morally relevant sense. It might even be argued that lack of restraint and constraint of an external sort are not *sufficient* conditions for an act or choice being plausibly classified as voluntary, though of course they are *necessary* conditions.

5.19) involves the absence of constraint or restraint;

5.20) presupposes the probability of genuine alternatives having occurred to the agent;

5.21) such acts are voluntarily performed by the agent.

5.22) Main supporting arguments:
5.23) sufficient condition of moral relevance and responsibility;
5.24) makes generally reliable prediction of moral choices possible.
5.25) Main criticism:
5.25a) that such freedom is a necessary but not sufficient ground of moral responsibility, which applies only if it would have been actually (and not merely theoretically) possible to have acted otherwise:
5.25b) an act that was both voluntary and determined would not be one for which the agent had any actual alternatives.

5.26) Agent causality:

5.26a) freedom as self-determination under the influence of motives which are never the sufficient causes of responsible choice or action;

5.27) while there is no action apart from motives, the agent himself decides by consent which motives prevail;

5.28) since the agent is the deciding cause, the agent could always actually have acted otherwise;

5.29) an agent free in this sense can choose to succumb to the strongest motive, but there is no necessity that the agent do so.

5.30) This view is libertarian incompatibilism.

5.31) Main supporting argument: moral responsibility implies the efficacious causality of

A third point of view regarding the morally relevant sense of freedom is called the *agent causality* view. According to this position, freedom in the morally relevant sense is self-determination in view of (or under the influence of) both external and internal motives (a motive is any operative influence on an agent that tends to incline a person toward a given act or choice), but which, irrespective of their strength of appeal, are never by themselves the sufficient cause of the agent's choice. No agent, on this view, can act apart from alternative systems of motives which tend to incline an individual toward a certain pattern of choice or action; but it is the agent, as the personal subject of action, that, by consent and choice, decides which set of motives will receive his or her affirmative response. In other words, freedom here is the agent's capacity to self-initiate an efficacious inclination toward (or away from) a set of influencing motives. A free act or choice is, then, not an uncaused act or choice: the agents themselves are the deciding causes; and, irrespective of the relative strength of alternative sets of motives, the agents always *actually could* have acted otherwise, since no system of inclining motives is sufficient in itself to decide an act or choice in the morally relevant sense. Of course, such transcendentally free agents can, by self-mediated decision, *allow* themselves to succumb or yield to the strongest set of influencing motives, and perhaps moral agents often or even characteristically do just that by a sort of habitual moral inertia; but, while alternative sets of motives make an option for choice possible, they cannot by themselves cause that choice in a morally relevant sense without the consent of the agent, even in cases in which the choice has become so habitual as to be barely conscious to the agent. Succumbing or yielding is *also* a choice the sufficient cause of which always includes the self-initiated causality of the agent so that whatever the agent chooses, that person could always and unexceptionably have chosen otherwise. This position is obviously *libertarian incompatibilism*, but without the contra-causal, indeterminate aspect of the first view discussed. Both views stand in contrast to the equally obvious *compatibilism* (whether weak or strong) of the second view. The main argument (generally stated) in support of this view is that it regards a morally relevant act or choice as one for which the agent can be held genuinely responsible, partly because the agent alone is the efficacious cause of the choice, and partly because, just for that reason, it would always have been possible for the agent *actually* (and not merely theoretically as in the second view) to have chosen otherwise; thus the view preserves both causal universality and genuine moral responsibility without any contradiction between them. The main argument against the agent causality view is that, while it purports to preserve causal universality by making the agent the decisive cause of a free act in the morally relevant sense, nevertheless it involves indeterminateness or contra-causality at the highest level, since by definition it holds that the agent's final and decisive causality, as self-initiated inclination, has no ground or reason that determines it to one choice rather than another, so that any choice, as indeterminate in this way, is unintelligible from a causal point of view. This counter-argument can be put as a kind of dilemma: either the agent's decisive, efficacious choice among motives has rational grounds, or not; if it does have such grounds, then they determine the choice; if it has no such grounds, then it is indeterminate and unintelligible in the sense that no explanation can be given for the occurrence of this particular choice as over against its alternatives.

The fourth (and final) view of freedom to be discussed here can be characterized as *necessary self-determination*, or perhaps *internally sufficient self-determination*. Regardless of terminology, however, this position holds that an act or choice is free if the sufficient (and therefore also necessary) cause of the act or choice is internal to the agent in the sense that it is the expression of the agent's nature, states, and character traits. This view differs from view three in that, on this perspective, these internal factors are necessary aspects of the agent's nature and individuality, so that there follows here no radical capacity to have acted otherwise; in fact, the acts and choices of an agent follow necessarily from his or her nature and are wholly self-determined. Yet the agent is morally responsible for every such act or choice, since it springs, in its determinateness as an act or choice, wholly from the agent's own character as the sort of individual he or she is; precisely because—on this view over all others—the act is the agent's own, the agent can be held morally responsible for it. This is determinism; but it is a determinism wholly self-contained in the agent by

the agent and therefore also his or her real and actual capacity to have chosen otherwise.

5.32) Main criticism:
5.33) that the agent's choice has no sufficient determining cause and is therefore indeterminate and contra-causal;

5.34) that a dilemma emerges: either the choice is determined or it is causally inexplicable.

5.35) Necessary self-determination
5.36) An act or choice is free:
5.36a) if its sufficient and necessary cause is internal to the agent as a self,
5.36b) so that, although there is no capacity to have acted otherwise, the agent is nevertheless morally responsible because acts or choices spring from his or her character;

necessity. In other words, the truth of freedom is necessity, and the truth of necessity is freedom—as Hegel so aptly claimed in espousing this view, along with Leibniz and many other thinkers in the tradition of philosophical idealism. The view is obviously a variety of what I have called *strong compatibilism*; and yet it clearly stands in contrast to view 2, the other compatibilist view discussed. The main argument in support of this view is that it purportedly combines determinism with objective moral responsibility without any logical contradiction or inconsistency: the act is wholly self-determined by factors internal to the agent, and for that very reason, the agent is wholly responsible for it in the moral sense. This is the strongest conceivable sense of moral responsibility: the slightest tinge of contingency or indeterminateness would in fact lessen and compromise the degree of responsibility. For this view determinism is not only compatible with moral responsibility; it is, in fact, entailed by moral responsibility, so that the denial of either would be the denial of the other (although the view need not be stated quite this strongly). The main argument against the necessary self-determination view of freedom is that it appears possible to claim that no act or choice of a finite agent is ever absolutely self-determined in the exclusive way envisioned by this theory; it is only the Absolute Mind of Hegel, or the Infinite Self of Bradley, or the Personal God of Leibniz (perhaps also Jonathan Edwards, or even Christianity generally) that possesses such absolute and wholly intrinsic freedom. And in the end these thinkers seem clearly to admit this, since they claim (at least in the case of Hegel and Bradley) that it is only by recognizing and accepting ourselves as aspects of the self-unfolding or self-manifestation of the Absolute or Infinite Self that we can participate in that sort of freedom. But this raises two serious questions. First, have we, in that case, left the freedom and moral responsibility out of account in the end? And second, can we unflinchingly pay the price of such an absolute idealism in which, in the end, all moral distinctions are transcended if not obliterated? So much for the elaboration of the principal views concerning the morally relevant sense of personal freedom.

Our next task will be to develop an analysis of the main varieties of determinism, which then will need to be related

Margin notes:

5.36c) hence, strong compatibilism.

5.37) Main supporting argument:

5.37a) that this view combines rigorous determinism with moral responsibility;

5.37b) that the degree of internal determinism is the degree of moral responsibility, and vice versa.

5.38) Main criticism:
5.38a) that no act of a finite self is ever absolutely self-determined, so that only the absolute Self or God would be morally free and responsible;

5.38b) that thus the freedom and responsibility of the finite self are left unaccounted for.

to the alternative perspectives concerning personal freedom. In my opinion there are (at least) four distinguishable varieties of determinism that are relevant to the issues of freedom and moral responsibility; and I will summarize them in the order of what I will call their rigor or strength, the least rigorous or extreme being considered first, and so on, to the most rigorous. In general, the more rigorous senses of determinism subsume the less rigorous as aspects of their own determinism, so that we are confronted here, not with the question of which of several mutually exclusive alternatives is the most plausible, but rather with the question of how far to go in the direction of greater rigor. The first (and least rigorous) meaning of determinism construes this concept as logically equivalent to what I will call *causal universality*: that an act or choice is determined simply means that it is susceptible of causal explanation. In general, this position holds that every originated state of things is the effect of antecedent and/or contemporaneous factors which account (i.e., provide a sufficient reason) for its existence, rather than not, and for its being as it is, rather than otherwise. A moral act or choice on the part of an agent is, of course, an originated state of things (or affairs) and therefore must have a sufficient ground for its existence as having the character it possesses. If that is so, then, by definition, the act or choice is causally determined (i.e., susceptible of causal explanation). The only one of the four previously analyzed senses of freedom, with which this meaning of determinism would be incompatible, is the view that defines freedom as causal indeterminateness; all the other views regard freedom (in the morally relevant sense) as compatible with the claim that acts or choices of a moral sort can be both free and causally determined or explained. Furthermore, the second and third views of freedom (avoidability, agent causality) hold that this sense of determinism is consistent with the claim that, for any moral act or choice involving the responsibility of the agent, it would have been possible (at least theoretically and perhaps actually) for the agent to have made a different choice; only the concept of freedom as necessary self-determination would deny this claim, while at the same time insisting that moral acts or choices are causally explainable. The main argument in support of determinism interpreted as causal universality is that the denial that moral acts

5.39) Four views of determinism, considered in an order of increasing rigor and inclusiveness:

5.40) Causal universality

5.41) Thesis: an act or choice is determined if it is capable of causal explanation.

5.42) This view is compatible with all the senses of freedom except indeterminateness, and is consistent with the claim (of two of the senses) that the agent could have acted otherwise, a claim denied only by the necessary self-determination view.

5.43) Main supporting argument: that the denial of causal

determinateness to moral acts and choices is both generally and morally unintelligible, so that moral responsibility would be eliminated.

or choices have causes is both generally and morally unintelligible: it is generally unintelligible because there is then no way to explain the occurrence of the act or choice as an originated state of affairs; it is unintelligible morally because it would thus remove the power to produce the act or choice from the causal control of the agent (the agent could not, that is, be the cause of the act or choice), so that the agent could not be held morally responsible for it. The main argument against this view of determinism is the claim that if moral acts or choices are the effect of causes which ensure necessarily and sufficiently that they exist, that thesis would seem to imply that such acts or choices, given their determinate causes, could not be otherwise, so that either moral responsibility is denied or else such responsibility is morally and logically conceivable in the absence of the capacity to act otherwise.

5.44) Main criticism: that causal determinateness would be incompatible with the ability to have acted otherwise, so that moral responsibility would (again) be eliminated.

5.45) Physicalistic or naturalistic determinism

5.46) Thesis: an act or choice is determined if its occurrence is completely explainable by the operation of physical and/or biological causes which are themselves similarly determined.

The second view regarding the nature of determinism accepts the thesis that moral acts or choices are causally explainable, but then proceeds to claim that these causes are basically physical and biological in character in such a way that the causes can be in principle analyzed by means of an empirical description, however difficult that might be in practice. It is no small task to find a satisfactory term to designate this perspective: but I will call it *physicalistic determinism*, or *mechanistic determinism* (provided that the latter term is not interpreted to imply that biological organisms [in this case, human organisms] are wholly explainable in terms of elementary material particles), or even *naturalistic determinism* (since this view holds that all operative causes are natural states of the physical universe). On this view, the universe is composed of a succession of extensive and complex physical states each of which is the necessary effect of similar previous states and itself a part of the necessary cause of succeeding states in accordance with certain recognizable descriptive regularities which, when formulated as propositions, are called the laws of nature. Hence, assuming the actual past (previous physical states of the universe) and the laws of nature (descriptive regularities in the relationships among those physical states), the succeeding states of the universe are necessarily and uniquely determined; that is, each succeeding state of the universe is wholly the effect of previous states and could not

5.47) For this view, assuming the actual past (previous physical states) and the laws of nature (descriptive regularities), each succeeding physical state is the

be otherwise on the assumed conditions. So-called moral acts or choices on the part of human agents are among these necessarily and uniquely determined effects, and therefore also could not be otherwise, given the actual past and the laws of nature. This view is clearly a more rigorous determinism than the previous view of causal universality, since it specifies the detailed nature of these causes as physical and interprets them as operating to ensure a unique future that excludes any alternative to what actually occurs. Of course, if the actual past and/or the laws of nature had been different, succeeding states of the universe might be different (or put alternatively, there might be a different universe). However, in that universe its actual past and its laws of nature would ensure nevertheless a unique, though different, result; and in any case, the conditions hypothetically supposed are contrary to fact—the actual universe is the one in which we find ourselves. It is clear therefore that this position eliminates any actual (or real) possibility of an agent's having acted or chosen differently, and any view of moral responsibility that entails that actual possibility. Hence, this sort of determinism is incompatible with the first and third views of freedom (indeterminateness, agent causality), but compatible with some versions of freedom as avoidability or even necessary self-determination. But the most likely result of this perspective would be a hard determinism that eliminates both any morally relevant sense of freedom and any notion of objective moral responsibility that is not culturally relative. The main argument in support of such a physicalistic or naturalistic determinism is that some such view of causal necessity underlies the whole of physical and biological science, and is logically required to underwrite its enormous predictive and manipulative success; science, in other words, entails such a rigorous determinism and would be inexplicable without it, irrespective of the consequences for the concepts of personal freedom and moral responsibility. The main argument against this position, from a moral standpoint, is precisely that it cannot accommodate ethical objectivity, morally relevant personal freedom, and moral responsibility or accountability: such determinism may be applicable at sub-personal levels of the universe, but it cannot accommodate the unique status of personal beings as moral agents.

effect of previous states of the universe and could not be otherwise, and moral acts or choices are such states.

5.48) This view is more rigorous than causal universality, since it excludes any alternative to what actually recurs.

5.49) It follows that:
5.49a) no agent could actually have acted differently, and
5.49b) moral responsibility cannot involve such a possibility.

5.50) Such a view would typically be a hard determinism that eliminated both moral freedom and objective moral responsibility.

5.51) The main supporting argument is the claim that such a determinism is implied by the scientific enterprise.

5.52) The main criticism is that this view logically eliminates ethical objectivity, freedom, and responsibility.

5.53) Teleological or religious determinism

5.54) Thesis: an act or choice is determined if its occurrence is decisively explainable as an unalterable consequence of purposive divine decree by means (in part) of operative natural causes.

5.55) This divine agent may be construed as either personal or impersonal, and is either contingently or necessarily operative,

5.56) but the choice, once made, is completely and inflexibly determining for the entire realm of contingent being.

5.57) Not all transcendental religious worldviews are committed to such a determinism: but the present concern is with those that are thus committed.

The third position concerning the nature of determinism I will characterize as *teleological determinism* or *religious determinism*. According to this perspective, while causal universality is accepted, and there is an extensive context of reality in which the intermediate causal forces that explain particular states of affairs are properly described as physical, mechanical, and natural, still there is a purposively directive force or agent that is the ultimate ground of events and natural laws, an agent that operates through, or in, or by means of nature in the form of what I will call purposive divine decree. On some views this agent is personal (in Hebrew-Christian theism, for example), on other views impersonal (in Stoic pantheism, for example); on some views this agent could have chosen differently concerning the production and operation of the entire contingent order of being (the universe in its entirety), while on other views the contingent universe follows with metaphysical and moral necessity from the ultimate character of the agent, so that a different choice would not be actually possible, though it might be theoretically and provisionally possible. But however these issues are resolved, this ultimate agent—in religious language, God—has by an eternal fiat or decree determined all the reality and detail of the entire contingent realm of being, including the moral acts and choices of finite moral agents like ourselves. And the inclusive, all-comprehensive divine choice, thus made, is invariable and inflexible, so that all things are as they must be to fulfill God's purpose, and no detail could (metaphysically considered) be different without the contravention of that purpose (which, of course, is for this view unthinkable). It is very important to point out that not every transcendental religious worldview (not every concept of God, whether theistically or pantheistically construed) involves such a rigorous determinism of divine decree as that which I have described; but in this context I am concerned only with those religious perspectives that *do* involve such a determinism. There are so many alternative approaches to this sort of teleological determinism that it is very difficult to identify with confidence the main arguments either in support of, or in opposition to, this kind of perspective; I can therefore do no more than make a tentative judgment call in both cases. In a sense, of course, one would need to confront the whole question of the basis for belief in a transcendent religious reality in general (natural theology, or arguments for the existence of God). But since I have dealt with this issue in two earlier books,[1] I will make no attempt of this sort here, although I will later consider certain varieties of normative ethical theism. Instead, I will provisionally assume that some sort of transcendental religious perspective is plausible as a general metaphysical position; and I will consider arguments pro and con only within the framework of this hypothetical assumption. In effect, this will narrow the present issue to the question whether such a religious worldview is more plausibly aligned with the sort of determinism described above, or more plausibly construed as opposed to that determinism. Within these limits, the main argument in support of teleological determinism is that, unless there is such a comprehensive determining of all contingent reality, the ultimacy and sovereignty of God would be compromised. How can God be logically construed as the absolutely necessary, self-existent, and self-explanatory being, the Ground of all else, if God's causality does not extend to every detail of the contingent world order? The main argument against teleological (religious) determinism in this context is that if all the acts and choices of finite agents are thus determined by divine decree (however complex the instrumental means may be), then this determination would relieve finite agents of all moral responsibility for such acts and choices: if finite agents are not, in some applicable sense, the decisive causes of their moral acts and choices, the supposition that they may justly be held responsible for committing them is morally (and perhaps logically) absurd. This difficulty can then be expanded to the question whether the God who is viewed as both omnipotent and essentially good (both morally and metaphysically) can actually possess those attributes (or, since the attributes are essential to God's nature, can actually *be* both omnipotent and essentially good), if God is viewed as having unchangeably decreed the occurrence of the morally evil acts of finite agents. Defenders of teleological determinism have certainly claimed that God's all-inclusive determinism is morally and logically consistent with the moral accountability of finite personal agents: they have claimed,

5.58) From a critical point of view, the plausibility of belief in a transcendent religious reality of some sort is here provisionally assumed.

5.58a) So considered, the main supporting argument for teleological determinism is that its denial would compromise the absoluteness and sovereignty of God;

5.58b) while the main criticism is that the divine determinism of the acts of finite moral agents would relieve the latter of both moral responsibility and moral accountability.

---

[1] *The Resurrection of Theism; The Reconstruction of the Christian Revelation Claim.*

in other words, to be strong compatibilists. But the thrust of the negative criticism previously described would call that claim into question and insist instead that comprehensive divine determinism is inconsistent with the moral accountability and morally relevant freedom of finite moral agents: it implies, in other words, that incompatibilism is true in this context, and that one must logically choose between any such determinism and any genuine moral responsibility.

5.59) Logical necessitarianism

The final and most rigorous view of determinism is that which subsumes the explanation of all occurrences (including moral acts and choices) under the notion of *logical necessity* and might therefore be called *logical necessitarianism*

5.60) Thesis: an act or choice is determined if its occurrence is entailed by logically necessary implication from rationally necessary causes, and whatever is the case is thus determined.

or *logically formal determinism*. On this view, reality is a complex of logically necessary relationships which, by virtue of that logical character, exclude any and all alternatives. A truth is said to be logically necessary if its denial would be logically self-contradictory or inconsistent or incoherent. As Spinoza claims: whatever is, is logically necessary; and whatever is not, is logically impossible. So of course, no finite agent ever logically could have chosen or acted differently than he or she actually did act or choose, on pain of a metaphysical contradiction; and hence, therefore, all versions of the morally relevant sense of freedom are eliminated except for the last version, which identifies freedom with necessary self-determination. Thinkers like Spinoza and Hegel exemplify of this sort of perspective, and given their presuppositions, which identify logical truth with reality, they are strong compatibilists, although their views of logic are strikingly different in ways that need not concern us here in detail. Suffice it to say that Spinoza's view of logico-metaphysical necessity is interpreted by him (mistakenly, I think) as eliminating all purposive or teleological explanation: if everything follows by logical necessity from the nature of absolutely infinite Substance (or Nature, or God), then these consequences eliminate purposive intent, both in God and in finite moral agents; just as the axioms of geometry do not purposively intend the logically entailed theorems of that science, so absolute Substance does not purposively intend its entailed metaphysical consequences. Thus Spinoza's view here is an exception to the generalization that the more rigorous last two views of determinism absorb the earlier views but then transcend them: for his

5.60a) Such determinism excludes all senses of freedom except that of necessary self-determination;

5.60b) hence, this view is a restricted type of strong compatibilism.

5.61) Spinoza and Hegel represent this view, but the former regards logical necessity as eliminating purposive or teleological explanation,

5.61a) while the latter (Hegel) regards the logically necessary structure of

view has no place even provisionally for teleological determinism as even a partial truth. But with Hegel it is quite different: for he sees teleological determinism as just such a partial truth, and this truth is absorbed and transcended in a more inclusive and adequate complete philosophy. A transcendental religious and teleological worldview is the Absolute Spirit in its self-actualization as religion, while philosophy, as the final phase of that self-actualization, recognizes such a view as part of the total truth in which all conceptual perspectives are reconciled in a comprehensively compete explanation of reality. In a way, this self-actualization of the Absolute as successively and implicatively Logic, then Nature, then Mind, is purposive intent brought to fruition in all its phases. The main argument in support of logical necessitarianism is the cumulative overall case for the general metaphysical explanation of which such a determinism is a part. If, as both Spinoza and Hegel, for example, claim, everything follows from the logico-metaphysical starting point (Substance or Absolute Spirit), in conjunction with clarifying definitional and self-evident axioms of the system, by logically necessary implication, that necessity epistemologically guarantees that all the details of the logical consequences of the starting point are invested with the same necessity as the starting point itself, since there logically can be no logical accidents (contingent effects that might for that reason have been different) in such a system. If the only reason for anything at all lies in such a self-evident logico-metaphysical starting point, and if otherwise there logically can be no reason for anything, then it follows that, given that reason, everything logically must be as it is and nothing could logically be otherwise; and hence moral agents, with all their morally relevant acts or choices always are as logically they must be. Outside of the system thus understood, there can be no reason(s) for preferring that system rather than some different one, since all reasons are internal to the system: the objective justification of the system consists therefore in its comprehensive explanatory power. If a system explains everything with a smaller residue of unexplained problems than any alternative system, that is the sole justification of its claim to truth—and that is what thinkers like Spinoza and Hegel claim for their nevertheless discernibly different systems. The main argument

reality as the virtual embodiment of purpose.

5.62) The main supporting argument for this view is an appeal to the comprehensive explanatory power of a system of logical entailments.

5.63) The main argument against this view consists of an attack on the logical adequacy of such a system to explain the world of particular things and events as deducible from logically necessary starting points, against this sort of logical necessitarianism is again an attack on the comprehensive metaphysical scheme that provides its context. In this connection, critics characteristically claim that purportedly complete systems of this sort have many logically arbitrary parts whose relations to the starting point and axioms are clearly not solely deductive and logically necessary; that the starting points and axioms of different systems are themselves different and irreconcilable with each other, so that there is no way to decide among alternative axiom sets and starting points in a rationally plausible manner; that systems of this sort which are obviously opposed to each other in basic structure might have at least approximately equal explanatory power, while yet logically they could not all be justifiable as true; and that all such systems reject in principle the intuitively plausible and widely held thesis that there logically could be a plurality of logically possible worlds which shared logically necessary truths, but differed in contingent details. This last point can be differently put by pointing out that it seems impossible in both principle and practice to deduce particular truths about the actual world from logically necessary principles and concepts. In relation to moral issues specifically, there logically could not be, in a logically necessary system, any real distinction between right or wrong, good or evil, in the moral sense, since whatever happens is equally the logically determined effect of the starting point and axioms of the system;

5.63a) while ethically such a system destroys all moral distinctions and any notion of moral responsibility.

and of course, there could, it seems, be no such thing as moral responsibility for having failed to act otherwise than one did act, or even for having acted as one did, since any alternative would be logically and metaphysically out of the question. Of course, one could define moral responsibility as equivalent to the sum of one's acts and choice; but it is difficult to see how this sort of responsibility would be morally relevant.

5.64) A summary of the relationships between the four views of freedom and the four views of determinism

Perhaps a summary of the logical relationships, between the four views of morally relevant personal freedom and the four views of determinism, would be a helpful clarification at this juncture. The least rigorous version of determinism, namely, *causal universality,* is logically consistent with three of the views on personal freedom and inconsistent only with the view that identifies that freedom with sheer indeterminateness. What I have called *physicalistic* (or *mechanistic* or *naturalistic*) *determinism* implies the claim that nothing which occurs *actually* could have been otherwise given the actual past and the laws of nature, although alternatives at all levels are logically conceivable. Hence, this kind of determinism is consistent, in some versions, with freedom as avoidability and even with freedom as necessary self-determination; but such a determinism is clearly inconsistent with freedom as indeterminateness, since it denies all indeterminateness for the whole of nature, and it is also inconsistent with freedom interpreted as agent causality, since that view involves the claim that, whatever the agent's choice, the agent actually could have acted or chosen differently in the same or relevantly similar circumstances. *Religious* or *teleological determinism* would clearly follow the same pattern as the previous view. That is, it would be consistent with some versions of freedom as avoidability and with freedom as necessary self-determination; but it would be inconsistent with freedom either in the sense of indeterminateness (God's purposive intent is all-determining) or in the sense of agent causality (since God decrees all the acts and choices of the agent, not to mention the actual being of the agent). Finally, *logical necessitarianism* entails freedom as necessary self-determination, and excludes all other views of personal freedom that I have discussed.

A Proposed Resolution of the Problems Concerning Determinism, Personal Freedom, and Moral Responsibility

While I have summarized the main arguments, pro and con, with regard to the four views of both personal freedom and determinism, I have neither drawn nor defended any conclusions concerning these issues. The time has now come to do exactly that, since I would regard myself as seriously hampered in the discussion of normative ethics if I could not operate with at least a provisional resolution of these problems. At the outset I will disclose at once that I accept the agent causality view of personal freedom and the causal universality view of determinism, and that I regard these two perspectives as entirely consistent with one another. Because I have extended the concept of determinism to include, as one of its species, the position of universal causality, then

5.65) The classification of the agent causality view of freedom and the causal universality view of determinism.

5.65a) If freedom and determinism are so defined and defended, the resultant view would be theoretically a variety of strong compatibilism;

theoretically my view would be a variety of strong compatibilism in the sense that I regard both universal causality (determinism) and agent causality (personal freedom) as true and logically consistent, and I also hold that if determinism in this sense were not true, then the agent causality view would not be true either. Yet my position on these issues would not be regarded as *either* determinism *or* compatibilism by most interpreters, who hold a different view of freedom and a more rigorous and restricted view of determinism. If determinism is restricted to the physicalistic, teleological (religious), and logical necessitarian types, then the agent causality view of freedom, as I interpret it, is logically inconsistent with those types of determinism; and that would make my view a variety of *in*compatibilism, as well as a variety of libertarianism, which holds that such a restrictive determinism is false and that the morally relevant sense of freedom (agent causality, in my view) is true as a necessary and sufficient ground (sufficient in the context of ethics, that is) of moral responsibility. So on my definitional terms, my view is a variety of strong compatibilism; but on the definitional terms of most other interpreters, my view is a variety of libertarian incompatibilism. Terminology, however, is far less important than philosophical substance or content: a rose by any other name would still be a rose and smell just as sweet! So let the reader think of my view on either set of definitional terms that he or she finds conceptually comfortable, but let the reader do so with enlightened understanding. However, I myself, in concession to the general philosophical community, will from henceforth call my position *libertarian incompatibilism*; but let it be recognized that my view of personal freedom is definitely *not* a contra-causal view, since I hold that the decisive cause of a morally free choice or act is the transcendental causality of individual agents themselves.

Since therefore I join those thinkers who regard any contra-causal view of freedom as critically inadequate in the moral sense, I therefore also join those same thinkers in rejecting any position that defines freedom (in the morally relevant sense) as indeterminateness: an act or choice that is not under the causal control of the agent in some significantly pertinent sense is not a morally responsible act or choice with the consequences of which an agent can with

5.65b) but since my position would not be regarded as either determinism or compatibilism in the usual senses, and since my view of freedom is incompatible with all the more rigorous and restricted types of determinism, it is preferable to call the view here defended a variety of libertarian incompatibilism;

5.65c) but whatever the terminology, it is essential to recognize that the view of freedom involved is not a contra-causal view.

5.66) Since the agent causality view implies both that moral acts and choices are under the agent's causal control and that the agent could always actually have acted otherwise than

rational justification be morally credited or charged. On the other hand, I also side with those thinkers who hold that an agent's causal control over an act or choice means that, however the agent's choice or act eventuates, nevertheless it was open to that agent to have acted or chosen differently in the same or relevantly similar circumstances—and this capacity means not merely that *theoretically* the agent could have chosen or acted otherwise, but rather that the agent *actually* could have done so. Since freedom as theoretical avoidability is therefore too weak to support genuine moral responsibility, and since freedom as necessary self-determination excludes the *actual* capacity of the agent to have acted or chosen otherwise without contradiction, I therefore regard both of those positions as critically inadequate. It is further the case that determinism, in any sense more rigorous than universal causality, also excludes that same actual capacity and thus, in my view, undermines moral responsibility. I therefore reject those other views of determinism. Hence, for all the views of personal freedom and determinism that I thus find wanting, I accept the counter-arguments against them as stated in the previous section.

A helpful way of summarizing my view, regarding personal freedom, determinism, and moral responsibility, consists in answering, for that view, the six questions with which our inquiry began.

1) Mature human persons *are* properly and correctly held responsible for their moral choices, acts, rules, principles, and character traits,

2) just to the extent that they exercise a voluntary causal role in originating these elements, so that the degree of that responsibility is directly proportionate to their personal freedom in these respects.

3) The morally relevant sense of freedom consists in the capacity of persons, as moral agents, to self-initiate an effective inclination to one of any given set of alternative influential systems of motives which are live options to the agent in question, although no such system of motives provides a sufficient cause of the agent's act or choice, except in conjunction with the

he or she did, the view involves the rejection of:
5.66a) (a) freedom as indeterminateness, or theoretical avoidability, or necessary self-determination;

5.66b) (b) any view of determinism more rigorous than causal universality.

5.67) In summary, the position defended involves:

5.67a) genuine moral responsibility proportionate to the degree of personal freedom as agent causality;

5.67b) the agent as the decisive cause of moral choice under the influence of alternative motives but undetermined by the motives alone;

exercise of the self-initiating capacity of the agent, who is therefore the decisive cause of the realized act or choice in such a way that it would always have been actually possible for the agent to have acted otherwise (i.e., in favor of one of the other alternative live options).

5.67c) the universal causality view as the only plausible sense of determinism, since other views threaten both agent causality and moral responsibility.

4) and 5) The only sort of determinism which is logically consistent with this view of personal freedom is that which limits determinism to universal causality: a morally free and responsible act or choice is not uncaused or contra-causal, since the agent *per se* is the decisive cause of that act or choice in relation to alternative systems of influencing motives. Other, more rigorous types of determinism are less plausible than the universal causality view, because they all imply, implicitly or explicitly, that the finite agent in question could not *actually* have chosen or acted differently, with the result that both the agent's decisive causality and the agent's moral responsibility with respect to the act or choice are called into serious question.

5.67d) Rational plausibility and/or logical probability are the highest degree of certainty achievable regarding such theoretical claims.

6) The morally relevant senses of both freedom and determinism are all susceptible of being critically examined or subjected to rational deliberation; the justification of any particular view about these issues, while it may be hypothetically necessary under a set of prescribed conditions or assumptions about the issues involved, cannot be regarded as logically demonstrative in a comprehensive sense, since such prescribed conditions or assumptions, however plausible to rational deliberation, are not themselves logically demonstrable. Hence, any such justification will be merely approximative, provisional, tentative, and always (under finite human conditions) subject to revision: in other words, rational plausibility or logical probability are the most that even the keenest investigators may reasonably aspire to. On such issues, I accept Joseph Butler's oft-repeated claim that probability is the guide of life, and (I add) therefore also the arbiter of moral theory.

Since the agent causality view, as I understand it, stands opposed to the other views of personal freedom, and since it is also inconsistent with the more rigorous versions of determinism, I propose to provide the only sort of justification possible for this view (or any alternative to it) by analyzing a number of supporting arguments for that position in relation to its alternatives concerning either freedom or determinism; next, I will analyze principal critical objections proposed by the opponents of agent causality, again concerning either freedom or determinism; and finally, I will attempt to respond to these critical objections in such a way as to reaffirm both the agent causality view of freedom and the causal universality view of determinism. Except to the degree that is relevant to this procedure as thus indicated, I do not intend to expound in detail or critique extensively the comprehensive metaphysical perspectives that provide a context for the critical objections to which my counter-arguments purport to respond. To some extent, I will undertake this task, in a degree limited by my concern with moral philosophy, when I analyze the normative ethical views connected with these comprehensive outlooks. I also intend to limit the sort of objections I consider by presupposing that certain issues have been at least provisionally settled in earlier discussion: I have, for example, already defended (in my discussion of general meta-ethical theories) the concept of ethical objectivism over against any variety of radical ethical relativism, whether individually or culturally oriented. As a result, I will not discuss any objection to my views about freedom or determinism that is based on such an ethical relativism. For the same reason, I will assume that the only sort of moral responsibility meriting consideration is the sort that bases such responsibility on whatever, in normative ethics, that objective (not individually or culturally relative) standard of moral goodness or rightness turns out to be. As an extension of this restriction, I will also assume that if, as I have argued earlier, there is an ultimate and objective standard of moral value or worth, rational moral beings like ourselves are in fact morally obligated to the highest fulfillment of that standard of which their faculties and powers make them capable. I will not therefore bother myself critically about objections to the genuineness of moral responsibility itself as thus characterized; and I will therefore assume that any objection, which

5.68) Thus the justification of my position will involve the consideration of supporting arguments, counter-arguments, and a response to such counter-arguments;
5.69) but such a justifying procedure (a) will involve only a limited consideration of metaphysics,
5.69a) and (b) will regard some issues as provisionally settled:
5.70) moral objectivism (*vs.* radical ethical relativism),
5.71) moral responsibility as dependent upon an ultimate objective standard to the fulfillment of which moral beings are obligated, so that any objection that reduces to hard determinism is rejected in principle on grounds previously argued.

stems avowedly from, or even reduces implicitly to, hard determinism and the consequent denial of the objective reality of moral responsibility, has been adequately rebutted merely by showing this to be the case. I am, in other words, not operating in a vacuum here; instead, I am arguing in a context that is already partly in place by reason of previous consideration. Of course, on different assumptions, or in a different context of previously argued conclusions, no doubt very different consequences might be forthcoming. But no one can be expected to start from scratch in the consideration of every new philosophical problem; and if any critics or defenders claim to do so, either those critics are (perhaps innocently) self-deceived, or their criticism and/or defense are philosophically vacuous. But I decline to pursue such hermeneutical issues any further, since I have already done so in my earlier writings to which I have previously referred. I now turn therefore to the agenda I have proposed as a methodology for resolving the intricate problems concerning determinism, personal freedom, and moral responsibility.

Arguments in Support of the Agent Causality View of Personal Freedom

5.72) Argument from the elimination of misunderstandings of the agent causality view:

The *first argument* in favor of the agent causality thesis consists in removing certain misunderstandings to which the view has been characteristically subjected by critics (or even by proponents) in their efforts to elaborate on the meaning of the agent causality position (I can only be intellectually responsible for my own version of this view, however much buttressing I may have borrowed from alternative versions). The first misunderstanding is contained in the claim that the agent causality thesis is merely a sophisticated version of the concept of freedom as indeterminateness (i.e., of freedom as excluding causal explanation or involving the denial of causal universality). If in the end there is nothing that determines an agent in the exercise of the agent's self-determining causality, it is claimed, then a free act will turn out to be an act for which there is no antecedent ground either in the sense of a sufficient cause or in the sense of a prevailing reason; and hence the act (which by nature is specific and determinate as being a certain particular act over against all others) will be indeterminate in the sense that

5.73) the view is not a disguised version of freedom as indeterminateness, nothing explains why (in a causal sense) the act occurs as it does with the descriptive qualities it possesses. But this explanation is simply and clearly a misinterpretation: free acts are not acts that have no cause, reason, or ground; they are rather acts of which agents themselves are the cause in the exercise of their self-determining causality as such agents. In the case of all finite agents, that a given agent exists and possesses this capacity for exercising self-determining causality, is itself the effect of whatever ultimate and/or proximate causes account for the agent's dependent being. Given the existence of such an agent, there is nothing extraneous to the agent's status as what I will call a transcendental self, which causes the agent to act on one option rather than another; it is rather the agent who fulfills that active causal role. But of course (and here I address the second misunderstanding), agents do not create *ex nihilo* their alternative options, nor do they exercise self-determining choice entirely apart from systems of inclining motives that exercise influences upon them. Freedom, for any given moral agent in a particular situation, is limited to a set of available alternatives which are live options for that agent (a live option is any available alternative that makes an appeal to the agent as providing a provisionally plausible direction for choice or action). To a considerable extent, the range of these options, though partly determined by the agent's previous choices and the habits or dispositions of response formed by those previous choices (what might be called the formed character of the agent), are also partly determined by the environmental and even biological context in which the agent makes a choice, however decisive the agent's causality may be in the determination of what line of motives to follow in making that choice. Some proponents of agent causality have supposed that a genuinely free act, in the morally relevant sense, must be an act of which the agent's self-determining efficacy is the sole causal factor, entirely apart from the influence of motives. But this seems clearly a mistaken claim: moral agents do not act or choose freely in a dispositional or motivational vacuum; instead they act in view of motives without being extraneously determined by them. The agent's transcendentally free causality operates as the decisive cause for a commitment to one line of motivation as over against another. Even

5.73a) since free acts are not contra-causal but are rather determined by agents' self-causality;

5.74) nor is the range of available options entirely a product of the agent's self-causality,

5.74a) since, although the available options are partly determined by the agent's dispositions and habits, they are also partly determined by the environmental and biological context;

5.75) thus the agent's choice is not the sole causal factor, because agents always act in view of motives;

in a case of moral temptation, it is not a question of motivation (whether from desire, formed character, provocative stimulation, or whatever) over against moral duty; it is rather a question of the motivation of duty over against other lines of motivation which incline the agent in a different direction. All these lines of motivation, so far as they are live options for the agent, are aspects that form a part of the cause of the agent's choice by providing an occasion for that choice. The agent's self-determining causality consists in the fact that none of these lines of motivation (not even that of moral duty) is a sufficient cause of the agent's choice, so that in the end it is the agent who turns a necessary condition into a sufficient condition by lighting its causal fuse. The agent causality view of freedom is therefore neither a disguised form of the indeterminateness view, nor is it in any relevant sense a contra-causal position.

5.76) while the free causality of the agent determines which line of motives is chosen,

5.77) so that no line of motivation is a sufficient cause of any morally relevant choice.

The *second argument*, in support of the agent causality view of personal freedom, is the claim that this position (perhaps uniquely among the four views I've discussed) is not only consistent with the concept of objectively grounded moral responsibility, but that this sort of freedom is a necessary condition of such responsibility, so that any version of determinism more rigorous than that of causal universality is false as a consequence. This complex claim has been a stock contention of libertarianism, and its denial is a common strategy of rigorous determinists. The argument has, furthermore, been formulated in a large number of alternative ways. But I can assume intellectual responsibility only for my own version of the argument; and I will therefore make no attempt either to formulate or access any of these alternative versions. Neither will I consider it in any sense incumbent on me to deal with negative criticisms that have been directed against those alternatives by opponents. My version of the argument can be stated briefly and simply as follows:

5.78) Argument from agent causality as a necessary ground of objective moral responsibility:

5.79) the argument stated in summary form;

Premise 1:
  No agent can be justifiably held to be morally responsible (or accountable) for an act or choice, unless it would have been *actually* (and not merely theoretically) possible for the agent, either directly or indirectly (immediately or mediately),

5.80) agents can be held morally responsible only if they could actually act or choose otherwise than they do;

to have acted or chosen differently in the same or relevantly similar circumstances.

Premise 2:
Agents can be justifiably held to be morally responsible for some of their acts or choices (namely, those which have moral relevance and with respect to which the agent actually could, directly or indirectly, have acted or chosen differently in the same or relevantly similar circumstances).

5.81) agents are morally responsible for some of their acts or choices;

Premise 3:
If any version of determinism more rigorous than the universal causality version were true, it would be false that any agent actually could have acted or chosen differently than the agent did in the same or relevantly similar circumstances.

5.82) if rigorous determinism were true, no agent could ever act otherwise than he or she does (or did);

Premise 4:
No agent can be justifiably held to be morally responsible in the relevant sense unless the self as agent is the decisive cause of the efficacious inclination that results in an act or choice for which he or she is thus regarded as morally responsible (the central thesis of the agent causality view).

5.83) no agent can be held morally responsible for an act or choice unless the agent is the decisive cause.

Therefore:
a. moral agents are morally responsible for their morally relevant acts or choices only if they are the decisive causes of those acts or choices in the indicated sense (i.e., only if the agent causality view is true). (1, 4)
b. The agent causality view is true. (2, a)
c. Any version of determinism more rigorous than that of the causal universality view is consequently false. (3, a, b)

5.84) Hence the agent causality view is true,

5.84a) and rigorous determinism is false.

Although I have not stated this argument in standard deductive form, I take it to be correct to claim that its premises logically entail the conclusions indicated, and that if the

5.85) Are the premises (and therefore the conclusion) true?

5.86) It is assumed that finite moral agents are sometimes morally responsible for their acts or choices in an objective sense (premise 2).

5.87) If premise 1 were denied: the choice or act would be removed from the agent's control, and moral responsibility would be undermined;

premises, understood in their intended sense are true, the conclusions drawn are also true. Are the premises true, then? On the basis of previous explanation and argument I will simply regard premise 2 as true without further attempt at justification: I am assuming, in other words, the truth of the concept of objective moral responsibility as applicable to finite moral agents under the indicated conditions. I will, however, argue out the truth claim of the other premises. Premise 1 is the claim that moral responsibility is correctly ascribable to an agent, only if the agent actually could have chosen or acted otherwise than the agent did in the same or relevantly similar circumstances. If this claim is denied, then the making of the choice or the execution of the act would be removed from the effective control of the agent; the agent would, in fact, be reduced to the status of a mere instrumental or proximate tool of the operation of causes whose functioning the agent was impotent to modify in their outcome. But then there is no justifiable basis for holding the agent responsible, since the agent would lack the effective and directive control which moral responsibility implies in the subject (agent) to whom it is ascribed. An agent possesses this requisite control only if, under the circumstances, there was at least one live optional alternative that the agent actually could have chosen and on which the agent could have acted. Nor is it sufficient to accept the claim of the avoidability view to the effect that it is sufficient, for the ascription of moral responsibility, if such an option is merely conceivable in the sense of involving no logical contradiction and no contravention of empirically given circumstances, even though the option is not in fact possible in the circumstances. For that would be tantamount to saying that agents would be morally responsible if they were ignorant of the necessitating causes and could thus deceive themselves into falsely thinking that they have genuinely possible live alternatives. The

5.87a) deliberation about moral choices would be nonsensical, since it logically presupposes a plurality of genuinely possible alternatives;

same conclusion emerges if persons analyze their own attitudes when they are to make morally relevant (or often even prudentially relevant) choices about matters of substantive importance (marriage, life vocation, etc.). Invariably, if the persons do not act on impulse, they find themselves deliberating or reasoning with themselves about what to do or which choice to make. The assumption of such deliberation or reasoning is, of course, that the agents believe themselves to have genuine (i.e., actually possible) choices among two or more available alternatives, any one of which could be actualized in the circumstances. If the persons did not at least implicitly believe this, they would cease to deliberate, since such deliberation would have no rationally intelligible object if no such genuine choice were possible. If it is objected that we sometimes do deliberate about objects whose status we believe to possess a necessity that excludes all options (for example, we sometimes deliberate about the solution to a problem in pure mathematics, or about whether a certain chemical is in fact chlorine, etc.), then the answer is that we deliberate in such cases only because we are trying to decide which of a number of initially plausible or *prima facie* alternatives actually possesses the requisite necessity, and the deliberation ceases when that issue is settled. But no agent deliberates about a moral choice on the supposition that he or she is attempting to decide which of several alternatives is the only one logically and empirically possible; or if an agent does, that is not the sort of deliberation which settles a genuine moral issue—instead it is the sort of deliberation which comes to recognize that there is no moral issue to settle. In either case (whether or not the objects of deliberation have a presumed status of necessity), the deliberation would continue only if persons believed themselves capable of making *either* a right *or* a wrong decision (whether logically or morally), so that they deliberate to avoid a wrong decision of which nevertheless they believe themselves genuinely capable. If there is no genuine option involved, then there is no rational deliberation to be done. Hence, the fact that we often deliberate about our moral choices entails that we believe ourselves to be facing more than one genuinely and actually possible alternative. I conclude therefore that premise 1 is true as the most satisfactory and intelligible account of genuinely objective moral responsibility. On the other hand, I do not claim to have demonstrated that premise with absolute logical finality, since I do not regard such demonstration as realistically possible except in pure logic or mathematics.

If premise 1 is accepted as true in the sense indicated, it will not be difficult to ascribe that same status to premise 4, which claims that premises 1 and 2 can be plausibly regarded as true only in terms of the agent causality view of personal freedom. If agents can be justifiably regarded as

5.88) premise 4 follows as a logical entailment of the truth of premises 1 and 2: if the agent actually could have acted differently, then

morally responsible for given acts or choices only on the condition that they could actually have acted or chosen differently in the same *or* relevantly similar circumstances, then it must be the case that none of the systems of motives supporting the influences of the various alternatives of choice or action would have been sufficient to cause them to choose as they did without some active and selective role played by the agents themselves. And that means in turn that, while the various systems of motives provided an occasion for choice or action, and exercised a degree of influence variable in strength for the different alternatives, nevertheless the self-determining capacity of agents (or the agents themselves actively exercising choices) would have to be the decisive causes which operated to make one of the available options into a prevailing option, so that this decisive causality of the agents, acting under the influence of various motivational alternatives (which would be necessary in the sense that choice logically could not take place without any such alternatives), becomes the sufficient cause of the choices among the various alternatives. But this is precisely the agent causality view of personal freedom, according to which a genuinely free and responsible moral choice is a choice of which, in the last analysis, the agent is the decisive cause. If anything other than this self-determining causality of an agent were the decisive cause of a choice or act, then it would simply not be true that an agent as such could actually have chosen differently. Premise 4 is therefore true as the most plausible explanation of what occurs in free and morally responsible choice. Again, as in the case of premise 1, this conclusion is not an absolutely conclusive and finally demonstrated result.

That leaves premise 3 to be considered: this is the claim that if any version of determinism more rigorous than the universal causality view were true, it would simply be false that any agent could actually have chosen or acted differently in the same or relevantly similar circumstances. But our previous analysis has, I think, provisionally established as plausible just exactly the proposition that would be false if such a rigorous determinism were true, namely, that at least in the case of morally responsible choices, agents invariably have the capacity to have chosen or acted differently in the same or relevantly similar circumstances. This

---

5.88a) none of the motivating alternatives could be a sufficient cause of the choice, and

5.88b) the self-determining causality of agents must be the decisive cause of the choices actively made.

5.89) Premise 3 would have to be true and rigorous determinism would have to be false, if any agents have ever made choices for which they were morally responsible in the objective sense.

means, in effect, that personal agents logically could not possess the sort of freedom relevant to the ascription of moral responsibility if any such version of rigorous determinism were true. Such determinisms are therefore individually and collectively false if any personal agent has ever been justifiably held to be, in an objective sense (the only sense meriting consideration), morally responsible for any act or choice whatsoever.

Peter Van Inwagen has occupied himself, in a large part of an entire book (*An Essay on Free Will*), with showing that the conditional proposition of premise 3 is true (although, of course, he did not designate it as such). In so doing, he operates on the version of determinism that I have designated as physicalistic or naturalistic determinism. But his principal arguments (in support of what I call premise 3) are adaptable without substantive modification to both the transcendental religious and logical necessitarian views. In fact, these latter versions of determinism acknowledge forthrightly that, on their view, no agent ever actually could have acted or chosen differently than the agent did in the same or relevantly similar circumstances: if either the immutable decrees of a transcendent divine reality or the operation of unmitigated logical necessity causally determines all that occurs, then the acts and choices of moral agents, along with all else that takes place, are swept into the jaws of such an inescapably omnivorous causality. (If anyone is offended by my emotive rhetoric, I apologize for the form, but not for the substance, of my comment.) In general, Van Inwagen argues in three ways which all come to the same point or conclusion: namely, that libertarian incompatibilism is true and that, given the relevant sense of moral freedom, determinism in the rigorous sense is false. Since all three ways in which Van Inwagen argues differ only as expressing three different modes or structures of the same argument, I shall present the argument common to all three modes without concerning myself with these alternative forms of expression; and, as is my usual custom, I will present an informal statement of the argument which is not necessarily in standard deductive form. Determinism as here considered is simply the view that any given event or statement of the universe is the wholly and uniquely determined effect of previous states in accordance with the laws of nature which express descriptive

5.90) Van Inwagen's defense of premise 3: that the morally relevant sense of freedom is true, and that rigorous determinism (especially the naturalistic version) is false.

5.91) Determinism is the view that, given the actual past and the laws of nature, any subsequent occurrence is the wholly and uniquely causal effect of that conjunction;

5.91 a) any choice made by an agent would be such a determined occurrence; b) for an agent to have a genuinely free choice, he or she would have to have a choice about either the actual past or about the laws of nature; c) since no agent has any choice about either of these, it follows that no agent has any free choice about anything at all; d) but the freedom essential to moral responsibility involves just such an actual choice between alternatives.

5.92) If determinism is so related to the relevant senses of freedom and moral responsibility, then incompatibilism is true.

5.93) It follows that premise 3 is true, and therefore that all four premises of my original argument are also true.

5.94) Thus it also follows that the agent causality view is true,

regularities among those previous states. Differently put: given the actual past (the succession of previous states) and the laws of nature, any subsequent future event or actual occurrence is a wholly and uniquely caused effect of that conjunction. A choice made by an agent would be such an actual occurrence as a wholly and uniquely caused effect of the conjunction of the actual past and the laws of nature. For any agent to have an actual choice at a given point (for a person to be confronted with a genuine alternative of choice or action at that point), the agent would also have to possess at that same point a choice either about the actual past or about the laws of nature. But it is indisputably the case that no one, at any given point, has an actual choice about the actual past (which, once it has occurred, is unchangeably fixed); nor does anyone have, at any given point, a choice about the laws of nature (which, after all, are simply statements of the regularities that have characterized past occurrences). It therefore follows that no finite agent has had, now has, or ever will have an actual choice about anything at all, including alternatives or moral decision or action. But the minimal free will thesis essential to moral responsibility involves precisely the possession of an actual choice (a genuine decision between alternatives). If then determinism in the indicated sense is true, this minimum free will thesis is false, and so also is the relevant sense of moral responsibility. Now if this whole argument is sound, incompatibilism is true (i.e., determinism is logically inconsistent with the relevant senses of personal freedom and moral responsibility). And if, finally, those relevant senses of freedom and responsibility are true, determinism in the rigorous sense is consequently false. I therefore take it that, at the very least, premise 3 is true, since that is the principal conclusion of Van Inwagen's three arguments for incompatibilism. Obviously, then, I judge the central thrust of those arguments as sound, although I have only presented one of the arguments in my typically informal fashion. If, furthermore, I have in any sense misinterpreted Van Inwagen's case, I will nevertheless go with the argument in the form in which I have (accurately or inaccurately) presented it.

In my opinion, therefore, all four premises of the moral responsibility argument for the agent causality view are true, so that the claim that the agent causality view is the only view that supports moral responsibility, in the objective and relevant sense, is also true as a conclusion. If that is the case, then, since rigorous determinism is logically incompatible with this view of freedom, any such view is also consequently false; and the agent causality view of personal freedom is, at the same time, true.

My *third argument* in support of the agent causality view is the claim that freedom, as self-determination in the precise sense of that view, is a necessary or essential condition for the recognition of objective truth and for the rationally objective justification of truth claims on the part of an agent considered as a knower. The recognition, by a knower, that a proposition is objectively true consists, subjectively or psychologically, in the knower's believing that proposition to be true in that sense. The rationally objective justification of a truth claim consists, again subjectively or psychologically, in one or other of two processes: either in the knower's belief that the proposition's truth is immediately evident either empirically or logically (an empirical example—the immediately evident perception of the sense quality yellow; a logical example—the rationally self-evident truth of the law or principle of contradiction); or in a complex set of beliefs to the effect that the premises of an argument are true, that they conjunctively entail the truth of the conclusion, and that the conclusion is therefore true. In all these cases, the processes involved take the form of beliefs on the part of the agent as a knower. Now beliefs, considered not with respect to their content (important as that may be), but rather with respect to their status as subjective or psychological occurrences, states, or dispositions—beliefs, in this respect, have causes. And the question why anyone believes a certain proposition to be true can be taken as equivalent to the question, what causes that person to believe that particular proposition to be true? For the purpose of my present discussion, it is important to divide the causes of belief into two kinds, which I will call rational and non-rational. A rational cause, in the case of a belief, consists either in the grounds (or some part of the grounds) of the belief's proposition(s) being objectively true quite apart from the fact that the proposition is being believed (for example, the cause or ground of a geometrical theorem's truth consists in its being logically entailed, directly or indirectly, by the

and rigorous determinism is false, if objective moral responsibility is accepted as a premise.

5.95) Argument from agent causality as a necessary condition for the recognition and justification of objective truth by a knower:

5.95a) from a psychological point of view,
5.96) the recognition that a proposition is true is a belief of the knower,

5.97) and the claim that it is rationally justified, either as immediately evident, or as following logically from what is thus evident, is a belief of the knower;
5.98) but beliefs thus construed have causes of two kinds—rational and non-rational;
5.99) the rational causes of a belief are the grounds of its being true (if it is), or of a knower's knowing it to be true;

axioms, definitions, and postulates of the geometrical system); or on the grounds (or some part of the grounds) of a personal agent's knowing that the proposition is true by reason of some logical relation to such grounds in the previous sense (for example, the wetness of the streets under specified conditions can be the cause of a perceiver's knowing that it has been raining, although the wetness is the effect, not the cause, of the rain). A non-rational cause, on the other hand, in the case of a belief, is a cause which, though it accounts for the existence or the occurrence of the belief on the part of the agent, has no logical relation to the grounds of the belief's proposition being objectively either true or false. The illustrations of this type of cause for belief are legion indeed: a person can be caused to believe a proposition by being brainwashed or otherwise forced into submission; or by simply trusting the word of another person; or by being induced into believing on the basis of strong and prevailing desires or emotional preferences; or as a result of hypnosis or even medical tampering with his or her central nervous system (especially the brain); and so on indefinitely. But all such causes are non-rational because, although they partly or even decisively account for the occurrence of the belief on the part of the person affected, they have nothing to do with the belief's being objectively either true or false.

5.100) the non-rational causes of a belief are logically independent of the grounds of its being either true or false;

Now while it is true that the operation of some non-rational causes requires the express or implicit consent of the agent under specified conditions (for example, yielding to one's desires, or deciding to trust another person's word, or surrendering to force); yet in the case of many (perhaps most) non-rational causes of belief there seems to be no express or implied consent at all on the part of the agent affected. In these last cases, given the general causal context of an agent, the non-rational causes, operating without the agent's consent, are, in the given context, the sufficient cause(s) of the occurrence of the belief in question. But in the cases involving express or implicit consent, the non-rational causes are insufficient to bring about the belief except in conjunction with that consent. Under normal circumstances, agents need not yield to their desires, or trust another person's word, or surrender their inner thoughts and beliefs to external force; agents have a choice about such matters, however difficult that choice may be. And what is

5.101) in the case of some non-rational causes of belief, and in the case of all rational causes of belief:

true of this limited class of non-rational causes for belief, is universally true of rational causes of belief: the grounds of a proposition's being objectively true or false, or the grounds of a person's otherwise knowing that a proposition is objectively either true or false, can never constitute the sufficient *cause* of a personal agent's *believing* that proposition to be objectively true or false, as the case may be. Agents, as knowers, must opt for (or choose) believing on grounds they are willing to accept as sufficient for their commitment in a particular case. In other words, the decisive cause of the belief, in conjunction with the recognition of objective rational grounds, is the agent's effectively operative self-determining causality—and that means that freedom, in the sense defined by the agent causality view, is an essential or necessary condition for the recognition of a proposition's being true on objective rational grounds.

Suppose, hypothetically and to the contrary, that this claim to agent causality freedom is not true in the case of belief. That would mean that all beliefs, on the part of knowers as agents, would be wholly the determined product of causes with respect to the effect of which the agent could exercise no control. Aside from the fact that an individual would not really be, in that case, the agent (active cause in the decisive sense) of his or her belief but merely its passive receptacle, there would then be no objective method for distinguishing between true and erroneous beliefs, no way even to distinguish between rational and non-rational causes of belief, and certainly no way of reassessing belief commitments to correct errors; since all beliefs, whether true or erroneous in some way inaccessible to knowers, would be equally the effect of wholly determining causes with respect to which the agent was wholly passive, if not inert. Rigorous determinists would be caught in this trap also, since, if determinism were thus inaccessibly true, they would have no way of knowing that such was the case. All their supporting arguments would be to no avail: for, given the truth of determinism, the beliefs expressed in those arguments would be wholly determined effects of causes over the effect of which the causality of determinists as agents would have no control or even capacity to recognize as true on objective grounds. If they did possess that freedom of agent causality which enabled them to aim at rational objectivity in the pursuit

5.102) the causes are insufficient to produce the belief without the agent's consent;

5.103) thus the decisive cause of the belief is the agent's effectively operative self-determining causality: hence, the agent causality view of freedom.

5.104) If this were not the case, then:

5.105) all beliefs would be determined by causes over which the agent could exercise no control;

5.106) there would be no objective method for distinguishing between truth and falsity.

5.107) Even rigorous determinism would be unrecognizable as either true or false, and unsupportable by objective rational argument;

5.108) the agent causality view of freedom is thus a necessary ground of the claim to rational objectivity in belief.

of truth, their dogma of determinism would simply be false, as our previous argument has attempted to show. The agent causality view of personal freedom is therefore true as an essential ground of the capacity to aim at rational objectivity in the pursuit of truth; and if anyone rejects that ideal of rational objectivity as a realistic ideal for finite knowers to aim at, that person certainly cannot claim that rational objectivity for the act of rejection itself, but must recognize it as the logically arbitrary effect of causes over whose operation the person could, by his or her own hypothesis, exercise no control. That is not to say, of course, that, given the agent causality view of personal freedom, all will be smooth sailing to the port of rational objectivity of the sort made possible in principle by that agent causality view. Such rational objectivity is an ideal for finite knowers; the best any devotee of that ideal can hope for in practice is an approximation which though pointed in the right direction, never fully reaches its mark. But that is no excuse for failing to expend one's highest efforts on the task; and it is certainly no reason for starting out with an inadequate perspective (rigorous determinism) that makes such an approximation impossible in principle.

5.109) Still, rational objectivity, as an ideal, can only be approximated;

5.109a) but rigorous determinism would make that approximation impossible in principle.

5.110) The aim at rational objectivity implies the self's capacity to sublimate non-rational causal influences on belief;

This conclusion to agent causality, as a necessary condition of aiming at rational objectivity, can be reinforced by a consideration of the self as agent in its attempt to offset, or compensate for, those non-rational causal influences that would have the effect of militating against the pursuit of rational objectivity as a goal. All sorts of such factors exert an influence on any given knower: aside from an imposing array of external distractions and pressures of many different sorts, there is an equally (if not more) extended multiplicity of internal disturbances in the form of impulses, desires, subconscious propensities, mood variations, and so on. Not all of these non-rational factors need be thought of as opposed in any consistent way to the aim at rational objectivity; some may actually support and buttress that aim. Many of these factors exercise their influence, whether distractive or supportive, without the agent being fully conscious or even conscious at all of the operation of such influence, although there is no fixed limit on the number and variety of such influences of which a given agent can become aware through disciplined and persistent

5.111) not all of these influences are negative in their cognitive effect, though many of them operate without the explicit awareness of the agent.

attention and investigation. However, in the case of those influences of which the agent is or *becomes* deliberately or otherwise aware, the agent is, by means of that awareness, in a position to compensate for those influences in various ways by arranging his or her circumstances so as to minimize their effect on the agent's effort to approximate rational objectivity. Just as an archer can compensate for the effect of the wind on the trajectory of an arrow he shoots, and just as a swimmer can compensate for the effect of the river's current on her attempt to reach a fixed point on the opposite shore, so a thinker, by conscious and deliberate effort, can compensate, within limits, for the effect of destructive or distractive influences on his or her aim at rational objectivity in thinking, provided the thinker is aware of these influences. In some cases, it might even be possible to suspend the effect of certain non-rational factors altogether by an act or policy of deliberate sublimation: a student, struggling to understand philosophy, can deliberately turn off a stereo, avoid prolonged exposure to friends, or refuse to become involved in extracurricular activities—so as to avoid the distracting influence of such facts on the student's efforts at concentration (and many students would be well advised to take these and many other similar steps for the sake of their scholastic goals). On the other hand, an agent can simply succumb blithely to such non-rational influences and allow his or her goal of rational objectivity to be restricted, distorted, or even largely dissipated as a result. But the point is that it is up to the agent, in an extended variety of cases, to determine which way the agent will go in his or her response to the effect of non-rational influences. Except in those cases in which the agent's response is externally and unavoidably forced, to the point of destroying the voluntary character of his or her response, the agent is the decisive cause of the direction the agent takes; and apart from the giving or withholding of consent, those non-rational factors, however strong in their influence, are impotent to determine the agent's direction. But this is precisely agent causality at work: that an agent can control, sublimate, or even totally disarm non-rational influences under the conditions described, is possible only because the agent as such is the decisive cause that allows such influences to operate effectively or not. Here again the possibility of approximating

5.112) If the agent is aware of such influences, the agent has the capacity to compensate for their effect on the aim at rational objectivity within limits;

5.112a) an agent can often deliberately offset such effects,

5.112b) yet the agent can also succumb to them;

5.112c) but what the agent will do often depends on the agent's self-determining consent, apart from which non-rational factors are impotent to function as motives.

5.112d) This process is precisely agent causality in application, and this sort of causality is a necessary condition of the ability to aim at rational objectivity.

rational objectivity in thinking depends on the freedom of the knowing agent in the sense defined by the agent causality view. If this sort of agent control or sublimation were an illusion, then the ideal of rational objectivity would be an illusion as well, since the determination of the agent's response would be out of the agent's control and totally produced by whatever non-rational factors might predominate over others. Rational causes, we saw previously, can operate only with the consent of the agent, since reasons can be persuasive to a thinker but cannot as such be the sufficient cause of an agent's response. If an agent had been non-rationally determined to aim at rational objectivity, it would be a fortuitous stroke of circumstance; and if not, the agent would in either case be an impotent captive of those non-rational forces, and for that reason not truly an agent at all.

5.113) Argument from the nature of self-consciousness as an essential attribute of personal being;

5.114) two qualities of personal being:

5.115) self-determination, which is virtually the same thing as agent causality by definition;

5.116) and self-consciousness.

5.117) Self-consciousness:
5.118) by definition, an awareness of one's self as agent or decisive cause of one's acts.

5.119) If every state of the self were a passive effect, there would be no active agency;

My *fourth argument* for the agent causality view is the claim that the very nature of self-consciousness, as the central core of personal being, implies this position with respect to personal freedom. In what, it may be asked, does personal being consist from a functional point of view? In my opinion, the essential features of personal being as such are self-consciousness and self-determination, though of course finite persons never actualize these properties completely. Since self-determination is the issue at stake in the present discussion, I will build no argument on it in this context, although in fact I believe that the concept of self-determination is precisely the concept of the capacity to choose freely one's goals (within certain limits) and then to direct one's subsequent activity toward the goals thus chosen by the individual—and this involves precisely the agent causality view as a clarification of the notion of that self-determination which is essential to personal being. But what about the other essential attribute of personal being, namely, self-consciousness? It seems fair to define it as awareness of one's being as the agent of one's acts; that is simply what it means to be a personal self, to be an ego or an 'I' that immediately discerns itself as agent or decisive cause of one's acts. If, to the contrary, it were the case that whenever an agent appears to itself to act, it is rather the case that each state of the self is the passive effect of previous states which are themselves related in the same way to still more previous states (along with external causal factors understood in the same passive way), that would be tantamount to claiming that there was no active agency involved at all. But in that case, what has become of self-consciousness, or the awareness of the ego or 'I' as an agent? That each of us clearly is aware of our own respective self (at times when we turn our attention to the question) as such an ego, seems indisputable; but then either this sense of active agency is an illusion of universal human proportions, or the genuineness of such an active agency at the core of human selfhood must be acknowledged. But it seems impossible to explain an illusion or mistake except as itself an expression of active agency on the part of a person: otherwise, who made the mistake or became involved in the illusion? If, in the case of selfhood, all is passively determined effect, where is the subject of the awareness of such effects? I am not being naïve: I realize that there are those who deny that there is such a thing as consciousness, much less self-consciousness; and I realize that there are those who claim (Hume, for example, or perhaps even John Stuart Mill) that the self or person is merely a succession of passively determined contents. But I simply regard such views as nonsensical. In the first case, who is it that expresses his or her active conscious agency in the denial? In the second case, how can such successive contents constitute a single self? And where is the awareness of the self—can one passively determined content be aware of another and still be merely a passively determined content? Such suggestions are indeed beyond my scope of comprehension (and, I suggest, anyone else's scope of comprehension). No: denials and affirmations are the work of an active conscious agent, an ego, a personal self—and this again is the agent causality view.

But suppose we carry the suggested denial of active personal agency even further. Suppose there is no such active causality: in that case, every state of things would be the passively determined effect of previous states and so on *ad infinitum*. But in that case there could, in turn, be no adequate explanation of all these successive passively determined states. A domino can fall because it has been struck by another which falls because it in turn has been struck by still another, and so on. But if, underlying the series, there is no self-determining active causality as the ground of these passively determined effects, those effects are left totally

self-determining causality: hence, the agent causality view of freedom.
5.120) but that would make the immediate sense of such agency an illusion,

5.121) while an illusion itself is explicable only as an effect of active agency;

5.122) nor can the sense of active agency be coherently denied,

5.122a) since denial and affirmation are themselves intelligible only as effects of active agency.

5.123) If the notion of active self-determining causality is denied in general,

5.124) that would lead to an infinite regress of passively determined effects which would themselves have no adequate causal explanation;

5.125) if the series is (quite plausibly) traced up to God or the Absolute, as wholly self-determining, that self-determination would be precisely agent causality.

without causal explanation in any adequate sense. 'Aha!' responds a critic, 'That is just a version of the cosmological argument for the existence of God, and who can take *that* seriously?' My answer is, 'Who can fail to take it seriously if they fully realize what they are doing?' In any case, I have defended a properly formulated version of the cosmological argument in my earlier books, and I will not repeat myself here. But suppose it all comes back to God or the Absolute as, in either case, wholly self-determining: but the problem recurs at that level as well, since nothing but the active causality of God or the Absolute determines God or the Absolute. So either the view of God or the Absolute as self-determining active causality fails or else no plausible and decisive objection can be brought against the concept of self-determining active causality. In the first alternative we are left with a causally unintelligible infinite regress; and in the second alternative we find ourselves right back at the agent causality view of freedom.

5.126) The activity of conscious awareness transcends its own content or states of awareness;

5.126a) even if the contents are passively determined, the agent *per se* cannot be the effect of such states, since all the states inhere in the agent as contemplated by it;
5.126b) thus active or agent causality is a necessary condition of there being personal awareness at all;

5.127) Agent causality as the conclusion of all four arguments

But the argument from the nature of self-consciousness has still another aspect. It has been argued by many otherwise diverse thinkers (with all of whom I agree on the point) that the activity of conscious awareness on the part of a personal self (and also that self as the pure subject of awareness) by its very nature transcends every content of the awareness of the self in the sense in which agency invariably transcends (or is distinct from) its object. Now while these contents or objects may be passively determined states, the agent and its activity of awareness cannot themselves be the effect of previous states of awareness, since it is the agent in whom all such states inhere, and it is the activity of awareness which contemplates all such states. Active or agent causality is therefore, in this way also, a necessary condition for there being any awareness at all. And again we find ourselves back at the position I started out to defend. And if someone replies (perhaps in shock): Shades of the transcendental ego! So let it be: it is substance, not labels, that is important in the search for truth! I therefore conclude that the very nature of self-conscious awareness implies, in the way indicated, the agent causality view of personal freedom. And, more generally, I conclude that the agent causality view emerges as the clear conclusion to all four of the arguments I have considered, whether those arguments are taken separately or in conjunction. Of course, I take them primarily in the latter way, since all the arguments intertwine with each other at the periphery and thus compose a single comprehensive structure of plausibility.

Criticisms of the Agent Causality View of Personal Freedom (and Response to Those Criticisms)

Many standard criticisms of the so-called free will doctrine are either inapplicable to the agent causality view by reason of the fact that they are directed toward a different version of libertarianism, or else they are irrelevant because they involve a misunderstanding or a misinterpretation of the agent causality thesis in the form in which I have explained and defended it. As far as I can discern, the most basic of these interpretive errors is the assumption that for an act or choice to be free in *any* relevant libertarian sense, it would have to be uncaused as a necessary condition of its being undetermined in the sense pertinent to the rejection of rigorous determinism. It is, on that assumption, not difficult to construct a slew of arguments to the effect that an act or choice thus construed could not really be attributed to an agent at all, since the agent would have, by definition, no capacity to bring about its occurrence (which would be to cause and thus determine it); or that such an act or choice could not in any case be a *free* production of the agent, since the agent would have no choice about whether it occurred or not; or that the concept of an act or choice that was undetermined in the sense of being uncaused was an unintelligible concept, since any originated state of affairs could actually occur only through the operation of a sufficient cause or ground. One might even maintain plausibly that causal universality is a necessary principle of reason; or that the consequences of such uncaused acts or choices would 'crack the back' of the entire enterprise of scientific explanation, since such uncaused events would themselves totally disrupt any ordered account of occurrences by themselves producing effects that could not even in principle be mathematically formalized (which, after all, is the ideal of scientific explanation). But none of these alleged difficulties are applicable to the agent causality view of personal freedom; for on that view a free act is not, when properly interpreted, an uncaused act, since

5.128) Some criticisms of free will do not apply to agent causality except through misinterpretation: if it is assumed that a free act is uncaused, then many obvious objections occur;

5.129) such an act could not be attributed to the agent as its cause,

5.130) nor would he or she have any choices about its occurrence.

5.131) The notion of an uncaused event is unintelligible;

5.132) uncaused acts would be incompatible with the ideal of scientific explanation;

5.133) but such objections do not apply to agent causality.
5.134) The agent is the active and decisive cause of the act,

the agent is the decisive and active cause of the act. Nor is it the case, strictly speaking, that an act or choice *as such* is either uncaused or undetermined (or even free) in the relevant sense: for on the agent causality view it is the agent who, as a personal self, is free with respect to acts or choices which are in turn caused and determined in the decisive sense by the agent's active causality, although the agent always exercises that determining causality in view of alternative systems of motives of varying strengths of influence. All the criticisms listed apply as serious difficulties for the view that a free act or choice is uncaused or undetermined (in that sense); but they are clearly not difficulties for the agent causality view, which is totally consistent with the doctrine of causal universality, and which maintains that acts or choices are properly viewed as free only as effects of the self-determining causality of personal agents. Nor is it the case that causal universality logically entails rigorous determinism, unless the question is begged so as to fallaciously eliminate the agent causality view at the outset. It would be a further mistake, also growing out of confusion about causality, to think of personal agents themselves as, in their existence or being, standing outside the framework of universal causality: finite agents are themselves causally originated beings and owe their existence and qualities to a complex of productive causality that I will not attempt to clarify here, since I have dealt with this issue in the philosophically relevant sense in my earlier writings. But even though finite persons are themselves a product, in being and nature, of extraneous causality, they possess, as persons, and because they are persons, the unique capacity of self-determining active causality in a range of acts or choices of which they are themselves the decisive cause. I have not attempted to provide anything even approaching an exhaustive list of the mistaken interpretations about causality and determination that have resulted in the sort of confusion I have been attempting here to dispel. But I have given a sufficient set of illustrations, I trust, to point the serious investigator in what I sincerely believe to be the logically (and perhaps morally as well) right direction.

It has been regarded as an equally serious criticism of the agent causality view that, while, if true, it provides an adequate basis for the justifiable ascription of moral

5.135) the agent causality view is wholly compatible with causal universality, which does not entail rigorous determinism;

5.136) finite agents are themselves causally originated,

5.136a) but they possess the capacity of self-determining active causality.

5.137) It is objected that the agent causality view exceeds

responsibility to an agent, nevertheless the strong sense the view gives to the concept of ability to have acted otherwise in the same or relevantly similar circumstances (i.e., requiring that the agent *actually*, and not merely *theoretically* in the empirically and logically conceivable sense, could have chosen or acted differently under the prescribed conditions)—such a view exceeds the logically sufficient conditions for the ascription of moral responsibility. It is quite enough to understand the capacity to have acted otherwise in a sense that is either indifferent to the controversy between rigorous determinism and its opponents, or else is straightforwardly committed to some version of determinism which involves the claim that no actual alternative to what in fact happens is literally possible (for example, given the actual past plus the laws of nature, a unique and exclusive future is the only one thus literally possible). In other words, either weak or strong compatibilism will function quite adequately to vindicate the ethically pertinent meaning of freedom and therefore also of moral responsibility. And if that claim is true, then the agent causality view, while clearly not falsified by such an avoidability view of freedom, would nevertheless become superfluous and irrelevant, so that, given the effective exercise of Occam's razor (explanatory entities are not to be multiplied beyond necessity), the agent causality view would become a dead issue. I have, of course, already argued in a previous context that no such view of freedom and moral responsibility, as compatible with rigorous determinism, is adequate to the purpose (and I refer the reader to that context). But to complete my previous case, I judge it strategically important to consider some of the main arguments for the avoidability view, and then respond to those arguments critically.

One such argument, which has been expressed in a variety of versions whose differences I will simply not explore, is the claim that the various phrases we employ to ascribe freedom and moral responsibility to persons, are phrases that derive their meaning from (or whose meaning consists in) the usage of those phrases in appropriate circumstances. These concrete situations become *paradigms* both for determining the meaning of such terms and phrases, and for learning that meaning on the part of persons not yet adequately advised about the usage of the terms and phrases involved

the logically sufficient conditions for ascribing moral responsibility;

5.138) it is claimed that either weak or strong compatibilism is sufficient to vindicate the ethically relevant sense of freedom and moral responsibility.

5.139) In support of this claim, it is argued:

5.139a) that the meaning of terms is either a function of, or is identical with, their usage in actual linguistic practice;

('The meaning is the use,' *à la* Ludwig Wittgenstein). Since usage in this way thus justifies meaning and serves as its criterion, and since persons do in fact, under appropriate conditions, describe themselves and others as acting freely and therefore being morally responsible, or as having had the capacity to have acted otherwise or chosen differently or avoided what was done, it follows that these terms and phrases can be used to make legitimate claims which no philosophical sophistry or (less emotively) analysis can dissolve, since the standard and customary usage establishes the legitimacy of the concepts. And when we examine the usage of such terms and phrases in context, we find that an act or choice is said to be free and morally responsible if it is both logically and empirically conceivable (we ordinarily do not use such philosophical jargon, of course) that other alternatives were available in the circumstances, and for a person with the general abilities and knowledge of the individual in question. At this point the argument can branch off in at least two (if not more) different ways: it can, for instance, be claimed that such conditions can be fulfilled quite independently of whether or not some version of rigorous determinism is descriptively true with respect to the act or choice that actually ensues in the case in question; but it can also be claimed (to go on with the Wittgensteinian type of line) that in situations that provide the meanings of the terms and phrases in question, no reference is characteristically made to rigorously determining causality or its denial (perhaps it might even be claimed that no such reference is *ever* made except in the specialized context of either philosophical or scientific discussion), and that therefore the legitimacy of the concepts involved, since they are justified and constituted by the context of usage, need not (or perhaps cannot) involve the issue between rigorous determinism and its denial. For either way of proceeding here, the question of rigorous determinism is left open; and it is also the case that, if there were solid reasons for accepting some version of rigorous determinism, its acceptance would generate no inconsistency with the relevant meanings of personal freedom and moral responsibility. Hence the agent causality view (which yields the denial of rigorous determinism) is superfluous and impertinent.

In response, the general plausibility of the previous

5.139b) that persons do describe themselves and others as free and morally responsible if alternatives were logically and empirically conceivable in relevantly similar or the same circumstances;
5.139c) that it is the case, either that these conditions can be fulfilled whether or not rigorous determinism is true; or that in the usage of the relevant terms no reference to rigorously determining causality is characteristically made,
5.139d) so that the legitimacy of the concepts (freedom, moral responsibility, etc.) need not involve the issue of rigorous determinism;
5.140) and therefore the agent causality view is itself overly rigorous and superfluous.

argument depends on the widely disputed Wittgensteinian claim that standard linguistic usage is the criterion of the meaning and legitimacy of concepts. I am on the side of those who challenge this claim; but I cannot, in a treatise on ethics, become involved in an adequate statement of the challenge to such a pervasive hermeneutical and epistemological claim—it would simply take me too far afield from my present purpose. However, I will mention some general reasons for my discomfort with this 'ordinary language thesis,' as it is often called. Wittgenstein and his sympathetic interpreters both admit and flatly assert that standard usage, in the case of any commonly employed term or phrase, is an elusive prize indeed. The reference of such terms is characteristically vague, imprecise, fuzzy, and even indeterminate: at the most there is a multiplicity of uses (for the same term or phrase) but no element of content or reference that is common to these uses, and at best we are in a position merely to recognize and again (vaguely) to describe any 'family resemblances' that occur among these uses. Now if all this analysis is correct, it involves the implication that standard usage (for any term or phrase, and therefore also for terms and phrases pertinent to moral issues such as personal freedom and moral responsibility) can provide no conceptually clear and determinate analysis of any such set of terms or phrases (in a universal fog of ambiguous usage, all is indeterminate, imprecise, and fuzzy). But the determination, that terms are logically consistent or opposed in their meaning in their relation to the same states of affairs, requires (logically necessitates) the very sort of conceptual precision and determinateness that the Wittgensteinian analysis denies. Propositions composed of terms and phrases whose meanings are indeterminate actually make no definite assertions and therefore cannot be either opposed to, or opposed by, the claim presumably expressed by other propositions. Of course, propositions purporting to express the meaning of rigorous determinism will themselves be indeterminate and non-definitive in meaning and will therefore also be neither compatible nor incompatible with any other propositions. The result of all this will be that no clearly determinate philosophical view will even admit of formulation, so that no plausible (or even implausible) judgments about the logical relation between any (fuzzy) concept of

5.141) In response:

5.142) the argument depends on the claim that standard usage is the criterion of meaning;

5.142a) but this claim can be challenged: since it is admitted that standard usage is vague, imprecise, and indeterminate, it would follow that no clear and determinate analysis of terms so construed will be possible;

5.143) but the determination of logical consistency or opposition depends precisely on the sort of clarity and determinateness denied.

5.144) It will thus follow that no plausible conclusions about compatibility or incompatibility will be possible.

personal freedom and any (equally fuzzy) concept of either moral responsibility or determinism will even be possible in principle. Surely an argument with premises that generate such implications can produce no reasonable argument for either compatibilism or incompatibilism (or any other clearly definable position).

5.145) The recognition that standard usage is imprecise implies a criterion of clarity and determinateness which exceeds that of standard usage, as a basis for discerning the imprecision;

On the other hand, the recognition of the inadequacy, ambiguity, and imprecision of 'standard usage' clearly implies as well a more rigorous standard of conceptual clarity than, by hypothesis, the ordinary language thesis itself makes possible in either principle or practice. To make such a recognition possible, one must be operating, at least implicitly, with a criterion of conceptual and linguistic clarity in standard or ordinary use in degree of precision, determinateness, and relative (perhaps even total) freedom from ambiguity; otherwise the 'fuzziness' of standard usage could not be intelligibly predicated. Yet the claim that 'the meaning is the use' would certainly appear to eliminate such a standard, which, by the very nature of the case, would be distinct from, and more logically precise than, that of such standard or ordinary usage. If there is *no* such independent standard of conceptual and logical clarity, then the main claim of Wittgensteinian thinkers about linguistic imprecision would be unintelligible and therefore unassertable; but if there *is* such an independent standard, then the further claim that 'the meaning is the use in ordinary discourse' is overturned, since that independent standard exceeds ordinary discourse in conceptual clarity and precision. Thus the 'ordinary language thesis' as a whole, embracing as it does both claims, is internally inconsistent and therefore highly implausible. Acceptance of this criticism, however, does not, as might be supposed, commit one to the clearly implausible thesis that any actual finite thinker could in practice actualize that standard of fully precise conceptual clarity across the board (in all of a person's thinking and predication); it is enough to recognize the ideal in principle, and then aim at the closest possible approximation in practice.

5.146) it follows that the standard usage view is inconsistent in claiming that standard usage is both imprecise and also the criterion of meaning;

5.147) yet the recognition of such a standard of logical precision does not mean that any actual thinker realizes the standard completely in practice.

5.148) If standard usage is itself unclear, how could a person be confident about the presence or absence of a veiled reference to determinism?

Quite aside from any question about the soundness or effectiveness of the previous criticisms, the original criticism, of the agent causality view of freedom, seems flimsy and inconclusive even if we play by Wittgensteinian rules. If the standard or ordinary usage of terms and phrases is, as claimed, riddled with ambiguity, imprecision, and fuzziness, how can any judge of the implications of such standard usage, with respect to moral terms and phrases, be so confident that talk about available alternatives with respect to which the agent could have chosen differently carries no veiled implication about whether the acts or choices in question were or were not rigorously determined? As to the claim that, since no reference is characteristically made to the determinism issue in contexts of usage that constitute the meanings of terms and phrases such as 'free,' 'morally responsible,' 'could have acted otherwise,' 'had available alternatives,' and so on, it therefore follows that the meaning of these phrases could not be logically dependent on any resolution of the determinism issue. This claim seems clearly false from one point of view, and highly questionable from another. It appears simply false, if we recognize that in any context of conceptual and linguistic usage, the resolution of an indeterminate number of unmentioned issues is clearly presupposed as a foundation or ground for that particular context; it is impossible in practice to spell out all the assumptions underlying, and presupposed by, any assertion in any context of usage—in fact, even indispensable presuppositions characteristically go without explicit reference, either because they are so obvious as not to merit such reference, or because it is in any case impossible to develop and apply with reasonable confidence any criterion of indispensability or essentiality. The mere failure to mention an assumption or presupposition does not entail its logical irrelevance to the issue at hand. From another point of view, it is highly questionable whether or not reference to the determinism issue is characteristic of contexts of usage in which the meanings of the relevant moral terms or phrases are, from a Wittgensteinian point of view, constituted. Even if one could recall a hundred (or even a thousand) linguistic situations in which the relevant moral terms or phrases were used, say, without reference to the determinism issue, that would settle nothing to the point, since the contexts of usage for such terms or phrases constitute a vast ocean of usage in comparison with which any individual sampling would be a mere drip. And why should we not count as counter-instances all the explicit reference to the determinism issue, in precisely the relevant context, on the part of philosophers, theologians, scientists,

5.149) Even if there were no such reference to determinism, that would not entail its irrelevance;

5.150) every context of usage presupposes a network of assumptions which, though pertinent, are not explicitly stated;

5.151) even a sampling of cases of choice in which determinism was not mentioned would be only a fragment of the whole context of usage.

5.152) What about all the explicit references to determinism by philosophers and other scholars?

linguists, philologists, and so on? I would even venture the following conjecture: if persons involved, in contexts of usage taken as definitive of the meaning of moral terms and phrases, were asked whether the determinism issue had any bearing for them on the meaning of phrases and terms like 'free,' 'morally responsible,' 'could have acted otherwise,' 'had alternatives,' and so on, and if the implications of the determinism issue were clearly explained in an unbiased way, I have no doubt whatever that, to a man, they would all answer in the affirmative, no matter what view they ended up adopting on the issue. Since, to my knowledge, no sufficiently comprehensive poll on the issue has ever been taken under appropriate statistical controls, I suppose my opinion on the conjecture is worth at least as much as that of a critic who takes the other side of the question. More seriously, it seems likely that what actually emerges from all this discussion is the highly plausible conclusion or claim that, while statistical linguistics can, at least in principle, make an instructive but revisable judgment about terminological usage, it cannot settle any issue of philosophical substance, whether about the correct conceptual meanings involved in moral thinking, or, for that matter, about any other such substantive issue.

A more direct method of supporting the critical claim that the agent causality view of personal freedom oversteps the bounds of sufficiency, for legitimizing the concept of moral responsibility, consists in bypassing the Wittgensteinian backdrop of the previous line of support, and then instead claiming forthrightly that, while avoidability (the capacity to have refrained from performing a morally significant act) is essential as a basis of moral responsibility, it need not involve either the denial or the affirmation of either rigorous determinism or its opposite (however that may be construed). For to say that an act was avoidable on the part of a given agent, or to say that the agent had alternatives or could have acted otherwise, means simply that if the agent had made a certain choice, which in fact the agent did not make (in place, that is, of the choice the agent did make), the action in question would not have occurred (although some other action, broadly understood to include merely refraining from acting, would have occurred pertinent to the choice which in fact was not made). Since the

5.153) Anyone to whom the issue was explained would probably recognize the clear relevance of the determinism question.

5.154) The most plausible conclusion would be that statistical linguistics can make a tentative suggestion, but can settle no substantive thesis about this.

5.155) As for the claim for the general avoidability view that agent causality is superfluous:

5.156) it is claimed that the freedom essential to moral responsibility is expressed in the thesis that if the agent had chosen differently, he or she could and would have acted differently;

conditional 'if' clause is counter-factual (the choice referred to in the 'if' clause did not occur), the entire conditional sentence does not imply that the choice (and subsequent act) that was made was not wholly determined; neither does it imply that it was wholly determined. What is implied is that if the agent had made a choice different from the one the agent *did* make, the agent would not have performed the act he or she did perform, and, furthermore, the agent would have performed a different act (again, broadly construing the notion of an act). Thus the claim, that an agent could have avoided a certain act, must be expanded into a conditional (hypothetical) proposition to express its full meaning: if (contrary to fact) the agent had made a different choice, then the agent *would* (and therefore also *could*, since no agent would be capable of performing an act that he or she could, for some empirical or logical reason, not perform) have performed a different act (or could/would have acted on a different alternative, or could/would have done otherwise than he or she did). All this is presumably to make clear that, for the avoidability view, it is *not* being claimed that any agent *actually* could have chosen or acted differently than that agent did (so that the view is consistent with rigorous determinism), but merely that, conditionally or theoretically, the agent could have acted differently *if* he or she had chosen to do so. On the other hand, the avoidability view, as here explained, does not claim that it is false that either choice (the actual one, or the hypothetical one) might be free in a sense that would involve, as in the agent causality view, the denial of rigorous determinism. Whether the choice or act, in either case, is rigorously determined or not, remains an open and therefore unsettled question. Hence, the agent causality view becomes superfluous in the sense that its truth (or that of any other similar theory) is not an essential presupposition of the legitimacy of moral responsibility.

In response to this criticism, what it boils down to, in my opinion, is the claim that it is *not* a necessary condition for the ascription of moral responsibility that the agent in question was *actually* capable of making a different choice in the circumstances (or that the agent was actually capable of avoiding the choice and act which occurred). Since the *condition* of avoidability is contrary to fact, according to the

5.157) since the thesis is counter-factual, it does not imply that either the choice or the act was either determined or not in the rigorous sense.
5.158) It is rather implied that a conditional follows— *viz.*, if the agent had chosen differently, the agent would or could have acted differently;

5.159) this does not mean that the agent actually could have chosen or acted differently.
5.160) Hence, the view is consistent with both rigorous determinism and its denial.

5.161) In response:
5.162) since the conditional expressing avoidability is contrary to fact, it follows that the avoidability itself, if conjoined with rigorous determinism,

is contrary to fact, and that would entail the denial of moral responsibility.

theory itself, it follows that the *avoidability* (which the condition alone makes possible) is also contrary to fact, if one opts for rigorous determinism in the case of either the actual or the hypothetical choice or act. And if therefore it was the case that the agent could not actually have avoided his or her choice or act (because both were rigorously determined, or the agent was rigorously determined in making the choice that precipitated the act), then of course it follows that, if avoidability is an essential condition of moral responsibility, then either rigorous determinism is false, or there is no such thing as objectively justifiable moral responsibility. Thus the criticism of the agent causality view (on the ground that it exceeds the sufficient conditions of moral responsibility) simply collapses. If, on the other hand, one opts for the alternative thesis (both options are purportedly left open by the avoidability view) that the agent was the active cause of the choice (and therefore also of the act through the choice) in such a way that the agent could have exercised that causality differently in the circumstances, that is precisely the agent causality position. And if a theory or interpreter leaves both options open (agent causality and rigorous determinism), the consequence is that the genuineness of moral responsibility is open and unsettled as well.

5.163) If, on the contrary, the avoidability is conjoined with the denial of rigorous determinism, that would entail the agent causality view and the vindication of moral responsibility.

In response to this same criticism against the agent causality view, however, I wish to draw attention to another and often discussed objection to the effect that any explanation of an agent's capacity to act otherwise, in a given situation, as equivalent logically to a conditional or hypothetical claim, appears to involve either an infinite regress or an incurable ambiguity (or perhaps both). Consider the claim that an agent could have chosen and/or acted differently than the agent did in a particular set of circumstances. If this claim is equivalent to the claim that 'if the agent had made a different choice, the agent would/could have chosen or acted differently in the circumstances'; then either the 'could have' in the second claim has the same meaning as in the first claim, or not. But if it has the same meaning, then we would require a more complex conditional sentence to explain the meaning of the first conditional claim, then a still more complex conditional sentence to explain that, and so on *ad infinitum*. One way of expressing the first of these more complex conditionals might be: 'If the agent had

5.164) In any case, it is questionable whether a 'could/would' claim can be analyzed as equivalent in meaning to a conditional containing 'could/would' as well:

5.165) if the 'could/would' has the same meaning in both occurrences, this would entail an infinite regress of conditionals to complete the analysis (which would be absurd);

chosen to choose differently, then the agent could have chosen differently; and if the agent had thus chosen differently, the agent would/could have chosen or acted differently.' There seems no obvious (or even covert) way of completing the series of clarifying sentences or propositions. And hence there emerges not only an objectionable infinite regress; but it also turns out to be the case that no succeeding complex conditional provides any explanation in full of the meaning of the previous complex conditionals and therefore also no adequate explanation of what it means to claim that an agent could have acted otherwise in a particular set of circumstances. But suppose, on the other hand, that the 'could have' in the very first conditional above does not mean the same thing as the 'could have' in the original proposition: in that case, it will convey no unambiguous explanation of the first 'could have,' because the meaning of the second 'could have' is undesignated and therefore unclear, so that its conceptual relation to the first 'could have' is equally unclear. It is however clear that the second 'could have' would have to entail the first 'could have,' if the conditional claim is to be logically equivalent in meaning to the original claim. Yet it is difficult to see how a person could carry through with all this clarification, if it is even possible. In any case, the logical equivalence of the original claim to the first conditional claim is highly questionable. So whether one opts for the two 'could haves' possessing the same meaning, or two different meanings, it is highly implausible to claim that the original claim (to the effect that an agent could have chosen and/or acted differently) is equivalent in meaning to any one or any number of supposedly clarifying conditional sentences. For all the reasons I have developed, therefore, I conclude that any such equivalence hypothesis provides no decisive or even plausible objection to the agent causality view of personal freedom.

At this juncture I wish to consider a serious criticism to the effect that the agent causality view itself (or any view involving the denial of rigorous determinism) involves an objectionable infinite regress that vitiates the position. My own acquaintance with this objection is grounded in a particular philosophical and theological context in the writings of Jonathan Edwards under the title, *Freedom of the Will*. Edwards himself is a strong compatibilist, since he holds that

5.166) if the 'could/would' has a different meaning in the two occurrences, then no clear analysis of either occurrence is achieved, though the second 'could/would' must entail the first if the two propositions are to be logically equivalent (which is highly questionable);

5.167) thus the equivalence hypothesis is not a plausible criticism of agent causality.

5.168) It is objected that the agent causality view itself entails an infinite regress. 5.169) The context of the objection in Jonathan Edwards.

5.170) this view is strong compatibilism combining uninhibited voluntary action (no constraint or restraint) with rigorous determinism by means of internal influences or motives,

the freedom of the agent, in the morally relevant sense, consists in the agent's capacity to execute his or her voluntary actions without external constraint or restraint and without any pertinent defect of understanding or knowledge with respect to the act or object of voluntary choice. He also holds, as perfectly compatible with this sort of freedom, that the choices and acts of agents necessarily occur only in the presence of sufficiently and wholly determining causes which account for the existence of the choice or act, and for its being as it is rather than otherwise, so that, of course, given the effective operation of those causes, the choice or act could not logically be otherwise than it is. The causes that determine morally relevant choices or acts (Edwards calls them *moral causes*) are such internal influences as biases, dispositions (habitual or not), inclinations, tendencies, motives, together with the objects of all these, however such states may originate in the agent (or, in Edwards' term, the soul). At the same time, Edwards does not initially insist that the will is in every case necessarily determined by the strongest conjunction of such influences; but even if the will can itself be determined by sufficient and therefore prevailing causes to oppose the strongest conjunction in a particular case, nevertheless it is always possible to conceive, in any given instance of volition, a strength or influence or motivation sufficient to establish a sure and perfect connection between moral causes and the relevant volitions that result from those causes. When this is the case, the connection is called moral necessity. Now Edwards is arguing the view thus summarized against an opposed theological position which he calls the Arminian view of liberty. On his interpretation of this libertarian position, it involves three elements in the notion of freedom or liberty in the morally relevant sense: first, a self-determining capacity that the willing agent has in the formation of its own choices or acts of volition; second, an indifference or equilibrium of the willing agent in relation to motivating influences prior to the act of volition; and third, a contingency, in the occurrence of any such volition, which is opposed to any necessity, or fixed and certain connection of the volition in relation to any previous ground, reason, or cause. This libertarian view is not necessarily indistinguishable from the agent causality view as I have developed it previously; and in some versions

5.170a) although the strongest conjunction of such influences sometimes prevails and sometimes does not.

5.171) Edwards pits this view against the Arminian view of liberty, which involves: (a) self-determining volitional agency, (b) motivational equilibrium, and (c) contingency of volition in relation to any prior reason or cause.

of the Arminian view, as discussed by Edwards, the difference is even striking. But I cannot here concern myself with such details; suffice it to say that it is possible to interpret the general definition above in such a way that the agent causality view would fall under it as a species. The agent causality view is in full accord with the claim that the relevant sense of moral freedom attributes self-determining, active causality to the agent with respect to its choices and acts as emerging from the exercise of that active causality. But the agent causality view does not represent the moral agent as necessarily in a state of indifference or equilibrium with respect to influence and motivation, since the view regards the agent as choosing or acting only under the influence of alternative sets of inclining motives: the only indifference or equilibrium would consist in the fact that it is the intrinsic and active causality of the agent that determines which of the possible alternative directions the agent takes, and, whatever the agent's self-determining choice, it would always have been possible for the agent to have exercised that causality differently, always have been actually possible for the agent to have opted for a different alternative. But I freely acknowledge that such is not the sort of balance or equilibrium that Edwards attributes to the Arminian perspective. As for the contingency of the agent's choice, it is contingent, on the agent causality view, only in the sense that none of the alternative systems of motives would be sufficient to determine the choice apart from the agent's causality or consent; and hence this means that such contingency is equivalent to the qualified sense of equilibrium or indifference mentioned just above.

How then does Edwards attempt to argue that such a view of personal freedom involves a logically objectionable infinite regress? In order to exercise self-determining causality in producing a choice that is free in the requisite sense, the agent must produce a volition which, in turn, is either itself free in the requisite sense, or not. If that volition is thus free (i.e., if the agent is thus free in forming it), then it must be dependent for its status on another formed volition of the agent in order to be free in this sense, and so on *ad infinitum*. But if, on the other hand, the original formed volition is *not* free in the requisite sense (so as to yield the infinite regress), then any choice or act resulting from its

5.172) The agent causality view can be interpreted as one possible species of the general Arminian position, although the agent causality view involves indifference only in the sense that the active causality of the agent decisively determines which inclining motive prevails,

5.172a) so that no system of motives is a sufficient cause of act or choice.

5.173) The infinite regress objection claims that the exercise of agent causality can operate only through producing a volition which, if free, would require another volition, and so on to infinite, but which, if not free, cannot result in a free choice or act;

formation will not be free either, even in a derivative sense, since it is caused by a volition that is not itself free in the indicated sense. So the libertarian position leads either to an infinite regress of prior volitions (which is contradictory and absurd) or to the denial of the requisite freedom in the original volition and the choice and/or act emerging from it (which would contradict the libertarian view of freedom originally posited).

5.174) In response:

5.175) the objection turns on an ambiguity in the concept of volition as being either a produced volition or a producing act on the part of the agent;

In response to this criticism, so far as it is applicable to the agent causality view as an objection, I answer that the alleged infinite regress does not logically follow because its emergence rests on an ambiguity in the notion of volition. The term *volition* can stand *either* for the active exercise of causality by a willing agent, or it can stand for the result produced by that active exercise, that is, for *what* is willed or voluntarily produced by the agent as active cause. It is true that a *produced* volition is free, in the relevant sense, only in relation to an *act* of volition on the part of the agent; but the active exercise of causality on the part of the agent is simply not, on the agent causality view, a *produced* volition; it is instead a *producing* volition (i.e., it is the operation of the agent's active causality as will). If, on the contrary, every *produced* volition required an antecedent *produced* volition as its ground, there would be no active or agent causality at all. But that is precisely what the agent causality view denies: the causal explanation of a produced volition terminates in the active causality of the producing agent, so that no infinite regress is involved at all. If it is then objected that this answer leaves the existence of the finite personal agent as possessing that originative capacity unexplained; then the answer is that, as I previously argued in a much earlier context, the existence or being of any finite personal agent has, of course, a cause (or causes) that explains that being or existence. But that cause does not determine the producing volitions of the agent thus originated, since in that case there would be only *produced* volitions, and no producing personal agency at all. I conclude, therefore, that the type of infinite regress objection argued by Edwards collapses, since it rests for its (specious) plausibility on an ambiguity in the notion of volition.

5.176) since the explanation of the produced volition terminates in the active causality of the producing agent, there is no infinite regress.

The distinction between *produced* volition (that which is willed by the agent) and *producing* volition (the active exercise of the agent's self-determining causality) also provides part of the answer to a different but related objection (also developed at length by Jonathan Edwards). It has been claimed by critics that the concept of agent causality veils an unanswered question in its insistence that the agent as such is the active cause of morally significant actions and choices. That the agent determines the choice, among alternative courses of action, may explain *in general* why the agent makes a choice (since it is predicated that an agent as such is the decisive cause of any morally relevant choice); but it does not explain why he or she chooses one particular course of action rather than others that were actually possible in the situation. Now, so the objection runs, either the agent chooses and acts for a reason the agent judges sufficient to ground or determine a particular choice, or not. If there is such a reason which determines the choice, it is not free in the libertarian sense (which implies the denial of rigorous determinism); but if there is no such determining reason, that is tantamount to the claim that there is nothing that explains the particular choice as over against others, so that the choice is irrational. In the former case, the agent causality view of freedom is contradicted; and in the latter case, the occurrence of the particular choice (as opposed to others) is left without rational explanation. Yet a choice is an occurrence and therefore requires such an explanation—unless we are prepared to drop the doctrine of causal universality, a doctrine which the agent causality view, on my version of it, opts to maintain (perhaps even as a necessary principle of universal reason).

In response to this critical objection, I answer that the insistence to the effect that there must be a sufficient cause of a particular choice (other than the causality of the agent which, by hypothesis, is common to all choices and thus, it is alleged, cannot explain one particular choice in contrast to others) again blurs the distinction between *produced* volition and *producing* volition. What the objection claims is that the agent's volition must be a *produced* volition (i.e., have an extraneous and sufficient causal ground). But if that were the case, there would be no *act* on the part of the agent at all, no active causality, since the putative agent would be wholly passive with respect to the volition and thus in no sense its productive cause in such a way as

5.177) It is objected that the agent causality view can offer no causal explanation as to why the agent made the particular choice he or she did make among the alternatives;

5.178) either the agent acts for a determining reason judged sufficient or not;
5.178a) if so, the act is not free in the relevant sense;
5.179) if not, there is nothing that explains the particular choice, which is thus irrational.
5.180) Hence, either agent freedom is contradicted, or the act has no cause;

5.181) In response:

5.182) this objection blurs the distinction between *produced* and *producing* volition;
5.182a) the agent's volition is a producing, not a produced, volition since otherwise there would be no active agency;

to be charged with responsibility for the action. Yet this response does not, as the objection implies, involve the consequence that the agent must be choosing without reason. Those reasons are found in the various influences that motivate the agent in relation to the various alternatives available in a particular situation. Such motives will have degrees of influencing strength, variable from alternative to alternative. Among these motives are the judgments of the agent about the moral worth, goodness, or rightness (or the denial of such) involved in the various alternatives and their predictable consequences. The agent's personal freedom, in the morally relevant sense, consists, for the agent causality view, in the fact that none of these systems of motivation are sufficient in themselves to be the cause of an agent's choice or act without the producing volition of the agent's self-determining causality and consent. Of course, an agent exercises that active causality, in any sense involving moral responsibility, only because the agent judges the supporting reasons to justify that exercise (although the agent's judgment may be either correct or incorrect, right or wrong). And that judgment, conjoined with the firm resolve to choose and act accordingly, *simply is* the active causality of the agent in morally responsible exercise. In a qualified sense, it may even be said that the agent acts according to the strongest motive; yet not in the sense that implies rigorous determinism and the destruction of the agent's capacity actually to have acted or chosen otherwise. For the agent's judgment, consent, and resolve are jointly what constitutes the prevailing strength of the motive in question. I therefore judge the veiled and unconsidered question charged by the critic to be fully answerable and answered by the agent causality view.

It has frequently been claimed, as a criticism of libertarianism and therefore also of the agent causality position, that if one accepts any sort of metaphysic (theistic or pantheistic) in which the ultimate ground of being is a self-existent Mind or Spirit or God that possesses the attribute of omniscience, defined in such a way as to include all future events and states as objects fully and perfectly known, then such a thinker ascribes to God an exhaustive foreknowledge (perhaps an ambiguous and misleading term) that would be inconsistent with the concept of personal freedom in

5.182b) there are reasons judged sufficient by the agent as a basis of choice, but no set of such reasons is productively sufficient without the agent's active consent;

5.183) the agent's judgment, as an exercise of active agency, tips the balance for a particular set of motives.

5.184) It is objected that if one accepts the reality of an ultimate mind that is omniscient, such omniscience would imply the rigorous determinism of events thus foreknown as certain to occur.

the agent causality view, since the foreknowledge of future events as certain to occur would imply the rigorous determinism of the events themselves and therefore the rigorous determinism of all the volitions, choices, and acts ascribable to finite personal agents. In other words, divine foreknowledge would imply what I have designated as religious and teleological determinism, which is incompatible with the agent causality view. There are, of course, many complex issues connected with this claim: issues, for example, as to whether such a metaphysical perspective is itself a rationally defensible worldview in any form in which it might be espoused. But I have no intention of pursuing such issues in a treatise on philosophical ethics in connection with the freedom/determinism problem: partly because my interest here is merely to consider objections to the agent causality view, and then to respond to them; and partly because I have already dealt with this issue in my previous books. For these reasons, I here restrict my consideration to the question whether, if there is an omniscient God with exhaustive and perfect foreknowledge of future events, that conclusion would entail rigorous (teleological) determinism and therefore the denial of agent causality. This is certainly the claim of Jonathan Edwards and many thinkers in his philosophical/theological tradition.

5.185) As discussed here, the issue can only be hypothetical: *viz.*, whether an omniscient knowledge of future events would entail rigorous determinism *per se*;

The objection, stated as a criticism of agent causality, contends that if God (I will use theistic language primarily for the sake of expository simplicity, but partly also because this is the perspective in which the problem is most often posited) has an infallibly certain foreknowledge of the future volitions, choices, and acts of finite moral agents, it follows that such future events must necessarily occur (i.e., their non-occurrence is not actually possible under the prescribed circumstances), since otherwise the divine prescience or foreknowledge would not be infallibly certain as predicated. If the term *foreknowledge* is taken with bald literalness in the temporal sense, then God's foreknowledge of any future event (including the future volitions, etc., of finite moral agents) would itself be temporally past relatively to such events. But since the past is necessary in the sense that, once transpired, its occurrences, as irreversible, cannot be otherwise than they were, it follows both that God's foreknowledge is necessary in the same sense; and if that is

5.186) if divine foreknowledge is temporally prior to the events foreknown and also infallible, that would entail the necessary occurrence of the events thus known, since such knowledge would be irreversible as such;

5.187) if foreknowledge is viewed metaphorically and as thus transcending time, the immediately evident status of the knowledge would render it and its objects necessary and irreversible also; even if God's knowledge is non-causal *re* the events, the infallible certainty of the knowledge would render the events necessary on pain of self-contradiction.

the case, then the foreknown event must be equally necessary, in the same sense, as an essential condition of the necessity of the divine foreknowledge. If, on the other hand, the term *foreknowledge* is interpreted as metaphorical with respect to its temporal implications, and God is viewed as transcending time so that God's timelessly certain knowledge does not in fact literally antedate temporally future events (God, in other words, would, in timelessness, be contemporaneous with all events—past, present, or future), it will still follow, even more directly, that God's knowledge of events, as thus immediately evident to God's awareness, is possessed of an infallible certainty which is necessary and irreversible, so that the event apprehended is equally necessary and irreversible. If, on the contrary, a critic objects that knowledge of an event as certain does not causally determine the event as necessary, so that God's certainty of events does not determine them as necessary in the causal sense and that therefore the events are after all contingent so far as divine knowledge is concerned; then the answer is that, even if God's knowledge is not as such causal, nevertheless that knowledge as certain and infallible proves the necessity of the event, since it is impossible that certain and infallible knowledge could be fallible or possibly mistaken, which is contradictory. Hence, even if God's knowledge is viewed as non-causal, it nevertheless proves or establishes the objects of that knowledge as necessary and incapable of their being otherwise than they are apprehended by God. But of course, if the volitions, choices, and acts of moral agents are thus necessary as certainly and infallibly known by God, it follows that it would have been impossible for them actually to have occurred otherwise than they did.

5.188) In response:

5.189) this objection confuses epistemological necessity with metaphysical necessity: events as foreknown by God are necessary in the former (epistemological) sense, but not in the latter (metaphysical) sense as such;

In response to this criticism, I answer that, given the transcendental religious metaphysic presupposed in the context of this discussion, the criticism, as directed toward the agent causality view of personal freedom, is fallacious because it depends on a misleading ambiguity in the concept of necessity. Given the infallible certainty of God with respect to temporally future events, it is a necessary conclusion (*epistemologically* necessary) that the events will occur as thus certainly known; but the knowledge as such does not determine the occurrence of the events as necessary in their being or existence (as *metaphysically* necessary). Whether events thus known to God are, in relation to their causes of being, necessary as the unalterable consequence of the operation of those causes, will depend on what sort of events they are and what sort of causes are relevant to their occurrences. No doubt God determines many events as necessary through the exercise of causal power. But their metaphysical necessity is the consequence of that active causality and entirely relative to it; such necessity is not, clearly, the consequence of divine knowledge. In fact, it is the other way around: the certainty of divine knowledge, though dependent in part on God's omniscience as a divine perfection, is, in a different sense, consequent upon the nature and qualities of the events known. If there are, as I have extensively argued previously, appropriate reasons for believing that the volitions, choices, and acts of finite agents, so far as they are morally relevant, are contingent in the sense that the agent is their decisive cause and could have acted otherwise under the same circumstances, then there is no contradiction in supposing that God has an infallibly certain (and therefore epistemologically necessary) knowledge of events which in themselves are contingent metaphysically in the morally relevant sense. God's knowledge, *as knowledge*, is absolutely necessary (i.e., infallibly certain); but the objects of God's knowledge are conceivably some of them necessary in their being in relation to their causes and some of them contingent in their being in relation to their causes. God necessarily knows objects as they are: causally determined objects God necessarily knows as necessary relative to their antecedent and contemporaneous causes, and contingent objects God necessarily knows as contingent in the indicated sense. But there is only confusion to result if, as in the original criticism, these two senses of necessity are not distinguished. I conclude therefore that divine foreknowledge in no sense implies either rigorous determinism or the denial of the agent causality view of personal freedom.

In all of this discussion of determinism, personal freedom, and moral responsibility, I have, of course, not even begun to exhaust the proliferation of all the possible positions, arguments, and counter-arguments. But I have analyzed what I judge to be the principal positions, arguments, and counter-arguments, so far as I am acquainted with them and understand them. My conclusions are therefore tentative

5.190) it is wholly consistent to hold that: (a) God determines some events as metaphysically necessary through an active causality, (b) and that God has an epistemologically necessary knowledge of other events as contingent in relation to their causes;
5.191) thus there is no contradiction involved: God necessarily knows objects as they are—either as causally determined or as contingent.

5.192) From the analysis of all five objections it is tentatively concluded that:
5.193) agent causality is the sole adequate basis of personal freedom and moral responsibility;
5.194) rigorous determinism is incompatible with both.

and I myself am surely fallible as a thinker. I do not therefore regard myself as having absolutely demonstrated anything about the issues involved. But I am convinced that the only plausible sense of determinism is that of causal universality (I reject all rigorous determinisms in moral context), and the only sense of personal freedom that supplies an adequate basis for genuinely objective moral responsibility is that of agent causality. For me, rigorous determinism simply excludes the morally relevant senses of personal freedom and moral responsibility.

General Meta-Ethical Conclusions

Although there are elements of plausibility in all of the meta-ethical alternatives that have passed in review and been subjected to criticism, and although I have made no claim to indisputability in my analysis, nevertheless I have come down on a particular position on all the main meta-ethical issues. My general meta-ethical theory I have designated *modified teleological intuitionism*: it is *intuitionist* in maintaining that the basic concepts and principles of moral philosophy can be apprehended in their meaning and truth (respectively) only through immediate rational apprehension by moral agents operating in a context that involves as full an apprehension of relevant nonmoral facts and circumstances as is possible for the individual agent. The theory is *teleological* in maintaining that the rightness (or wrongness) of a morally significant act or proximate moral principle (rule) is a function of the goodness, worth, or value (in the moral sense) of the consequences of performing that act or following that rule or principle. But this teleological claim is *modified* by the recognition (a deontological concession) that the ultimate standard of moral value must be self-evident in its worth and therefore, as already indicated, apprehended by immediate rational insight. On the controversy between ethical objectivism and radical ethical relativism, I have concluded on the side of ethical objectivism by maintaining that all plausible moral truth claims are ultimately grounded in a criterion of moral value which has its status as such a criterion entirely independently of individually and culturally variable states of opinion, preference, feeling, or

5.195) Modified Teleological Intuitionism:
5.195a) intuitionist

5.195b) teleological

5.195c) modified

5.196) Ethical Objectivism *vs.* Radical Ethical Relativism

response; and I have therefore concluded as well that radical ethical relativism is false, while that claim is wholly compatible with the view that an indeterminately extended number of moral beliefs (as distinguished from moral truths) are in fact individually and culturally relative in precisely the sense claimed by the relativist in the case of all moral principles without exception. And finally, with regard to determinism, personal freedom, and moral responsibility, I have accepted determinism only in the very limited sense involved in the doctrine of causal universality, while I have rejected every version of rigorous determinism (every version which involves the claim that no finite moral agent ever actually could have acted otherwise then he or she did in a designated context of circumstances). I have, in turn, defended personal freedom on the terms granted by my interpretation of the agent causality view, while I have rejected as inadequate any version of freedom that identifies it, in the morally relevant sense, with causal indeterminateness, theoretical avoidability, or necessary self-determination. I have, in fact, adopted these positions in general because they are, in my opinion, the only adequate grounds for the recognition of genuinely objective moral responsibility—a recognition which, in its turn, I judge to be an essential condition of the intelligibility of moral discourse in human experience. Again, in all of this, I claim no demonstrated finalities, no logical clinchers, no unchallengeable results: I am, after all, as are all of my readers, a fallible human being, and I have therefore nothing but my cautiously considered and hopefully reasonable opinion to offer. At the same time, the views I have presented *are* my opinions, and the arguments I have offered are intended to explain why I sincerely believe them to be more highly plausible conclusions than the alternatives I have tried fairly to criticize. In any case, I intend to use these conclusions as premises in all that follows.

5.197) Causal Universality, Agent Causality, and Moral Responsibility *vs.* Rigorous Determinism, and Freedom as Indeterminateness or Necessary Self-determination

Part II

Normative (Substantive) Ethics:
Alternative Conceptions of the Ultimate Moral Ideal

Chapter VI

*The Principal Classifications of
Normative Ethical Theories*

The Central Concerns of Normative Ethics

In the long history of moral philosophy in western philosophical tradition, the sharp distinction between meta-ethics and normative ethics did not become clear until about the end of the nineteenth century, and even then it was largely limited to the English-speaking philosophical community with what became, by the 1930s, its virtual obsession with philosophical analysis and its concern with linguistic and conceptual meaning. Yet this is not to say that previous thinkers were not interested in clarity of meaning; it is merely to say that for Plato or Aristotle, Aquinas or Kant, Spinoza or J.S. Mill, this concern with meaning was interwoven with the normative ethical discussion that constituted the main thrust of traditional moral theories. One thing was clear enough from the time of Plato onward, as I see it: that any concern, with the meaning and logical status of ethical terms, judgments, and arguments, was subordinate to normative ethical claims in two ways: first, had there been no normative ethical claims, no actual judgments of moral value (as distinguished from discussion about them from a linguistic and logical point of view), there could be nothing

6.1) The clear distinction between meta-ethics and normative ethics, while it emerged in the late nineteenth century, was implicit from the time of Plato,

6.2) but for these earlier thinkers, meta-ethics was subordinate to normative ethics:

6.3) the former could not exist without the latter.

6.4) The purpose of ethical analysis was to serve as a means of clarifying normative ethical claims;

6.5) yet clarity and truth (or substance) belong together, even though it is important to distinguish them.

for meta-ethics (as it finally came to be called) to analyze and clarify, so that in this way meta-ethics is parasitical to normative ethics; second, the ultimate purpose of ethical analysis, in its aim at clarity, was to use that clarity to state, develop, and assess (or argue) actual moral claims or normative judgments. Of course, it seems impossible in principle to achieve any plausible normative results without a clear understanding of the meaning and logic of the terms and propositions that expressed those claims. But it is even more evident that analytic clarity is not enough, since a meaning understood, unless attached to a claim expressed, would be quite pointless: truth without clarity may be misconstrued or misdirected, but clarity without truth is devoid of any substance to be either construed or directed. Of course, in actual practice, the two—analytical clarity and substantial truth—grow up together like children in the same family context, each providing an influence for the growth and development of the other. Still they can be, and, for clarity's sake, they ought to be, distinguished, though never divorced: meta-ethics, as such, makes no substantive moral claims, but the making of those claims, at the level of general principles, is precisely the main concern of normative ethics.

6.6) General elements of a normative ethical theory

6.6a) The justification of specific moral claims by an appeal to ultimate principles of goodness or rightness whose truth is self-evident;

What then is involved in the development of a fully worked-out normative ethical theory, once the framework of linguistic and conceptual meaning (meta-ethics) is provisionally and operationally clarified? Any moral claim, even if very specific and particular (for example, 'you ought to spend more time studying your school lessons, and less time merely enjoying yourself') provokes the question, why?, and involves a standard or criterion of moral value or worth as its ultimate basis. A fully satisfactory basis of this sort, in answer to the question, why?, identifies an ultimate principle of goodness or rightness, the worth or obligatoriness of which is intrinsic or self-contained. Along the way to this basis there may be many extrinsic or instrumental values expressed and appealed to, and many a limited and intermediate principle whose authority is subordinate to that of more inclusive principles and thus requires both justification as a rule of procedure and restriction to a particular context. But it seems plausible to argue, as Aristotle did, that in the end, all instrumental values and intermediate principles find their basis and justification in some highest good or some ultimate principle of moral obligation, whose moral authority is wholly self-contained and the knowledge of which (if the standard or principle is to have any function in moral practice) is, in principle for a morally sensitive person, wholly self-evident: it must be good in itself or right in itself, since otherwise there would be an objectionably infinite regress of values or principles, each of which was in turn subordinate to some still higher value or principle *ad infinitum*. The central concern of normative ethics is to identify this ultimate ideal of moral value or obligation, and explain how it is logically related to all lesser values or principles which involve the application of that ethical ultimate in a particular context or in a particular set of circumstances. But of course, since there is an extended plurality of such normative ethical ideals, their mere self-development, in the way indicated, would leave the inquiring thinker with a stalemate on the question of resolving the competing truth claims of the various alternatives. So a fully worked-out system would provide a structure of argumentation in support of its claims, and, at the same time, a clarifying evaluation of alternative theories judged to be critically less adequate. One might say, it is a matter of positions, arguments, and counter-arguments—in my opinion, that is the gist of what philosophy in general is all about, and therefore the gist also of what moral philosophy is all about.

6.6b) the critical adjudication of competing truth claims among alternative normative ethical theories;

Yet, as I pointed out at the beginning of my treatise, it is not the business of normative ethical philosophy, *as philosophy*, to give specific moral advice about particular issues and problems of moral practice. Philosophy provides a context for that application, while it is the business of the individual moral agent to determine its employment in actual moral decision and action. The agent may, of course, find plenty of help from others along the way. But in the end it is the agent's own personal responsibility, which he or she cannot reasonably delegate to another.

6.6c) the limitation of philosophical ethics to providing a context of principles for the resolving of specific moral issues by individual moral agents.

It might appear initially to be the case that, if the ultimate value or principle, which provides the basis and ground of all less inclusive and intermediate values or principles, is necessarily self-evident and self-justifying in its moral authority, there would be no way to settle, in a rationally objective fashion, the competitive claims of alternative theories concerning that ultimate value or principle, since any and all

6.7) Even though ultimate ethical principles must be self-evident, there are formal, logical criteria for their comparative assessment;

such alternatives would have equal right to the categories of self-evidence and self-justification, and thus there would be no neutral criterion or standard of critical evaluation. But, as I see it, this qualm turns out to be largely unfounded. For it is quite possible to identify, with a high degree of at least provisional plausibility, a set of formal logical properties which, because they are essential to the notion of an ultimate moral value or principle as such and in general, are quite adequate to serve as criteria or standards for the comparative assessment of alternative theories concerning that ultimate moral value or principle. For example, no value or principle that depends for its objectivity and authority on anything other than itself can possibly qualify, since such a dependence would be incompatible with its purported self-evident and self-justifying character. Again, no quality or attribute which, by its very nature, is variable or changeable, will do either, since any criterion which is to function as a standard must be fixed and changeless as an essential condition of its applicability. Nor can the ultimate value or principle be restricted in scope or admit of exceptions to its applicability within the moral sphere; for if it were restricted or exceptionable, its limited applicability would have to be justified by some more inclusive moral value or principle which would therefore be more ultimate than itself—which would be self-contradictory. It is further clear that any value or principle that is radically relativistic by its very nature, so that it depends on variable states of opinion, preference, feeling, or response, cannot possibly be eligible as the ultimate moral value or principle, since then it would be subjectively dependent in the sense precisely opposed to its required objective independence. Finally (although I do not claim that my list of formal criteria is logically complete), the ultimate moral value or principle must be universally compossible, in its application as a criterion, for all responsible finite moral agents, so that no ideal, whose approximate actualization by a limited number of persons would preclude its actualization by the whole remaining class of persons capable of moral decision and choice, could conceivably be the ultimate moral ideal, since that ideal must be accessible and applicable for all finite moral agents without exception. None of these criteria, either singly or collectively, is itself a moral standard in its own right, and hence

6.8) thus an ultimate ethical principle must:

6.8a) contain the whole ground of its objectivity and authority in itself;

6.8b) be fixed and changeless as a criterion of worth;

6.8c) be unrestricted in scope and unexceptionable in application;

6.8d) be free of radically relativistic dependence on variability of preference;

6.8e) be universally compossible for all finite moral agents.

none begs the question in favor of any particular theory as to the identity of the ultimate moral ideal. If, however, it should turn out (an exceedingly unlikely possibility, in my opinion) that more than one version of the moral ultimate should satisfy these criteria (and any other plausible criteria of the same logical sort) equally well, one would be left with a logically arbitrary choice between such alternatives; but it would be at least an open question whether the alternatives in question were in reality substantially different at all, but were merely different ways of verbalizing one and the same moral ideal. After all, they would be, from a moral point of view, operationally indistinguishable.

6.9) But these logical criteria are not themselves moral principles or standards, so that they are not question-begging; 6.10) it is questionable whether more than one ultimate moral principle could satisfy the criteria.

A Proposed Scheme of Classification for Normative Ethical Theories

Normative ethical theories are characteristically segments or parts of some inclusive metaphysical worldview perspective, and there are inevitably logical and conceptual relations (not always formally deductive) between the ethical perspective and the rest of the system. Partly for this reason, and partly for the sake of clarity in exposition, I find it useful to classify normative ethical theories by means of associated metaphysical categories. Metaphysical theories in general may themselves be usefully classified as naturalistic, idealistic, and theistic; and I propose to use the same terms to classify normative ethical theories about the ultimate moral value or principle. However, it is extremely important to explain the precise meanings of these terms in the context of ethics, in order to guard the interpreter against confusion. I designate any normative ethical theory as *naturalistic* if it identifies the ultimately good or right as something (process, relation, or type of entity) within the natural empirically discernible realm of things and events in space and time, or with that realm as a whole. In turn, naturalistic ethics is itself divisible into subtypes of various kinds. Among these I plan to consider *hedonistic* naturalism (the ultimate good is identified with realized pleasure and the absence of pain as qualities of conscious experience), *humanistic* naturalism (the ultimate good is identified with individual and social human well-being as the realization of authentic personal selfhood), *evolutionary* naturalism (the

6.11) Since normative ethical theories tend to be parts of metaphysical perspectives, they can be usefully classified by metaphysical categories as naturalistic, idealistic, and theistic.

6.12) Normative ethical naturalism identifies the ultimately good or right with something within nature or with nature as a whole: 6.12a) (a) hedonistic

6.12b) (b) humanistic

6.12c) (c) evolutionary

6.12d) (d) religious.	ultimate good is identified with the highest actualization of living reality at the culmination of evolutionary process as increasingly successful environmental and internal adaptation), and *religious* naturalism (the ultimate good is identified as the rationally necessary and perfect order of nature itself considered as an object of religious respect or veneration on the part of moral agents who are themselves aspects of that natural order).
6.13) Normative ethical idealism identifies the ultimately good or right with something that transcends nature as value or principle:	I designate any normative ethical theory as *idealistic* if it both denies that the ultimately good or right can be identified as anything within the natural order or as that natural order itself, and therefore claims that the ultimately good or right, whether as value or principle, transcends (is logically and/or metaphysically independent of) the natural order in some identifiable sense. In turn (once again), idealistic ethical systems are classifiable into various sub-types. Among
6.13a) (a) essentialistic (Plato)	these I plan to consider *essentialistic* idealism or *Platonic* idealism (the ultimate good is identified with a transcendent form, essence, or property which is itself the ground of the being and intelligibility of the particular things and rela-
6.13b) (b) absolute (Hegel)	tions that compose the natural order), *absolute* idealism or *Hegelian* idealism (the ultimate good is identified with the wholeness or totality of being viewed as all-inclusive [but impersonal or supra-personal] Mind or Spirit), and *ratio-*
6.13c) (c) rationalistic (Kant)	*nalistic* idealism or *Kantian* idealism (the ultimately right is identified as conformity to the law of rational self-consistency or coherence, whose unconditional moral authority is rendered more fully intelligible by the postulational beliefs in freedom, immortality, and God, although these beliefs do not extend our genuine metaphysical knowledge).
6.14) Normative ethical theism agrees with ethical idealism in maintaining that the good is transcendent but identifies that good with ultimate personal mind.	I designate any normative ethical theory as *theistic* if it agrees with ethical idealism in rejecting any and all normative ethical naturalisms, but holds that ethical idealism, though plausible within limits, nevertheless requires systematic completion through carrying the notions of essence, spirit or mind, and rational principle, logically upward to their integration in the concept of an ultimate personal being or (in theistic religious language) God as absolute (but personal) Mind. Ethical theism, therefore, does not reject any of the versions of ethical idealism outright and completely; it merely transcends what it regards as the critically inadequate and incomplete aspects of ethical idealism, while

combining its critically adequate and fragmentary aspects in the notion of a transcendent personal God, whose essence is absolute goodness itself. As before, ethical theism in turn subdivides into numerous varieties, all of which regard the ultimately good or right as grounded in the being and character of a personal God (it would be better to say: *the* personal God, since there can be, for theism, only one). In analyzing these perspectives I will draw mainly on insights of the Hebrew-Christian tradition as expressed in the philosophies primarily of Augustine, Thomas Aquinas, and Søren Kierkegaard. But in all of these ethical traditions (naturalistic, idealistic, and theistic) the thinkers I choose to discuss, though my choice is admittedly highly selective and in that sense arbitrary, are intended to represent a much more inclusive scope of thought than their own verbal expression explicitly encompasses and embraces. In consequence my exposition, and my criticism as well, will aim at being applicable as much to that broader scope as to the thought of the paradigmatic or exemplary thinkers with whose thought I deal explicitly.

6.15) Augustine, Aquinas, and Kierkegaard

6.16) In all of the normative ethical traditions, the thinkers analyzed are illustrations of a far broader perspective.

Chapter VII

Normative Ethical Naturalism

Naturalism, in normative ethics, has already been defined generally as including any normative moral view that identifies the ultimately good or right with something within the natural, empirically discernible realm of things, or with that realm as a whole. Now while there is a certain relationship between any such view and some metaphysical perspective in which nature is a central concern as well, it is nevertheless very important to point out that the relation between ethical naturalism and metaphysical naturalism is not one of simple and reciprocal logical implication. I define metaphysical naturalism as the view that the natural, empirically discernible realm of things, processes, and events in space and time constitutes the whole of reality. For such a view there is and can be no realm of being that transcends nature or is metaphysically independent of nature; and furthermore, on this same view, the ultimate elements of all substantially real entities are material or physical in nature and are therefore either physical particles or physical forces. Now if a thinker is committed to such a metaphysical perspective, and if he or she has a developed moral philosophy, that philosophy will, barring any blatant contradiction, necessarily be a variety of ethical naturalism, since, for a metaphysical naturalist, nature is the only conceivable context within which moral values and principles can be construed.

7.1) The logical relation between metaphysical naturalism and normative ethical naturalism

7.2) Clarification of metaphysical naturalism:

7.3) If one is a metaphysical naturalist, one logically should be an ethical naturalist (if one has a normative ethical position);

But it does not work the same way if we begin with ethical naturalism: a thinker who is an ethical naturalist is very often a metaphysical naturalist as well; but there is no deductive logical inference to that conclusion, since a thinker with a non-naturalistic metaphysic may nevertheless be an ethical naturalist. Aristotle, for example, believed in a transcendent God as prime mover or final cause of all the processes in the natural universe—he was not therefore, by my definition, a metaphysical naturalist; but since he made no significant use of the concept of God in ethics, no reference to any transcendent basis for moral claims, he was an ethical naturalist. Something of the same sort could be said of John Stuart Mill, who believed in a transcendent but finite God as a partial ground or cause of the natural universe (and hence was not a metaphysical naturalist), but who was an ethical hedonist and thus defined the good naturalistically as identical with pleasure taken as the sole intrinsic and ultimate value (and hence *was* an ethical naturalist).

It is equally important to realize that meta-ethical naturalism (naturalistic definism) and normative ethical naturalism are clearly distinct and do not reciprocally entail each other either. A thinker can identify the ultimately good or right with something within nature (normative ethical naturalism) without claiming that ethical terms are equivalent in meaning with any conjunction of non-ethical terms (which would be meta-ethical naturalistic definism). On the other hand, if a thinker is a meta-ethical naturalistic definist, he or she will clearly be, barring any blatant contradiction again, a normative ethical naturalist as well, if indeed he or she has any developed normative ethical theory at all. If therefore a writer claims to be an ethical naturalist, without explicit qualification, it will be, in the case of current writers on ethics at least, incumbent on the reader to determine whether this is meant in the meta-ethical sense, in the normative ethical sense, or both—the context alone will determine the reference. Only confusion can arise from any failure to recognize these distinctions.

Hedonistic Naturalism

Outside of religious circles, I would judge some variety of hedonism as the most widely held normative ethical

---

7.4) but one can consistently be an ethical naturalist without being a metaphysical naturalist.

7.5) Again, a thinker can consistently be a normative ethical naturalist without being a meta-ethical naturalistic definist, but if one is a meta-ethical naturalistic definist, one should logically be a normative ethical naturalist as well.

7.6) Clarification of the meaning

theory in the English-speaking philosophical (if not total intellectual) world. At the outset, hedonism seems to be a logically simple normative ethical perspective, since it holds that the sole ultimate, self-justifying, and intrinsic good is pleasure (taken as a collective abstract term for any complex of experiences sharing a positive feeling tone for sentient beings, whether human or sub-human). Clearly enough, hedonism in whatever form is a straightforward teleological theory, since it holds that the moral rightness of an act or the moral rightness of a rule consists in the degree to which performing the act, or acting in accordance with the rule, would predictably tend to maximize pleasurable consequences and minimize painful consequences for all the sentient (or at least human sentient) beings likely to be affected by the proposed conduct, or, alternatively and on a different version, for the moral agent per se. In the unlikely possibility that all available alternatives for choice and action involve only different degrees of painful consequences and thus have no positive value as pleasures, the hedonist thesis would regard as morally right that act or rule which would generate the least degree and smallest amount of painful consequences. What makes all these procedures morally right is the intrinsic value or goodness of the resultant pleasure and/or the intrinsic disvalue of the resultant pain, since, on the hedonistic theory, pleasure and the absence of pain are the only intrinsic locus of moral value.

But even this preliminary formulation raises a number of clarificatory questions whose answers will subdivide different and partly opposed versions of hedonism itself. (1) The first question raises the issue as to what sort of pleasure should be pursued relative to degrees of intensity and immediacy. What I will call *activistic* hedonism holds in general that a person should morally pursue those pleasures that involve the propensity for sensualistic indulgence (food and sex are obvious examples) and that offer the most immediate temporal prospect of fulfillment and the highest quantity of realization (the greatest amount of intense pleasure at the earliest possible time). Aristippus and the ancient Greek school of Cyrenaicism were reputed to have held this sort of view. And even the philosophy of Jeremy Bentham included, among his criteria for measuring the quantity of pleasure, the standards of intensity

of hedonistic naturalism:

7.6a) identifies pleasure (and the absence of pain) as the sole intrinsic moral good.

7.7) This is clearly a teleological theory, since pleasure and pain are consequential;

7.8) if the consequences are all painful, the morally right course would be the one with the least painful effect.

7.9) Contrasts within hedonism:

7.9a) activistic *vs.* passivistic hedonism: 7.10) pleasure as active and immediate sensualistic indulgence *vs.*

and temporal immediacy (which he generally called propinquity), although he moderated these standards with others that tended to balance out the calculation in such a way as to avoid any extremes that might result from intensity and propinquity alone. In contrast to activistic hedonism there is the interpretive slant that I will designate as *passivistic* hedonism: this perspective emphasizes the passive and, in a way, negative ideal which construes the ideal of pleasure as tranquility or serenity along with freedom from pain, so far as that can be achieved. The worst pains are regarded as those that involve psychological turmoil, anxiety, and disorientation, and the greatest pleasure is found in a peace of mind or soul from which all this is absent. The Greek philosopher Epicurus and his later Roman disciple Lucretius represent this outlook; and in fact, most later hedonists have tended to de-emphasize the pleasures of active sensualistic indulgence, even if they did not oppose those pleasures in the fashion of Epicurus and Lucretius. And this de-emphasis and opposition are not without good reason: opting for the most intense present pleasures is in numerous ways counter-productive. Indulgence in such immediate pleasures is subject to the law of diminishing returns: the more frequent and full the indulgence, the less the amount of pleasure—even to the point of ennui and boredom which involve no positive pleasure at all. It is also a well-known feature of sensualistic indulgence that it brings many painful consequences in its wake; and hence the pursuit of such indulgent pleasure is a mark of shortsightedness even from a more balanced hedonistic point of view. There is, furthermore, the danger and even the likelihood that the pursuit of active sensual pleasures will make the individual into a slave of his or her passions and thus destroy the self-control that seems essential to the morally good life. Finally, and perhaps worst of all, the disintegrative effect of sensual pleasures as ends in themselves deprives a person of the very serenity or tranquility of mind that, for these critics, will bring the individual the greatest quantity of pleasure in the long run, not to mention the least amount of pain.

7.10a) pleasure as passive or negative tranquility or serenity

7.11) The arguments of Epicurus and Lucretius against activistic hedonism:

7.12) Egoistic *vs.* altruistic hedonism: pleasure for oneself *vs.* pleasure for all sentient creatures likely to be affected;

(2) A second question that arises from the general definition of hedonism is the question as to whose pleasure the individual hedonist is morally obligated to pursue. *Egoistic* hedonism is the view that it is the moral obligation

of individuals always to choose and act in such a way as to maximize pleasure and minimize pain *for themselves* in the long run. This does not mean that egoistic hedonists will never act in such a way as to promote the hedonistic well-being of other persons (much less that they will set out to act on principle in such a way as to undermine the hedonistic well-being of those others); but it does mean that their reason for pursuing anyone else's well-being will always be that doing so is the most effective way of pursuing their own. And there is the widely debated doctrine of the spontaneous harmony of all egoisms, according to which, if individuals truly and wisely act in such a way as to maximize pleasure and minimize pain for themselves in the long run, then, barring any error of calculation, they also are acting in such a way as to achieve the same result for all other persons likely to be affected by the consequences of their choice or act. I do not know whether this doctrine is invariably born out in practice; but, if we assume the plausible thesis that most persons are out to feather their own nest at whatever cost to others, it would appear that no even approximately stable social order would be possible at all unless such a spontaneous harmony held true for the most part. In any case, an egoistic hedonist who follows out this theory in practice is not necessarily (or even at all) a blatantly selfish individual, even though he or she is self-promoting in policy. On the other hand, *universalistic*, or *altruistic*, or *utilitarian* hedonism is the view that individuals are morally and directly obligated to act in such a way as to maximize pleasure and minimize pain, not only for themselves, but for all persons whose well-being is likely to be affected by their choices and/or acts. They themselves are to be counted in the calculation, but they are to be counted as no more than one among others, each of whom possesses the same right to consideration as the utilitarian hedonists themselves. The modern classical defenders of this view were Jeremy Bentham and John Stuart Mill; but many subsequent thinkers, especially in the English-speaking philosophical community, have embraced this tradition as well, including especially Henry Sidgwick, S.E. Toulmin, J.J.G. Smart, and even John Rawls. These various utilitarian hedonists are divided on the question whether every individual act should be judged by the principle of utility (the greatest hedonistic good for the greatest

7.12a) the egoistic justification of promoting the well-being of others: the spontaneous harmony of egoisms:

7.12b) The utilitarian or altruistic version of hedonism:

7.13) Act-utilitarian *vs.* rule-utilitarian views:

number)—that view is called *act* utilitarianism—or whether it is general rules that should be judged in their hedonistic utility—that view is called *rule* utilitarianism. While I think this an important distinction, the exploration of it is so involved and technical that my exposition, comprehensive and general as it purports to be, can give it only modest consideration. The main argument in favor of act utilitarianism is the claim that rules are themselves in fact merely shorthand summaries of individual judgments about the rightness and wrongness of particular acts, so that while such generalizations may be very useful rules of thumb for application to moral decision and choice, nevertheless these rules take no priority over the moral judgments about individual acts of which the rules in fact are the summary. The main argument for rule utilitarianism is the claim that whenever individuals judge a particular act to be right or wrong, they are, whether consciously or not, subsuming it under a universal rule, since they are assuming that any act of the same description in morally relevant similar circumstances would and should be judged to have the same moral property as the act they are judging; for otherwise, their judgment would be merely the idiosyncratic expression of their own personal preferences, and not therefore a properly moral judgment at all. While I myself am strongly inclined to the rule version, I will carry the issue no further in this context, since I do not regard a decision on the matter as seriously affecting the question of the overall plausibility or implausibility of the utilitarian theory in general (although I recognize and respect the position of those who differ with my opinion, I myself will not treat the issue as crucial in my criticism). It is more important to ask for a defense of universalistic hedonism against the contrasting view of egoistic hedonism. In general, there seems to be no objective reason to give exclusive moral consideration to one person as over against giving equal consideration to all persons likely to be affected by the choice or act of the agent. Any plausible argument for treating oneself as an end (as being intrinsically valuable in the moral sense) will be just that plausible as an argument for treating any and all persons as ends in the same way, since such an argument will invariably ground itself in qualities that persons share rather than in purely idiosyncratic characteristics. It can even be argued that a perspective that

7.14) Defense of universalistic hedonism against the egoistic version:
7.15) no plausible reason for selecting one person (rather than another) as a moral end;

radically relativizes moral judgment exclusively to a particular individual (the agent) is not really a moral perspective at all, since it places the agent under no objective principle of universal moral obligation. A further argument, to similar effect, is that egoistic hedonism (or any other egoistic ethical theory) would totally pervert the institution of moral advice and counsel—which is an important, if not essential aspect of morality as a whole. For if egoistic hedonists consistently follow out their theory, they will be bound to give any moral advisee or counselee the advice that would further their own personal hedonistic well-being rather than that of the person being advised—and that is not the point of moral advice at all. More generally, egoistic hedonism is involved in a pervasive incoherence or existential contradiction, since it holds universally that every agent should act (and choose) in such a way as to maximize pleasure and minimize pain for that agent, while in fact if persons formulating the theory were actually following this theory in the formulation consistently, they should be claiming that they alone should act in this way and that all other agents should act in such a way as to further, not their own, but the egoistic hedonist's well-being. That comes very close to saying (if it does not actually say) that no one can recommend egoism as a universal moral practice without rendering impossible its practice in his or her own case and in the case of any other person making such a recommendation. This is seemingly an inescapable predicament for the egoistic hedonist.

(3) A third question raises the issue as to whether the only morally significant differences among various sorts of pleasure are merely quantitative in nature, or whether some pleasures are intrinsically better than others as such, irrespective of quantitative considerations. I shall use the designation *quantitative* hedonism to refer to the view first mentioned, to the effect that pleasures differ in worth or value only in a quantitative sense, and the designation *qualitative* hedonism to refer to the view that, while the quantitative aspects of pleasure are morally significant, nevertheless certain types of pleasure are in themselves of greater moral value, irrespective or regardless of their evaluation by purely quantitative standards. In particular, John Stuart Mill, the principal defender of qualitative hedonism in classical philosophical history, claimed that mental pleasures

7.16) egoistic view incapable of formulating a universal objective principle;

7.17) egoistic view makes the giving of moral advice impertinent;

7.18) egoistic view is contradictory in holding that every agent universally should act out of self-interest, since that would undermine his or her own self-interest;

7.19) quantitative hedonism *vs.* qualitative hedonism: pleasures differ only in quantitative respects *vs.* some pleasures qualitatively superior to others.

7.20) Mill's defense of the qualitative superiority of mental pleasures on the ground that those capable of fully experiencing both kinds of pleasure invariably prefer mental over bodily pleasures

(intellectual understanding and aesthetic appreciation, in particular) were in themselves and as such of greater moral worth than bodily pleasures, entirely apart from quantitative criteria of assessment. It would be better to be Socrates, capable of the highest mental pleasures but frustrated in the fulfillment of them, than to be a pig, wholly satiated with the pleasures of sensualistic indulgence but incapable by nature of enjoying mental pleasures at all—better, as he put it, to be Socrates dissatisfied than a pig satisfied. And if the pig were (per impossible) of a different opinion, that would only be on the ground that the pig was incapable of the higher pleasures attendant upon the fullest exercise of human mental capacities. Should anyone ask for a supporting argument for such a qualitative hedonism, Mill's best answer is that persons capable of experiencing both mental pleasures and bodily pleasures invariably regard the former as intrinsically better than the latter, even though they might prefer that indulgence in the two types be moderately and harmoniously balanced. It is often claimed that the position of Epicurus (and Lucretius) was essentially qualitative hedonism as well. But that is not the way I read either the fragments of Epicurus or the treatise (*De Rerum Natura—On the Nature of Things*) of Lucretius. Both of these thinkers agreed with the claim that mental pleasures were better than bodily pleasures; but as I interpret them, they thought so on the ground that mental pleasures would, on the whole and in the long run, produce a greater total quantity of pleasure for the individual, as well as a smaller quantity of pain. As Epicurus and Lucretius saw it, mental pleasures involved none of the disadvantages of bodily pleasures: the pursuit of them brought no painful consequences in their wake, it was not subject to the principle of diminishing returns, and it certainly produced no ennui or boredom for the truly wise and committed. Quite the reverse in fact, since Epicurus, followed by Lucretius, held that the study of philosophy was by far the most pleasant of all experiences for those who had the capacity and the will to undertake it; and rather than losing its appeal in the continuation of its pursuit, philosophy became but more stimulating, exciting, and challenging, since, unlike the pursuit of bodily pleasures, the same amount of energy expended in philosophical reflection brought an even greater hedonistic return with the passage

7.20a) Epicurus' and Lucretius' defense of mental pleasures on quantitative grounds

of time. Yet, despite their preoccupation with mental pleasures, Epicurus and Lucretius were nonetheless quantitative hedonists and would have disagreed with Mill's claim that mental pleasures were better regardless of quantitative considerations; but they would have held as well (no doubt Mill would have agreed) that the most satisfied pig would, in the same stretch of time, have enjoyed a much smaller quantity of pleasurable consequences over painful ones than even a moderately indulgent devotee of mental pleasures and especially of philosophy. Certainly Jeremy Bentham was a quantitative hedonist as well and thus also disagreed with his brilliant student, Mill. For him, quantitative considerations alone were of valuational and moral consequence. Thus he developed a calculus of hedonistic measurement involving a plurality of standards for making the calculation: intensity, duration, degree of certainty, temporal proximity, productiveness of other pleasurable consequences, elimination of painful consequences (purity, he termed it), and social extension. Indeed, Bentham virtually immortalized his view in one of the most quoted philosophical epithets of all time: 'The quantity of pleasure being the same, pushpin [a simple game] is as good as poetry!' But of course, Bentham never seriously supposed that, with the same expenditure of time and energy by those capable of appreciating both pushpin and poetry to the full, the quantity of pleasure would ever actually *be* the same. So much, then, for the clarification of hedonism as a normative ethical perspective. 7.20b) Bentham's defense of quantitative hedonism as essential to moral calculation

What supporting arguments, then, can be offered in support of this grand moral tradition? The main argument that has been offered in support of ethical hedonism historically (and which I have found expressed in either explicit or implicit form in all the hedonistic writers I have investigated) involves a logically distinguishable doctrine called *psychological* hedonism, which is not an ethical doctrine at all but a piece of purportedly descriptive psychology. This is the doctrine that the decisive causal influence or ground of every consciously motivated human act is the desire to pursue (or maximize) pleasure and avoid (or minimize) pain for the agent himself. In its strongest version, the claim is made that human agents are psychologically incapable of bringing themselves to decisive action on any other basis. But of course this is not to say that individuals always or 7.21) Arguments in support of hedonism:

7.22) the argument from psychological hedonism;
7.23) the decisive and determining cause of every consciously motivated human act is the desire to pursue pleasure and avoid pain;

even characteristically succeed in realizing this objective; it is merely to say that this is always their intended (but not necessarily acknowledged) objective. If they fail, it is always because of some kind of ignorance on their part: either an ignorance of relevant facts, or an ignorance of the predictable effects of their actions, or a failure to take a long-range view of the hedonic elements of those consequences. Individuals regularly claim, indeed, that they are following other motives (duty, or selfless love, or benevolence, etc.); but all these alternative motives can be reinterpreted as hedonistically motivated. And when individuals are wholly frank and honest in assessing their own motives, they invariably acknowledge the same to themselves, although most persons manage to avoid this sort of blatantly honest self-assessment. There is, in fact, an easily performed mental experiment, that any reflective person can perform, which will support psychological hedonism. Suppose you are trying to control the behavior of other persons: it is clear that, if you assume that, like angels, they will always act with unexceptionable self-disinterestedness, your predictions of their behavior will fail miserably; but it is also clear that if you assume that they will act in such a way as, in their own opinion, to maximize pleasure and minimize pain for themselves in the relatively short range with which most people are alone concerned, your properly drawn predictions of their behavior will turn out to be astonishingly accurate. Indeed, applied social and political sanctions are invariably employed on this latter assumption. Teachers like myself, for example, realize this all too well: that is why they give examinations to constrain students to do, from the threat of penalty (pain), what they would rarely if ever do out of enlightened self-interest, since they are incapable, for the most part, of even envisioning it.

In any case, the first premise of our argument is the claim that psychological hedonism is true. The second premise is that psychological hedonism implies (at least in a loose and informal sense) that ethical hedonism is also true, that individuals ought always to act on such hedonistic motivation. Strictly speaking, of course, even if it were a fact that individuals always acted and chose on hedonistic grounds in their own behalf, that would certainly not entail directly that they ought morally to act on such grounds, unless one supplies an additional premise or premises. And some of the

7.23a) any failure is due to some kind of ignorance;

7.23b) all other purported motives are reinterpretable as hedonistically based;

7.23c) attempts at behavior control on this basis are generally successful and characteristically used in social control;

7.24) psychological hedonism loosely implies (or renders plausible) ethical hedonism;
7.25) this is not a strict logical entailment, since it reasons from a factual premise to a moral premise.

proposed candidates for filling in this blank are certainly implausible, if not downright fallacious. Mill, for example, argued in a notorious passage that, just as the only evidence for an object's being visible consists in the fact that people actually have a visual experience of it (they *see* it), so all the evidence needed to show that pleasure is morally desirable consists in the fact that people actually (and universally and unexceptionably) desire it. But this argument, as it stands, is clearly invalid, since the 'ble' suffix in the term *visible* is used with *one* meaning ('capable of being seen'), whereas in the term *desirable* it is used in an entirely distinct sense ('worthy of being desired'); yet that ambiguity is exactly the point at issue—namely, whether an end is *worthy* of being desired, in the moral sense, merely on the ground that it *is* desired (and of course therefore 'capable of being desired'). It would appear that this could be the case only if one accepted a hedonistic version of naturalistic definism—a position already judged critically inadequate in our previous discussion. But perhaps one could make the transition to ethical hedonism by arguing in the following way: if we suppose that there is *some* way in which persons ought morally to act and choose, and if acting on self-directed hedonistic motivation is the only way they ever *do* act or choose (or, more strongly, the only way they are *psychologically capable* of acting or choosing), and if it is absurd to argue that they ought to act in some way that they either never do act or psychologically cannot act; then it must be that acting in such a way as to maximize pleasure and minimize pain for themselves is the way they morally ought to act. To soften the shock of this bold claim, it has been pointed out by ethical hedonists that other supposed ultimate principles (almost) invariably include hedonistic well-being as an aspect or consequence of some supposed more inclusive moral ideal, that no ethical theory (not even that of Kant) regards hedonistic well-being as totally irrelevant to moral value, and that no end of human activity in the moral sense would be regarded as the true, complete, and ultimate good, if it totally excluded hedonistic well-being from its scope—a person, for example, who completely fulfilled his or her non-hedonistic duty, but was hedonistically miserable, would be regarded by no person of sense as living the morally best life conceivable. Putting this all together, the transition from psychological

7.26) Mill's argument, that pleasure ought to be desired merely because people generally desire it, is clearly fallacious and rests on an ambiguity in the term 'desirable.'

7.27) The transition would require hedonistic definism;

7.28) the transition from psychological to ethical hedonism seems more plausible:

7.29) if it is observed that no one can have a duty to act unless he or she is capable of doing so:

7.30) if it is noted that virtually all moral ideals include hedonistic well-being as an aspect.

hedonism to ethical hedonism, when supported by such supplemental considerations as premises, seems highly plausible, even if it is not a logically formal entailment. Or so it is claimed by ethical hedonists, at any rate.

There are, of course, a variety of other arguments for ethical hedonism, although most of them draw some degree of support from this main argument, as I have termed it. Jeremy Bentham, for example, claimed that the greatest happiness principle (the greatest hedonistic well-being for the greatest number of persons likely to be affected by an act or choice, or by its consequences) provided a universally applicable and objective standard of moral worth in comparison with which all other proposed standards would reduce in the end to subjectively variable and idiosyncratic preference. The principle is applicable in the sense that the hedonistic calculus involves a determination of moral worth through quantitative criteria, conformity to which is capable of being empirically measured, at least in principle, though it might be difficult in practice. The principle is objective in the sense that the truth value, of propositions expressing predictable quantitative increments of pleasure, is independent of any person's subjectively variable opinions or preferences; and it is also objective, in its utilitarian version, in the sense that it is universally and impartially applicable to all likely-to-be-affected persons, without giving any restricted or special consideration to a limited group of persons. Bentham also buttressed this argument by claiming that arguments used to support other supposed moral standards commonly appealed to the hedonistic consequences of conforming to those standards as a justification of those standards themselves, which therefore became subordinate to the greatest happiness principle; or if those arguments failed to make that appeal, they provided no effectively operative motive for conformity to the recommended principle in question. Presumably he regarded no motive as effectively operative if it did not appeal to self-interest, and he interpreted every appeal to self-interest as ultimately taking hedonistic form. Whether this procedure begs the question, for the main thrust of his argument, is at least a plausible critical challenge.

A standard criticism of hedonistic ethics is the claim that while hedonism regards the pursuit of pleasure as the sole object (directly or indirectly) of desire in general, it

7.31) The argument of Bentham from the universal applicability and objectivity of the hedonistic standard:

7.32) pleasure can be quantitatively measured by empirical criteria;

7.33) propositions expressing increments of pleasure are thus objectively either true or false;
7.34) the standard is impartially applicable;

7.35) arguments for other moral standards either appeal to hedonistic motivation or supply no effective motivation at all.

nonetheless seems evident that personal agents actually desire many other ends besides pleasure and pursue them as ultimate and intrinsically valuable ends—for example, the love of, and obedience to, God, or the pursuit of duty for its own sake alone. But if personal agents do in fact consciously pursue other ends than pleasure (for its own sake), that would appear to dislodge an important prop in support of at least psychological, and therefore indirectly ethical, hedonism. However, both John Stuart Mill and Henry Sidgwick acknowledge the factual basis of this critical claim: for them, as hedonistic utilitarians, we do often consciously pursue ends other than pleasure, and frequently we do so for the sake of those other ends themselves without any conscious reference to pleasure as the sole intrinsically valuable end. But this is no serious criticism of hedonism, since those other ends thus pursued can be reasonably construed as themselves parts or aspects of ultimate hedonistic well-being. It is not, for example, that, at our moral best, we pursue duty as an end with a view to achieving greater hedonistic happiness; it is rather that we pursue duty for its own sake as a fundamental constituent of hedonistic happiness. Furthermore, some of the most significant pleasures are best realized through the pursuit consciously of non-hedonistic ends. If, in fact, persons pursue duty, or friendship, or artistic appreciation, or even truth, with their minds consciously fixed on pleasure as their goal, they will render themselves less capable of pursuing these ends to their fullest; but if persons pursue them for their own sake, they will end up deriving more hedonistic happiness from them in the process. With a recognizably different slant to the same effect, Sidgwick argues, with regard to the principles Justice, Prudence, and Benevolence, that all three, as properly stated formal principles, are intuitively self-evident principles of moral obligation; but he argues, at the same time, that these principles supply no content or substance for the moral good to which they refer, and that the content needed can be supplied only by the pleasure principle of utilitarian hedonism. How else could one construe the determinate nature of the good to be impartially dispensed (justice), or to implement self-regard (prudence), or to will the best for other persons (benevolence)? In other words, intuitively self-evident and (in themselves) non-hedonistic

7.36) Argument from the interpretation of all other pursued ends as themselves aspects of hedonistic well-being, broadly construed;

7.37) if other ends than pleasure are pursued, even for their own sake,

7.38) they are fairly interpretable as elements of pleasure,

7.39) and their conscious pursuit of hedonistic grounds reduces the amount of pleasure achievable.

7.40) Other moral principles, even if self-evident, derive their content or substance from the pleasure principle;

moral principles depend, for their application in practice, on the hedonistic principle of happiness. Other moral ends than pleasure, therefore, are either themselves constituent elements of pleasure (hedonistic well-being), or they are channels through the principled structure of which such pleasure or well-being flows.

7.41) the argument from the approximate conformity of hedonism with the elements of popular morality, and the use of the hedonistic standard for solving popular moral conflicts;

Perhaps the most intriguing argument in support of ethical hedonism is again supplied by Sidgwick in his contention: first, that the virtues and ethical goals recognized in any well-developed system of popular morality exhibit a rough approximation or correspondence (sometimes even highly precise) to those that would be plausible on utilitarian hedonistic grounds; second, that, where popular morality is either ambiguous or inconsistent, opposing moral opinions, in any civilized society, are decided on utilitarian hedonistic grounds; and that, therefore, such a utilitarianism presents the most plausible explanation of all the data of human moral experience, while at the same time this ethical perspective provides an ethical ideal for the improvement and reconstruction of the popular morality which it thus explains. Of course, this complex contention is difficult to assess, since its empirical, anthropological, and sociological claims are so intricate and involved. It might well turn out that, since all normative ethical theories take the moral beliefs and practices of civilized societies as fundamental data, all well-formulated theories that take moral objectivism seriously (as utilitarian hedonism purports to do) would exhibit roughly the same degree of correspondence to popular morality, and provide roughly the same leverage for the recognition and elimination of the ambiguities and inconsistencies of popular morality. That would put all such theories on an equal par as satisfactory explanations of moral data, and would leave the systematic oppositions among the theories unresolved. None of this would surprise me: I have long since noticed, in my own reflections on such matters, that ethical theories as different as those of Aristotle, Kant, and Sidgwick might well exhibit a close and extensive correspondence in the actual moral advice provided in principle with regard to specific moral issues; and therefore, factoring in a correspondence of all of them to various schemes of popular morality would merely provide more ground for my observation, though it

7.42) this argument is difficult to assess, since all well-developed normative ethical theories, taking popular moral beliefs as data, may be expected to exhibit an analogous conformity;

7.43) this would leave the theoretical oppositions among different theories unresolved.

would contribute little (if anything) to resolving the issues at stake among various normative ethical theories. So much, then, by way of supporting arguments for hedonistic ethical theories of one sort or another.

By way of critical response to hedonistic ethical perspectives, perhaps the best starting point consists in raising the question how we are to construe the notion of pleasure and what kinds of intrinsic satisfaction are to be included in the range of that notion. It has already emerged that there is a striking difference between the immediate enjoyment of sensualistic indulgences, on the one hand, and the sort of developing satisfaction that comes from intellectual understanding, artistic appreciation, or personal friendship, on the other. At some level and to some extent, any activity or pursuit that human beings are motivated to indulge in on a continuing basis will involve a sustaining sense of satisfaction as an aspect of that activity or pursuit. Persons who, for example, after considerable moral struggle, firmly resolve to carry out a recognized moral duty, just because it is right that they do so, will achieve an elevated sense of satisfaction and delight in self-respect about which persons, whose chief satisfaction lies in a scheme of sexual promiscuity, know nothing. If therefore pleasure is construed so broadly as to include in its range every sort of satisfaction of which human agents are capable at every level of response, whether primarily physical and intense or primarily mental and moderate, then some sort of psychological hedonism will become true virtually by definition, since every positive (or even negative) feeling tone or satisfaction (or frustration) will become hedonistically relevant. It will be impossible, then, to think of any conceivable human activity with respect to which no such positive or negative influencing factors are pertinent. Whatever one decides to do, for whatever acknowledged motive, will be reinterpreted as grounded in hedonistic inclination or disinclination, or some combination thereof; there will thus be no conceivable counter-instances, no conceivable acts or choices that could possibly escape the universal trap of hedonistic motivation.

Now this outcome is a serious difficulty for psychological hedonism, which purports to be an empirically grounded psychological description of human motivation. But a genuine empirical generalization must be such that it is, at least

7.44) Criticisms of ethical hedonism:

7.44a) if pleasure is defined so broadly as to include every conceivable sort of satisfaction one might find in choosing or acting, then psychological hedonism would virtually be made true by definition, and could not be interpreted as an empirical generalization:

in principle, falsifiable: there must be conceivable instances of human motivation which, if they took place, would tend to disconfirm the generalization; and other conceivable instances of course, which, if they took place, would tend to confirm the generalization. If this were not the case, and if the doctrine of psychological hedonism were therefore compatible in principle with every conceivable instance of motivated human action, then the doctrine would not really be a descriptive empirical generalization at all, but an arbitrarily presupposed or quasi-*a priori* interpretive principle, a metaphysical dogma, if you please. Yet the doctrine is not the sort of formal principle of reason (like the law of contradiction, or the principle of causal universality, for example) that could reasonably be viewed as a genuinely *a priori* principle of reason. Whether the doctrine of psychological hedonism is plausible on these terms or not, is a question which I will leave to the thoughtful reader for decision.

7.45) for an empirical generalization must be, at least in principle and conceivably, falsifiable by possible counter-instances;
7.46) otherwise the doctrine would be an arbitrary presupposition or *a priori* dogma;

If, on the other hand, the doctrine of psychological hedonism is interpreted as an empirical generalization, and if negative counter-instances are therefore conceivable in principle, then two results will emerge, I suggest: the first is that the transition from psychological hedonism to ethical hedonism would be far less plausible then on the assumption that psychological hedonism is a universal and unexceptionable dogma or first principle, since now it will be possible in principle to conceive a vast range of motivated human actions that are not determined by the desire to maximize pleasurable consequences and minimize painful ones—the most that could be claimed empirically would be that personal agents often act out of hedonistic motivation, a thesis that few reflective thinkers doubt, but also a thesis from which any inference to ethical hedonism would be flimsy indeed. The second result would be that it is not at all difficult to identify actual types of human motivation which, in their operation, are not determined by the hedonistic principle. It is certainly clear, in fact, that, consciously at least, persons often desire other objects than pleasure, and that they also sometimes do so with no awareness, on their part, of pleasure as an end, much less the sole ultimate end. A lengthy list is unnecessary, but a few examples would be friendship, artistic beauty, knowledge of the truth, and ethical love. In some cases, these goals can be reinterpreted as

7.47) if psychological hedonism is subject to genuinely conceivable counter-instances,
7.47a) then in this weakened form, the doctrine would hardly provide any basis for ethical hedonism;

7.47b) persons often desire other objects than pleasure;

unconsciously or subconsciously being motivated by the desire for pleasure as an end. But this ploy merely leads to the difficulty previously discussed, since it tends to deprive psychological hedonism of its purported status as an empirical generalization. Furthermore, it is equally possible to qualify the examples in such a way as to exclude hedonistic motivation—that would be at least as plausible as the hedonist ploy. In any case, a person can never be *merely* desiring pleasure as such as his or her end, since then there would be no basis for desiring or choosing one object rather than another when the hedonistic yield is approximately the same for both; yet we often make such choices—choosing to listen to a symphony, let us say, rather than eat a meal from which we might expect approximately the same hedonistic result. Nor is it the case that we characteristically are conscious of any hedonistic calculation at all in such circumstances: one might prefer the symphony to the meal, but one would rarely cite any hedonistic estimate as the ground of one's preference. Perhaps it would be correct to say that we virtually never desire something as an end for the sake of pleasure: it may rather be the case, as both Aristotle and Joseph Butler maintained, that we choose things because we desire them as good in contributing to our own well-being in general, and that we derive pleasure from them because we desire them in the way indicated, rather than desiring them because we expect to derive pleasure from them. The case of the desire for the knowledge of the truth is a particularly apt example of this claim: when persons, aiming at rational objectivity in their judgment, attempt to decide a question of truth in a particular situation, they would find it necessary to suspend all influences involving non-rational desires, since failure to do so would be expected on the whole to distort that aim at rational objectivity in judgment. If it should be the case that their judgment as to the truth of a proposition were determined by whether or not, if true, the proposition would maximize their hedonistic yield, they could not themselves respect the decision they had made; and the rest of us, if we were privy to this situation, would regard them as clearly having failed in their aim at rational objectivity. Now while it is sometimes the case (often, we hope) that an objectively true judgment turns out to affect our hedonistic yield in a positive way, it is surely never the

7.48) surely one can never merely be desiring pleasure, since then we could not choose in cases for which hedonistic yield is the same for different alternatives:

7.48a) it is always possible to claim that we choose things for other reasons and, as a result, find pleasure in them;

7.48b) desire for truth is a plausible example;

7.49) in such a case the hedonistic motive would be counter-productive.

case that the judgment of it as objectively true can be justified on that happy hedonistic result. And if a critic claims that, just because of hedonistic determination, we can never put solid confidence in our attempt to realize rational objectivity in our judgments, that will be a good reason to put no confidence in his or her own judgment to that effect. Here then at least, in the case of the aim at rational objectivity, psychological hedonism is way off the mark.

7.50) Pleasure fails to conform to the logically formal criteria for valuational assessment;

In an earlier context, I mentioned and explained a set of logically formal criteria for rationally assessing alternative theories about the ultimately good or right in the moral sense: criteria such as objectivity, intrinsic or self-contained worth or authority, and fixity or changelessness. Does the criterion of pleasure as the sole ultimate good satisfy these criteria in the morally relevant sense? The term *pleasure* is an abstract term for a collection of feelings or emotive experiences on the part of sentient human beings. Now since feeling is wholly dependent on the awareness states of human subjects and is in that sense wholly subjective in its dependence on a particular person's psychological states, and since pleasure, for any given individual, is an interrelated collection and accumulation of such feelings, it seems clear that pleasure is not objective in its value or worth in the relevant criterial sense. The mere fact that there are objectively true propositions describing such states does not ground the requisite objectivity, since the value of a feeling experience clearly does not consist in the objective truth of propositions describing it; its worth rather consists in the subjective satisfaction derived from the feelings themselves by the person experiencing them. Thus the value of pleasure (as feeling experiences) is radically relative to the individual subject in precisely the relevant sense that is opposed to objectivity. And since the worth or value of pleasure is therefore not objective, then by the very nature of the case the value or worth or authority of pleasure is not intrinsic or self-contained; for even if the notion of a pleasure of which one is not aware is intelligible (which I doubt), such a pleasure has no worth or value in itself. As to the question of fixity or changelessness, and the criterial unity that a dependably fixed standard implies, pleasure, understood as a collection and accumulation of feeling experiences, is clearly transitory, variable, and intricately multiplied in its species. It is

7.51) as a collection of states, pleasure is subjective rather than objective in the relevant criterial sense, and is thus radically relative to the individual experiencing it;

7.52) as subjectively relative; the worth of pleasure is not self-contained;

7.53) nor is pleasure fixed or changeless as a criterion, since the satisfaction derived from it is radically variable for different individuals

perhaps the case that there are certain experiences that are regarded as in some degree pleasurable for all persons capable of having those experiences at all. Still the same experience, descriptively considered, involves markedly different levels of satisfaction for different individuals under approximately similar circumstances, and even for the same individual under even moderately altered circumstances; and the same sort of thing could be said about experiences generally regarded as painful for all persons. Furthermore, various types and degrees of pleasure (and pain) are so different from each other descriptively that no objective unit of measurement seems universally applicable to them; as a result pleasures are incommensurate and insusceptible of being cumulatively conceived or culminated in a unified totality. How, for example, would a person compare and judge, by means of a single fixed criterion, the hedonistic satisfaction derived from eating a dish of vanilla ice cream with that of making progress toward the solution of a complicated philosophical problem? The question seems unanswerable. In summary, pleasure, understood descriptively as experienced by actual persons, simply does not conform to the logically formal properties that are requisite for an objective standard of the ultimately good or right.

To consider a further difficulty of ethical hedonism which, as a difficulty, is closely related to the previous critical problem, it is important to note that the practical applicability of the pleasure principle in the solution of particular moral problems depends on an empirical estimate of the hedonic consequences of alternative options for choice or action. But the possibility of such a calculation holds with such imprecision that it makes appropriately grounded judgments of moral goodness or rightness all but practically impossible. This is partly due to the previously noted problem that pleasure as a standard lacks the logically formal properties required for functioning as such a standard. But it is partly based on other grounds as well: since the hedonic consequences of an act are indefinitely extended into the future, it is not at all clear whether even the most careful investigator could judge any calculation as objectively sufficient to support a judgment of moral rightness or wrongness that could be expected to hold up under the scrutiny of future experience (in a sense, of course, this difficulty

and for the same individual at different times and in different circumstances;

7.54) various types of pleasure are so different that their relative worth cannot be compared.

7.55) An empirical estimate of the hedonic consequences of an act or choice is all but practically impossible:

7.56) partly because pleasure is radically subjective;

7.57) partly because the consequences are indefinitely extended;

applies to any teleological version of the relation between rightness and goodness, although the difficulty is especially acute for hedonism, since it functions with a criterion which is itself incapable of functioning as a single unified standard). Again, the judgmental capacity of an individual, in making such a calculation, is so radically variable with unpredictable mood swings and changes of overall emotional state, that any chance of achieving rational objectivity of moral judgment under such circumstances is a distant prospect indeed. Pertinent, as well, to the practical possibility of calculating the hedonic consequences of alternative options, is the empirically observed fact that a person's conscious preoccupation with empirical estimates of pleasure is self-destructive in actually altering the amount of pleasure or pain derived from various types of action. Persons would hardly derive the same amount of pleasure, for example, from sexual intercourse with their spouse (or anyone else, for that matter), if they were throughout preoccupied with calculating the exact amount of sensual pleasure derived from the experience, if indeed they were capable of having the experience at all under such circumstances. As Spinoza long ago observed, the most effective way to disarm the appeal of an emotionally charged experience is to subject it to objective rational scrutiny in the process. For all these reasons, one might well ponder whether, on such hedonistic grounds, persons could ever make a moral judgment with any rational confidence.

7.58) partly because the judgmental capacity of an individual for the calculation is radically variable;

7.59) partly because conscious preoccupation with hedonistic calculation is counter-productive.

Suppose, in the next place, that John Stuart Mill is right in regarding mental pleasures as intrinsically better than sensual and bodily pleasures regardless of quantitative considerations (suppose, in other words, that qualitative hedonism is correct): if that were the case, as many critics have pointed out, then there would have to be some standard, other than the pleasure common to both types, to establish that qualitative valuational superiority for mental pleasures (the pleasures attending the exercise of our higher faculties). But in that event it would follow that pleasure as such would not be the sole intrinsic good, since that alternative standard would take valuational precedence over mere pleasure: and that in turn would be the end of a consistent ethical hedonism. If, on the other hand, qualitative hedonism is denied, so that, as Bentham contended, 'pushpin is

7.60) If some pleasures are qualitatively superior to others, a non-hedonistic criterion is implied,

as good as poetry,' there will be no plausible way to explain the obvious incongruity or incommensurateness of different sorts of pleasure as markedly distinct as the enjoyment of a favorite food and the satisfaction of contemplating a work of art like Beethoven's Ninth Symphony. So hedonism in ethics is faced with a baffling dilemma: either to accept the qualitative distinction between mental pleasures and bodily pleasures, and thus undermine the consistency and universality of the hedonistic criterion, or to reject that distinction and attempt to conflate all qualitatively distinct types of pleasure into a single type subject to a unitary standard, quantitative in nature, and thus implausibly ignore the distinctions in question. I have no vested interest in arguing this issue further, except to say that I am on Mill's side of this issue, and to observe that either horn of the dilemma poses a serious, if not insuperable, difficulty for any doctrine of ultimate ethical hedonism.

7.61) while, if this superiority is denied, it seems impossible to explain the incongruity of different types of pleasure.

A final critical difficulty of ethical hedonism in general can be spelled out as follows: any adequate normative ethical theory is logically responsible for providing a reasonable explanation, in terms of its ultimate ethical standard, of all the significant functions of moral reasoning and judgment, one of which is the concept of moral obligation or moral oughtness. Does ethical hedonism make sense as a standard of moral obligation or moral oughtness? Or, put another way, can the pleasure motive ever form an adequate basis for assigning a moral duty as incumbent on a particular individual? Under certain realistically conceivable circumstances one might argue that the hedonistic consequences of an act would justify the act as right in the sense of being morally permissible (or morally acceptable). But is it plausible to claim that a person has a moral *obligation* to maximize pleasure and minimize pain for himself? I might, for example, justify being a teacher rather than an insurance salesman (assuming I have the capacity for both occupations) on the ground that I would derive greater hedonistic satisfaction from being a teacher. But surely no right-thinking person would say, on that hedonistic ground alone, that I had any moral *duty* to be a classroom teacher, however justified morally I might be in making such a decision. A critic might ask about the consequences of my choice for other persons besides myself in this connection.

7.62) Pleasure, as an ultimate criterion, cannot provide a justifying basis for judgments of moral duty or obligation;

7.63) while the pleasure principle might render the pursuit of pleasure morally permissible, it could never render it morally obligatory;

It is, I think, wholly reasonable to claim that I ought not to inflict unnecessary suffering or pain on other persons, and that obligation would then be a moral duty. But is it at all clear that my duty in this sense is grounded in any moral obligation to maximize pleasure and minimize pain for all other persons likely to be affected by my act? The moral duty to avoid inflicting unnecessary suffering on other persons, as a purely negative duty of refraining, even if carried out as fully as possibly, would not necessarily even minimize pain, much less maximize pleasure, although it would presumably involve less pain or suffering for those likely to be affected. Hence, the moral obligation involved (the duty to avoid inflicting unnecessary pain or suffering) neither entails the hedonistic standard nor is it grounded upon that standard, so that the obligation must have some other basis or ground, although I will not speculate at this point as to what that other foundation might be. I therefore take it that no moral obligation or duty, whether to oneself or to any other person, is incumbent on any individual to actualize (or attempt to actualize) the hedonistic standard, even though, under a wide variety of realistically conceivable circumstances, it would be morally right (i.e., permissible) and even good (i.e., commendable) either to do so or to attempt to do so. Actions that have the full hedonistic aim are, when performed, supererogatory deeds; that is, it is morally good to perform them, but not morally obligatory. On reflection, I cannot identify any moral duty, that any individual has in ordinary circumstances, to follow the full hedonistic aim in his or her actions; and I suggest that any reader who disagrees should attempt to provide some clear example of such a duty, always bearing in mind that the fact that an act is morally commendable does not provide a sufficient ground for judging it to be morally obligatory as well. Of course, if one adds some non-hedonistic stipulation that does not itself follow from the hedonistic principle, the situation changes. Suppose I voluntarily promise or agree to attempt always to follow the full hedonistic aim in my dealings with others; in that case, I would be obligated to do so, and thus I would be what is often called a philanthropist. But the duty would rest on my *prima facie* obligation to keep my promise—an obligation quite independent of the hedonistic principle. I therefore conclude that ethical hedonism

---

7.64) there is a duty to avoid inflicting unnecessary pain or suffering, but it is not clear that this duty is hedonistic in its basis, since the duty certainly does not entail the hedonistic standard;

7.65) at most, a hedonistically grounded action might be right as permissible, but never obligatory as a moral duty, unless supported by some independent moral principle;

provides no adequate foundation for a very large class of moral judgments, namely, those that assign or recognize moral duty or obligation.

I have already argued in an earlier context that utilitarian or universalistic hedonism is right in rejecting any egoistic version of hedonism. Whatever reason there is for believing that one person's hedonistic well-being is good objectively is at the same time a reason for believing that every person's hedonistic well-being is good objectively, so that to whatever extent it is a duty morally to actualize one's own well-being hedonistically (a point I have just challenged above, however), it would also be a duty morally to actualize the hedonistic well-being of other persons likely to be affected by one's choice or action, so far as that is possible in a given set of circumstances. But that does not mean that hedonistic utilitarianism itself is unblemished as a normative ethical perspective. It is, for instance, very difficult to see how hedonistic utilitarianism can reasonably count on any support from the doctrine of psychological hedonism; for there seems to be no way of arguing plausibly that persons, who by hypothesis are always motivated efficaciously to pursue their own hedonistic well-being (assuming knowledge of that well-being and of the most effective way of achieving it), have any moral obligation or duty to pursue the well-being of all other persons likely to be affected by one's own pursuit, except so far as one does so as a means merely to one's own hedonistic well-being (but that would be egoistic hedonism, not utilitarian hedonism). Yet that is exactly how John Stuart Mill and many other hedonists do in fact argue, and hence argue fallaciously. As Sidgwick argues, the only way to support the utilitarian claim, that persons have a moral obligation to support the hedonistic interests of other persons, is to suppose that, quite independently of the hedonistic principle, persons have a moral obligation to support the personal well-being of others as such on the basis of non-hedonistic moral principles (like justice and benevolence), and that the only plausible way of acting in accordance with those independent moral principles would consist in acting on the hedonistic principle itself. But this would be a seriously compromised utilitarian hedonism, since it involves the recognition of non-hedonistic moral principles, so that pleasure would not be the sole ultimate good after all.

7.66) while universalistic hedonism is logically preferable to egoistic hedonism, the former is subject to criticism:

7.67) it cannot logically derive support from psychological hedonism.

7.68) It could be argued plausibly only in conjunction with other non-hedonistic moral principles (such as justice and benevolence).

7.69) Utilitarian hedonism does not as such provide any means of deciding among alternative methods of distributing hedonistic well-being;	Closely related to this last criticism is the oft-mentioned fact that the principle of utilitarian hedonism contains a serious ambiguity which, it appears, cannot be resolved on hedonistic grounds alone. The principle as such is concerned with maximizing total pleasurable consequences and minimizing total painful consequences for all those likely to be affected by one's choice or action. But the principle in itself does not entail any means of distributing hedonistic well-being among such persons as are affected in a particular case. Are those persons to be considered individually or as a group? Suppose a set of alternatives such that, on one alternative, the total positive hedonic consequences for the group of those affected are much larger in quantity then on the other, but the amounts are very unevenly distributed among the individuals in the group; while, on the other alternative, even though the total positive hedonic consequences are much smaller in quantity, nevertheless the available amounts are more evenly distributed among the individuals composing the group, all of whose members have a positive hedonic balance. What would be the morally right choice under such circumstances, and on what basis could the choice be justifiably made? There seems to be no way of answering this type of question (and other similar types of question) on hedonistic grounds alone and without the introducing of a non-hedonistic principle of justice or equality of consideration for individuals considered separately. On hedonistic grounds alone, the first alternative would be morally correct, but impartial moral judges would most certainly opt for the second alternative, precisely because showing impartiality involves the sort of principle of justice or equality of consideration just indicated. It would seem that utilitarian hedonism provides no adequate basis of judgment concerning alternative means of distributing increments of hedonistic well-being.
7.70) even if an uneven distribution produced a larger total quantity of pleasure, a more even distribution with a lesser total might be reasonably deemed more just.	
7.71) In any case, the hedonistic principle could provide no method of distribution, except through a supplementary non-hedonistic principle of justice or equality of consideration.	
7.72) General conclusions about normative ethical hedonism: 7.73) critical difficulties summarized;	What general conclusions, then, can be drawn as to the adequacy of hedonism, either in general or in its specific types, as a normative ethical theory? In the light of critical examination, I judge ethical hedonism to be seriously inadequate as a comprehensive normative ethical perspective: its dependence on the doctrine of psychological hedonism, as its main argumentative support, provides little or no foundation for ethical hedonism, partly because psychological

hedonism does not imply ethical hedonism, except in conjunction with highly debatable additional premises, and partly because psychological hedonism is itself a highly debatable doctrine; pleasure, as a standard of moral judgment and assessment, lacks the principal formal characteristics requisite to any purportedly objective moral standard, and in fact pleasure, as a standard, implies the radical subjectivity of all such judgment and assessment, so that it reduces to radical ethical relativism in the end; the practical problems, attending the estimation of the relevant hedonic consequences of any given act or choice with a view to the formation of any moral claim, are so extensive as to make the formation of any such claim all but unachievable in practice; and finally, ethical hedonism provides no adequate basis for judgments of moral duty or obligation on rationally plausible grounds. Furthermore, while utilitarian hedonism is philosophically far more plausible than egoistic hedonism, the former is itself attended by numerous problems that appear unresolvable, since it depends on non-hedonistic principles for whatever plausibility it possesses, and since it cannot, in principle, supply any objectively reasonable ground for distributing the means of pleasure among individual persons. For all these reasons, it seems appropriate to conclude that pleasure is not the sole ultimate and intrinsic good, on the foundation of which all objectively formulated moral judgments can be reasonably grounded.

And yet, even though pleasure, as a standard of moral evaluation, lacks comprehensive and systematic adequacy, there is no good reason for regarding the hedonic consequences of human behavior as morally irrelevant altogether. Pleasure may not be the ultimate, intrinsic, and supreme moral good; but it nevertheless is a good (one among others) that must be taken into consideration in the formulation of moral judgments, since it seems so obviously an ingredient in what I will call complete and total human well-being. No one, I have previously argued, has a moral obligation to maximize pleasure and minimize pain either for oneself or for anyone else, but each person has a moral right to pursue goals that bring pleasure (and the relative absence of pain) in their wake more fully than alternative courses of conduct open to him or her, *unless* the pursuit of it in this indirect way would contribute to either one's own self-destruction as a person

7.74) but pleasure is nevertheless a good in the morally relevant sense, and an essential ingredient in human well-being;

7.75) while following the pleasure motive is never a duty as such, it is a permissible goal, unless its pursuit runs counter to other aspects of moral goodness;

Normative Ethical Naturalism

or that of others, or would bring unnecessary pain and suffering on those likely to be affected by the consequences of one's action. Furthermore, it is certainly morally permissible and even morally commendable to perform, whether occasionally or habitually, such supererogatory deeds as will tend, in all probability, to increase pleasurable consequences and decrease painful ones (with the same restrictions just noted above) for other persons; even if no person has any moral obligation to do so. Moral duty or obligation is an important and major element in moral philosophy; but it is not the whole of it, and humanity is fortunate indeed that many persons extend their own moral goodness by going far beyond the call of sheer duty in subserving the well-being of other persons. Certainly a life that exhibited the fullest conformity humanly possible to moral duty, but was totally devoid of any satisfaction or enjoyment in the pursuit of it and of other morally inconsequential activities, would not be the best sort of human life even from the point of view of an entirely moralistic standard of evaluation. Not only the pleasures attending the exercise of our higher faculties, but also those deriving from the morally appropriate satisfaction of our propensity for sensualistic indulgence, can be and are positive aspects of the fullest morally good life conceivable. To eat, drink, and be merry, therefore, is not the ultimate end of life; but it can be and is an element in the achievement of the complete and perfect moral good.[1] For all this there is a time, a place, and a situation, even though it is not for every time, place, and situation.

7.75a) this includes both the pursuit of one's own pleasure as well as the furthering of pleasure for others;

7.75b) the morally best life would include hedonistic satisfaction as an important element;

7.76) the range of morally permissible pleasure extends even to sensualistic indulgence within the limits set by other aspects of the moral good.

Humanistic Naturalism

7.77) Humanistic naturalism identifies the ultimate good (for humans) as the actualization of the propensities and capacities of human personhood in both individual and social harmony;

If, therefore, it seems lopsided and unbalanced to suppose that a person's true moral good is grounded upon, and capable of completion through, such a limited value as pleasure, then perhaps it will be deemed more reasonable to suppose that pleasure is a segment of a much more complex ideal of goodness, through all the aspects of which the multiple, varied, and especially the distinctive capacities of human persons, can be brought to a balanced and integrated fulfill-

---

[1] But of course only within the limits implied earlier in the paragraph, so that any kind or degree of eating, drinking, or merriment, that results in or tends toward either personal destruction or unnecessary suffering, is excluded.

ment in a comprehensive ideal of human personhood that involves the realization of the harmony of all these elements in both individual persons and the social relationships in which they stand to each other. That the ultimate and objective good for human beings consists in such an ideal of authentic personhood, is the claim of humanistic naturalism. On such a vision of the true and ultimate good, individual persons are regarded each as intrinsically valuable in the eyes of all (ideally, at least); but at the same time each person must earn his or her right to respect as intrinsically valuable by aiming at such an ideal of human personhood as an individual and by attempting to implement and reinforce a complex of social relationships in which every other person, at least in principle, has the opportunity realistically to strive toward this same goal, so that human beings are both means and ends, each to all and all to each, in a comprehensive social community (which, for the fullest such vision, embraces the whole of humanity). Hence, such a perspective is properly designated as *humanistic* in its sole and comprehensive concern with such an ideal of human personhood. Yet the vision is *naturalistic*, since all the elements of the moral ideal are embraced in the various aspects of human existence as itself emerging in and sustained by the natural order, of which human beings (at least relative to *our* experience) may properly be viewed as the crowning achievement: here there is no transcendent essence of moral and metaphysical goodness, no timeless and eternal law of universal reason of which humanity is, in some sense, the projected shadow, and no self-existent personal God whose moral nature provides the clue and ground of human moral goodness (although a humanist like Aristotle believes in a personal God, but makes no significant use of the idea in clarifying the ideal of human moral goodness). On the contrary, humanity's entire potential for moral goodness is intrinsic and self-contained, yet in such a way that a person should view this central core of humanity's being *qua* humanity as constituting the moral authority through which that being can be actualized through intelligent and self-disciplined effort and struggle.

Thinkers who share this moral and social vision are individually characterized by unique and even contrasting emphases that distinguish them each from the rest. My intention is to develop four paradigms of the moral ideal I

7.77a) human beings are reciprocally regarded as intrinsically valuable, although each earns his or her right to respect from others by acting to implement the well-being of all;

7.77b) as focused on humankind (humanistic) and grounded in nature (naturalistic), this view rejects any transcendent basis for moral goodness.

7.78) Varieties of humanistic naturalism:

have summarized in general terms. The first, which I shall designate as *realistic* humanism, is provided by the moral philosophy of Aristotle (384–322 BC); the second, which I shall designate as *pragmatic* humanism, is exemplified in the ethical perspective of the American philosopher John Dewey (1859–1952); the third, which I shall designate as *existential* humanism, finds its focus in the work of the French philosopher Jean-Paul Sartre (1905–1991); and finally the fourth, which I shall designate as *evolutionary* humanism, confronts us in the philosophy of Friedrich Nietzsche (1844–1900). The choice of these model thinkers for the discussion of ethical humanism, is of course to some extent arbitrary; but the selections represent, in my opinion, both the most widely discussed and the most effective versions of the perspective, while at the same time (perhaps) illustrating some of its typical critical shortcomings. I probably could have used other models and emerged with generically (at least) the same results.

> 7.78a) realistic (Aristotle)
>
> 7.78b) pragmatic (Dewey)
>
> 7.78c) existential (Sartre)
>
> 7.78d) evolutionary (Nietzsche)

Realistic Humanism: Aristotle

> 7.79) The doctrine of real essences, modified to deny the subsistence of those essences apart from particulars, provides the basis (metaphysically) for Aristotle's theory of value and therefore his normative ethic;
>
> 7.79a) every class of particular things has a set of defining properties which defines its essence;
>
> 7.79b) while all things aim at 'the

As a pupil of Plato, Aristotle accepted the doctrine that there are forms, real essences, or natures of all the classes of particular things or relations, and that the form of any class or type of thing consists in the defining properties that make the thing what it is rather than any other sort of thing with a different set of defining properties. But while Plato held that the forms or real essences had real being independently of the particular things or relations that exemplified them (although of course, he did not think that these transcendent forms or essences were themselves particular things, but rather logical properties), Aristotle held that essences or forms were real only in particular things, as their natures or defining properties, and in knowing minds as the objects of class concepts: he denied, in other words, that the forms were metaphysically transcendent, or subsistently real in themselves. According to Aristotle, every identifiable class of things has an essence or nature generically common to all members of the class; and every class of things has a different essence or nature. In the most general sense and from the standpoint of worth or value, 'the good' is that at which all things aim; but since a thing (or class of things) can only aim at 'the good' within the limits prescribed by its essence, 'the good' is specifically different for each class of things. In fact, the good of each class of things consists, for Aristotle, in the fullest actualization of its essence as the distinctive sort of thing it is. This is true of natural objects—the best horse, for example, is that particular horse which most fully actualizes the defining properties that constitute the essence of what it is to be a horse; but it can also be ascribed to artifacts (things produced by the art, skill, or craft of an agent)—the best guitar is that particular guitar which most fully actualizes the defining properties that constitute the essence of what it is to be a guitar. It goes without saying that, for any given class of things, some specimens of that class are therefore better than others and some worse than others: some horses are better (or worse) than others, and some guitars are better (or worse) than others. In each case, the recognizable and principal essence of the class provides the standard for evaluative comparison among the members of that class.

And what about human beings? Well, of course there is a recognizable and principal essence (here and in other cases, Aristotle called it an entelechy) of humanity as well. If, therefore, we wish (as we do) to know what the good is for human persons explicitly, it will be necessary to identify the defining properties that constitute the essence of a human being (or person, as we would say). Human beings have, of course, both a vegetative aspect and an animal aspect; but since these are shared with other forms of living things, they do not constitute the distinctive properties of the human essence as over against other classes of living things. Man (*anthropos*—Aristotle's generic term for humanity) is certainly an animal, but he is a special kind of animal in terms of the distinctive aspect of his essence; that aspect is rationality. In a sense, other beings and things are rational as well in being subject to determination by rational principles (such as the laws of logic and the essences of the classes to which they belong); but man is rational in certain unique ways that he does not share with other beings or even with other living things, since he is capable of conceptually understanding things in terms of the rational principles that determine their being, and also capable of voluntarily subjecting himself to the authority and direction of rational

good' in general, 'the good' of any particular class of things consists in the fullest actualization of its essential properties.

7.80) Clarification of the good for human beings:

7.80a) the distinctive essence of man is rationality;

7.81) other beings and things are rational in the sense of being determined by rational principles;
7.82) but humans are subjectively rational:
7.82a) through the capacity of conceptual understanding,

7.82b) and through the capacity of voluntary subjection to rational principles.	principles in both the formation of his character (habitual dispositions) and the guidance of his conduct toward recognizable ends or goals. Man, in other words, is, one might say, subjectively rational, in his capacity for rational apprehension and action, in a sense in which other living things are not subjectively rational. Hence, Aristotle defined (specified the essence of) man as rational animality, in the special senses of rationality just explained.
7.83) In general the good of humankind is well-being as relative to the human essence of rationality;	In what then does 'the good' of a human being consist? Aristotle claims that verbally at least, there is general agreement as to the answer: 'the good' of man consists in well-being or *eudaimonia* (sometimes translated into English by the word *happiness*—a very unfortunate choice, since for many English readers the term connotes a hedonistic notion of well-being—which would certainly be a perversion of Aristotle). But this agreement is of little help, since the term *well-being* is merely a synonym of the term *good*, and the question is to determine precisely in what the well-being or good of man consists. That good must be a function of man's essence or nature as distinctly rational, since the specific good of anything (man included) is relative to its essence. Now reason, according to Aristotle, has two principal functions in the sense of the subjective rationality unique (among living things) to man: the highest or logically purest and most independent function of reason is simply rational apprehension, together with knowledge as the result of the exercise of that capacity; the second, logically less pure and less independent in its operation, is the use of reason to guide conduct through the rational control of our desires, passions, impulses, and active propensities. Accordingly, the fullest actualization of reason (in the sense in which it is unique to man among living beings) would result in two sorts of virtue (excellence of quality) proportionate to these two functions of reason: *intellectual* virtue would be the habitual pursuit of knowledge as an end in itself, while *moral* virtue would be the rational control of our desires, passions, impulses, and active propensities. Because a human person is less dependent on external objects of any special sort in the pursuit of intellectual virtue than in the pursuit of moral virtue (anything at all can be the object of knowledge—including our passions, etc., while our passions themselves, etc., have severally special objects with
7.84) human reason has two principal functions: 7.84a) rational apprehension and knowledge, 7.84b) the rational control of desires, impulses, and active tendencies; 7.85) hence, two sorts of virtue:	
7.85a) intellectual (the pursuit of knowledge as an end), 7.85b) moral (rational control of active and passive tendencies).	

respect to the presence and effect of which our voluntary control is very limited and restricted), Aristotle held that intellectual virtue was the more excellent of the two. But it is clear that, in Aristotle's view, the complete and total good of a human person would consist in the parallel and interrelated realization of both kinds of virtue by the same person in the context of social relationships with other human beings similarly motivated. Since it is customary to use the terms *moral* and *ethical* far more broadly than Aristotle did and to use them in an approximately synonymous sense, in our parlance the chief good for human persons in the moral ethical sense would include both intellectual and moral virtue in Aristotle's sense.

Now there seems to be no special need to clarify the pursuit of intellectual virtue any further here except to recognize (as Aristotle also did) that the capacity to achieve intellectual virtue in its most effective exercise clearly varies from individual to individual, so that a person's moral responsibility is limited, in this respect, to the degree of that capacity and the significant opportunity for its exercise. But moral virtue is different, not only in the sense that the capacity for its achievement (so far as it depends on variations of individual ability) seems more evenly distributed among human beings, but also in the sense that a further clarification is required to explain how in general the rational control of our passions, desires, impulses, and active propensities is to be carried out with moral propriety. Some philosophers have supposed that, at least with respect to passions, desires, and emotional impulses, the proper office of rational control would consist in suppressing or at any rate sublimating their influence on our choices and actions. But Aristotle held that since the capacity to experience such elements and the actual experience of them are natural and, to a considerable extent, involuntary for human beings, neither the capacity nor the experience could be judged as morally virtuous or vicious as such. And he went on to conclude that the rational control of these aspects of human response would consist in moderation, that is, in aiming at a mean or intermediate state between excess and defect, either of which would be vices, while the mean would be the virtue in the range of responses for any given passion, desire, or emotional impulse. In regard to the desire for food,

7.86) Intellectual virtue, as more self-sufficient in its pursuit, is more excellent,

7.87) but the complete and total human good would include both types of virtue in the context of social harmony.

7.88) As for the virtues:

7.89) the responsibility for intellectual virtue varies with intellectual capacity;

7.90) moral virtue:
7.90a) is more evenly distributed in terms of capacity;

7.90b) involves the rational control of tendencies natural to humans;

7.90c) consists in moderation (aiming at the rational mean);

for example, it would be an appetitive and moral vice to eat either too much (gluttony) or too little (call it self-deprivation), while to eat enough would consist in a moderate indulgence between the two extremes—which would express the virtue of temperance. Nor is the mean to be construed mathematically as exactly equidistant, so to speak, from the two extremes, since the appropriate mean for a given person is always relative to a range of relevant circumstances, such as the state of one's health, the amount of exercise a person has engaged in, the availability of appropriate food, and so on. And of course, the mean and the extremes would differ for different persons according to variation in their relevant circumstances: the mean or intermediate amount of appropriate food for a tall, 200-pound man, for instance, would be far and away an excess for a woman of short stature and small frame. Or take as a somewhat more appropriate example from the moral point of view—the willingness to risk danger in regard to the emotion of fear. Again the extremes are vices: a reckless swashbuckler who rushes heedlessly into a clearly insurmountable situation of risk with no fear is said to have the vice of foolhardiness, while a timid and hesitant person who is paralyzed by fear, at the thought of the slightest risk of danger, is said to have the vice of cowardice. Once more the virtue is a mean involving the intelligent willingness to take calculated risks to the degree that is proportionate to the significance of the result to be achieved and to the realistic chances of success in accomplishment—that is the virtue of courage. But of course the scheme will falsely appear to break down if the desire mentioned is so specific that in itself it involves either an excess or defect at the outset and in principle, or else a virtue which by its very nature excludes the notion of moderation. Assuming that adultery, for instance, is already a vice of excess, there can be no mean of indulgence in it which constitutes a virtue; and assuming that fidelity is a virtue whose very nature admits of no exceptions, even a moderate indulgence in infidelity would be a vice.

In reflecting on the doctrine of the mean between extremes, a person may concentrate either on the virtue (or vice) of the agent or on the virtue (or vice) of the individual action. An action can be morally virtuous, for example, by expressing and actualizing the mean between extremes

7.90c1) the mean is relative to the person and his or her circumstances.

7.90c2) Very specific desires may be excessive or defective by definition, and certain moral qualities imply an extreme that excludes moderation;

7.90c3) while individual acts may be virtuous, an agent is virtuous only if such acts spring from habitual dispositions or states of character:

relative to the relevant circumstances in a particular case of moral choice—it could, for instance, be a temperate act or a courageous act and thus be the morally right thing for the agent to do in the circumstances. But that does not necessarily mean that the agent has the virtue of either temperance or courage, since a given agent is said to be virtuous (or vicious) with respect to the indulgence in a given passion or desire only if his or her actions are based in large measure on habitual dispositions or states of character. To take one of Aristotle's own slogans out of context, just as one swallow does not make a summer, so one virtuous act of courage does not make a courageous agent, although it may be indicative of that virtue in the agent, provided the act is the expression (with the agent's voluntary consent) of a settled or habitual disposition of the agent. Hence, Aristotle, in his doctrine of moral virtue, emphasizes the virtue (or vice) of the agent rather than that of an individual act. Thus the effective exercise of rational control consists primarily in the disciplined formation of character states or habitual dispositions; and to become a morally good human being is to exercise rational control in the formation of such habits of response as aim at the mean between extremes in particular actions across the whole spectrum of desires or passions.

7.90c4) hence, Aristotle's emphasis is on the agent rather than the act.

Aristotle summarizes all this in a widely quoted and highly clarifying formulation in which he claims that '[moral] virtue, then, is a state of character concerned with choice, lying in a mean, i.e., the mean relative to us, this being determined by a rational principle, and by that principle by which the man of practical wisdom would determine it...'[2] As I indicated above, here Aristotle is focusing on virtue, not in the sense in which it can be predicated of an individual act, but rather in the sense in which it can be predicated of a personal agent—hence his emphasis on virtue as a state of character or habitual disposition. In effect, he is claiming that the rational way to exercise appropriate moral control over one's passions, desires, impulses, and active propensities, is to aim at moderation or a mean between extremes of excess and defect, always recognizing and taking into account that the rational mean is both individually and circumstantially variable, and in that sense relative. Of course, this is not, at least on the surface, the

7.91) Summary on moral virtue;

7.92) moral virtue as a relative mean (between extremes) determined by reason;

7.93) there is a relativity to the individual and his or her circumstances, but this (purportedly) is not radical ethical relativism;

---

[2] *Nichomachean Ethics*, bk. II, chapter 6.

relativity of radical dependence upon individual cultural opinion, but rather it is what would now be called situational relativity. In other words, Aristotle does not intend here to subscribe to the radical ethical relativism which I subjected to exposition and criticism in the earlier context of meta-ethical issues. Yet Aristotle recognizes here a certain vagueness or imprecision in the notion of the 'rational principle' which is to serve as a standard for recognizing the appropriate mean: in a sense, perhaps, the rational principle referred to simply *is* the principle of moderation itself; but in a further sense, it is the criterion for judging what the moderate course of action is. And in this latter sense, Aristotle recognizes, but does not specifically identify, a principle to which reason, as a capacity of apprehension that characterizes a personal agent as such, looks for guidance in determining the mean. Since the vagueness thus lingers still, Aristotle attempts to alleviate it by referring the moral inquirer to an ethical model. If we are confused about how our own reason should be guided in aiming at the morally appropriate mean, he advises that we look to the 'man of practical wisdom' as a moral example, and he recommends that we follow the principle that we observe such a person to be employing in guiding his own moral choice and action. Of course, the man of practical wisdom is simply a morally virtuous person; and it would appear, at least, that, since what makes a person morally virtuous, is precisely aiming at the mean through the correct rational principle, it would follow that a moral inquirer would have to know (at least implicitly) what that rational principle was in order to identify such a moral exemplar. Now if, as I am suggesting, Aristotle is actually reasoning in a circle here, it may well be that the vagueness he intended to eliminate is still present in his formulation. It may also be, of course, that this imprecision illustrates Aristotle's thesis that in moral philosophy one can achieve no more than an approximation (something considerably less than absolute rational certainty) in identifying the mean in particular cases of moral decision, and that in this respect ethics stands in sharp contrast to logic or mathematics. He certainly held, as well, that it was very difficult to achieve the mean in practice and to do so out of a stable disposition of moral character, since finding and conforming to the

7.94) the determination by reason, or rational principle, is vague, so that Aristotle recognizes 'the man of practical wisdom' as a model, though it is not clear how a person would identify such a model without already possessing the requisite moral knowledge.

7.95) The knowledge of moral virtue in specific cases is no more than approximative and hence it is very difficult to become a morally good person in knowledge and practice;

mean in relation to a given range of passion or desire involves not only balanced moderation in the indulgence of the desire in question, but also directing it toward its morally proper object at the right time, with the right motive, and in the right way—hardly an easy accomplishment even in the case of a single morally relevant act.

While Aristotle is certainly not a hedonist, he nevertheless regarded pleasure and pain as significantly related to the achievement and the assessment of moral virtue. Although human beings are often motivated by the experience or expectation of pleasure or pain, nevertheless it is clear, according to Aristotle, that pleasure is not the intrinsic and ultimate moral good for human beings, nor is pain the intrinsic and ultimate moral evil. For it is evident that persons are lacking in virtue of character if they take pleasure in activities that are morally evil, or are pained (perhaps even lacking in pleasure without pain) in the performance of activities that are morally good. And on the contrary, persons are judged to be morally virtuous if they take pleasure in habitually being disposed to acting rightly in the moral sense, as well as in acting accordingly in particular cases; and persons are furthermore virtuous if they are pained at the prospect of performing morally evil acts, or at the supposition that they feel any habitual inclination toward the performing of such evil acts. That is the reason why, in the process of morally training those who are lacking in virtue (ourselves, others, or young persons) we deliberately contrive to make moral vice painful in its effect and moral virtue pleasant in its effect with respect to the performance of individual acts. For by that process, hopefully, such training will condition us to take pleasure in morally good acts and experience pain in morally evil acts even when this deliberate contrivance is suspended.

But even though pleasure is not therefore the sole ultimate and intrinsic good, it is nevertheless related to the characteristic activities that both form and express the virtues (intellectual and moral) that constitute the good or well-being of human persons. For pleasure completes, in a morally appropriate way, the various activities (moral and nonmoral) that are natural to human beings. In the case of the operation of our sense organs, for example, when a well-conditioned organ functions in the sensing of its proper objects

7.96) while pleasure is not itself the moral good, it is related to that good.

7.97) Virtue involves taking pleasure in morally good acts and being pained at the prospect of morally evil acts;

7.98) pleasure completes the activities that are natural to human beings and even intensifies these activities.

in the most effective way, the activity involved is completed by the pleasure and satisfaction that are correlated with the activity as a culmination of its appropriate operation. The same is true with the higher activity of reflective or contemplative thought: the pleasure involved intensifies the activity and is proper to it, although it is also true that, for all human activities (sensory, contemplative, and so on), alien pleasures (pleasures proper to a different activity or directed toward an immoral activity) can obstruct and frustrate the completion of the original activity and diminish or even eliminate the pleasure proper to that activity. It is also clear, finally, that pleasures differ in kind in proportion to the corresponding difference in the activities they complete. Again in this context Aristotle refers to the model or paradigm of a morally good man (i.e., a person who is effectively exhibiting both intellectual and moral virtue): the pleasures experienced and enjoyed by such a person are the morally appropriate pleasures when they are experienced and enjoyed (as they are by the morally good person) with integrative moderation and harmony.

7.99) The achievement of moral virtue is only possible in a well-ordered society in which others share this moral goal.

Of course, this comprehensive ideal of human well-being (the good proper to a human person), as depicted by Aristotle, can hardly be actualized outside the context of a well-ordered society or community of persons who, on the whole, are striving for the same ideal themselves and are therefore willing to contribute to a structure of social relationships and institutions that make the realization of that ideal possible, in principle at least, for all. Man is, after all, a political animal and can realize his fullest individual and communal good only in a well-ordered society.

7.100) Supporting arguments:

For the most part, I have included Aristotle's supporting arguments, for his ethical perspective, in the exposition of the position itself, and there is no need to repeat those arguments here even in summary form. But a few general comments about the basis of the ethical view may be helpful. It

7.100a) Aristotle's ethics is based on his metaphysical doctrine of real essences, since the good of any sort of thing is relative to its essence, and consists in its actualization;

should be obvious that Aristotle's ethic is squarely oriented in, and grounded upon, his metaphysical commitments. If there were no essences or natures that distinguished different classes of entities from each other, the notion of a good or well-being proper to each class of thing would be unintelligible, since that good or well-being consists, for Aristotle, in the fullest actualization of the distinguishing properties of any given thing which make that thing what it is rather than something else. There is, for Aristotle therefore, no universal and determinate common good, participation in which would account for the good of each class of things, since the determinate good of each class of things is relative to the defining properties of the class. And that is the reason, at least with respect to ethics, that Aristotle rejected Plato's doctrine of an absolute idea of the Good—which would be too abstract to account for the differing goods of different classes of things. Yet there must be real essences in things in order to account for differences among distinguishable classes of things. I cannot here undertake an analysis of Aristotle's whole doctrine of real essences (that is why I have designated his ethical view as *realistic* humanism), since that would take me far beyond the scope of my purpose in a work on moral philosophy. Suffice it to say that if there are no real essences, Aristotle's ethic would be without reference and logically groundless; and to add that I find that to be no negative criticism of Aristotle, since I share with him the belief in real essences, and, if anything, I would go beyond his version of the doctrine in the direction of the Platonism he rejected or at least drastically qualified (perhaps because he did not fully grasp Plato's doctrine in its most effectively stated version—but that too is another question not directly relevant here). Of course, if the doctrine of real essences in general is rejected, that would mean that there was no human essence either and also therefore no identifiable human virtue, whether intellectual or moral; at least, therefore and on Aristotle's terms, there could be no objective and ultimate moral good for man.

On the other hand, if the metaphysical doctrine of real essences is accepted as philosophically plausible, then Aristotle's ethic, as far as it goes, may appear (or even actually be) highly reasonable, at least within the parameters of normative ethical naturalism. In that case, there will be a human essence or nature in relationship to which human goodness or well-being may reasonably be construed: surely it is obvious that the good or well-being of anything, man included, must be relative to the distinctive nature that it possesses and must involve the actualization of that nature or essence; it is equally obvious that any distinctive difference of nature or essence implies a parallel difference in the

7.101) thus there is no universal and common good of all things (contra Plato);

7.102) without essences, Aristotle's ethic would be groundless,

7.103) since there would be no ultimate moral good for man.

7.104) If real essences are presupposed, Aristotle's ethic is highly plausible as a version of ethical naturalism:

7.105) the goal of anything must be relative to its defining properties;

determinate content of the good for the class involved. And since it seems clear that the distinguishing essential property of man is rationality (in the particular senses clarified by Aristotle), the good for man will involve the proper actualization and operation of rationality, both in the pursuit of knowledge as an end (intellectual virtue) and in the rational direction of man's desires, passions, impulses, and active propensities. Jackasses, being different in nature or essence, may, as Aristotle suggests, prefer sweepings to gold; but human beings will prefer gold as a more versatile instrument for achieving a wide spectrum of objectives pertinent to human purposes. And the man of virtue (the morally good person, in Aristotle's sense) would prefer the balanced and simultaneous achievement of both intellectual and moral virtue to either sweepings or gold, if it became necessary to choose; but in the end, according to Aristotle, both food and economic means are necessary instrumental means for the achievement of the human well-being which, relative to man's nature as rational, gives them whatever worth they possess. Perhaps a central appeal of Aristotle's ethic is that its moral ideal precludes no genuinely human capacity from its balanced and moderate fulfillment in conjunction with all the rest.

But my enthusiasm for Aristotle's ethic, while genuine, is not totally unqualified, although I think that some standard criticisms of his ethical philosophy are either undeserved, or irrelevant, or both. It is commonly claimed that, in his contention that the morally good man is the person who habitually acts, under the guidance of reason, in a cool, calm, and deliberate fashion, keeping all his non-rational propensities from exceeding their limited bounds as dictated by the principle of moderation, Aristotle has recommended a lifestyle which, while implementing a certain dimension of genuine human value, would lead to the virtual (if not actual) elimination of some of the most worthwhile (and in that sense valuable) experiences that are realistically possible for human beings. Some morally legitimate desires, it is insisted, depend for their worth, in the fullest sense, on being indulged of an extreme degree that would be incompatible with Aristotle's doctrine of the mean or policy of moderation. An Olympic athlete, for example, cannot pursue the goal of winning a gold medal without throwing moderation to the winds and

7.106) man's defining property is rationality in the pursuit of knowledge and in the direction of passions and actions;

7.107) thus the true human good consists in the achievement of both intellectual and moral virtue, so that all the aspects of human capacity receive balanced and moderate fulfillment.

7.108) Critical objections:
7.109) It is commonly objected that the emphasis on rationally directed balance and moderation would preclude the realization of certain values that depend on an extreme degree of their fulfillment;

7.110) for example—athletic excellence, or genuine friendship;

giving him or herself entirely to the intended purpose. Or, to take a more commonplace example, the full value of genuine friendship at its best depends on a reciprocal and totally uncompromising commitment whose only bounds or extremities are set by the circumference of permissive moral rightness. The person who pursues either athletic excellence or friendship, with consciously (or even subconsciously) restricted moderation, will simply render himself or herself incapable of achieving the highest possibilities of the sport or the full value of the relationship. Now I have tried to state this criticism in what I regard as its most persuasive form; but nevertheless, even as thus expressed, I regard it as an inane criticism. In fact, it seems to me to be based on a perverse interpretation of Aristotle; for as I interpret him, he is not intending to exclude the most indulgent expression of a passion or desire, provided that expression is within the limits of moral propriety as determined by the principle of moderation or the doctrine of the mean. Here the concept of moderation or the mean involves indulgence in the right circumstances, in relation to the right person, with the right proportion of investment by way of time and energy relative to one's other morally legitimate pursuits. Aristotle does not, I think, intend to be interpreted as claiming that acting with moderation should lead a person to indulge morally legitimate desires in a relatively uninvolved and unenthusiastic or guarded fashion. It is perfectly consistent with his position to recognize that athletic endeavor should be pursued with enthusiasm and verve, or that having a true friend should involve genuine commitment across the board. But if a man (with the possible exception of an Olympic athlete) became wholly involved in competitive sport, to the preclusion of any other significant activities, or became so involved in a friendship as to surrender himself to the extent of a complete emotional dependence that destroyed his own integrity as a separate individual person, these extremes, for Aristotle, would violate the doctrine of the mean and be immoral indeed. On the other hand, there are, for Aristotle, both extremes and means that are immoral in the indulgence of desires, precisely because their indulgence to any extent lies outside the bounds of moral propriety: adultery, thievery, the use of performance-enhancing drugs, and even using friends merely as tools of one's own selfish ends, are all

7.111) but this criticism misinterprets Aristotle;
7.112) for moderation does not exclude extremity in the pursuit of that which is truly valuable;

7.113) it rather excludes excessive preoccupation with a limited range of values at the expense of overall human well-being;

appropriate examples here. On the grounds of the original criticism, therefore, I regard Aristotle as not guilty on this score: perversely or mistakenly understood perhaps, but not philosophically guilty.

> 7.114) yet this criticism does have a real point:

Still the above criticism does, I think, allude to a real point, even though it is inappropriately expressed. The doctrine of the mean, or the principle of moderation, seems to work reasonably well with respect to virtues related to acts and character formation in relation to the rational direction of passions, desires, impulses, and active propensities; but does this context cover the whole range of moral goodness and/or rightness in the most inclusive sense? Are there not

> 7.114a) virtues involving duty or obligation seem incompatible with the notion of moderation or limited fulfillment—e.g., fidelity in the keeping of promises, the telling of the truth, or the fulfilling of assumed obligations to others.

virtues, especially those that involve duties or obligations to other persons, to which the concept of a mean between extremes does not plausibly apply? I am thinking in particular about what I will call the virtue of fidelity understood in the broad sense of dependability with respect to the obligations to keep one's genuine promises to other persons, to tell the truth to them in an unambiguous and non-misleading fashion, to fulfill consistently the voluntarily assumed obligations of special relationships (such as marriage, or parenthood) into which one enters with other persons, or even, in general, to recognize and further the genuine moral well-being of other persons, so far as that well-being is likely to be affected by our choices, actions, or habitual responses.

> 7.114b) In these cases moderation seems incompatible with the nature of the obligations involved;

Here, in all such cases, any sort of moderation in commitment seems incompatible with the very nature of the obligations involved: a person whose promises are only partly or sometimes dependable, or whose word can be depended upon only to a limited extent, or whose commitment to the obligations of voluntarily assumed relationships is inconsistent—such a person could hardly be called morally virtuous in these respects. It is not that such obligations are absolutely unconditional and unexceptionable, since there are conceivable circumstances in which one might be exempted from them in particular cases. It is rather that such exemptions call for a reasoned justification on moral grounds, and that the habit of indulging oneself in such exceptions without the requisite justification is essentially immoral. In the absence of any such moral justification for an exception, the duties involved are indeed unconditional and unexceptionable (i.e., they are *prima facie* duties of this sort), and the

> 7.115) any exceptions must themselves be morally justified in terms of some more inclusive and overriding obligation;

> 7.116) otherwise the notion of exceptions is morally out of the question.

thought of making exceptions on the ground of one's non-moral (or even immoral) self-interest is simply out of the question morally. How then does the notion of an intermediate mean enter into the nature of such virtues of fidelity as those mentioned? Hence, as the previous criticism suggests, there are moral values to which the idea of moderation does not seem to apply, but they are not the values involved in the indulging of our morally justifiable desires and passions; they are instead the values involved in a range of duties and obligations that we have toward other persons.

Perhaps the problem with Aristotle's ethical perspective in this regard is due to the fact that his whole emphasis in ethics is self-regarding in the sense of focusing on how an individual may become a better person morally through the exercise of disciplined and rationally directed control, with the intent of achieving a basis, in one's habitual dispositions, for a morally justifiable self-respect. That, of course, is morally commendable; but it seems to bypass other-regarding virtues, except so far as they tend to implement this self-regarding objective, or perhaps also in the sense that one aims at a social order in which any person (including especially oneself) has the opportunity to actualize such a self-regarding ideal. Is Aristotle's ethic therefore overweighted in the direction of ethical egoism, even if the overweight is not hedonistic?

7.117) Perhaps Aristotle's ethic is overweighted in the direction of self-regarding virtues at the expense of other-regarding virtues that involve such duties and obligations;

In any case, this same imbalance seems to generate a further difficulty with respect to moral obligation, not this time toward other persons, but rather toward, or in regard to, oneself. If I let my mind glance across the whole spectrum of typical passions, desires, impulses, and active propensities that characterize human persons, and if I think contemplatively about the corresponding virtues paralleling these tendencies; it seems obvious to me that, while there are some of these proclivities that are inevitable and indispensable for all persons, nevertheless many of them seem clearly optional for a great many persons, when considered from a moral point of view. Aristotle's ideally good person is presumably a person who finds a place, determined by reason or a rational principle, for the expression of all the varied and typical tendencies that generally motivate human beings. But is it plausible to suppose that this lofty and commendable ideal is in any sense incumbent upon, or obligatory for, particular individuals in the moral sense? Or more generally, if one

7.118) on the assumption that some human desires and tendencies are optional (in the sense that their indulgence is not essential to human life as governed by reason), do particular individuals have any moral duty or obligation to express all these desires and tendencies?

7.119) Can Aristotle's view provide any adequate basis for duty or moral obligation at all?	begins with the problem of the morally good life as Aristotle sees it—namely, how to exercise appropriate rational control over the expression of our non-rational propensities, will one be able to find any adequate place for the notion of duty or moral obligation at all? On what basis, from Aristotle's point of view, is a person morally obligated to give any expression at all to passions, desires, impulses, or active propensities which seem clearly optional in the sense that there is no clear moral reason why a particular individual ought morally to indulge them at all, since their expression is not essential to human life even as governed by reason? It would
7.120) At most, one might claim a conditional obligation to indulge such desires and tendencies with moderation, if the individual elects to indulge them at all.	seem that the most one might reasonably claim is that, if any person does indulge such optional propensities, that person should do so in a rationally controlled and moderate way (in Aristotle's sense of moderation already explained). In other words, the obligation is conditional, not only on a person's having the desire in question, but also on that person's electing to indulge it at all; but there seems no moral obligation to the indulgence at all on moral grounds and relatively to optional tendencies. Here again, as in the case of our criticism of hedonism, such indulgence may be right in the sense of morally permissible, but it is clearly not morally obligatory. What criterion then does Aristotle's moral philosophy offer for distinguishing between the morally permissible and the morally obligatory?
7.121) Might not there be other models of the moral ideal besides balanced indulgence of all of one's propensities, since some human excellences involve a relatively exclusive preoccupation with their achievement?	A closely related set of problems concerns the question whether the moral ideal might not vary for different persons with different abilities, different relative strengths of the various non-rational but typically human tendencies. Why should every individual have to be a jack of all trades here by aiming at a balanced indulgence of all his or her propensities across the board? Are there not some distinctively human excellences that depend for their realization on a relatively exclusive preoccupation with their development to the similarly relative neglect of many other tendencies and inclinations? Perhaps the serious pursuit of knowledge (either in general, or in a particular field) is an especially significant example of such an excellence, though there are many others. How can one become a real scholar without consigning the bulk of one's other passions, desires, and impulses to a very small corner of one's life? And yet the pursuit of this and other similar excellences is surely morally commendable.

Can Aristotle's moral ideal find a place (a morally appropriate place) for all this? There seems to be some reason to doubt it, even if, as I do, one accepts the thesis of Aristotle that the morally good life must be a rationally controlled and directed life.

A final criticism of Aristotle's ethic, but one which I will not attempt to develop fully in the present context (since it will come up again in connection with idealistic and theistic theories of ethics), concerns the question whether reason, as a formal structure of apprehension on the part of a knowing agent, can itself function as an adequate criterion of the ultimately good or right (in the moral sense) in the determination of that which is morally appropriate in particular cases of moral decision and action. If I understand Aristotle's concept of reason correctly, it is a name for the mind's whole power of knowing (understanding and apprehending) as both active (or agent) intellect and passive (or receptive) intellect. In itself, therefore, reason is a formal or structural capacity and consequently depends for its operation on being directed toward an object that supplies its content. Of course, in the case of personal beings, reason can be directed toward itself as one object among others, since self-consciousness is an essential property of persons; but in the case of such self-awareness, a person would, in his or her awareness of reason itself, merely apprehend its own nature as involving whatever structural capacities make apprehension possible. But reason would still be left without any objective content to function as a standard or criterion of knowledge. Certainly the structure of rationality provides a sort of negative criterion or standard of knowing: it prescribes, for example, that no rationally incoherent or self-contradictory thesis can possibly be true, that nothing can be rationally known unless the apprehension of it is clear and precise rather than indeterminate and vague, and so on. But that is not a positive content; it is merely a set of necessary conditions for genuine apprehension. If therefore reason is to make judgments about moral value (goodness or rightness), it must be directed toward a positive content as a standard or criterion that may appropriately guide reason toward the realization of genuinely objective human well-being. But Aristotle's ethic puts forth no such content, except again to state that reason should aim at well-being, and that

7.122) Can reason, as a formal structure of apprehension, be itself an adequate criterion for ethical judgment?

7.123) As a purely formal or structural capacity, reason depends on being directed toward an object for its content;

7.124) what reason in itself supplies as a criterion is simply the negative requirement to avoid incoherence and lack of clarity.

7.125) In relation to value, reason provides no positive criterion of human well-being.

the well-being of anything consists in the actualization of its distinctive essence. Yet the distinctive essence of human persons is precisely rationality; and hence, we have come full circle, as it were, back to the rational capacity whose objective value standard was to be clarified in the first place. And thus there is clearly no positive content of moral value here by which reason is to be guided, other than the purely formal structure of rationality itself. Perhaps therefore Aristotle was too quick to dismiss his master Plato's concept of an absolute Good to which reason could look as a guide and standard for morality and all other objects of apprehension. But that has yet to be explored in a later context.

7.126) Conclusions regarding Aristotle's moral philosophy:
7.126a) His ethic is more plausible than hedonism, since it finds a place for pleasure as an aspect of the morally good life;
7.126b) but his view is incomplete:

As a preliminary conclusion, I certainly regard Aristotle's ethic as, on the whole, far more plausible than any version of ethical hedonism, since he finds a place for pleasure as a sort of fulfilling radiance on the face of the ideal moral life, while recognizing that it is nevertheless not the central core of that life, whose essence is rationally directed moderation, harmony, and balance with respect to all the characteristic human capacities and propensities. Perhaps the most appropriate critical conclusion to draw about Aristotle's realistic humanism is not that it is in any central sense clearly mistaken, much less perverse; but rather that it is incomplete both in its compass and in its basis. As to compass, it

7.126b1) in compass, because it fails to account for moral duty, or for the possible plurality of models for the good life;

fails to deal adequately either with the notion of duty (or moral obligation) or with the possible plurality of models for an ideally good human life, since some forms of the good life may be morally commendable without involving the inclusive and balanced moderation emphasized by Aristotle.

7.126b2) in basis, because it provides no positive criterion of moral goodness.

As to basis, Aristotle's ideal of rationality needs a positive (rather than a merely formal) standard or criterion of moral goodness which, however, he fails to provide. In a word, Aristotle's ethic seems clearly right-minded as far as it goes; it simply does not go far enough in certain clearly relevant directions. Whether any other form of humanism, or even of ethical naturalism in general, can compensate for this incompleteness, is an issue now to be considered.

Pragmatic Humanism: John Dewey

Even though Aristotle and Dewey are separated by a considerable cultural gap and by a historical stretch of some

2300 years, and even though the metaphysical and terminological contexts of the two philosophical views are remarkably different, it is nevertheless striking that the substance of the two normative ethical perspectives is in many ways remarkably similar, as will shortly appear. Both purport to find the central clues to ethics in human nature (though in Dewey there is no talk of real essences); both appeal to reason as the instrument of arriving at ethical insight (though Dewey has a purely functional view of reason and views it as roughly involving 'the scientific method'); both reject the notion that there is a single ultimate and intrinsic end or good on which all values are finally based; both view the morally good life as involving the rational direction of human desires toward their balanced and harmonious expression both in the individual and in the social order (though Dewey's emphasis on integrative harmony is perhaps more extensive and comprehensive than Aristotle's, since the former envisages the moral ideal as encompassing all human civilization and culture, rather than, as in Aristotle, a single body politic like the Greek city-state). All this is not to minimize the differences of metaphysical and terminological expression I have already alluded to; it is merely (but importantly) to say that in their ethical thinking these two intellectual giants largely bridged the gaps that otherwise separated them.

And yet Dewey appears, at least, to begin his ethics by rejecting what Aristotle purports to accept as a starting point: namely, that since all rational human activities are directed toward the realization of ends or goals, it is important to realize that there must be a supreme end or good toward which all lesser ends are directed and for the sake of which they are pursued. Dewey blatantly and explicitly rejects the notion of such a *summum bonum* (supreme good), regards it as grounded in the notion of an ordered cosmos in which rest is higher than motion (a notion he rejects in the name of science), and recommends that we advance to the notion of a plurality of goods and ends that are continuously changing, each end in turn becoming a means to further ends without assignable logical limit. More particularly, Dewey rejects even the concept of a distinction between intrinsically valuable ends that are thus worthwhile in themselves, on the one hand, and instrumental goods

7.127) Aristotle and Dewey:

7.127a) In general they have basically similar ethical perspectives in that:
7.128) both emphasize human nature as foundational:
7.129) both regard reason as the instrument of moral insight;
7.130) both deny a single universal good;
7.131) both regard the good life as the rational direction of desire toward balanced and harmonious expression;

7.132) but Dewey appears to reject Aristotle's doctrine of a supreme good for man;

7.133) he recognizes instead a variable series of ends which in turn become means;

that function merely as means to the realization of intrinsic ends. In his opinion, this distinction collapses if the notion of a single supreme good is rejected, as Dewey recommends. The result of keeping the distinction would be to divorce intrinsic goods from the interests of daily human life and activity. In any case, and in actual practice, while all human activity is goal-directed (in agreement with Aristotle), any ends or goals actually achieved invariably become means to further ends and so on as human vision and aspiration expand. Thus nothing is ever merely a means (it has its own intrinsic worth) and nothing is ever merely an end (it always contributes to some further and more expanded objective).

7.134) still, Dewey recognizes individual and social well-being as an all-inclusive objective;

In spite of all this, however, Dewey does, after all, envision an all-inclusive objective, the content of which however is continually changing and developing: that is, the implementation of individual and social welfare or well-being, partly through the achievement of an increasingly adequate adjustment to our natural and social environment, and partly through the intelligent reconstruction and ordering of human desires so as to achieve integrative individual and social harmony. In other words, the goal or end is a collective concept that subsumes under itself all the goal-directed activities of human beings in society, with all the change and development implied in that ongoing process. Aristotle,

7.135) but Aristotle, for his part, identifies the supreme good for man with that same sort of well-being,

on the other hand, while arguing, as we have seen, that all pursued ends are subsumable under a *summum bonum* or supreme good, nevertheless defines that good (for human beings) as individual and social human well-being, and then proceeds, like Dewey two millennia or more later, to clarify the nature of that well-being, as involving the rational control and direction of desires, along with human capacities and propensities in general, toward a rationally determined moderation in the exercise of those capacities and propensities. Nor is his perspective without a clear emphasis on society (and especially the political state) as a necessary context for the realization of this ideal by individual

7.136) so the difference seems more apparent than real.

persons. So perhaps the apparent disagreement between the two thinkers, regarding a supreme good, is precisely that—more apparent than real (at least in substance). Aristotle begins with the abstract concept of a supreme good which he then diversifies into lesser ends involved in the rational direction of life; Dewey begins with a changing and successive variety of means and ends which he then collects together under a comprehensive notion of individual and social human well-being that involves the balanced harmony of realized human desires in the individual and among individuals in society. As I see it, Aristotle would not object to Dewey's emphasis on the changing diversity of limited human ends, and Dewey would not object to Aristotle's notion of a supreme good as simply an abstract term for the realization of those same ends.

Dewey rejected both the empirical and the absolutist theories of ethics, as he designated them. By the empirical theory of value he meant any theory that uncritically identified the fact that a thing was desired with the claim that the thing was, for that reason alone, a value in the morally relevant sense. But, argues Dewey, that a thing is desired by, or satisfying to, some individual or group, merely raises the question as to whether that thing is desirable or satisfactory in the valuational sense. The judgment that something is desired is, in a particular case, the statement of an isolated fact, whereas the judgment that it is desirable is the making of a valuational claim that aims at providing guidance for conduct in the moral sense—it is to say that it *ought* to be desired, that it meets certain conditions of expectation or leads to certain consequences that implement individual and social human well-being. But some things that are desired would, if acted on (or perhaps even if obsessively contemplated), lead to the perpetuation or origination or increase of conflict, obstruction of effective action, and, in a word, the relative disintegration of human well-being. It is not that there are any values that do not involve the realization of desires and the experience of satisfaction; it is rather that only those desires which result in integrative and effective operation, on the part of individuals in harmonious relationships with other persons, are to be critically judged as genuinely valuable, desirable, and satisfactory in the moral sense. And these desires can achieve that status only through the direction of a rational control based on the knowledge of the conditions in which the desires emerge and the consequences to which their realization leads. To identify desires with values point blank is to eliminate all moral criticism and appraisal in the objectively relevant sense.

7.137) Criticism of the empirical theory of value: 7.137a) that anything is desired only raises, but does not settle, the question as to whether it is morally desirable;

7.138) the latter is a function of conditions and consequences that have a causal relation to human well-being;

7.139) all values involve realized desire and satisfaction, but that is not a sufficient condition of genuine moral value.

7.140) Criticism of the absolutist theory of value:
7.140a) Absolutist principles are too abstract and general to provide effective moral guidance, and hence they are ignored in moral practice;

As for the absolutist theory, Dewey regards an ethic as absolutist if it builds its proximate rules of practical application on some purportedly fixed, ultimate, and changeless ideal of goodness, principle of reason, or moral authority. His objections to any such view are multiple: such a principle, in order to make plausible its claim to universal moral applicability, will be so abstract and general that it will provide no effective guidance in making actual moral decisions in everyday human experience, and as a result, while the principle may be revered or respected, it will be ignored in practice and replaced by arbitrary impulse, the customs of tradition, or the propensity for immediate and rationally undirected pleasure or enjoyment. As for the moral authority of religious, political, or social institutional structures, there will be no objectively reasonable way of deciding among conflicting claims to such authority, and the authority actually accepted will be the one powerful enough to enforce its way on the broadest social segment. On the contrary, the only plausible moral rules will be those that are capable of functioning as flexible hypotheses which, though providing some stability of structure, are subject to modification in the light of altered experiential circumstances. No fixed and intrinsically unalterable ideal or principle can even conceivably face up to the expanding, growing, and shifting front of changing social conditions. So opposed is Dewey to anything fixed or static or permanent that, although he purports to build his ethic on an analysis of human nature, he nevertheless denies (*contra* Aristotle) that human beings have a fixed nature in the sense of a permanent essence, or that the human self is distinct as an enduring agent over against its activities and propensities, or even that there is such a reality as consciousness as distinct from habits, impulses, and tendencies. Not even in human nature, as a dynamic, interactive conjunction of habits, impulses, desires, and tendencies, is there any permanent element on which any sort of absolutist ethical view could be grounded.

7.140b) there is no way of deciding among conflicting 'absolute' authorities;

7.140c) moral rules must be flexible hypotheses, if they are to cope with social change;

7.140d) there is no fixed basis for morality in human nature, which is itself a changing combination of habits, impulses, and tendencies.

7.141) Characterization of the moral good:
7.141a) Moral problems result from the obstruction of unified activity toward intelligently formulated goals;

How, therefore, should the moral good, understood in general as individual and human well-being, be characterized, according to Dewey? Moral problems arise in situations where unified activity, toward intelligently formulated aims, is obstructed, diverted, or threatened by conflict, either through tension with other persons or the natural environment, or else through opposing desires, impulses, or tendencies in the individual. This conflict and tension constitutes the set of problems toward which moral deliberation directs itself. But the aim of that deliberation is not to calculate, with respect to various alternatives of conduct, sums of future or anticipated feelings as consequences—that would be the utilitarian procedure which Dewey rejects as both irrelevant (because it fails to distinguish between the desired and the desirable) and impossible in practice (since the calculation required is too complex to carry through to a clear resolution). Instead, the work of moral deliberation consists in the sorting out of present tendencies to act in such a way as to restore unified activity through the rational and balanced harmony of all those tendencies, each of which is given proportionate and impartial consideration in the integrated continuity of action. Present experiences of pleasure and pain (in contrast to anticipated future feelings) certainly play some part in this process, so far as they are correlated with imaginatively projected alternatives of action. The moral good is precisely the meaningful fulfillment that emerges when the various conflicting tendencies are reconciled in such an impartial way as to result in an orderly release in action. Thus the good for the individual is achieved through the realization of inner personal integration, and the good for society is achieved in the reconciliation in action of the opposing tendencies of individuals; that is precisely social integration. Personal and social integration together constitute the ordered and harmonious functioning in which genuine human well-being or goodness consists. Thus the good is not a distant goal but a present harmony of action, or, as Dewey claims, the good (in the morally relevant sense) is now or never!

 The answer to two further questions will complete the clarification of the substance and basis of Dewey's humanistic ethic. The first concerns the issue as to whether this perspective, although opposed to any sort of changeless absolutism in ethics, is nevertheless a modified form of ethical objectivism, or, alternatively, is a variety of the sort of radical ethical relativism which in the end grounds all moral claims on the contingent and variable states of individual and cultural opinion, preference, feeling (including desire), and response. In general, Dewey's position purports to go

7.141b) moral deliberation consists, not in the calculation of future feelings as consequences,

7.142) but in the harmonizing of present tendencies to act with a view to restoring unified activity;

7.143) the moral good is the restoration of unified activity through the rational reconciliation of conflicting tendencies to act.

7.144) The result is personal and social integration,

7.145) so that the good is a present harmony of action.

7.146) On the question of objectivism *vs.* relativism:

7.147) It is claimed that morality has both subjective and objective aspects;	through the horns of this dilemma by arguing that there is a middle way between the extremes of rigorous objectivism (which, in his opinion, always ends up with a transcendental standard that is disconnected from human choices and circumstances) and a sheer subjective relativism (which, in his opinion, permanently sets the habits and propensities of persons over against the facts of their objective environment in conjunction with which alone such human habits and propensities can achieve effective and appropriate expression). Moral values are, on the one hand, subjective, both individually and culturally, in the sense that they would be impossible without the desires that lead to the pursuit of certain goals and the satisfaction experienced in the achievement (to whatever degree) of those goals. On this subjective side, desire and satisfaction lead to the formation of habits of response that direct their fulfillment. But for these habits to be operative in overt activity, they must function under the guidance of objective conditions and consequences that are based in the environment of the agent. The harmonious balance between habit (subjective) and environment (objective), if that balance has been achieved in certain circumstances, can, however, be disrupted: for environmental conditions and anticipated consequences can change in such a way that the habit loses its objective support. In such cases, the agent attempts to restore that support, partly by the revision and restructuring of the habit and partly by the attempt to change existing circumstances to reconstitute the support. If this sort of reconstruction and change do not take place, then the result is a purely subjective morality cut off from its objective basis by habits that sustain this opposition more or less permanently. Yet no individual or social group is ever totally at odds with the environment; for while harmony is disrupted at certain junctures, it is nevertheless maintained in a larger framework of objective conditions and goods—otherwise, functional human activity would be impossible across the board. That morality is only possible through such a shifting relationship between habit and desire, on the one hand, and objective conditions, on the other, means that moral achievement is never more than partial and approximative, not to mention uncertain and inexact. So Dewey's ethic claims to be a developing marriage of sorts between
7.147a) moral values are subjective in being contingent on desire and satisfaction;	
7.147b) but they are objective in being contingent on objective conditions and consequences. 7.148) These aspects call for continual reciprocal adjustment;	
7.148a) otherwise habits tend to lose their objective support,	
7.148b) although some correlation must continue if functional human activity is to be possible at all;	
7.148c) the correlation, however, is always changing and tentative.	

subjective and objective factors: a marriage that never transcends its tentativity.

The second question, which rounds out Dewey's normative ethical perspective, concerns the issue as to whether the conditions, both objective and subjective, that make the achievement of moral ends possible, can be significantly fulfilled in a causal context which is pervasively deterministic in some scientifically plausible sense, or whether, alternatively, moral values are significantly achievable only if moral agents possess a sort of contingent personal freedom that is incompatible with any universal and rigorous determinism. On the whole, Dewey takes the position that the morally significant aspects of freedom are realizable by human agents irrespective of whether existence in general is completely determinate in some universal and rigorous sense. In the terminology I previously developed in my earlier analysis of the freedom/determinism controversy, Dewey combines *weak compatibilism* with the *avoidability* view of freedom. As he sees it, the morally relevant aspects of freedom are three: the first is efficiency in action involving the ability to carry out plans without external constraint or obstructing obstacles; the second is the capacity to alter plans, redirect choices, and experience novelties, even if this involves risk and uncertainty to a considerable degree; the third is the confidence that desire and choice can be factors in bringing about certain events rather than others, that such desire and choice can count in shaping conditions and producing consequences. But none of these, rightly understood, requires the sort of metaphysical freedom or contingency of the will that would be incompatible even with rigorous determinism: deliberation, desire, and choice can be significantly free in relation to conditions and consequences, even if these elements of freedom are themselves completely determined. For moral purposes, it is simply not necessary to decide between thoroughgoing determinism and the open-ended contingency that would introduce uncertainty, doubt, and novelty into the objective world order: empirically speaking and from a subjective point of view, all these elements of contingency are aspects of the thinking and experience of human agents, since they do not know in advance what all the details of a determined objective fixity would be. At the same time, Dewey inclines toward open-ended contingency

7.149) On the question of freedom and determinism:

7.150) Dewey combines weak compatibilism with the avoidability view of freedom, so that the morally relevant view of freedom holds whether or not rigorous determinism is true;

7.151) freedom involves:
7.151a) efficiency of action without obstruction;
7.151b) capacity to redirect choices;
7.151c) confidence that desire and choice can shape events.

7.152) All these aspects of freedom can hold whether the world is characterized by rigorous determinism or open-ended contingency;

7.153) but Dewey inclines toward the latter and rejects any sort of logical necessity as determining events.
7.154) Yet human agents are not permanent conscious subjects;
7.154a) a human agent is the conjunction of habit and impulse under the guidance of intelligence;
7.154b) intelligence provides impulse with direction, and the latter provides intelligence with options;

7.155) human well-being is integrative individual and social harmony.

7.156) Critical evaluation:
7.157) In agreement with Dewey:
7.158) situational relativity of intermediate moral rules;

7.159) values motivated by desire in relation to genuine human well-being;

even in an objective sense, since he believes that only a sort of rationalistic deductivism (which he rejects as a pragmatic empiricist) would provide any plausible basis for complete determination and finality.

It is important to point out that, according to Dewey, the human agent, who possesses freedom in a morally relevant sense, is not an enduring and permanent pure subject of conscious experience. For, as he sees it, there is no enduring subject of awareness, no transcendental ego: the conjunction of formed habits with impulsive reaction and desire under the direction of intelligence (construed as involving scientific knowledge) provides an adequate functional basis for human agency. Intelligence is neither the slave nor the master of impulse: not the slave because impulse and desire in themselves are blind and gain their direction only under the guidance of intelligence; not the master because all the options open to intelligent direction are provided by the thrust of impulse and desire, for which intelligence acts as clarifier and liberator through insight into the conditions and consequences that provide the context in which alone impulse and desire can effectively operate. In the end, human well-being, both individually and socially, involves an integrative harmony in which individuals achieve the balanced fulfillment of those desires, impulses, and propensities which support that harmony with the coherent and unobstructed pursuit of goals, and in which society achieves an order in which such individuals respect and implement the rights of other persons to do the same. That, after all, is the sort of naturalistic human moral good that Dewey envisions as constituting the only sort of true human well-being that is dependably achievable by human agents.

If now we attempt a critical evaluation of Dewey's normative ethical perspective, there is much here with which a soberly thoughtful person can surely identify: that proximate and intermediate moral rules or principles are situationally relative in their application to changing conditions and that they are therefore both limited in scope and subject to continuous revision and progressive reconstruction; that moral values are ends that are fueled by desires, impulses, and propensities, while at the same time only those desires (impulses and propensities) which in their fulfillment implement genuine human well-being are morally desirable and morally worthy of pursuit, so that moral value is not wholly constituted by the fact of desire (or impulse or propensity); and that the good for human persons consists in the actualization of human nature resulting in the achievement of an integrated personal selfhood through an individual and social harmony accomplished through the impartial, rational consideration of opposing tendencies and conflicting claims which are thus adjudicated in that harmonious balance—all this becomes plausible as a part of any adequate normative ethical perspective on the sole condition of its being clearly and adequately stated. For it is merely to say that persons as persons possess intrinsic moral worth, and that our overall moral responsibility is the fullest actualization of personal selfhood through the balanced expression in character and activity of what it is to be a human person. With all this I have no quarrel whatever, since the pursuit of any goal deemed significant presupposes, whether consciously or not, such an intrinsic personal worth in the agent and by that very fact in other human agents as well.

 But my enthusiasm for the central thrust of Dewey's perspective is not entirely untarnished. Dewey purports to reject any notion of a supreme good that is changeless and fixed: there are only limited, particular goods each of which, though functioning as an end initially, becomes a means to some further end without assignable logical limit. Now if this claim is merely a descriptive thesis to the effect that characteristically (or at least frequently) in human experience what starts out, as a goal or end, becomes, to whatever degree it is achieved, a means to some further, more comprehensive end, then I have no objection to such an empirical generalization, since that does often happen. But Dewey's claim is much stronger: it involves the denial that there is any fixed ideal or principle of moral goodness, any ultimate intrinsic moral value. Yet if that were actually the case, it would become impossible to justify any particular moral claim in decisive terms. For if each goal or end is a means in turn and nothing is an end in itself (nothing is an intrinsic moral good or an intrinsically reasonable moral principle), then the logical process of justifying any particular moral claim would involve an actually infinite series of successive means, no finite set of which would provide

7.160) integrated personal selfhood as the good for human persons, who possess intrinsic worth.

7.161) Critical difficulties:
7.162) Dewey purports to reject any ultimate moral good or principle;
7.162a) it is rather the case that ends achieved become means to further ends and so on without limit;

7.162b) but if that were the case, there would be no way of justifying any particular end, since an infinite series of means and ends would be generated (which is logically absurd);

any adequate moral justification—and yet any actual set accessible to us is always finite. Unless there is some ultimate intrinsic good or ultimately reasonable moral principle, there could be no justifiable means. If, to avoid this logical impasse, it should be argued that no ultimate moral justification is ever possible, and that the only sort of provisional and tentative justification possible even in principle is provided by recognized transitory ends which are in turn and without limit replaced by others in some later context, then I would respond with the question whether such a position would not involve the surrender of even any sort of moderate ethical objectivism—a step which Dewey clearly does not want to make, for he himself (correctly, in my opinion) criticizes the so-called empirical theory of moral value by claiming that there is an objective standard for determining which desires, impulses, and propensities are morally justifiable pursuits. That objective standard is the concept of integrative individual and social harmony as constituting essential human well-being: and is not that the very sort of ultimate moral goal or principle that Dewey seems to be arguing against? It seems therefore reasonable to claim that either there is no vestige of ethical objectivism at all, or else there is after all such a rationally recognizable ultimate moral good or principle. Were that not the case, there would be no identifiable method of setting limits to the network of provisional and proximate moral rules that are involved in all moral reasoning. For example, one ought always to tell the truth, except when some more inclusive and higher good or principle would be compromised by doing so; and we ought always to act in conformity to that broader principle, except under analogous conditions, and so on. But not without logical limit, for in that case there could be no rational justification for making an exception to any particular moral rule whatever.

7.162c) if any sort of ethical objectivism is rejected, that would contradict Dewey's own concept of integrative individual and social harmony as constituting genuine human well-being.

If my previous argument in criticism of Dewey seems reasonable, then we have clearly a way of responding to the brunt of his criticism of all absolutist ethical principles; namely, that such principles are either so general and abstract that they provide no moral guidance at all, or else that they are so specific that they clearly admit of morally justifiable exceptions. For if a moral rule admits of justifiable exceptions, it is simply not an ultimate (absolutistic) moral

7.163) Dewey argues that, because particular moral rules admit of exceptions, there are no absolute moral principles:

principle, but a limited and proximate moral rule to be followed within certain restrictions, but not beyond them. Yet there would be no logically plausible way of justifying exceptions to such limited and *prima facie* moral rules, if there were no unexceptionable and unconditional moral good or principle at the base of all such moral reasoning. By the very nature of the case, the ultimate moral good or principle will be very general precisely because it is completely universal. And its application to particular moral issues will be situationally relative to the relevant circumstances in which any particular moral decision is to be made. It is the function of limited and proximate moral rules to provide circumstantially relative guidance in applying the ultimate moral principle to particular situations and cases. Dewey's legitimate complaint is against transforming such limited moral rules into absolute principles (which they are not); but his mistake lies in supposing that, since particular moral rules admit of justifiable exceptions, it follows that there is no such thing as an ultimate moral good or principle (which it does not).

Dewey's moral ideal is the actualization of human nature through the achievement of personal and social integrative harmony. But does he operate with an adequate concept of human nature? He denies that human nature either is or has a fixed essence; yet he gives a descriptive analysis of the properties that he regards as universally predicable of human selfhood. He holds, for example, that the human self is a dynamic process that consists in the integrating of various habits, impulses, and tendencies into a unified response in overt activity toward morally justifiable ends. If this is a universally applicable description which defines human selfhood (which Dewey takes it to be), then is not this precisely what would be meant by a fixed essence of human nature? The recognition of a defining essence of humanness does not, as Dewey wrongly implies, eliminate creative development and integrative growth; instead, it provides a framework within which such development and growth become possible, a set of parameters that provide a structure for dynamic change and the achievement of individual uniqueness in a plurality of focal points that vary from person to person and for the same person at different times. Thus human nature is indeed in the process of its actualization; but this process is the unfolding of a universal and common human

7.163a) but this conclusion does not follow, since particular rules which admit of exception are not universal moral principles;

7.163b) it is further the case that exceptions can be objectively justified only if there is an unconditional moral principle at the base of moral reasoning.

7.164) If, as per Dewey, the moral ideal is actualization of human nature,
7.164a) do not the enduring descriptive properties of human nature constitute the sort of enduring human essence that Dewey denies?

7.164b) The recognition of such an essence need not entail the denial of growth and development;

7.164c) the human essence is rather the context in which such processes occur;

7.165) nor is it plausible to deny an enduring subject of conscious awareness;
7.165a) for that is required as a basis of sustained personal identity to serve as the subject of moral duty and responsibility.
7.165b) It is also necessary for the sublimation and direction of desire;
7.165c) if persons are transitory biological products, how can they possess intrinsic personal worth (as Dewey claims)?

7.166) As Dewey sees it, integrative personal harmony requires the resolution, in the individual, of conflicting habits, impulses, and tendencies;
7.166a) the harmony is achieved through giving each such element equal consideration and expression:
7.166a1) this assumes an analogy between conflicting claims of different persons and the claim of tendencies within the same person;

essence which is diversified in the virtually endless variety of individual focal points. Dewey, on the other hand, claims that there is no enduring subject of conscious awareness, but that consciousness is merely the conjunction of habit and impulse (desire, propensity, etc.) under the direction of intelligent guidance. But does not that locus of habit and impulse, as well as that directive intelligence, imply an enduring self-conscious agent or pure subject of experience? If there is no such permanent (though developing) self, what will function as the center and basis for the achievement of moral character and the subject of moral duty and responsibility? If personal selfhood has no such enduring core, how do persons achieve a sustained identity of awareness through memory, present experience, and future anticipation? And how do human agents develop the capacity to sublimate and redirect the otherwise determining influence of impulse and desire? If, finally, persons are merely and entirely transitory products of material and biological forces, what basis is there for recognizing intrinsic personal worth as the center of the moral ideal (a center that Dewey seems clearly to recognize)? While therefore I agree with Dewey that the moral ideal involves the actualization of human nature, I seriously doubt that his restrictive and limited concept of human nature can bear the full weight of that moral ideal even on Dewey's own terms.

A further criticism emerges in connection with Dewey's development of the concept of integrative personal harmony. Dewey envisions an individual human agent as being influenced by different and sometimes conflicting habitual, impulsive, and even intellectual claims that require appropriate adjudication and resolution if integrative personal harmony is to be achieved. As he sees it, each conflicting tendency has a right to due and fair consideration if a just and fulfilling balance is to be achieved, and a unified, effective response in overt activity is to be accomplished. As Dewey considers the situation he seems to be drawing an analogy between the just resolution of conflicting claims among different persons, on the one hand, and the opposing impulsive tendencies in a single person, on the other hand. It appears that his only standard of fairness in either case (social harmony or individual harmony) consists in the degree to which honoring or acceding to a given claim would contribute to integrative harmony. The social case seems plausible enough, since the rights of individuals against each other's conflicting claims cannot extend to the indulgence of claims that would result in the disintegration of social harmony, precisely because individuals as persons possess intrinsic worth and therefore also reciprocal rights and responsibilities. But within a given human agent or person, impulses, desires, propensities, and habits are clearly not possessed of any such status of intrinsic personal worth; instead, such influences are morally relevant only as means to the actualization of the selfhood of the individual and the achievement of harmony with other individuals. No doubt one such mode of achieving integrative personal harmony would be the one Dewey envisions—giving to each impulsive tendency a balanced and moderate place in personal development (a little of everything, but not too much of anything). But surely there are other paths to inner personal harmony, such as the sublimation of many impulsive factors to the domination of a single overwhelming drive for the sake of some noble and morally worthwhile goal such as intellectual excellence, artistic creativity, or self-sacrificing service to other human beings. Surely we cannot accuse Thomas Aquinas, or Michelangelo, or Mother Teresa of any inner moral tyranny for opting to devote themselves to such sovereign and overriding goals, since, after all, impulses, desires, and tendencies have, as such, no rights that are neglected in such dominating pursuits. Indeed, many of the most important achievements of outstanding individuals might never have been accomplished at all without some such sacrifice in the indulgence of various impulsive tendencies which, though morally permissible or even innocent in themselves, would, as preoccupations, have distracted such individuals from their most significant achievements.

Of course, the realization of unified response, through the overriding domination of some single consuming goal, could conceivably be directed toward an objective whose actualization could reasonably be judged as morally defective or even morally perverse. But that result is equally possible for an individual who balances all of his or her habits, tendencies, and impulses into a harmony of unified response by giving to each its 'place in the sun' in a justly determined order of priority. And that is just the point:

7.166a2) the standard in each case is integrative harmony. 7.166b) But while persons, as intrinsically valuable, have reciprocal rights and responsibilities, tendencies within a given person have no such worth as a basis for claiming expression;

7.166b1) so, while balanced expression of all tendencies is one moral possibility,

7.166b2) it can claim no precedence over the subjection of various tendencies to the pursuit of a single morally worthwhile goal which is dominant;

7.166c) either model (balanced moderation or subordination to a dominating goal) could lead to a morally perverse or evil result;

7.166c1) thus unified response requires an objective moral standard beyond itself as a criterion.	personal integration in unified response, though essential to the progressive achievement of the moral ideal, is not sufficient for that result. For unless unified response, however accomplished, is guided by some further standard of moral value or goodness, such a response may end up opposing the highest conceivable moral ideal, rather than supporting it.
7.166c2) Likewise in the case of social harmony:	The same would be true of the achievement of social harmony: history is replete with cases in which entire societies, cultures, and bodies politic have been harmoniously integrated in the pursuit of what reflective judgment could reasonably judge to be morally evil and perverse.
7.167) while Dewey claims to reconcile ethical relativism (dependence of value on desire) and ethical objectivism (dependence on environmental support),	And now what about Dewey's proposed marriage between ethical objectivism and ethical relativism? On his view, moral values are subjective and relative in the sense that they are crucially dependent on desires, impulses, and tendencies, since the pursuit of any goal invariably involves an indispensable inclination of some sort toward that goal. On the other hand, moral values are objective in the sense that their pursuit as objects of desire is only possible through the support provided by objective environmental correlates and conditions, since it is only in a very limited and short-lived sense that individuals can set themselves in opposition to such environmental support in their pursuit of goals (moral or otherwise).
7.167a) yet this kind of objectivity is, though, not adequate to constitute objectivity in the morally relevant sense, since, if it were, it would justify any environmentally possible action or goal (which is clearly absurd);	But surely Dewey is mistaken if he thinks that this kind of objectivity (dependence on environmental support), though necessary, is sufficient to constitute objectivity in the morally relevant sense. If it were sufficient, then any organized set of dispositions (desires, impulses, etc.) would be morally objective if environmental conditions made their fulfillment possible. Yet surely many environmentally realizable desires are morally wrong in their actualization (for example, murder, theft, deception): objective environmental possibility simply does not entail objective moral goodness. For that a further standard, logically independent both of subjectively relative desire and of objective environmental possibility, is necessary as the basis and principle of such moral goodness. On the other hand, Dewey's concept of the relativity of moral goodness to subjective desire (impulse, etc.) does indeed make his perspective a variety of radical ethical relativism, even if he does hold that not all desires (empirical fact) are desirable (moral worthiness). Of course, the realization of value involves, as

Dewey maintains, an operative and sustained inclination toward an objective; but if the inclination constitutes as such its own goal, rather than recognizing that goal as a morally worthy object of pursuit quite apart from the inclination itself, then surely every vestige of moral objectivism is surrendered and radical ethical relativism takes its place. It is analogous to the case of visible perception: if the perceptual mechanism, on subjective psychological grounds, generates its own object through imagination, then even though objective conditions make this whole process possible by sustaining the existence and operation of the perceiving process, there is nevertheless in such a case no genuinely objective entity that is the referent of that perceptual process. So also with moral value: if there is no genuinely objective referent of moral judgment and of moral desire through pursuit to be recognized, there is no objective moral value involved. Thus Dewey's view seems in the end to exclude moral objectivism in favor of radical ethical relativism, even if he sometimes claims otherwise.

Finally, on the question of Dewey's view of the relation between rigorous determinism and the morally relevant sense of personal freedom, it will be recalled that Dewey accepts, in this context, the sort of view which I term *weak compatibilism*, according to which even a rigorous determinism would not be logically inconsistent with the morally relevant sense of personal freedom, while at the same time Dewey is inclined to be suspicious of any rigorous determinism of the sort in question. In Chapter 5 I have already subjected this and other compatibilist views to extensive criticism, and I have really nothing to add to that analysis. I simply cannot regard any view as plausible that attempts to defend moral responsibility, while either denying or questioning the decisively free causality of the particular agent who is to be held morally responsible; and that is what relevant versions of compatibilism (including Dewey's) all do. If moral responsibility is conceivable only on the basis of contingent and genuine agent causality, then Dewey's compatibilism and all the others are philosophically and morally questionable.

On the whole, then, Dewey's normative ethical perspective, while containing some centrally sound elements of great importance, becomes logically defective primarily because his position either compromises the claim to ethical

7.167b) but Dewey's view does result in radical ethical relativism precisely because he recognizes no genuinely objective good at which desire and inclination aim:

7.167c) if there is no objective referent of moral judgment, there can be no objective moral value.

7.168) Dewey's attempt to reconcile rigorous determinism with the morally relevant sense of freedom is as unsuccessful as other forms of compatibilism, since genuine agent causality entails the denial of rigorous determinism.

7.169) Summary conclusion on Dewey's ethic

objectivity and thus reduces to radical ethical relativism; or else it rests on a core of moral objectivity that centers in the concept of the intrinsic moral worth of personal being, while this emphasis is weakened critically by an inadequate view of the sort of personal selfhood essential to such a concept of personal worth. Could these problems find their solution, not merely in Dewey's version of ethical naturalism, but also in any version of ethical naturalism as such? The answer to this question remains to be clarified.

Existential Humanism: Jean-Paul Sartre

7.170) The meaning of existentialism as a context of Sartre's ethic:

7.171) existentialism is not a metaphysical doctrine, but an attitudinal slant:
7.172) the traditional slant involves:
7.172a) the ideal of rational objectivity;
7.172b) the determination of thought by being as discerned by a disinterested spectator;
7.172c) the subordination of particulars to universal laws and principles.
7.173) The existentialist slant involves:
7.174) the rejection of the ideal of rational objectivity in favor of a radical subjectivity for which the truth about being is a self-projection of the individual, who himself is involved in the being he tries to explain;

If I refer to Sartre as an existentialist, I am only using the epithet by which he designated himself. But that a position is referred to as existentialist does not identify it as a particular worldview perspective with a particular doctrine of the meaning of being; for existentialism, as a term, designates an attitudinal slant, rather than a doctrinal content. Much of traditional western philosophy has had as its attitudinal slant the ideal of a detached pursuit of rational objectivity in the understanding of being and truth; a supposition that being should determine our thought and conceptualization about it, so that the knower should be a disinterested spectator who, once informed of the truth about being, can then adopt interests and goals that are rooted in being as thus understood; and the assumption that explanation should view particular existing entities, personal or non-personal, as exemplifying universal laws and principles which constitute the structure and framework of being. But the existentialist attitude stands in stark contrast to such an attitude of disinterested rational objectivity and universal explanatory principle. For a typical existentialist holds that, since all thought is a project of particular individuals, and since such individuals are inextricably involved in and bound to the being they are trying to explain, it follows that the ideal of rational objectivity is a kind of pipe dream that can never be significantly fulfilled by persons who thus cannot stand disinterestedly outside of being in order to explain it. Hence all thought about being by particular persons is a kind of self-projection and self-creation pervasively veiled by the individual who, instead of being bound by being in his or her thought, has the radical freedom to bind being with his or her own intellectual (emotive and volitional) project. Being does indeed bind the individual through constituting the structural framework in which the individual is involved; but the individual, precisely because of this involvement, is reduced to, and at the same time is radically free in, interpreting being through his or her own creative intellectual projection, so that, in this sense, truth, for the individual, is constituted through responsive personal decision and choice (truth as subjectivity). Nor is the starting point for this projection to be thought of in terms of universal principles, categories, or essences; it is rather I myself, this particular existing individual, together with other such particular individuals, that is the starting point for understanding existence. If principles, categories, and essences are part of the fabric of explanation, then it is the individual thinker who has woven them into that fabric in the exercise of his or her radical freedom. Thus the notion of a rationally objective system of principles (etc.) which explains existence and being, is not merely foreign to the thinking of the existentialist; it is, in fact, an illusion, so that philosophy is a kind of prosaic poetry which somehow illuminates existence and being, but which is incapable of providing an objective description of it. Of course it is an understandable preoccupation of this attitudinal stance to dwell on the anguish, the despair, the dread, and the sense of being threatened that are the consequence for the individual of realizing all this.

7.175) the rejection of universal principles as a starting point in favor of the particular existing individual who thus possesses radical freedom in his or her interpretation.

But it is important to point out that the radical subjectivity of the existentialist attitude, in virtue of its emphasis on thought as individually creative, while it provides as it were ample wings for intellectual flight, provides strikingly different landing places for different individuals whose course is thus of their own making. A Søren Kierkegaard, for example, sets his craft down on the terrain of a theistic view of the world in the framework of traditional orthodoxy (and we have yet to deal with that in a later context). But not so with Jean-Paul Sartre: for him it is atheism, a world with no God as creative ground or providential director, no essences (especially not an essence of humanity, which would objectionably restrict the individual's radical freedom) for individual persons and things to actualize, no logically necessary principles to choke and restrain either thought or being, and thus also no rationally objective laws of moral duty

7.176) The existentialist slant leads to different results for different thinkers:

7.177) Kierkegaard opts for theism,

7.178) while Sartre is an avowed atheist.
7.178a) This means that there are:
7.178a1) no real essences in an objective sense;
7.178a2) no logically necessary principles;

7.178a3) no objective laws of duty; 7.178a4) and, in general, no rational objectivity.	or obligation to limit the open-endedness of individual decision and choice. As Sartre sees it, the whole enterprise of the ideal of rational objectivity collapses with the recognition of the non-existence of God (in any transcendental and theistic sense): objective principles would be possible only if they were grounded in a transcendent realm of essences, and such a transcendent realm of essences would be thinkable only if God existed to conceive those essences, more or less on the analogy of there being plans or goals for human beings only if agents exist to conceive them (which in the human case, they do). But if God does not exist, as Sartre supposes (how he could know this on his own radically subjective ground, is a serious question), then the whole basis for rational objectivity in the traditional sense vanishes just as sunlight vanishes in the grip of darkening night. Most importantly for ethics, there is no human essence (transcendental and eternal) to determine what persons ought to be: first there is existence, the fact that individual agents exist; and then the essence of any human being is what he or she becomes through radically free choice.
7.179) God would be required as the basis of all of these, but God does not exist;	
7.180) in particular, since there is no human essence prior to human choice, man is radically free.	
7.181) For Sartre, human beings are both totally free and totally responsible;	All this means that human beings possess a creative, though dreadful, freedom in the exercise of which they are totally responsible for what they become. There is no God whose commands, purposes, and character traits provide an objective moral ought, no Kantian rational principle of moral duty or obligation to provide that basis either; hence, there is no objective support whatever for moral decision and choice. Persons cannot even fall back on the moral advice of others, except in a purely secondary sense; for individuals themselves must choose their own advisors with no objective basis. Hence individuals are *totally* and *wholly* responsible, according to Sartre, for their own moral decisions and choices: that is why their freedom, though complete, is dreadful and involves anguish and forlornness—since individuals can blame only themselves for their choices and the results of those choices; and in the process they are creating their own essence in the only sense in which they have one.
7.182) since there is no objective support for moral principles, individuals are totally responsible for their own decisions and their consequences,	
7.183) but in legislating for oneself, one also legislates implicitly for all humanity, since only thus can one take one's own legislation seriously;	And yet no human agents can morally legislate for themselves alone; for in choosing or legislating an essence for oneself, persons are, at the same time, choosing and legislating for the whole of humanity. For individuals cannot take their own moral self-legislation seriously unless they believe

that they are, in doing so, choosing an image of humanity as it generically ought to be, unless in choosing they affirm in some approximatively objective sense the value of what they choose. If I understand Sartre's point here correctly, and if I can assume that he is not deliberately and blatantly contradicting himself (although he may nevertheless actually be contradicting himself in some less directly obvious sense), then what Sartre is actually claiming is that persons have to believe in the objectivity of the moral values they legislate, even though that belief is in some ultimate sense false for an existential analyst who 'sees through' moral values to their inevitably radical subjectivity as depending entirely on individual decision and choice.

But if persons accept their total moral responsibility and develop scales of values for which they alone are the basis, then, in the persistent courage that they thus display, they are achieving a genuinely authentic selfhood in the moral sense. By universally legislating moral values, by accepting the entire responsibility for the selves they become and the environment they face (which after all has meaning for them only so far as they interpret it as a structural framework for their decisions and choices), individuals take the whole weight of the world on themselves in the recognition that they choose and act entirely on their own with no objective support whatsoever; and to face up to one's own existence in this way is precisely to achieve authentic selfhood as a human being. Individuals are thus responsible for everything except the facticity of their existing as responsible agents: for they are not the foundation of their own being. At the same time, individuals can either deliberately or inadvertently refuse or fail to face up to their responsibilities in explicitly self-conscious ways; and in that case they do not achieve authentic selfhood, no matter how this failure occurs—in defiance, in uninvolved passivity, or in consciously acceding to some external authority (be it religious or secular). In all these modes of diversion and aversion, persons entangle themselves in the sort of 'bad faith' that rests on some variety of pervasive self-deception. And although they fail to achieve genuinely authentic selfhood, they nevertheless are still entirely responsible, since all these avenues are the consequences of their own choices, even if that fact becomes veiled in their own consciousness. Radical personal freedom

7.184) if one chooses with full awareness of one's own responsibility, one achieves authentic selfhood;

7.185) thus one is responsible for what one becomes and how one takes one's environment;

7.186) but one is not responsible for one's sheer existence.

7.187) If one refuses to choose, he or she misses authentic selfhood, but is still responsible for what one becomes;

7.187a) in this case, one acts in 'bad faith' and becomes self-deceived;

7.188) hence, radical freedom is inevitable in any case.

7.189) Critical evaluation of Sartre's ethical perspective:

7.190) briefly, either his claims are themselves merely his own subjective projections and are thus devoid of genuine critical significance, or those claims are themselves rationally objective and therefore contradict themselves;

7.191) in the former case, the claims would be comparable to judgments of preferential taste which are admittedly subjectively relative;

7.192) in the latter case, the claims would constitute exceptions to their own assertions, and hence be contradictory.

is therefore inevitable, whether persons courageously affirm it with settled conscious resolve, or, along one of the multiply possible routes to aversion, fail either to recognize or exercise that freedom explicitly.

The criticism of any moral perspective which, like that of Sartre, explicitly surrenders the ideal of rational objectivity and substitutes radical freedom and subjectivity in its place, is certainly not a logically straightforward matter for the would-be critic. On the one hand, it could be regarded as a short project: for if Sartre's propositions and arguments are not to be regarded as themselves rationally objective truth claims, then they cannot be regarded as a critically significant challenge to any opposing viewpoint, since by hypothesis (on Sartre's part) those propositions and arguments would thus be merely the subjectively relative projections of Sartre's own personal and creative intellectual legislation, a product entirely of his own individual subjectivity. And if that be so, if all of Sartre's thoughts, consistently with the viewpoint he projects, are subjectively relational in their logical status, then it might be more appropriate logically to say that his views do not logically oppose any other positions at all, much in the same way that judgments expressing matters of preferential taste (in food, music, clothing, etc.) do not logically oppose other judgments made by other persons and expressing different preferential tastes about even the same subject matter. On the other hand, if, in putting forth his doctrine of radical subjective freedom and relativity in the domain of thought, Sartre is to be understood as providing an objectively true analysis of the logical status of all human beliefs and truth claims, he would be involved in contradicting his own perspective by making his own analysis an exception to his own doctrine of subjective relativity. Hence we have a first-class dilemma: either Sartre's perspective is itself radically subjective and therefore devoid of critical thrust, or his perspective claims to be objectively true and therefore contradicts its own doctrinal content. And of course all this would apply to ethics as well, in which area, if anywhere, Sartre's radical subjective relativity is more explicitly asserted and spelled out than in other parts of his philosophical position: values (moral or otherwise) have, for Sartre, no objective support whatsoever. That, as I previously suggested, would be the short work of criticism; and in my opinion, a wholly serious and plausible critique.

At the same time, however, there are other longer routes of criticism, and the short route might possibly blind us to some important insights provided by Sartre's analysis. In my opinion, the main positive insight of Sartre is found in his doctrine of radical personal freedom and his claim that such freedom is a necessary (for Sartre, a sufficient) condition of genuine moral responsibility. My own case for this position has already been stated in Chapter 5 where I defended (perhaps in more rigorous terms than Sartre would find comfortable) the agent causality view of freedom. Yet in spite of my overall agreement with Sartre on the issue of freedom, I think he unreasonably overstates his case in several ways. For him, personal freedom is so unrestricted and absolute that, in consequence of it, individuals bear the weight of the whole world on their shoulders since, in the exercise of that freedom, individuals are the author of their own world by reason of the fact that they access that world solely through their own self-projected interpretation of it. But this claim seems clearly too extreme: there is a sort of environmental givenness about the world which, however it may be (subjectively or otherwise) interpreted by the individual, nevertheless imposes a structural framework of restriction on that individual's freedom. It is not my purpose to spell out these restrictions in detail, but I will mention some exemplary illustrations—individuals' options for choice are clearly limited by at least some objective circumstances over which they can exercise no control through decision or choice. For instance, such options are limited by accessible environmental means or instruments, by the individual's sheer empirical ability (I cannot choose to be the world's fastest runner, although I can choose to aim at it), by the lack of opportunity to exercise the ability he or she possesses (I may be completely preoccupied by some unavoidable project like economic or even physical survival), or by the mere absence of any options among which to make a choice (I may have no alternative to eating cold baked beans for lunch if they are the only food on my horizon). No doubt some of these limits are partly shaped by a person's previous choices and their consequences; but it would be difficult to make a case for the claim that they all were

7.193) Sartre is certainly correct in claiming radical personal freedom as a necessary condition of moral responsibility, but his case seems overstated;

7.194) for him the freedom of the individual is unrestricted and absolute, since the influence of the environment on an individual is relative to his or her totally subjective interpretation of it.

7.194a) but this overlooks the sheer givenness of the environmental world, over many aspects of which the individual can exercise no decisive control;

explicable in that way. There is at least a minimum framework of restrictions within the limits of which choices must operate and by which choices are limited. Nor is the facticity of being born with the potential of responsible agency the whole of the environmental givenness which limits choice; for the circumstances of one's birth are also restrictive—I was born into a middle-class family in upstate New York, and perhaps at the same moment some other child was born in poverty on the lower east side of New York City or in the jungles of central Africa. For both of us, these radically different circumstances significantly and inevitably influence our available options. It would perhaps not be too much to claim that, while the degree of genuine agent freedom sets the limit of responsibility, that freedom effectively operates within very narrow bounds, so that I am confronted after all (and *contra* Sartre) with a world context for whose elements I am simply neither responsible nor free.

7.194b) nor is it merely a case of the facticity of existing as an individual,

7.194c) for freedom operates within very narrow limits that differ for each individual.

It is possible to turn this point around and claim, again *contra* Sartre, that a freedom totally devoid of limits, utterly deprived of objective support, entirely cut off from all motivational restriction, would be a morally meaningless freedom in the last analysis. For there would be neither rational justification nor significant motivational influences as a framework for the operation of freedom; it would rather be like the view of freedom as total indeterminateness which would simply remove a so-called free act from the agent's control rather than placing it under his or her self-determined direction. If I may borrow (out of context) a simile from Immanuel Kant, it would be rather like the winged dove which, noticing that the atmosphere provided considerable resistance to its flight, imagined that flight would be totally unobstructed in absolutely empty space. Would it not be the same with an unrestrictedly free human agent? Would such a completely indeterminate act be a decision or choice at all in any morally relevant sense? Does not genuine and morally relevant freedom require a ladder of restriction and limit to make its ascent to authentic moral responsibility possible? So freedom in the agent causality sense, yes; but absolutely unlimited, unfounded, and undirected freedom, no!

7.195) A totally unrestricted freedom would be morally meaningless, since it would be undirected, unmotivated, and therefore indeterminate;
7.195a) this would remove the act from the agent's control;

7.195b) and it would not involve decision or choice in the morally relevant sense.

In further qualified agreement with Sartre, I find the complex claim—that rational objectivity (and the objective rational principles and categories it involves) is possible only on the basis of a transcendent realm of universal essences, and that such a realm is conceivable only if God (in the transcendent personal sense) exists as the locus of such essences—to be an entirely plausible process of rational analysis: no rational objectivity without essences, no essences without God. The Augustinian/Thomistic Christian philosophical tradition has argued this position virtually from time immemorial; and as a member of that tradition I have myself argued this same position in a somewhat modified form in two of my previously published philosophical works.[3] The remarkable thing is that Sartre regards this argument as logically valid. But this, of course, is where the agreement ends; for, on Sartre's terrain, the argument, though valid, is not sound, since its premises are not true. Indeed Sartre claims that God does not exist, that hence there are no transcendent universal essences, and therefore no rational objectivity (no rationally objective principles and categories). In contrast, a typical Augustinian-Thomistic formulation (but not the only possible one) would claim that there are objectively necessary principles of reason (for example, the logical principles of contradiction, identity, and excluded middle), principles which have a truth status that is independent of the existence of empirical particulars and therefore transcend the natural order as the whole realm of particular entities; that such objectively necessary principles can be transcendent only if they are themselves universal essences, although they hardly exhaust that realm which includes as well all logically possible properties, attributes, characteristics, as well as the classes they define; and that such essences in turn can be transcendent only in finding their locus of reality and being in the content and structure of the mind of the transcendent personal God (whose essence is, in one aspect of it, precisely that of objectively necessary reason). Thus if there are any objective principles of reason (i.e., necessary principles of all thought and being), there must be a realm of essences; and if there is such a realm, God must exist both to conceive and to constitute it. But the claim that there are no objectively necessary principles of reason is clearly self-contradictory, since the claim itself would be intelligible only

7.195c) Sartre seems clearly correct in arguing that rational objectivity is conceivable only if there is a transcendent realm of essences, which are in turn conceivable only if God exists as their transcendent locus and constitutive ground;

7.196) but for him (Sartre) the argument, though valid, is not sound, since God does not exist;

7.196a) but it can clearly be argued that, since there are objectively necessary principles of reason, essences must be real and God must exist as their ground.

---
[3] *The Resurrection of Theism; The Reconstruction of the Christian Revelation Claim.*

7.196b) The contrary claim, that there are no objectively necessary principles of reason, would either be self-contradictory (and therefore false), or it would be reduced to a subjectively relative projection.	through the principles it purports to deny, or else, alternatively, the claim would be a purely subjective and relative projection of some individual's arbitrary choice, in which case, as a radically relative opinion, it would neither state nor establish anything objective about the existence or non-existence of necessary principles of reason. Since no self-contradictory claim can logically be true, it follows that there are real essences and that God exists as their locus.
7.197) Sartre writes as if he knows that God does not exist (and that thus rational objectivity is possible);	But let us consider Sartre's position about reason, essence, and God from his own point of view. For Sartre, as we have seen, the ideal of rational objectivity is a myth, there are no universal and transcendent essences, and there is no transcendent personal God (or any other sort of ultimate and transcendent reality). Sartre writes as if he knows without question that God, in any transcendent sense, does not exist—he is no Humean agnostic in the sense of merely claiming that he does not know (or that no one knows, or even that no one can possibly come to know) that God, in this sense, exists, so that his opinion or claim is purely negative. The question then arises: on what basis, consistent with
7.197a) but Sartre, by hypothesis, could have no objective basis for this claim; 7.197b) his writings contain virtually no negative natural theology;	Sartre's doctrine of radical subjective relativism, can he plausibly make the claim that he knows that God does not objectively exist? I certainly do not find in Sartre's writings (the philosophical ones) any arguments of negative natural theology in which, from premises he claims to be objectively true, he validly concludes the non-existence of God. Instead I find rhetorical and literary diatribes about existence itself being irrational and senseless, without objective meaning. But again I find no explicit arguments leading to that conclusion either: it is instead stated as what he presumes to be obvious to anyone who reflects about being, a sort
7.197c) and if they did contain such arguments, the same dilemma would recur: 7.197d) either the premises would purport to be objectively true (and thus self-stultifying), 7.197e) or they would be subjectively relative projections.	of *fait accompli*. Yet suppose that Sartre were a sort of negative Thomas Aquinas whose writings bristled with the very sort of refutational arguments that are in fact essentially absent from his philosophical writings. Would we not (or even would *he* not) face the very sort of dilemma as before? Either these arguments would contain premises that purported to be objectively true and would involve a structure of formal logical validity based on logically and objectively necessary principles, or else the arguments would be subjectively relative opinionative projections (the only sort that Sartre, on his position, would have to work with). In the former

case, he would be contradicting his own doctrine of subjective relativity; and in the latter case, he would be providing merely a piece of descriptive psychology about his own beliefs, so that nothing would be established objectively about the existence or non-existence of God. Since Sartre's objections to real essences and rational objectivity are based on the premise of his atheism, and since therefore his case for atheism cannot consistently have any objectively plausible basis, it follows that, even for Sartre, if God exists, then real essences and rational objectivity (as an ideal) become plausible philosophical elements, so that the main thrust of his existentialist stance would be undercut.

7.198) Since Sartre's whole case depends on his atheism, for which there can be no objectively plausible basis, the foundation of his stance is, to that extent, undermined;

But Sartre's nominalistic rejection of real essences can be approached in another fashion that does not rest (at least explicitly) the whole case for or against real essences on the question of the existence or non-existence of God. Sartre makes the general claim that existence precedes (I suppose ontologically) essence, and that the only essence particulars have emerges in the progressively unfolding contingency of their being: the essence of non-human entities results from their subjectively relative interpretation by human beings, so that in themselves (and objectively?) they have no essence; the essence of human beings is, in the only sense in which they have an essence, the product of their radically free decisions and choices—at the outset I am nothing essentially, but I become something essentially as a consequence of how I use my freedom. Now all this seems to be highly questionable: real essences, if there are any, are universal properties, characteristics or attributes which in their meaning, are logically independent of the particulars that exemplify or instantiate them (if there were, for example, no such property as being alive, no particular living things could logically exist). But human beings (to limit myself to Sartre's main example) have initially and at the outset at least some universal properties: even in the upsurge of their brute givenness they are something determinate, something that is of one sort rather than another. Sartre himself regards them as, quite apart from their own choices, free and therefore responsible agents with the intrinsic capacity to recognize options and to act with respect to them; but this is surely a complex essential property of human beings, so that existence is possible only through the instantiation of essence.

7.199) quite apart from the question of God, Sartre claims that:

7.200) things have no essence apart from human interpretation;
7.200a) the essence of human beings is a result of their free decisions and choices;
7.201) but this is questionable;
7.201a) since essences (if there are any) are universal properties, and human beings have (even for Sartre) some universal properties that precede their choices,

7.201b) it follows that the only alternative to real essences would be total indeterminateness;	Nothing could exist if it were wholly indeterminate, wholly devoid of universal properties. Sartre's mistake here, in my opinion, consists in his supposing that genuine radical freedom is logically incompatible with determinateness (with possessing specific properties), and that therefore, at least in the case of free agents, there can be no essence. But that is surely wrong: free agency is itself a property, and the contingency of our significant choices is certainly not inconsistent with our possessing essential qualities which determine what it is to be a human being. I suppose this comes down to the same point as my earlier argument that freedom is intelligible only if it operates within limits and restrictions.
7.201c) but even the free agency that chooses is itself a property of human beings.	
7.202) Sartre rejects all varieties of ethical objectivism and is thus a radical ethical relativist;	Suppose now that we turn to the ethical implications of all this. Consistently with his concept of radical subjective relativity, Sartre, as a matter of course, purports to reject all varieties of ethical absolutism or objectivism, and he is therefore a believer in radical ethical relativism. I have already spoken my piece about ethical relativism *vs.* ethical objectivism in Chapter 4; and the arguments I present there, in support of objectivism and against relativism, are clearly applicable as a critique of Sartre on this point. To reject ethical objectivism *toto caelo* or across the board is, in my opinion, not to substitute one normative ethical perspective for another; it is rather to prescind the whole project of normative ethics, which, after all, aims at identifying and arguing for an objectively ultimate ideal of ethical goodness or rightness. So if every reference to objectivity is by hypothesis cut off in principle, there would appear to be no normative ethics (in the proper sense) to discuss, except from a purely meta-ethical point of view. But I will not further criticize Sartre for being an ethical relativist in the radical sense, since I have nothing more of substance to say about it.
7.203) but this is not a variety of normative ethics, it is rather the rejection of all normative ethics across the board;	
7.204) nor is Sartre a consistent ethical relativist; 7.204a) for he implies an objective standard in distinguishing between morally authentic and morally inauthentic self-actualization;	But consistency is an entirely different matter: is Sartre a *consistent* ethical relativist? In spite of his view that there are no objective moral values and that values are ultimately legislated by the creative self-projection of individuals, Sartre seems to imply and even assert an ultimate moral ideal that smacks of the ethical objectivity he purports to reject. He judges self-actualization to be morally authentic if it unfolds through the conscious recognition of the role of radical freedom and of the total responsibility of the individual for the choice, whereas self-actualization is morally inauthentic

if the individual accedes morally to some external moral authority. But what could possibly be the standard for making this distinction, if in fact moral choice has no objective criterion? Again, Sartre claims that when individuals legislate values for themselves they are, by that very fact, legislating value for the whole of humanity, since, as he says, nothing can be morally good for the individual unless it is morally good for all human persons—unless it is morally valid for every individual. But surely there can be no such universal moral obligatoriness or responsibility, if morality is devoid of all objective reference. If Sartre, as I suggested earlier, merely means in all this that a person must (falsely) take morality to be objective in order to take his or her own moral legislation seriously, then I agree with that and merely point out that this would be tantamount to admitting that normative ethics as such entails moral objectivity; and if there is no such objectivity, then there is no moral ideal in the genuinely normative sense, no moral ought or moral obligation or moral responsibility in the relevant normative sense. Finally, Sartre labors at great length that 'bad faith,' moral self-deception, is morally reprehensible and a sign of inauthentic selfhood. But is that claim plausible, in the normative sense, if there is no objective standard of moral judgment? From all of this I conclude that a huge shadow of logical inconsistency hangs over Sartre's radical ethical relativism, since he seems unable to manage his ethical perspective without elements of the very sort of moral objectivism that he purports to reject.

Of course, there is a descriptive empirical sense in which Sartre is incontestably correct about the subjective and cultural relativity of the moral beliefs of individual persons: clearly there is self-legislation, as well as cultural legislation (moral belief by external authority in the form of advice or behavioral sanction), and there must be elements of such relativity even in the moral beliefs of the most logically rigorous ethical objectivists. But since, as I long since argued, truths and beliefs are not identical in logical status, the relativity of even the majority of moral beliefs does not logically entail the conclusion that there are no objective moral truths. Indeed, if, with Sartre, we claim that there are no such objective moral truths or principles, it would seem questionable whether there could, in those terms, be any

7.204b) he also claims that when an individual legislates morality for himself, he is doing so for all humanity: and this implies either an objective standard or individual self-deception;

7.204c) yet he regards moral self-deception ('bad faith') as itself morally inauthentic;

7.204 d) but Sartre is clearly correct in claiming descriptively that many moral beliefs are individually or socially relative, though this fact is quite consistent with ethical objectivism.

Evolutionary Humanism: Friedrich Nietzsche

7.205) Nietzsche is generally unsystematic in his style, although it is possible to extract a definite ethical position from his writings;

7.205a) yet in the end he rejects all 'system' as perverse and cramping;

7.205b) nor is he a very good example of ethical humanism; 7.206) for him moral value is relative to creative human being, although the moral ideal is 'post'-human;

7.207) humans must create a potential for value that they do not possess merely as human.

It would be difficult to find a more striking, provocative, and disturbing philosopher than Nietzsche in all the annals of western thought. From an organizational standpoint the very form of his writing is non-systematic, chaotic, emotionally charged, artistically rhetorical, and often aphoristic. His style is merely to suggest, rather than delineate, any arguments that support his view; and his intent is not to persuade his readers of the reasonableness of his point of view, but rather to rouse them empathetically to identify with the range and impact of his feelings. And yet there is a definite position there to be distilled, as it were, from the unrefined ore of his actual writings; it can even be explained in a more or less systematic fashion, even though in the end it is an attack on all system in the philosophical sense. Fortunately his two most important ethical works (*Beyond Good and Evil, The Genealogy of Morals*), though not really systematic in form, are better organized than much of the rest of his philosophical writing. On the other hand, Nietzsche is not the clearest model of what I have called normative ethical humanism; for, although he clearly believes that human beings (the tyrannically dominant among them, at least) constitute the cutting edge of evolutionary advance toward the realization of value in his senses, and thus are the clue to the nature of that value, still he regards such human beings (even his so-called 'free spirits,' the creative aristocrats) as forming merely a provisional evolutionary phase on the way to the higher ideal which he terms 'the superman'; nor is he confident (at least not all that confident) that man as he now is, even at his human 'best,' has the intrinsic potential to achieve that evolutionary advance. Other ethical humanists want human beings, individually and collective, to actualize a potential that as humans they already implicitly possess, but Nietzsche seems to want the dominant aristocrats among human beings to *create* a potential they do *not* possess merely as human and to discard their mere humanness as a serpent discards its dying and now useless skin.

In a recognizably important way Nietzsche is (far ahead of his time) a forerunner of existentialism in general and of Sartre's variety of it in particular. Like Sartre, he rejects the ideal of rational objectivity (for him objective truth is a sheer myth), disdains all philosophical systematizing (naturalism, idealism, and theism *en masse*), and regards values as the creative self-projection of, if not human beings as such, at least of the aristocratic 'free spirits.' Again, like Sartre, he openly embraces atheism with a vengeance, though he proclaims his commitment by announcing that God is dead and by suggesting that he himself, Nietzsche (and other champions of the value of tyranny), may have contributed to God's demise; of course, what he really means is not that God, once quite alive, has at long last expired (other than in the minds of human beings), but that quite obviously God never really existed in the first place. At the same time, neither Sartre nor Nietzsche is merely a revised version of the other: for Sartre takes the idea of radical human freedom seriously in the ultimate sense, while Nietzsche is a rigorous universal determinist and even a believer, consequently, of the doctrine of eternal cyclical recurrence (when the space-time universe has run through all its logically possible evolutionary phases, the whole cycle repeats itself identically with determined necessity). Again, Sartre regards every mature human being as capable of achieving authentic selfhood, while Nietzsche believes that human beings at the forefront of evolutionary advance are a rare breed indeed, while the rest of humanity inevitably is to be discarded as mere evolutionary trash. Nor does Sartre regard with any intense disdain the Christian ideal of self-denying love, although he rejects the theistic metaphysic on which it is based; Nietzsche, on the other hand, is a self-proclaimed archenemy of the 'slave' morality of the masses, of which he regards the Christian ethic as the most despicable example.

To begin with, Nietzsche pushes radical epistemological relativism much more rigorously than Sartre, for Nietzsche blatantly and unabashedly asserts, in numerous contexts, that objective philosophical or even scientific truth does not exist. So-called truths of this sort are in fact non-rationally determined projections of the impulsive nature of the individual thinker. And the variation in scientific and philosophical views is a function of the parallel variation in the

7.208) In part, Nietzsche is a forerunner of atheistic existentialism: 7.209) thus (1) he rejects rational objectivity along with all philosophical systematizing; 7.209a) (2) he is an avowed and outspoken atheist;

7.210) but he contrasts with Sartre:

7.211) he rejects freedom in favor of determinism;

7.212) he rejects any universal ideal of authentic selfhood;

7.213) he exhibits disdain for the slave-morality of Christianity. 7.214) Nietzsche's radical epistemological relativism is extreme:

7.215) objective truth (of any sort) does not exist;

7.216) all truth claims are impulsive projections of individual thinkers with the tyrannical impulse being dominant;	relative strength of different impulses in different individual thinkers; behind all such impulses and variations is the dominating influence of the tyrannical impulse or will to impose one's own perspective on reality, so that, when different thinkers argue in opposition to each other, they are really engaged in the sort of power struggle that is the cutting edge of the evolutionary process itself. It may be, of course, that taking belief in objective knowledge and principles seriously is strategically necessary for human beings (well, at least for serious thinkers) in some pragmatic or regulative sense. As Kant himself said, synthetic *a priori* principles and categories are necessary presuppositions of all possible thought and being for us; but the necessity, according to Nietzsche, is not logically objective but rather instrumentally subjective as a tool in the struggle for domination. In fact, this wholly instrumental necessity is directly proportional (in a non-mathematical sense) to the actual (objective?) falsity of the principles and categories thus accepted, or rather seized upon. Nor does Nietzsche regard his own claims and arguments as exceptions to this radical analysis: he does not claim that the analysis is true, but freely acknowledges that it is his own tool in the intellectual power struggle. In one passage, he speaks of his 'darling thoughts' and expresses fear for them, lest they should become calcified or petrified into the mythological status of objective truths. He even proposes, in this connection, what I will call an inverted Hegelianism: Hegel was notorious for arguing that there are no false philosophies and that every viewpoint, though it appears false in isolation from other viewpoints, is a partial fragment of the whole truth (the Absolute) in which all dialectical oppositions receive final reconciliation; but Nietzsche turned this claim on its head by insisting that there are no true philosophies and that the hostile opposition of irreconcilable perspectives represents varying degrees of falsity in the intellectual struggle for domination. The ideal of rational objectivity would make sense only if there were indisputable logical starting points for all thought; but there are no such indisputable principles, since the claim that there are—or the claim that any particular principles are—such starting points, is merely the setting of an intellectual battle line for which there are always serious opponents straining for the fight. The opposition
7.217) the belief in objective knowledge may be necessary as a tool in the struggle for domination—such necessity is directly proportional to the falsity of its expressions.	
7.218) Nietzsche's own claims are admitted to be tools in his own struggle;	
7.219) contra Hegel, Nietzsche claims that all philosophers exhibit varying degrees of falsity; 7.219a) there are no indisputable starting points for thought,	

between opposing ethical perspectives is, of course, viewed by Nietzsche as merely a series of skirmishes in the larger battle among struggling total viewpoints; it is simply a 'military' tactic to assume hypocritically (or even unknowingly) the guise or mask of rational objectivity—merely a 'front' to deceive one's opponent! Nietzsche sees Immanuel Kant as a superb philosophical example of this disingenuous attitude; he asks us to imagine the 'tartuffery of old Kant' who, chafing at the bondage to moral law within himself, constructed his entire moral philosophy with the sole objective of binding the whole human race with the imaginary chains that he could not (or would not) himself escape.

To spell all this out in detail, as it applies to the development of Nietzsche's normative ethical perspective, involves the recognition that the subjective relativity of all beliefs, and therefore also of moral beliefs, becomes plausibly intelligible only if we view the impulsive and non-rational source of beliefs as itself an expression of the power principle which lies at the root of all evolutionary development and advance. From this point of view, power is the locus of value, not because it is a transcendently objective standard of value (as in traditional objectivist ethics), but because power is the locus of all real efficacy in action and because beliefs, rightly understood in their genesis, are the tools and operative channels of that power. So for Nietzsche, it is not as if *some* ethical perspectives are the product of non-rational impulsive factors, while others have a different and perhaps more respectable or more objective source; no, *all* ethical viewpoints are in general on an equal par in this respect, all are equally impulsive in their basis. But there is a difference between perspectives that acknowledge that impulsive source, even exult in it, and whose champions creatively put forth some scale of moral values that consciously express the self-esteem and life-affirming assertiveness of the 'free spirit' who is on the front line of evolutionary advance, on the one hand, and, on the other hand, those perspectives that perversely deny this impulsive foundation, ascribe their moral philosophy to some purportedly objective, transcendent, even religious source, and put forth the framework of their morality out of resentment for the self-assertive aristocrat and in support of the suffering, the helpless, and the defenseless, with the result that morality,

7.219b) but only struggles among projected beliefs;

7.219c) opposing ethical perspectives are elements in the larger struggle for domination.

7.220) Application to ethics:

7.220a) All beliefs are an expression of the basic tyrannical impulse or will to power;

7.221) power therefore is the locus of value in the sense that it is the locus of all efficacy in action, while beliefs are the tools of that power;

7.222) though all ethical viewpoints are impulsive, there is a distinction between:
7.222a) the master-morality which acknowledges that source;
7.222b) the slave-morality which depicts itself in the guise of some objective basis.

though actually produced by life-affirming impulse, is directed against its source through self-denying and life-obstructing rules and principles. Nietzsche designates the first of these types of moral standpoints as the master-morality of the aristocratic 'free spirit,' while he terms the latter type as the slave-morality of the masses; the first is creative, tyrannical, and life-fulfilling; the second is reactionary (a response to the other type), resentful, and ultimately life-destructive. The moral antithesis of the master-morality is that between *good* (whatever promotes power and domination) and *bad* (whatever frustrates these objectives); the moral antithesis of the slave-morality is that between *good* (whatever protects the suffering and helpless against aristocratic exploitation) and *evil* (whatever expresses and/or implements that exploitation to the detriment of the weak and helpless). The first sort of morality construes the true and the good as the exclusive possession of the strong and therefore not as any common or universally compossible end or goal; while the second type (the morality of resentment) moves in just the opposite direction, construing the true and the good as precisely common and thus universally compossible (realizable in principle by all human beings). But in reality both types are in fact expressions of the evolutionary will to power, so that the slave-morality (the project of what Nietzsche calls the ascetic or purportedly self-denying priest-philosopher), while claiming to be a self-preservative for the suffering, is only an apparent exception to the Nietzschean claim that all perspectives are the projection of tyrannical impulse, since the slave-morality actually is also life-affirming in a perverse and self-destructive sense. Nietzsche, of course, makes it clear that the master-morality is the higher (better?) type, since it consciously and self-assertively affirms the power principle on which it is based, while the slave-morality necessarily disguises and masks its true source—the will to power.

It is not Nietzsche's intent to provide rationally persuasive arguments for his own opinions and commitments: he even says quite abruptly that his opinion is precisely that—*his* opinion rather than anyone else's, and that another man has not easily a right to it, unless he pays the price of intense and agonizing struggle to make it his own, just as Nietzsche himself claimed to have done. But the impression, at least,

---

7.223) These two types stand in stark contrast to each other: the free spirits *vs.* the masses; 7.223a) the assertive and life-fulfilling *vs.* the reactionary and life-destructive;

7.223b) the good/bad contrast *vs.* the good/evil contrast; 7.223c) the good realizable only by the strong *vs.* the good as universally compossible for all human beings; 7.224) but even the slave-morality is life-affirming in a perverse and self-destructive sense, while the master-morality is higher because directly self-affirming.

7.225) Supporting arguments (although Nietzsche does not claim to give rationally persuasive arguments, the impression of such arguments is constantly alluded to):

of supporting argument is threaded through Nietzsche's writings to a considerable degree. I would describe his argumentative motif as genetic in character; that is, he regards the logical status of any belief as determined by its empirical origin. At times he argues on philological grounds, for example, that moral language was originally set in a nonmoral context of some sort—for instance in the economic language of creditor and debtor, so that the concept of obligation in the moral sense is based on the notion of economic debt. Again, as we have already seen, he argues extensively that moral beliefs are ultimately grounded in the biological impulses that, on his view, account for evolutionary advance from the lower forms of life to the human species. He also culls out of the history of philosophy and theology numerous passages that display rancor, spite, and enmity of one sort or another, and then he concludes from this attitudinal stance that such non-rational motives are, at least in large measure, the basis of the viewpoints that are propounded in this clearly emotional context. In general, from all of these lines of argumentation, Nietzsche repeatedly suggests, if he does not explicitly conclude, that beliefs which emerge from such motives cannot rise higher than their source, and that, since these sources are all non-rational in the relevant sense, any claim to rational objectivity for the substance of the beliefs is wholly implausible. Since he regards all beliefs (and therefore also all moral beliefs) as originating in some such impulsive and non-rational fashion, he intimates often, and sometimes flatly asserts, that there cannot be any rationally objective philosophical or therefore moral truths. Non-rational origin thus implies non-rational substance in the case of beliefs. If, for example, one could show that the belief in any sort of transcendent divine reality originated from, say, the desire of political rulers to control their subjects, or from the desire of frustrated persons to accept their bleak plight in life, etc., that would imply that there was no rational basis for believing in such a divine reality. In the moral case, if my sole basis for accepting moral principles turned out to be my respect for the authority of my parents (or any other such non-rational motive), that would support the claim that principles so arrived at could not be objectively true. I shall designate this general type of argument, in which origin implies truth

7.226) the arguments are basically genetic in character and assume that the logical status of a belief is determined by its empirical origin. 7.226a) such arguments may be cast in several contexts: 1. philological, 2. biological, 3. psychological;

7.226b) it is then claimed that all beliefs arise from such non-rational causes.

7.227) It is then argued (or claimed) that such non-rational causes invalidate any claim to rational objectivity for the beliefs involved, so that there cannot be any rationally objective philosophical or moral truths.

7.228) Applications of the genetic principle:

7.229) The question will then be whether geneticism is itself a valid form of argument.

7.230) Critique of Nietzsche's ethic:

7.231) the general question:
7.232) whether subjective relativism destroys its own thesis;

7.233) and whether any genuine normative ethic can be defined in this context;

status, as *geneticism*. And then the question will be whether geneticism is either a fallacy or a reasonable form of argument; but that question has yet to be considered. Hence, it is to the task of critically assessing Nietzsche's overall normative ethical perspective, and its basis, that we now turn.

As with Sartre, so with Nietzsche: since he rejects the ideal of rational objectivity and with it any notion of an objective moral norm, it is possible once more to raise the twofold question whether such a radical doctrine of subjective relativism in epistemology does not destroy its own relevance as a philosophical thesis by reducing itself to the mere impulsive projection of Nietzsche himself (or other similar relativists), and whether, if moral principles are, like all other beliefs, themselves also impulsive projections in the same way, Nietzsche can be said to propound any genuine normative ethic at all in the morally relevant sense, whether any wholly subjective moral principles could possibly provide a framework for a genuine moral ideal or any authentic basis for universal moral duty or obligation. Such questions are, in my opinion, simply unanswerable by Nietzsche's position in any logically consistent fashion. If the argumentative geneticism to which, as I have noted, Nietzsche repeatedly appeals is accepted as a plausible basis for criticism of views for which Nietzsche has disdain, it will, as a method, also carry Nietzsche's own views into logical oblivion along with those of his intellectual opponents. But I need not develop this sort of argument further in this context in any general way, since I already have developed this sort of criticism in several previous contexts and especially in my critique of Sartre.

7.234) as applied to Nietzsche:

7.235) the claim, that all propositions are false, is itself false by its own assertion; and if this is true, objections based upon it are all invalid;

Yet it is important to apply this criticism to Nietzsche's own discussion. If there is no such thing as objective philosophical truth, if any and all epistemological principles are as dispensable as they are false (and, vice versa, as false as they are dispensable), and if one opts for an inverted Hegelianism for which there are no true philosophies but only varying degrees of philosophical falsity; then it follows logically that Nietzsche's claims are themselves false by their own assertion, since they purport to be correct descriptions of the logical status of all propositions and therefore are rendered false by that very description. In other words, to claim that it is true that all propositions are false is to claim that this proposition itself is false, which is self-contradictory.

If Nietzsche were to argue that in fact he does claim that his propositions are precisely false in this very way, then it will be the case that these propositions make no epistemic claim at all and that they therefore constitute no objections whatsoever to positions (like the ideal of rational objectivity) that Nietzsche claims to reject. Another way to put this same criticism is to point out that unless the law of contradiction is recognized as itself a rationally objective and necessary principle of reason (or rather unless there is such a principle whether or not it is recognized as such), it will be impossible to make any epistemic or substantive claim. A proposition can be true (can claim that something is the case) only if its denial is not true (or in other words is false); hence, if, as Nietzsche claims, there is no essential logical opposition between true and false, no assertions can conceivably be intelligible. Nietzsche's own claims can therefore communicate intelligible assertions only on the basis of the very sort of rationally objective principles he purports to deny.

7.236) unless the law of contradiction is itself a rationally necessary principle, no intelligible assertion can be made.

Consider once again Nietzsche's geneticism. The underlying assumption of his method here is the thesis that the logical status of a belief or claim is wholly determined by the nature of the sources from which that belief or claim emerges; in other words, the history (whether cultural or individual) of a belief settles the question of its logical grounding. Thus if a belief originates historically or genetically from sources or causes that would provide logical grounds for the reasonableness of that belief (logically supporting reasons), then, the belief itself could, in principle, be regarded as rationally objective in its logical status; but if the sources or causes of a belief are non-rational and hence would not supply logically supporting reasons for the substance of that belief, then such a belief could not properly be regarded as rationally objective in its logical status. This, of course, raises the question as to how the distinction between rational and non-rational causes or sources can be clearly drawn. If the epistemic motive of a person who accepts a belief is grounded in appeals to rational coherence, compatibility with existing scientific knowledge (or at least adaptability with that knowledge through reciprocal adjustment), relevant empirical observation, or pertinence to solving a practical or theoretical problem, then the sources or causes as thus described would be rational because such appeals,

7.237) Nietzsche's geneticism assumes:
7.237a) that the logical status of a belief is determined by its origin;

7.237b) that there is a distinction between rational and non-rational causes of belief;

7.237c) that if the causes of belief were rational, the beliefs would have some claim to rational objectivity, but that if they were non-rational, the beliefs would not have such a claim;

if successful, provide relevant logical reasons for accepting a belief as true or rejecting it as false. But if the epistemic motive of a person who accepts a belief is grounded in appeals to personal preference, traditional instruction, authority (i.e., sheer testimony from another person), antiquity, or desire, then the sources or causes as thus described would be non-rational because such appeals do not supply (except in cases where these factors themselves are being analyzed) any logical reasons for accepting a belief as true or rejecting it as false. That, for example, I prefer a belief, that the belief has wide acceptance in my cultural sub-group, that some other person told me that the belief was true quite apart from any supporting reasons for his or her testimony, that the belief has been accepted over a long period of time in our civilization, or that I have a yearning or desire for the belief to be true—none of these sources or causes provide in themselves any logical basis for the belief's being either true or false. Now Nietzsche's argumentative thesis here is that, in the end, all beliefs are grounded in non-rational sources or causes, and that they therefore can lay no claim to rational objectivity precisely for that reason. In particular, philosophical beliefs (and therefore moral or ethical beliefs as a subset of them) are grounded in impulse and are therefore particularly vulnerable in this way; morality, for example, is grounded in social conventions which are themselves determined by prevailing impulses of individuals and groups, so that beliefs thus originated could not possibly be rational in the relevant sense.

7.237d) that all beliefs have non-rational causes and can therefore make no claim to rational objectivity.

7.238) In response:
7.238a) There is again the self-contradictory character of Nietzsche's claim;

Now in response to all this I need not now bring up again in detail the self-contradictory character of claiming that all beliefs are non-rationally originated, and also that certain beliefs (in religion and morality, for example) should therefore be rejected as false because they have such an origin, or even (more strongly) that such beliefs could not possibly be objectively true; for in that case, Nietzsche's own critical claim could, for that same reason, not possibly be objectively true and thus should be rejected as false. That I regard this as an appropriate and sound criticism has already been made abundantly clear, and I need to labor it no further. I shall rather urge that it is simply false that the originating causes of a belief, if non-rational, settle the question of its logical status as false. That which any belief claims to be the

7.238b) it is simply false that beliefs with non-rational causes cannot be objectively true;

case is logically distinct from the causes that motivated any given person to believe it. To develop this as a criticism, I will assume (what Nietzsche does not) that there are some rationally grounded beliefs (I will leave the reader to provide his or her own examples for the most part, but I have in mind such beliefs as two times two are equal to four, contradictory propositions cannot both be true, I am now writing this sentence, my parents once existed as human beings and progenitors, etc.). At the same time I will claim (even insist) that any given person could believe any or all of such a set of beliefs for reasons and in relation to causes that would provide no rational basis for their truth; that is, a person can, and often does, believe the right things (whatever is true or is the case) for the logically wrong or at least irrelevant reason—in other words, he or she could believe on non-rational grounds. But if that is the case, then it would be logically absurd to claim that a belief originated from non-rational causes (in the case of a given person) could not possibly be objectively true or that its origin in this way provides any evidence for supposing it to be objectively false. Most people, for example, start out and end up believing in the multiplication table on the authority of some teacher or textbook (or both); but of course the fact that their motivation in believing is non-rational in no sense settles any question about the logical status of multiplication products. In the same way, if a person believes in God from the motivation provided by respect for one's own father figure (of course, almost no one would give that analysis of one's own belief), that would clearly be a non-rational origin of the belief; but its being so (or even if it were so universally about virtually all believers in God) settles nothing about the truth or falsity of the belief in God. Of course, it is also true that purporting to believe something on clearly rational grounds does not of itself guarantee that a belief claim is true either, since even logically appropriate or rational grounds can be misconstrued or incorrectly used or even perverted—no doubt that happens quite regularly in a subject like philosophy. But the misconstruction of a generally appropriate rational method and the appeal to logically irrelevant reasons as a basis for belief commitment are two radically different types of mistakes; the former involves a built-in structure for revision and self-correction, while the latter does not. In

7.238c) there are some rationally grounded beliefs;

7.238d) a person could accept such beliefs on non-rational grounds (i.e., believe the right things for the logically wrong reason);

7.238e) it is absurd to claim that a belief resting on non-rational causes could not be objectively true, or that it is for that reason objectively false;

7.238f) nor does the claim to rational grounding guarantee truth either:

7.239) geneticism, as an argumentative method, is therefore basically unsound: psychological motive and philosophical basis are logically distinct, so that Nietzsche's genetic arguments are inconclusive.

any case, from all this we can reasonably conclude that the central thrust of geneticism as an argumentative method is basically unsound: the psychological motive that generates a belief and its philosophical basis (its rational or logical grounding), although they may occasionally coincide in particular cases, are entirely distinct in logical status, and neither logically entails anything positive or negative about the other. It is entirely possible to believe the logically right thing for the logically wrong sort of reason, and also the logically wrong thing for the logically right sort of reason. And if that is true, then Nietzsche's caveats against certain sorts of beliefs (or even all beliefs), on grounds of their genetic origin from non-rational causes, are seen to be logically irrelevant and inconclusive. This is especially the case for Nietzsche since he regards the belief in the principle of causation as itself an impulsive projection with no rationally objective status.

7.240) Regarding the thesis that power is the ultimate locus of all value:
7.241) as a purely descriptive account of how moral beliefs arise, this thesis makes no substantive moral claim;

But what about Nietzsche's central normative ethical thesis that power is the ultimate locus of all value (and therefore, via impulsive factors, of all moral perspectives, principles, and beliefs)? On one interpretation, Nietzsche's thesis should be understood as a purely descriptive and genetic account of how moral beliefs arise in the thinking of human agents, with the result that he is making no ethical or moral claim in the normatively relevant sense at all. Such beliefs are the determined product of various impulses (especially the tyrannical impulse), and these beliefs function therefore (either directly or indirectly) as both expressions and tools of those impulses, all of which are themselves facets of the power impulse. If that were the whole of Nietzsche's moral philosophy, then it would follow, on any other than purely instrumental grounds, that all moral beliefs and principles would be on an equal footing, so that none would be more or less adequate as moral beliefs than others, except in the sense of being more efficient expressions or tools of the power impulse. Consistently with that interpretation, Nietzsche would have to conclude logically that, in the relevant normative sense, master-morality would be no more adequate than slave-morality, the aristocratic morality of the 'free spirit' no more adequate than the morality of the masses. It might even be argued that, on purely instrumental grounds, the slave-morality was more pragmatically effective in achieving

7.241a) if all moral beliefs are products of the power impulse, they would be on an equal footing in terms of moral adequacy;

7.241b) on purely instrumental grounds,

its ends (the restraint of the aristocrats and the protection of the weak and suffering masses) than the master-morality in achieving its ends (subjection of the masses and domination over them). And in many contexts Nietzsche seems reluctantly to accede to these consequences.

But there are clearly other passages in Nietzsche's works that point in a radically different direction. He repeatedly exults in the aristocratic morality and regards it as vastly superior to the slave-morality for which he has only disdain and vitriolic critical rejection. He even gives reasons for this rather obvious value judgment: the aristocrat freely creates his scale of values as a direct expression of the tyrannical impulse, while the slave-morality takes the form of reactionary resentment against aristocratic values, so that such an ethic is indirect and externally dependent (since it would never arise apart from aristocratic provocation) rather than internally independent and freely creative; the values of the aristocrat are rare, individual, unique, and self-elevating, while the values of the masses are common, ordinary, universal (in a spurious sense), and relatively insignificant. Of course, Nietzsche gives one sort of argument for the aristocratic morality (and against the slave-morality) which represents a lapse or transition into his previously analyzed stance: the aristocratic style of morality is on the cutting edge of evolutionary advance which is made possible by domination, while the slave-morality is a vestige of the rubble which that advance leaves behind—indeed slave-morality actually obstructs evolutionary advance. Yet even this distinction is based on a normative value standard for identifying what would constitute advance rather than retrogression. Clearly all this is inconsistent with Nietzsche's earlier genetic explanation of the impulsive origin of all values and moral beliefs, since in arguing the superiority of aristocratic over slave-morality he is appealing to the very sort of objective normative standard which it was the intent of his earlier arguments to destroy. Doubtless Nietzsche would respond to this sort of argument by rejecting (again inconsistently) the rational objectivity of the principle of contradiction itself.

With some qualms, therefore, let us suppose that Nietzsche, however inconsistently, is actually propounding the normative ethical thesis that power is the ultimate moral good and thus the sole basis of all genuine moral worth. I

slave-morality might plausibly be judged more effective than master-morality;

7.242) Yet Nietzsche judges master-morality as superior:

7.242a) partly because it is creative and independent rather than reactionary and dependent;

7.242b) partly because it promotes evolutionary advance rather than obstructing it;
7.242c) but this value judgment rests on the very sort of purportedly objective value standard that Nietzsche's geneticism denies.

7.243) If Nietzsche is claiming that power is the ultimate moral good in an objective sense:

do not know, of course, whether Nietzsche would accept this interpretation of one segment of his pronouncements about morality. But if so, he would be involved in an even greater degree of incoherence. To begin with, power is by its very nature instrumental and extrinsic, rather than ultimate or intrinsic; it is always power to produce an effect or pursue an objective, it is always power for, or in relation to, some end beyond itself. It logically could not therefore, in the relevant normative moral sense, be the ultimate principle of goodness since, as the basis of all contingent goodness, the ultimate good must have the whole ground or basis of its worth in itself intrinsically or self-containedly. Again, the ultimate good, as universally obligatory on all rational moral beings (the basis of all moral 'oughtness') must be, in a general sense, universally compossible for all responsible moral agents. But since power in one person implies the subjection of those over whom it is exercised, power and its actualization by individuals cannot be universally compossible as the basis of moral obligation for all moral agents. And yet the universal moral good or right is precisely that which all moral agents are objectively obligated to pursue. Of course, Nietzsche would hardly be moved by any of this since he explicitly rejects the notion of the good as universally compossible: it is rather the unique, individual, and exclusive possession of the aristocratic free spirit and his self-projection. But if that is the case, then there is no normative ethic here in the proper sense at all. Further and finally, if the creative aristocratic morality of the 'free spirit' is the highest sort of morality, then that raises several unanswerable questions from Nietzsche's point of view: what is the standard of its high status in the normative sense? Again, how can such a position be plausibly argued, given Nietzsche's radical epistemological relativism? And especially, how can the notion of a freely creative aristocratic spirit be anything but a 'free-floating' myth in view of Nietzsche's rigorous determinism? Any answers to such questions would clearly violate one or other of Nietzsche's cardinal doctrines, or, as he calls them, 'darling dogmas.'

In retrospect, I find in Nietzsche, comparatively speaking, no really significant advance over Sartre as an exponent of ethical humanism; if anything, all the features of Sartre's ethic that raised critical questions for my reflection are

7.243a) this claim fails to account for the fact that power is always instrumental and extrinsic, rather than ultimate and intrinsic;

7.243b) nor is power universally compossible, as the moral good must logically be.

7.244) How is the notion of such a highest morality consistent with either epistemological relativism or determinism?

simply more exacerbated in Nietzsche and therefore more negatively provocative. The package includes radical epistemological relativism, equally radical ethical relativism and subjectivism, and elements of some sort of normative objectivism that are logically incompatible with this prior relativism. And then Nietzsche adds some 'genus' of his own by throwing in his brand of argumentative geneticism, rigorous determinism, and the grounding of all beliefs in non-rational impulse (especially the tyrannical impulse) and desire as expressions of the power principle. Any attempt to work this all up into a coherent normative ethical perspective seems clearly implausible at the outset. And if we should try to cure these ills by either discarding the relativism and leaving the normative objectivism, or by alternatively jettisoning the objectivism and preserving the relativism, then we are left either with a normative ethical theory (power ethics) that is implausible on its own turf, as I have previously argued, or with an epistemological stance that is in principle limited to describing and historicizing moral beliefs without providing any genuine moral theory of its own.

I do not claim that, in discussing Aristotle, Dewey, Sartre, and Nietzsche, I have covered all of the significant options for ethical humanism; but I do claim to have analyzed some of the most important and most widely discussed varieties of such a humanism. As is obvious, I have found them all critically wanting in complex and partly different ways from both a logical and a moral point of view. Hence I conclude that if there is a plausible normative ethical naturalism of the humanist genre, it has yet to come under our purview. At the same time, much that has the ring of genuineness has survived my critical understanding, much that surely will constitute a part of an adequate normative ethic even if that ethic goes beyond the limits of ethical humanism. Whatever the ultimately good or right turns out to be in a logically objective sense, if it is to be the good or right for human beings, it will have to be correlative with human nature, it will have to be a good that fulfills and actualizes that nature both individually and socially. In this I agree with all the humanists I have discussed with some qualifications and with the possible exception of Nietzsche. The good for humanity, even if it is objectively independent of human judgment and opinion, cannot be wholly external to human

7.245) In general, the elements of Nietzsche's ethical perspective are reciprocally inconsistent, while they provide no basis for resolving these inconsistencies.

7.246) Summary comments on ethical humanism:

7.246a) All the perspectives considered are judged critically defective from both a logical and a moral standpoint;
7.246b) yet genuinely valid elements survive:

7.246b1) the ultimate good must be correlative with human nature, since personal being possesses intrinsic worth;

nature or totally unrelated to it. Personal being in human agents, since it is contingent in its existence, may have an intrinsic worth or value that is derived and dependent in relation to some objective principle or standard; but such personal being, nevertheless and as thus constituted, does possess intrinsic moral worth as such, so that the moral good for humanity involves as an aspect the actualization of human nature in however wide a variety of ways. I myself am prepared to go along with Aristotle on this point (within limits) and speak of the good for humanity as a well-being that most fully actualizes the defining properties of the human essence and to regard those defining properties as centering in rationality.

7.246b2) many moral beliefs are relativistic and impulsive in their genetic origin,

Again, while I cannot accept the radical epistemological and ethical relativism of some humanists (especially Sartre and Nietzsche), it seems essentially correct to say that a vast compass of moral beliefs do in fact originate for given individuals in the way that such relativism suggests: many moral beliefs are (whether consciously or not) originated from desire, preference, and impulse. But since, as I have argued, genetic origin does not finally determine the logical status of a belief, the recognition of this point does not destroy moral objectivism; it merely bids us to be cautious about our moral commitments and to recognize that our best efforts to achieve rational objectivity in our moral thinking and reflection are approximate at best. Moral humility, after all, need not be the same thing as intellectual surrender and collapse.

7.246b3) although this does not determine their logical status.

Religious Naturalism: Baruch (Benedict) Spinoza

7.247) The metaphysical context of Spinoza's moral philosophy:

The title of Spinoza's chief philosophical work is: *Ethics Proved in Geometrical Order*. From such a designation one might be led to expect a treatise almost exclusively concerned with moral philosophy; and it is therefore surprising that the work is preoccupied in three of its five parts with the development of metaphysical and epistemological claims which provide the backdrop and context for the analysis of Spinoza's perspective on the human predicament and its proposed solution. In fact, Spinoza's first and principal object of concern is God, though hardly the God of traditional Christian theism: for Spinoza God is the rationally

7.248) centers in God as absolutely infinite substance or nature;

necessary and logically self-completed totality which he also calls Nature or Substance. Descartes had previously defined substance as that which requires nothing but itself in order to exist; he then proceeded to acknowledge that, strictly speaking by virtue of this definition, God would be the only substance. He then went on to claim that God, however, had by fiat created two types of contingent substances, thought and extension, mind and body, which required only the creating and sustaining activity of God in order to exist; and he added that thought (mind) and extension (body) were completely distinct types of substances having no common property, characteristic, or attribute aside from contingency on the creative power of God. Spinoza, however, while he had great respect for Descartes and derived much of his own philosophical inspiration from him, took the position that Descartes' views on these matters, though employing the appropriate concepts (substance and attribute), were inconsistent. He agrees with Descartes in defining substance as self-existent, self-explanatory being, and in defining God as absolutely infinite substance. But then he opts for Descartes' original thesis that accordingly God must be the only substance, so that thought (mind) and extension (body) could not be substances at all. If God is absolutely infinite substance, he must possess all logically possible attributes: that is, an absolutely infinite number of attributes; hence, whatever else is real must either be itself an attribute of God, or a mode (or way) in which God exists determinately or in particular. Nor could there be more than one substance, in any case: first because, if there were more substances than one, each would constitute a limitation on the being of the others, so that none could be really self-existent or self-explanatory (which would contradict the definition of substance and hence the definition of God); and second because, if there were more than one substance, each would possess all the same attributes in conjunction (since God as substance possesses all logically possible attributes) and would therefore be the same identical substance. So, for Spinoza, God is the one and only substance; and although God has an absolutely infinite number of attributes, thought and extension are the only attributes known to human beings as finite minds. What on Cartesian grounds would be called finite substances, Spinoza designates as finite (lim-

7.249) this begins with Descartes' definition of substance, which, however, Descartes did not work out consistently;

7.250) Spinoza claimed that God, so defined, must be the only substance, while all else must be either an attribute or a mode of that substance;

7.250a) though God must have an infinite number of attributes,

7.250b) thought and extension are the only ones known to finite minds;

7.251) individual things (minds, bodies) are therefore finite modes of God, each mode being the same thing under all attributes;

7.251a) the mind and body of a finite person are therefore the same entity under different attributes;

7.251b) this identity extends through all nature;

7.252) God is not an individual personal mind with purposive ends, but divine causality is, as logical necessity, all-inclusive;

7.253) finite modes follow from God by logical necessity, not by purpose;

7.254) the logically ordered succession of finite modes is itself God or Nature or Substance.

ited) modes or ways in which God exists. Each finite mode is a mode of Substance (or God) under all of his attributes; but the only finite modes of substance known to human agents are finite minds (modes of substance under the attribute of thought) and finite bodies (modes of substance under the attribute of extension). It is, however, one and the same mode that, from one point of view or under one attribute, exists as the substantially and identically same mode under all the other attributes. Thus, for example, the mode of substance that constitutes the mind of a given human person under the attribute of thought is the substantially same mode that constitutes the body of that person under the attribute of extension, so that the mind and body of a person are therefore substantially the same identical entity. Of course, all other physical bodies are identical with their mental correlates (and vice versa) as well, even though we have no direct insight into what those correlates are like in the case of non-personal bodies like stones or trees, for example. Finally, from an ontological point of view, Spinoza does not regard God as a personal mind who creates finite modes in accordance with some divine plan or purpose; and of course, God does not *create* his attributes since they are simply constitutive of his essence. Yet divine causality is all-inclusive in its scope: each finite mode follows from the essence or nature of God by logically necessary implication in the same way that theorems follow from the axioms, definitions, and postulates of a geometrical system by logical entailment; and just as the theorems are not the product of purpose or design but are merely logical consequences of those axioms, definitions, and postulates, so finite modes are not the product of God's purpose or design, but are merely the logical unfolding or development of what God is as absolutely infinite substance. And each finite mode follows in this logical way from God, not directly (like a fiat creation), but indirectly through some previous finite mode and so on to infinity. The logically ordered succession and totality of these finite modes is what we would call nature, while at the same time it is also God or Substance. Hence Spinoza's formula: God or Substance or Nature. Of course, since it all proceeds in accordance with logical necessity, Spinoza's metaphysic is a rigorous determinism: all that exists is absolutely necessary, and whatever does not exist (at some time or other) is logically impossible.

In the preceding analysis, I have presented only a brief sketch of Spinoza's metaphysical perspective—just enough to provide the backdrop or context for his moral philosophy. Spinoza's discussion of ethics operates at two levels: first, at the level in which he attempts to explain how the ordinary moral beliefs and distinctions of human persons arise in the mind; and second, at the level in which he describes the human moral predicament and attempts to provide a solution for it by clarifying the notion of an ultimate moral good in which the mind of a human person can find genuine rest and peace. At the first and descriptive level, it is appropriate to designate Spinoza as a qualified ethical relativist. Human persons, Spinoza notes by immediate experience, are characterized by desires and aversions; and they call those circumstances, which implement and further their desires (whether immediately or in the long run), *good*, while they designate as *evil* whatever obstructs or hinders the realization of their desires. From this point of view, *good* and *evil* refer to nothing that characterizes things or circumstances in themselves, but only relatively to our desires and aversions, so that goodness and evil are not objective properties but rather are subjectively relational terms (to use my own previous terminology). And if that were the whole substance of Spinoza's views about morality and moral terms, he would be a radical ethical relativist indeed.

But for Spinoza that is decidedly not the whole of the matter. For he contends that there is an ideal of perfection, a true and supreme good in which human beings can repose and find genuine peace of mind: and he proceeds to develop a model of human nature which, as progressively actualized by the individual, will result in this repose and peace. On the other hand, human beings in their common and ordinary state are in general far removed from this model and therefore, in varying degrees, deprived of true repose and peace. Hence, human beings are in a moral and spiritual predicament from which they need to be delivered or even saved (in numerous passages Spinoza refers to this deliverance by the use of the clearly religious term *salvation*). This predicament or plight is essentially twofold: first, individuals are in a state of more or less continuous emotional bondage to their passions and desires, with the consequent

7.255) Two levels of ethical analysis:
7.256) The level of ordinary moral belief;

7.256a) at this level Spinoza is a qualified ethical relativist;

7.256b) good and evil are relative to desire and aversion;

7.257) The level of ideal moral perfection;
7.258) at this level, there is a true objective good in which individuals can find genuine peace and repose;

7.259) the human moral predicament is twofold:

7.259a) emotional bondage to desire and the resultant frustration when desire is obstructed; 7.259b) ignorance of the necessary order of nature.

7.260) Ignorance of the necessary order of nature is the intermediate cause of emotional bondage, although Nature itself is the ultimate cause of both;

7.260a) emotional bondage results from supposing that reality could be otherwise than it is, so that the knowledge that reality is logically necessary breaks the grip of emotional bondage and its resultant frustration;

frustration, disappointment, and alienation they experience when the realization of those passions or desires is obstructed or denied by the circumstances of their lives; and second, individuals are in general ignorant of the necessary order of Nature, understood in Spinoza's previously elaborated fashion. Correlatively, moral and spiritual salvation would consist in deliverance from both emotional bondage (along with its disintegrative consequences) and ignorance of that necessary order.

Now Spinoza believes that emotional bondage and ignorance have a clearly recognizable relation to each other. For he thinks that ignorance of the necessary order of Nature is the proximate or intermediate cause of emotional bondage in the case of any particular individual (in the ultimate and final sense, of course, Nature itself [or God or Substance] is the causal ground of both ignorance and emotional bondage, since everything without exception follows by logical necessity from the essence of absolutely infinite Substance, according to Spinoza). The emotional bondage of individuals is grounded in their ignorance in two ways: first, if individuals are frustrated, disappointed, alienated, and so on, when their desires and passions are not realized, it is because those individuals suppose that their feelings and circumstances could have turned out differently had they (or other persons) chosen or acted differently, or had the larger frame of contextual circumstances been different (all of which these individuals regard as both logically and actually possible)—and these unrealized possibilities, as imaginatively pictured by them, result in the undesirable consequences. But suppose, on the contrary, that individuals had, in general at least, a knowledge of the necessary order of Nature (as Spinoza envisioned it) and that therefore they knew that every event, thing, and circumstance was a logically necessary consequence of the nature of absolutely infinite substance. No one becomes emotionally distraught or frustrated over that which one clearly regards as logically necessary or over the non-occurrence of that which one clearly regards as logically impossible: who ever 'fell apart' emotionally because he or she saw it to be logically necessary that triangles have three internal angles or that there are no triangles with four internal angles? But according to Spinoza, everything (event, circumstance, occurrence, etc.) is just that logically necessary: nothing could be otherwise than it is; and if individuals know that, not just in the sense of supposing it remotely plausible, but in the sense of being unconditionally committed to it as logically necessary, then this knowledge would not only dissolve their ignorance but would also break the grip of their emotional bondage. Your mother *had* to die when and as she did, your sweetheart *had* to 'throw you over,' your job *had* to be terminated, your child *had* to get cancer, and so on. And thus the knowledge of necessity 'breaks the back' of emotional bondage.

The second (and logically related) way in which ignorance causes emotional bondage is more complicated in its explanation. Obstructed passions and desires result in frustration (and so on) precisely because individuals are ignorant of the nature and causes of the passions and desires themselves, as well as of the nature and causes of their obstruction. Thus the path to liberation from such frustration consists in making our passions and desires together with their causes and those of their obstruction, objects of fully adequate knowledge on our part. And the (perhaps) surprising thing here is that, as persons try to understand their passions and desires in relation to their causes, those passions and desires proportionately lose their grip on them and their frustration at their obstruction is diminished, precisely because active contemplative understanding involves a sort of mental tranquility which is incompatible with the disturbance of mind occasioned by passions and desires, especially if and when they are obstructed. Hence, as that mental tranquility progressively pervades the mind, the disturbance and frustration progressively diminish, so that the more persons understand their passions, desires, and frustrations, the more they increase their control over them. If, on the other hand, individuals do not pursue the adequate knowledge of their passions, desires, and the causes of them, then just in proportion to their ignorance their emotional bondage will not only continue but actually increase. According to Spinoza, it is of the utmost importance in this connection to recognize a distinction between *active* emotions and *passive* emotions or passions. A passive emotion is conjoined by the mind with the idea of an external cause or causes through confused and inadequate thinking; for example, such an emotion is construed as caused by an external object or objects

7.260b) emotional bondage is further dissipated by making passive emotions and their causes objects of adequate knowledge;

7.261) active knowledge involves a mental tranquility that is opposed to the bondage and frustration of passive emotion;

7.262) passive emotion is conjoined by the mind with an external cause through confused thinking, while active emotion is conjoined with the mind itself as its adequate cause through adequate knowledge;

7.263) passive emotions and their causes cease to cause disturbance when they are made objects of active emotion through adequate knowledge.

through sensory awareness thereof, or alternatively it is attributed to some bodily response or condition. But an active emotion is, by contrast, conjoined with the mind itself as its cause through adequate ideas by means of which the mind understands that emotion, so that the mind experiences emotional pleasure and delight in its own adequate understanding. For Spinoza, it follows from this analysis that when persons make of any passion or desire or cause thereof an object of their own adequate knowledge, that passion or desire ceases to be a passive emotion and that external cause comes under the control of those persons precisely by means of their adequate knowledge of it. Of course, that does not mean that the objects or causes (even as external) cease to exist; but it does mean that the object no longer occasions a passion (or passive emotion) and that the cause no longer disturbs the mental tranquility of those individuals, since they have an adequate and therefore liberating knowledge of that cause. Passive emotions cannot thus be overcome simply by struggling against them; they can be overcome only through being overbalanced and dissipated by the active emotion generated through fully adequate understanding. Knowledge therefore is not external cosmic power, but it is internal and active emotional power, since knowledge, adequate understanding, and the tranquility of mind that they occasion, simply cannot coexist with emotional bondage in the same individual in relation to the same objects or causes.

7.264) The adequate and comprehensive knowledge of all things in God not only dissolves emotional bondage, but replaces it with the active emotion of intrinsic delight in that knowledge and in God as its object;

7.264a) this is the intellectual love of God;

For Spinoza, of course, the adequate knowledge that results in liberation or salvation from emotional bondage cannot consist of so many isolated bits of unrelated insight. Such knowledge rather expands to the comprehensive apprehension of the necessary order of all things in the being of God (or Nature or Substance) as the ultimate causal ground and reality of all that is. And individuals who have that vision not only break the grip of their own emotional bondage, but also replace it with the active emotion of intrinsic delight in that knowledge itself together with its object and ground (God or Nature or Substance). Spinoza designates this supremely satisfying and active emotion as the intellectual love of God; but of course, it is not love for God as a person, since God is the impersonal order of nature and therefore logically cannot reciprocally love individual persons in return, except in the sense that the persons themselves, along with others who share in the salvation originated by adequate knowledge, are, as persons, a part of God, so that, in *their* love for God, God (in that same identical love) loves them (individuals) in return. In any case, for Spinoza, this intellectual love of God is the ultimate and highest good subjectively for human persons, while objectively and in itself God (or Nature or Substance) is the true and ultimate good. For Spinoza, after all, the Good is Perfection, and Perfection is Reality itself. To know that with full adequacy and to rest in it is not only to be delivered from emotional bondage; it is to find salvation in the only intelligible sense in which it is available to human beings.

7.264b) this love is the highest subjective good, while God or Nature is the true and ultimate objective good.

Spinoza's normative ethical perspective is so closely and extensively attached to his general metaphysical point of view that any criticism of his ethic must concern itself in part with the question of the adequacy or inadequacy of that inclusive general outlook. At the same time, it is hardly my intention to offer here a critique of that entire comprehensive position; and I shall therefore concern myself only with those aspects of his general metaphysic that have a direct logical bearing on my critique of his normative ethic. My silence about other aspects of Spinoza's overall philosophy should not be taken either as approval or disapproval, consent or dissent. I have written enough on these other areas in my previous writings (to which I've already referred) so as to enable any serious reader to project for him or herself my critical assessment of those aspects of Spinoza's position. But it is important to point out that his metaphysic involves several morally relevant elements, such as (what I will call) immanental pantheism, rigorous logico-mathematical determinism, and thought/extension (or mind/body) identity (at the level of Substance). I define pantheism as the view that all reality is included within the being and nature of God, so that, independently of God there is nothing real; and I call Spinoza's obvious pantheism (in this sense) immanental because he regards the terms God and Nature as referring to the same and only reality and as being therefore co-extensive—God, in other words, has for Spinoza no aspects that are independent or transcendent of Nature in the largest sense, but the whole of God is present within and identical with Nature (hence, immanent). The doctrine

7.265) Critique of Spinoza's ethic:

7.266) Spinoza's metaphysical perspective has several aspects relevant to ethics:
7.266a) immanental pantheism;

of rigorous logico-mathematical determinism in Spinoza's thought I have already explained; it is simply the view that whatever and all that is the case follows from the essence of God with logical necessity and in a way that is analogous to the way in which theorems and propositions follow from the axioms, definitions, and postulates of a formal mathematical system (for example, Euclidian geometry). Finally, thought/extension or mind/body identity is, in Spinoza, the view that mind and body are not two different entities but one and the same entity considered from two different points of view or aspects.

I shall begin by stating point-blank that I regard all three of these closely related doctrines as seriously flawed from a critical standpoint, and that I regard them, both individually and conjunctively, as logically incompatible with any plausible form of normative ethical objectivism. But I will not try in this place to argue both of these claims in any inclusive sense; as previously indicated, I will concern myself only with their ethical dimensions. If immanental pantheism (in Spinoza's sense) is true so that reality, God, and Nature are all co-terminous, and if, as Spinoza claims, perfection (both moral and nonmoral) is reality itself, then it would follow either that there is no such distinction as that between morally good or right and morally evil or wrong, or that whatever is real or even conceivably the case is morally good or perfect when considered in its total context (in actuality, these two points are the same point differently stated). The first of these points would follow because, on Spinoza's view, there could be no conceivable basis for judging any state of affairs as either good or evil (right or wrong), for whatever is the case would be perfect, since being real and being perfect are identical in meaning; the second point would follow because everything would proceed from the nature of reality and therefore be an aspect of that perfection with which reality is identical. But Spinoza clearly believes that there *is* a moral ideal of human nature that defines the moral good for man and that any state of human existence that falls short of that ideal is less than morally perfect or morally good in the highest sense. And he also appears to believe that both emotional bondage and ignorance (or the lack of adequate knowledge) are morally evil (perhaps even morally wrong for the individual). Yet such moral distinctions cannot logically hold if all that is real or is the case is perfect for that very reason; the only view compatible with Spinoza's general position is that everything is as good as it could possibly be in its context. Hence, either the general view or the moral distinctions will 'have to go' or yield logical ground. Another way of putting all this is to say that if God is the supreme good, then that good logically cannot contain in itself any aspect that is even conceivably evil or wrong, for that would be to claim that good in its essence entails evil as an aspect, and how could evil be an essential aspect of the good? If, to avoid this contradiction, it is maintained that the so-called evil aspect is only evil from an isolated or limited point of view, but is essentially good from the standpoint of the whole, then that would eliminate the distinction between good and evil altogether. Such are some of the problems of Spinoza's pantheism from a normative ethical point of view.

As for Spinoza's rigorous logico-mathematical determinism, my whole earlier critique, of any sort of compatibilism which argues that rigorous determinism is consistent with the sort of freedom that is essential to moral obligation and responsibility, is relevant as a criticism of Spinoza's view as well, but it is especially problematic for Spinoza, since he holds that whatever is the case, and therefore whatever the moral condition of finite moral agents, that case and condition are the logically necessary consequence of the essence of God and hence could not logically be otherwise than they are. Now, as we have already indicated in the previous section, Spinoza clearly propounds a moral ideal (deliverance from emotional bondage and the realization of the moral good through adequate knowledge), an ideal that he presumably regards as realistically possible for human beings to pursue, since he repeatedly urges individuals to undertake that pursuit as a path to salvation. But clearly all this moral exhortation and advice on Spinoza's part must, from his own point of view as a determinist, fall on deaf ears. For if the choices and actions that human beings opt for are logically necessary, then it follows that they do not have the morally relevant freedom to choose and act otherwise than they do. If it is wholly determined that an individual will achieve the adequate knowledge to effect release from emotional bondage, then so be it; but it makes no sense to claim either that

7.270c) yet such distinctions are incompatible with the view that moral perfection is reality itself.

7.271) If rigorous logico-mathematical determinisms were true, the advocacy of a moral ideal would be irrelevant, since all human acts would be necessarily determined, and human agents would lack the pertinent freedom to respond to any such ideal;

7.271a) if human acts are wholly determined, then human agents logically cannot be morally responsible for acting as they do, rather than otherwise;

he can, or that he morally ought to, pursue such an ideal, since by metaphysical necessity it is a settled matter. And if it is wholly determined that an individual will persist in being a moral profligate enslaved by passion and desire, again, so be it; but it makes no sense to claim that he or she could have chosen differently, much less that he or she ought to have chosen and acted differently, since, as in the previous case, it is once more a settled matter. Yet presumably Spinoza claims that human agents ought to pursue the moral ideal and that they are morally responsible for their condition if they fail to pursue adequate knowledge as a way of deliverance. It is even possible (though this is debatable) that Spinoza regarded himself as morally obligated and responsible for disseminating the moral insight that he dispenses throughout the *Ethics*; but how, on his own deterministic premises, could such a conviction of moral obligation and responsibility be logically justified, since determinism implies that his choosing and acting as he did in writing his treatise was a necessarily settled matter?

7.271b) the determinism required for release from emotional bondage and frustration seems logically incompatible with the freedom required to change one's attitude on the basis of recognizing that determinism.

An even greater difficulty about Spinoza's determinism, from his own normative point of view, concerns his concept of the relation between adequate knowledge and the deliverance from emotional bondage. As may be recalled, Spinoza maintains that adequate knowledge of the necessary order and details of nature is the key to release from that emotional bondage which consists in the frustration experienced as a consequence of obstructed passion and disappointed desire. For if persons fully understand the logical necessity of every event and circumstance, they will be able to change their attitudes from one of frustration and alienation to one of rational acceptance, since no one can rationally be frustrated either over occurrences they understand as logically necessary or over non-occurrences they understand as logically impossible. And on Spinoza's view *whatever* occurs is logically necessary and *whatever* does *not* occur is logically impossible; hence, for the person who has fully adequate knowledge of that necessity and that impossibility, it will be possible to face all occurrences and obstructions with an attitude of rational acceptance and serenity. Now, since Spinoza urges human beings to pursue such knowledge and such an attitude, and since such urging would itself be irrational on Spinoza's part if the occurrence of that knowledge and that attitude were purely mechanical and automatic, I assume that Spinoza regards the pursuit of that knowledge and attitude as an open option which persons may or may not adopt or which they are genuinely able and free to adopt or not. Otherwise Spinoza's appeal would be ridiculously pointless. But this entire process involves an inescapable and insoluble dilemma in Spinoza's bailiwick. For unless rigorous determinism is true universally, there will be no all-inclusive necessity and/or impossibility the recognition of which by persons could lead to their deliverance from frustration; yet unless rigorous universal determinism is false, there will be no genuine option for persons freely to adopt (or not) in pursuing adequate knowledge and changing their attitude to one of rational acceptance and serenity. Thus rigorous universal determinism is a necessary condition for deliverance from frustration, while the falsity of such a determinism is a necessary condition for the genuine freedom required as a basis for rational choice in the pursuit of adequate knowledge and the effecting of changed attitude. But surely all this is a clear logical contradiction. If, on the other hand, the requisite knowledge and attitude are purely mechanical and automatic occurrences (for some, perhaps very few, persons), then all of Spinoza's moral writing and advice are themselves irrational, irrelevant, and inconsequential. Either way, the result for any thoughtful and meditative person would be one of confusion and befuddlement; for *without* the determinism the needed deliverance from emotional bondage is not possible, and *with* the determinism the needed freedom, to opt for the knowledge of necessity and the attitude of serenity, is eliminated. And I have long since made it clear that, faced with such a choice, I opt for the requisite personal freedom and reject the rigorous determinism: after all, my very choice in adopting this option is itself an example of the very sort of genuine freedom that the option involves.

But what about thought/extension or mind/body identity as it is defended by Spinoza? At the outset and from a purely metaphysical standpoint, it seems plausible to argue that if the identifying properties of mind/thought are not only entirely different from those of body/extension but also simply and across the board unpredictable of body/extension, while at the same time the properties of body/extension (as conceived by Spinoza) are likewise simply and across the

7.272) If thought/extension or mind/body identity were true;

7.272a) there would be no way of accounting for the fact that mind and body seem to have mutually exclusive properties, or for the claim that thought and extension are different attributes;	board unpredicable of mind/thought, then it would seem plausible to conclude that whatever is a body or an extended thing (in Spinoza's sense) could not possibly be a mind or thinking thing, and vice versa. And much less would it be conceivable for thought (mind) and extension (body) to be attributes in entirety of the same substance. Yet this very identity is what Spinoza asks us to accept; and since I regard the properties of mind and body (in Spinoza's sense) as mutually exclusive, I can only conclude that Spinoza is clearly

7.272b) it would be inconsistent to regard genuinely distinct attributes as attributes in entirety of the same substance;

mistaken about this purported identity. This too can be more narrowly stated as a sort of dilemma for Spinoza: if thought and extension are genuinely distinct and therefore mutually exclusive attributes, they cannot logically be attributes of the same substance; but if thought and extension are two different terms for the same thing or substance, then they cannot be as Spinoza maintained they were, genuinely distinct attributes; and in that case, the obvious fact that thoughts are not extended (in Spinoza's sense) and that extended things are not ideas or mental occurrences (in Spinoza's sense) will be left totally unaccounted for. I shall, however, not further 'extend' this purely metaphysical argument, since my interest here is principally moral or ethical.

7.272c) a mind that, in correlation with bodily states, is simply a succession of mental states, cannot be the sort of enduring personal agent or moral self that could be the subject of moral responsibility.

Now from that moral or ethical point of view, I shall merely raise the question whether the sort of mind, that can be regarded, on Spinoza's ground, as identical with the body of a particular person, can be plausibly construed as a moral self or as the subject of moral experience. Now, as I understand Spinoza, the term *body* is an abstract term that stands for a succession of physical states and occurrences (perhaps even motions), and it would follow that the term *mind*, if its referent is to be regarded as identical with the body, would have to be an abstract term that stands for a succession of mental states and occurrences (or as Spinoza calls them: ideas). A person's body would be a continuity of such physical events, and a person's mind would be a continuity of such mental events, with the stipulation that any given physical event would be numerically identical with its correlated mental event, and vice versa. On such a view, there would be no such entity as an enduring body in relation to its changing physical states, and therefore also no such entity as an enduring mind in relation to its changing mental states. And that would mean there would be no enduring subject or self that persisted as a continuing agent through the succession of its states. But it seems clear to me that there must be such a permanent self (I would call it a transcendental ego) both as the epistemological subject of experience and as the moral subject of ethical obligation, duty, and achievement. If there is no such enduring personal identity, then there cannot be an enduringly responsible moral agent. If the 'I' that acts morally today is not in some sense the same 'I' that acted yesterday, then how can the 'I' of today either have or be morally responsible for its previous acts? But on Spinoza's view of mind/body identity, there would be no such enduring personal identity and therefore also no enduringly responsible agent in the moral sense: the 'I' that claims adequate knowledge and changed attitude *now* cannot, on Spinoza's view, be the same 'I' that was in emotional bondage and ignorance previously. In fact, if the 'I' is merely a succession of ideas, there could not even be an 'I' as the subject of experience at any given moment. From all this I conclude that the sort of 'mind' which, on Spinoza's view, could be identical with the body, again on his view, is not the sort of 'I' (if it is an 'I' at all) that could be the enduringly responsible subject of moral experience; and without that moral self a plausible normative ethic of any sort seems unthinkable or even rationally inconceivable.

At the same time, Spinoza's account of normative ethics is, in my view, by no means entirely without philosophical merit. While I regard his pantheistic monism, his rigorous determinism, and his mind/body identity theory as both implausible in themselves and also disastrous for normative ethics (including his own), there are nevertheless some aspects of his normative ethical view that can be defended in modified form without such strong premises as those which he defends. Spinoza seems certainly right in claiming that ignorance and emotional bondage are ingredients in the human moral predicament, and in maintaining that knowledge and liberation from emotional bondage (at least in part and in principle) are indispensable elements in the solution to that predicament. Moral objectivism implies moral truth and its instrumentality in addressing the human moral predicament. Still that predicament involves further elements that Spinoza deals with only slightly if at all—elements such as moral obligation and duty, the

7.273) Spinoza's ethic apart from these metaphysical problems has considerable merit:

7.274) ignorance and emotional bondage are certainly aspects of the human moral predicament, although it also involves moral duty and responsibility (with which Spinoza deals only slightly);

liability to make amends for moral defects and faults, for example. While Spinoza is, in my personal judgment, clearly right in claiming that moral virtue is only intelligible in relation to a rationally objective ideal of moral goodness (a *summum bonum*), he is perhaps overly optimistic in supposing that it is just a matter of replacing ignorance with adequate knowledge, however difficult even that may be in itself; it is also a matter of character transformation and conformity to objective moral requirement.

7.274a) his moral objectivism is commendable;

7.274b) but adequate knowledge is hardly a sufficient cause of character transformation.

7.275) If we recognize that many of the causes of our emotional bondage are beyond our control, and that we possess the freedom to change what is within our control, we will be able also to reshape our attitudes and achieve a large measure of relief from emotional bondage;

Again, we can even preserve Spinoza's argument that the knowledge of necessity (within limits) contributes significantly to a person's liberation from emotional bondage, even if that knowledge is not as fully effective for this purpose as Spinoza supposes. If we replace formal logico-mathematical necessity with a practical necessity which consists in the fact that many of the factors which contribute to emotional bondage are quite beyond our personal (and often even our social) control, then the knowledge of even that limited sort of necessity can dissipate our frustration over influences on us about which we can actually do nothing. And if, bereft of Spinoza's rigorous determinism, we intellectually and practically realize that we have the genuine and contingent personal freedom both to reshape our attitudes about what we cannot control and also to direct and channel those of our circumstances that do fall under our own causality as moral agents, we may be able on that basis to achieve a large measure of relief in relation to all the causes of our emotional bondage, even though our efforts may never result in complete and total liberation. The other part of Spinoza's argument, about the relation between adequate knowledge and emotional bondage, may also be maintained in modified form without Spinoza's objectionably strong premises. It seems to be a clearly justifiable (even justified) empirical thesis, quite independently of Spinoza's rigorous determinism, that the more adequate our knowledge of our passions and desires, as well as of their causes, the weaker their grip and effect on us become, and the less likely we are to be frustrated when our passions and desires are obstructed. Perhaps this is because the tranquility of mind that is essential to the pursuit of rationally objective knowledge simply cannot co-exist with any degree of emotional turbulence that would unbalance our equilibrium; at least I find that to be

7.276) it seems also true that knowledge of our passions and desires (so far as they are destructive) involves a tranquility of mind that weakens their grip;

the case in my own existential struggles, and I recommend it to the reader as an emotional palliative even if it is not a universal panacea. Of course, even if reality has a structure and framework that are metaphysically necessary and could not be otherwise (the laws of pure logic, the ultimate categories of reason, the logical relations of formal mathematical systems, perhaps even the properties of space and time), and even if much that is contingent in the real world, and could therefore theoretically be otherwise, is quite beyond any practical control on our part, within these parameters there is yet, perhaps, a vast panorama of possibilities whose realization or not decisively depends on our own genuinely free though always motivated choice. At the very least, let no one assume at the outset that anything contingent is beyond their reach until they have given it their own best and disciplined effort; and since no one knows what the limit of that effort itself is in their own case, perhaps the assumption should never be made at all. At the same time (and possibly in disagreement with Spinoza), the attempt to dissipate the bondage of disabling, disintegrative, and disruptive passions or desires, need not and should not lead to the elimination of emotions (or even passions) that are strengthening, integrative, and fulfilling in their pursuit, even if they are sometimes intense and involve the possibility of personal risk—I am thinking of such emotions as love (not merely the love of moral commitment or of friendship, but even the love of romance), artistic enjoyment of various sorts (maybe even the chortling delight that some of us take in raucous music), and the intoxicating thrill of just being alive and in a state of vibrant health, to mention just a few (though important) examples. I would like to think that these and other positive kindred emotions, rather than being dissolved by knowledge, are in fact intensified and supported by it; Spinoza himself thought that was true of the active emotion he called the intellectual love of God. I think he was certainly right about this, but perhaps I would include in the scope of that love all those emotions that would enhance our personal and moral self-fulfillment and contribute to the same result in others. Spinoza might even agree; I rather think he would.

As I consider in meditative retrospect all the species of normative ethical naturalism that I have discussed and

7.276a) within the limits of metaphysical necessity and contingent possibilities that are beyond our control, there is much whose occurrence (or not) depends on our free and motivated choice, if Spinoza's rigorous determinism is rejected;

7.276b) but not all emotions should be eliminated; there are positive emotions that do not involve bondage and frustration, but are rather integrative and fulfilling;

7.276c) such emotions may be intensified and supported by knowledge, rather than dissolved.

7.277) Conclusions on normative ethical naturalism:

	attempted to evaluate, I am keenly conscious of other models that I have intentionally bypassed and still others that I have simply overlooked. But I sincerely think that the perspectives I have considered are sufficiently important and representative to enable me to draw some provisional general conclusions. Doubtless all of these typical thinkers have contributed elements that will form a part of any reasonably adequate normative ethical perspective; I have tried to mention these elements as I went along, and I will not repeat them here. Nevertheless there is something fragmentary and incomplete about normative ethical naturalism: many species involve a radical ethical relativism that is incoherent in itself and incompatible with any rationally objective moral ideal; others involve a determinism that would preclude the sort of genuine freedom of personal agency that is essential to moral duty and responsibility; and still others, like Spinoza, take wings that fly far beyond the limits of nature as any final locus of moral worth and thus effectively sever their naturalistic moorings. All this at least suggests that, if there is a highest good in the moral sense, then, although it must be applicable to and within nature, in its final basis and ground it must transcend that realm. Ethical idealism and ethical theism both follow that lead; and it is therefore to such views that I now turn in my investigation.
7.277a) the representative views discussed have many valid elements;	
7.277b) but these views are at the same time incomplete and fragmentary by involving:	
7.278) radical ethical relativism;	
7.279) or determinism;	
7.280) or elements that transcend naturalistic premises.	
7.281) Perhaps the highest good, though applicable within nature, yet transcends it.	

Chapter VIII

Normative Ethical Idealism

The basic thesis of normative ethical idealism is the claim that the ultimate basis and ground of all values, both moral and nonmoral, is situated in a realm that is logically (and perhaps also ontologically) independent of the natural, empirically discernible realm of particular things and events in space and time, so that in some sense (different for different ethical idealists) the locus of value, in its highest and most fundamental form, transcends nature. At the same time, the ultimately good or right, in the moral sense (with which we are primarily concerned), can be and is illustrated in, partly instantiated and actualized through, and applicable to the natural realm; *the* good or *the* right is indeed transcendent, but particular goods and individual right acts are immanent in the natural order. As far as humanity is concerned, human moral and spiritual personality is the crucial and decisive point of contact between the transcendent realm and the natural order; human selves are, as it were, rooted in both worlds, since they are a part of the natural order while at the same time in their rational, moral selfhood they are tangential to the realm of the transcendent in such a way that they are both capable of apprehending its principles (however imperfectly in particular cases) and also motivated to their fulfillment in their natural existence. Furthermore, human beings (at least in the stages of their maturity) have the

8.1) General aspects of ethical idealism:
8.2) the ultimate basis and ground of value transcends the natural order, although its principles are exemplified in the natural order;

8.3) human personhood is the point of contact between the transcendent realm and the natural order;

8.4) the mind is capable of apprehending transcendent principles, is motivated to their fulfillment, and is competent to act rationally in pursuing the good;

8.5) failure is due to the obstruction of rational control by ignorance and/or emotion;

moral capacity to govern their lives rationally in such a way as to direct them toward the realization of the transcendent good or right in individual and social human experience. If, on the other hand, human beings fail to aim at and approximate the good or right in particular cases and situations, it is basically due to the displacement or disorientation of rational control either through ignorance or through the influence of purely emotional or volitional factors.

8.5a) the ultimate good must transcend nature, because, as the fixed standard or criterion of all value, it cannot be identified with anything contingent or transitory.

If the question is now posed as to why the ultimately good or right, in the moral sense, must be transcendent rather than naturalistic, the answer is different in detail for each variety or even for each proponent of ethical idealism; and as our discussion continues we shall have to deal carefully with these different answers. But in general, ethical idealism argues that since the ultimately good or right is both the highest embodiment of value and at the same time the criterion of its fragmentary and limited presence in the natural realm, that good or right cannot be identified with anything that is transitory, ephemeral, contingent, or in process, since in that case it would be a limited and fragmentary actualization of value, rather than (as postulated) the ultimate criterion and standard by which all such imperfect actualizations are themselves to be judged and evaluated. But the whole of empirical nature, and all its constituent aspects, is precisely transitory, ephemeral, contingent, and in process, so that, if there is any rationally objective criterion of moral or ethical worth, that criterion must transcend this realm of perpetual flux.

8.6) Subdivisions of ethical idealism:

8.7) Two main types:

Beyond this general characterization, ethical idealism subdivides into distinguishable types, the arrangement and classification of which are to a considerable extent a matter of expository efficiency, convenience, and even arbitrary choice. From my point of view, the most significant distinction is between those views which (as in the case of normative ethical naturalism) start with the elaboration of a metaphysical worldview perspective and then derive their normative ethic from the structure and framework of that perspective, on the one hand, and, on the other hand, those views which, with no more than a structure of epistemological principles, develop a theory of normative ethics as (at least in the logical sense) autonomous and independent of any developed metaphysical standpoint; for this latter type it is characteristic to derive metaphysical beliefs themselves from the implications of normative ethics. For the first sort of perspective, one starts with metaphysics and then develops ethics as a derivative, and I shall therefore designate this approach as the *metaphysical orientation* in ethical idealism; for the second approach, one starts with ethics and then develops metaphysical beliefs as plausible postulates for rendering moral principles more fully intelligible from a rational standpoint, and I shall therefore designate this outlook as the *postulational orientation* in ethical idealism. It is my plan to discuss two main perspectives under the metaphysical orientation, namely, Plato's *essentialism* and the *absolute idealism* of G.W.F. Hegel and F.H. Bradley. The historical 'fountainhead' of the postulational orientation is Immanuel Kant's *transcendental idealism*. For my purposes, I will regard these perspectives as sufficient representatives of the whole tradition of ethical idealism; it is not, of course, an exhaustive but only an illustrative account, since my aim here is clearly not historical but rather conceptual completeness.

8.8) the metaphysical orientation (ethics based on a metaphysical perspective);

8.9) the postulational orientation (ethics as autonomous, while metaphysical beliefs are grounded in it).

8.10) Representatives of the two types:

The Metaphysical Orientation in Ethical Idealism: Plato's Essentialism

Plato's most famous dialogue, *The Republic*, was, if I recall correctly, the very first full-length philosophical work that I ever read in my very first philosophy class taught at Cornell University by Professor Edwin A. Burtt. Together both Plato and Burtt initiated my lifelong romance with philosophical contemplation, and both have been my intellectual friends and comrades ever since, Burtt as my historical contemporary with whom I kept in contact until his death well into his nineties, and Plato as one of a small circle of traditional western philosophers whose writings literally brought them alive to me in my contemplative thinking. I make this biographical point only to reveal how difficult it is, because of my deep admiration toward Plato, for me to be rationally objective in the exposition and critical assessment of his philosophical views. I shall certainly aim at that objectivity as fully as I possibly can; but the reader should nevertheless be warned that I have always a tendency to envision Plato's perspective in the best possible light, and perhaps I sometimes even foist upon Plato a more plausible posi-

8.11) Personal attitude toward Plato, and early exposure to Plato's philosophy:

8.12) the difficulty of being objective in evaluating Plato's views;

8.13) the 'Plato' discussed here is the Plato of the dialogues and especially of *The Republic*;

tion than the one he actually held historically, while at the same time I will sincerely attempt always to advise the reader when that is the case. The only Plato I know is, of course, the Plato of *The Republic* and the other dialogues of his mature years; I shall not even speculate as to whether the published Plato held the same views as those taught to the inner circle of his students or disciples, or whether, instead, that esoteric doctrine taught orally represented a quite different position. I do find a recognizably different Plato in the writings of his best-known student Aristotle; but I shall leave all these complications to the historians. The Plato I have always known and loved is the Plato of the dialogues that form a cluster around *The Republic* as their center; and it is that Plato whose ethical views I intend to consider, whether or not he was the actual historical Plato.

8.14) The theory of absolute ideas:

8.15) the distinction between:
8.16) particular (a concrete individual entity)

8.17) and universal (a logically independent and abstract property or essence): such a property Plato terms an absolute idea.

The central core of Plato's total philosophical outlook is found in his theory of absolute ideas (forms, or essences)—a theory which is primarily metaphysical and epistemological, but which provides as well the basis for his ethical views. It is very difficult to decide how best to elaborate the theory of absolute ideas; but I have found it pedagogically most useful to start with the distinction between particulars and universals. A particular is an actually (or possibly) existing concrete entity—the pencil with which I write, the table at which I eat, the bed upon which I sleep, for example. A particular is a thing that has certain properties, characteristics, or attributes that make it the sort of thing it is rather than some other and different sort of thing. But though any given particular exemplifies, illustrates, or even instantiates some set of properties (characteristics or attributes), the properties themselves are logically and ontologically distinct from and independent of the particulars that thus exemplify them. The complex property designated by the term *triangularity* is, in this way, logically independent of particular objects that are triangular in shape, and so on for other classes of particulars. Such a logically and (on Plato's view) ontologically independent property or class-defining characteristic is what Plato means by an absolute idea, form, or essence. If there were no such essence or complex property as triangularity, therefore, there could not logically be any triangularly shaped particular things or objects; hence, while such real essences do not provide a complete account of the existence of particular things, those essences are a necessary condition for the existence of particular things. However, it does not work the other way around: while particulars cannot exist without exemplifying essences (or universals, as they have long been called, though I cannot recall Plato ever having used the Greek equivalent of the term *universal* in this connection), there is no reason for claiming that universals or essences cannot be real apart from particulars that exemplify them, since otherwise there would simply be nothing logically prior that the particulars could exemplify in order to exist. Hence, on Plato's position, there can be essences that are not exemplified in particular things. In fact, Plato even held the view that no particular even fully actualized the essences it exemplifies; an essence, rather, is an 'ideal' that the particular approximates, though always imperfectly. In the dialogues Plato does consider the question as to how extended the realm of independently real essences is; his tendency is to suppose that real essences are both very general and very important or even valuable, such as truth, beauty, and righteousness, while it is hardly necessary to posit essences for such mundane things as mud, hair, or rocks, much less for human artifacts like tables and chairs, and still less necessary to posit very determinate essences such as the essence of 'face with rosy cheeks and brown eyes.' However, these limitations are put forth rather tentatively and hesitatingly by Plato. The inner logic of his position would lead to the claim that the realm of essences is indefinitely extended so as to include all logically possible class-defining properties or characteristics and all levels of generality from the least specific and determinate (in other words, the most general and inclusive) to the most specific and determinate (in other words, the least general and inclusive). Of course, this would mean that the actually existing realm of particulars would instantiate or exemplify a relatively limited set of real essences, and that the realm of real essences would be vastly more extensive than the realm of concrete entities. The mere fact, that human knowledge of essences is limited to those occasioned by the specific details of our mental and empirical experience, would place no restrictions on that realm itself; whatever is logically possible must be represented in the realm of essences, whether or not we humans actually conceive them. After all, from Plato's standpoint, the human

8.18) Absolute ideas are a necessary condition for the existence of particulars, although universals are real independently of particulars, which never fully exemplify the properties they illustrate.

8.19) While Plato suggests that absolute ideas are limited to the very general and the very valuable, the logic of his position implies that the realm of essences includes all logically possible class-defining characteristics and all levels of generality;

8.20) the actual world of particulars would include a limited set of exemplified essences;

8.21) the limitations of human knowledge place no restrictions on the realm of essences;

mind does not constitute the reality of essences; it merely recognizes that reality.

From a logical and ontological point of view, the essences constitute a logically ordered hierarchy such that the more inclusive essences constitute the logical ground for inferring the less inclusive, and the less inclusive themselves are the entailed consequences of the more inclusive; but while Plato makes this deductivist claim and gives some glimpses of what such a hierarchy would be like, to my knowledge he nowhere develops a scheme for displaying this logically ordered system of essences even in its general aspects. Perhaps he thought that, although the human mind can see that there must be real essences and that those essences must be logically ordered in such a way, the limits of our *de facto* awareness of essences would preclude any actual working out of the scheme in detail. But about one thing Plato is buoyantly confident, namely, that at the pinnacle of this hierarchy of essences is the absolute idea of the Good. In a sense, this idea is itself the highest and most inclusive of the essences; and yet it is not merely an essence or even merely the essence of all essences, though it is of course all of that. For the idea or form of the Good is itself ultimate Being and ultimate Truth, as well as ultimate Goodness; as such, it is itself the ground of the being or reality of all lesser essences (since they follow logically from the Good itself) and of all particulars as well (since they can exist only by exemplifying or instantiating essences), as well as the source of all intelligence and truth in knowing minds and of intelligibility in the objects of knowledge, and even the cause of whatever is right and good in lesser essences and in the realm of particulars. Thus for Plato the ultimately Real, the ultimately Good, and the ultimately True are ontologically identical; and in this identity we confront the transcendent criterion or standard of both moral and nonmoral goodness in the sense in which we are concerned with it in normative ethics.

But of course no one can make effective moral use of this standard or criterion unless the person either achieves adequate knowledge of the form of the Good or, less ideally, follows the ethical advice of someone else who possesses and models that knowledge in moral practice. And this consequence raises the question as to how the knowledge of the Good is to be achieved by the human self; and since the

8.22) the realm of essences constitutes a logically ordered hierarchy, in which the less inclusive essences are entailed by the more inclusive (and vice versa), although Plato never details this system.

8.23) The absolute idea of the Good is:

8.23a) the highest of the essences,

8.23b) the ultimately Real, True, and Good,
8.23c) the ground of all lesser essences, and of all particulars,

8.23d) the source of all intelligence in finite minds and all intelligibility in objects,
8.23e) the cause of whatever is right and good in lesser essences and in particulars;
8.24) thus the Good is the transcendent standard of all goodness (moral and nonmoral).

8.25) This raises the question how the Good, and essences in general, are to

Good is itself the highest of the forms or essences, this in turn raises the basic epistemological question as to how the knowledge of essences in general is to be achieved. Although Plato's epistemological views are extensively treated in the dialogues, I cannot here develop them in depth but can only consider them briefly as a context for addressing more directly moral aspects of Plato's overall philosophical position. For Plato, then, forms or essences are the only authentic objects of genuine knowledge, if the certainty of our knowledge is to be objective (rather than subjectively relative to the opinions and preferences of the knower), universal (rather than limited to a restricted group of particulars and their circumstances), and necessary (rather than contingent and merely possible). Plato did not deny that human beings possess empirical information about images or representations, and about sense objects; but he held that such information is not knowledge but merely opinion or (at best) probable belief, since such information is clearly subjectively relative (rather than objective), particular and restricted (rather than universal and unlimited), and contingent or merely possible (rather than necessary). But it is quite otherwise with the forms or essences. While empirically experienceable objects are always changing and the effectiveness of our sensory capacities always variable, forms or essences are by nature fixed and changeless, even though our grasp of them is subject to development and our language for referring to them subject to conventional change. Whatever triangularity or any other essence is (not the word, but its object), it is a timelessly necessary and unchangeable object of rational insight (not of sense). Of course, the properties belonging to a given particular can be exchanged for others (a circular object can become elliptical, for example, by reason of physical modification), but the properties themselves simply are what they are changelessly (circularity and ellipticality do not change into any other essence). And hence, if there are any real essences in Plato's sense, they are clearly necessary (they logically must be simply what they are) and universal (under no circumstances can they be other than what they are). But essences are not subjectively relative either; human minds do not create or constitute them, they merely discover them as determinate objects of rational thought, so that essences are objective in

be known (as a basis for their moral application).

8.26) Essences are the only authentic objects of objective, universal, and necessary knowledge;

8.27) empirical information is merely opinion or probable belief, since it is subjective, particular, and contingent;

8.28) but essences are themselves the fixed and changeless objects of rational insight, although our understanding of them is subject to development;

8.29) since empirical particulars only approximate the essences they exemplify, they can only be the occasion for knowing the essences;

8.30) thus the essences must be implicit in the mind prior to empirical experience, so that they are *a priori* in that sense and in the sense that they are logically independent of those particulars and of the minds that apprehend them.

8.31) While innate essences and principles make intelligible thought possible,

8.31a) the conscious knowledge of them requires disciplined training in which the mind turns away from sense objects toward rational objects, until the person has a dialectical vision of the forms or ideas—culminating in awareness of the absolute idea of the Good.

nature. And since, for Plato, no empirical particular (*this* table, or *this* chair, for example) fully exemplifies or instantiates any essence but merely approximates it, the knowledge of essences cannot be abstracted purely from our sense experience of particular objects. That we recognize any particular as approximating a given essence, implies that the essences are already implicit in the mind of the knower, so that the imperfectly actual particular merely becomes the occasion for bringing the knowledge of the essence into explicit consciousness. In the technical lingo of epistemology, the knowledge of essences is not *a posteriori* (empirical) but *a priori* (rational), both in the sense that essences are in the mind prior to and independently of empirical experience (though they are brought into consciousness through the occasioning influence of experience) and also in the sense that essences are ontologically prior to and independent of particular sense objects which after all can exist only by participating in or exemplifying essences. Thus essences are rational objects of intellectual contemplation. Essences, and principles of reason, make intelligible thought possible for the individual mind; but not every person who thinks intelligibly is aware of these essences and principles consciously, since they are not characteristically the objects we think about but rather the instruments or means by which we think of other objects, including particular empirical entities.

How then are essences to be known by the individual personal mind, since in the end this knowledge (and especially the knowledge of the absolute idea of the Good) is clearly essential for Plato to the living of the morally good life in the highest sense? As he sees it, the individual can achieve this knowledge only through an extended and disciplined training through which the mind is gradually turned away from its preoccupation with images and sense objects in the direction of the essences and principles that make both knowledge and actual existence possible, until at last the person has a dialectical or rational vision of the realm of forms culminating in awareness of the absolute idea of the Good. Without such a vision, which brings along with it the will to commit oneself to its moral implications and guidance, no persons can of themselves and intentionally either think correctly or act rightly either in their own life or in the affairs of social and political institutions. Plato also recognized that even though every rational human self has the intrinsic capacity for achieving this knowledge at least to the extent of having the modest ability to think intelligibly about the ordinary objects of experience, yet not every one has, whether from lack of opportunity or from inadequate mental discipline or even from limitation of mental ability, the competence and diligence to carry this embryonic capacity all the way to its intellectual birth in the achievement of the dialectical vision of the Good and of the whole realm of essences. Those who can and do succeed in this, and who go on to make it the basis of their thought and moral practice, are the true philosophers and are thus eminently qualified for the rational direction both of their own lives and of the political state. For the rest of us, whose various limitations block the achievement of such knowledge, we can at least recognize that wisdom (however imperfectly) and commit ourselves to the moral and political direction of those who possess it.

How, for Plato, should all this work out in the achievement of moral virtue by the individual person? Plato develops a distinction between the body (the biological organism) and the soul (the personal selfhood) of an individual human being. Now while Plato had no disdain for the so-called 'goods' of the body, such as physical health and the satisfaction of basic bodily appetites like food and sex, still he did not view the moral good for man as primarily rooted in the body, since it is the soul or self that constitutes man's distinctive being. The soul or self in turn, though it is one soul in each individual person, has three distinguishable and different parts, aspects, or functions, namely, *reason* (the capacity for conceptual and sensory apprehension), *spirit* (in the sense of active energy or drive), and *desire* (the various passive emotions, passions, and appetites). While the word *part* here should not be taken with physical literalness, as if the three were virtually separate entities though closely conjoined, many critics have blamed Plato for making some such 'committee' out of the personal self. Whether that criticism is justified I shall not be so bold as to decide; I shall simply assume, on the basis of Plato's strong emphasis on the unity and indivisibility of the soul elsewhere in his writings, that he did not intend the Greek equivalent of the word *part* in such bald literalness. What he did stress was

8.32) No one can think correctly or act rightly in the fullest sense without this knowledge;
8.33) but not everyone is equally competent to achieve this knowledge or put it into moral practice;
8.34) those who are thus competent are the true philosophers capable of the rational direction of life;
8.35) other persons must recognize that wisdom and follow the guidance of those who possess it.
8.36) The achievement of moral virtue:

8.37) The moral good for humanity is rooted primarily, not in the body, but in the soul.
8.38) The soul, though unitary, has three aspects:
8.38a) reason,
8.38b) spirit,
8.38c) and desire;

8.39) these three functions can incline a person in contrasting directions, but reason alone possesses the intrinsic self-directive capacity to rule the soul through its apprehension of the Good as moral standard.

that these aspects or functions were sufficiently different as to permit them to incline the individual person in contrasting or even opposed directions, desire, for example, often inclining a person to act differently from the judgment of reason. And this fact raises the question as to which function of the soul should assume the status of leadership or authority; according to Plato, spirit and desire simply lack any intrinsic principle of self-direction, so that the strongest active tendency or emotion always wins out, and the result is personal and especially moral chaos, while reason, in contrast, not only possesses but actually is such a principle of self-direction by virtue of its ability to apprehend and be guided by the absolute idea of the Good in its aspect as a moral standard or criterion. Hence it follows that a morally good or virtuous person is one in whom reason rightly and habitually governs active energy and desire in accordance with reason's knowledge of and commitment to the idea of the Good, and in whom active energy and desire accede to the authority of reason thus operating. Vice, in the moral sense, occurs when either active energy or desire usurps the authority of reason; but the self always has the ability to follow reason or rational judgment, even though in fact it does not always exercise that ability, while active energy and desire can exercise authority only with the passive consent and even the cooperation of reason wrongly used. This does not at all mean that the authority of reason should deny either active energy or desire; it rather means that it should direct and limit their expression through the rational vision of the Good. For Plato, in fact, the best life is not at all the mere life of the mind engaged in disinterested contemplative thought; it is rather a mixed life in which active energy and desire find their morally appropriate and balanced expression through the exercise of rational direction by means of a knowledge of the Good. In such a life there is room for all the characteristically human propensities and desires, as well as for the wide-ranging pleasures or satisfactions that attend their appropriate expression. When all this comes off, as it were, in the rationally and morally proper way, then each aspect of the self achieves its proper virtue: reason possesses the *wisdom* for the exercise of rational self-direction, spirit or active energy displays *courage* in the enlightened willingness to accept limited risks

8.40) A morally virtuous person is one in whom this rule operates effectively, while a morally vicious (or corrupt) person is one in whom active energy and desire usurp that authority;

8.41) yet active energy and desire are not to be suppressed but rather guided by reason to their appropriate and balanced expression.

8.42) Each aspect of the self has its proper virtue:
8.43) reason-wisdom,
8.44) active energy-courage, and
8.45) desire-temperance;

in the pursuit of truly valuable ends, and desire exemplifies *temperance* or rational self-control through the moderate indulgence of, and satisfaction in, the whole varied range of natural human emotions. The resultant ideal of moral virtue is not, understandably, all that different from the ideal of balance and moderation found in Aristotle's ethical perspective, except that for Plato all this is subject to the ultimate standard of transcendent Goodness, while Aristotle removed any such transcendent reference from his purely humanistic approach. For Plato, finally, the individual, in whom each aspect of the soul achieves habitually its proper virtue, is for that reason a just person, so that moral justice is precisely the synthetic virtue of this balanced and rationally directed self-expression. 8.46) the harmony of the three aspects is moral justice;

It is clear from the previous exposition that Plato is an ethical idealist with a metaphysical orientation and that he therefore rejects in principle any attempt to identify the ultimately good or right in the moral (and nonmoral) sense with something within the realm of the natural and the empirically discernible. Goodness, as the highest of all essences and their ontological ground, is precisely ultimate Being itself and therefore has a reality status that transcends and is independent of the realm of empirical particulars which could not themselves exist without approximatively exemplifying transcendent essences. Thus Plato bases his entire moral philosophy on the metaphysical doctrine of real essences and on the metaphysical thesis that human beings possess a rational nature which places them in contact with that transcendent realm of essences, even if they do not always or even characteristically activate the capacity which that contact implies. 8.47) Plato is therefore an ethical idealist in the sense previously defined.

And this brings us to the critical evaluation of Plato's transcendental essentialistic idealism in ethics. I suppose that a typical contemporary western philosopher of the late twentieth century, bound as he or she would likely be by the presuppositions of analytic empiricism (at least in the English-speaking philosophical community) in some Wittgensteinian vein, could hardly take any sort of Platonism in ethics or elsewhere as anything more than an important historical background and curiosity. Such a critic, steeped in an extreme nominalism (the doctrine that universal essences are merely general terms and are therefore

8.48) Critical evaluation of Plato's ethical view:
8.49) contemporary reactions:
8.50) Platonism in ethics is, in general, met with disdain in the analytic empirical tradition;

Normative Ethical Idealism

conventional in origin), would undoubtedly regard the doctrine of objective and transcendent real essences as pure balderdash; and since Plato's ethic rests precisely on such a doctrine of real essence, his moral philosophy would share the same fate at the hands of such a critic. But it is not so in the European continental tradition of Husserlian phenomenology refracted through the minds of such thinkers as Max Scheler (in both his earlier and later periods) and Nicolai Hartmann. Here the typical thinker moves easily with talk of rationalistically *a priori* principles of knowledge, real and transcendently objective essences, and a frank and open acknowledgment of indebtedness to Plato and the whole subsequent tradition of Platonism. The monumental ethics of Hartmann is boldly and without apology cast in this framework and is, in my opinion, the finest work of normative ethics to be produced by any western scholar in the twentieth century. Nor should we overlook the English-speaking philosophical tradition that springs from the work of Alfred North Whitehead; here too essences are clearly recognized as transcendently eternal objects in the absence of which there logically could not be an empirical world order. I mention all this historical backdrop only to disarm the pejorative attitude of those students of philosophy who may be tempted to laugh scornfully at any attempt (including my own) to take Plato seriously: Platonism in some modified form is still a live contemporary option; and even if it were not, it should be carefully noted that the truth or falsity, adequacy or inadequacy, of any philosophical perspective whatever is entirely independent logically of either historical or contemporary prevalence.

I confess therefore without hesitation or boggle of any sort that there is a vast panorama of concepts in Platonism and especially Platonic ethics that I can accept without cavil. On the doctrine of real essences, for example, I enthusiastically take my stand with Plato (as I have interpreted him) and his philosophical clan. Plato's claim, that particular empirical entities could not exist without instantiating or exemplifying universal essences (properties, attributes, or characteristics) that are logically and ontologically independent of those particulars and are for that reason a necessary ground of the being of such particulars, seems to me incontestable on any grounds that acknowledge, as I do,

8.51) but in the continental tradition of Husserlian phenomenology and in the Whiteheadian tradition Platonism is still taken seriously;

8.52) yet in any case, truth and falsity are not dependent on prevalence or its opposite.

8.53) Valid elements in Plato:

8.54) realistic essentialism; combined with the recognized reality of empirical particulars;

the rational intelligibility of being. Empirical particulars surely exist; but their existence is dependent and contingent upon the real universal essences which, as independent and necessary, make that existence possible, though without providing a complete account of it (essences are, as such, clearly not efficient causes). I am prepared to go even further with Plato in recognizing that the ultimately Good, the ultimately Real, and the ultimately True are, at the pinnacle of being, ontologically identical. From an ethical point of view, the ultimate Good must contain the whole ground of its worth in itself in order to constitute underived and intrinsic value (which it must be if it is to be the final and objective criterion or standard of both moral and nonmoral worth). But clearly it could not thus contain the whole ground of its worth in itself if it did not constitute its own ground of being, since, dependent in its being, it would *ipso facto* be dependent in its worth or value—which would contradict its status as the ultimate Good. The same would be the case with ultimate Truth: whatever is true of the ultimate Good = the ultimate Real, must be true of it wholly within itself, which would only be the case if it constituted ultimate Truth in itself and not dependently in any ontological sense. Hence, the ultimate Real = the ultimate Good = the ultimate Truth (or in Latin: *Ens est Bonum est Verum!*). Of course, I acknowledge that anyone who commits oneself to such an argument and conclusion must have traversed many conceptual waters in his or her epistemological canoe; and I also acknowledge that I have not provided a complete account of that journey either here or anywhere else. But if the reader combines what I have said here (and in other contexts of this entire treatise) with what I have said elsewhere in my other published writings, he or she will have a sufficiently adequate account of the journey at least. So go ahead and identify me as a sort of Platonist and whatever else I seem to be in consequence of my commitments here and elsewhere; I will not mind the designation at all, since I have certainly been described with less appropriate epithets.

And from this same positive or even enthusiastic point of view, what of the other facets of Plato's moral philosophy? Of course I share Plato's rationalistic apriorism (with some limitations), at least to the extent that I regard the human mind as intrinsically structured with interpretive

8.55) the ontological identity of the Good, the Real, and the True;

8.56) with some qualifications: rationalistic apriorism, to the extent that the mind is intrinsically structured with interpretive principles of reason as necessary presuppositions of all intelligible thought;

8.57) the mind's ability to know the ultimate Good as a basis for responsible moral decision and action;

8.58) but Plato seems clearly wrong in limiting adequate moral knowledge to those with dialectical vision;

8.59) a person would need minimal moral insight to choose moral advisors;

8.60) intellectual moral insight must be far more widely diffused than Plato supposed;

8.61) yet moral advice is of great benefit.

principles and categories that characterize the mind logically prior to and independently of any ground in experience—principles and categories that constitute the necessary presuppositions of all possible (and actual) thought and being, so that they make thought about the Good or anything else possible for the human self. Again, I have written extensively about these topics elsewhere in both an expository and critically defensive fashion, and I cannot take the time or space to traverse this old ground again here. But more specifically as regards moral knowledge, I again agree with Plato in regarding the human mind, thus equipped and constituted, as in principle capable of achieving a knowledge of the ultimate Good at least to the extent necessary for providing a sufficient basis for responsible and appropriate moral decision and action. At the same time I do not think (with Plato) that the only epistemological possibilities are either the knowledge of the Good in dialectical vision or the necessity of unreflectively following the advice of someone who possesses this knowledge in both theory and practice. For individuals must themselves be capable of recognizing those who are in a position to provide such moral advice; and this capacity itself would involve a degree of moral knowledge (knowledge of the Good, however fragmentary) that would make these individuals capable of making responsible moral decisions on the basis of their own ethical insight. If persons lack even that ability (to recognize qualified moral advisors and to assume responsibility for their own morally significant choices), it is questionable whether they could be held morally liable for those choices and their consequences, and equally questionable whether they possessed the capacity to make any actual moral choices. With all due respect to Plato, therefore, if, on the whole, mature persons are to be held universally and morally responsible for their morally significant choices and acts, the degree of intellectual moral insight essential as a basis for such liability must be far more widely diffused among human beings than Plato seems to have supposed. On the other hand, Plato is probably right in contending that human agents generally are greatly benefited by the moral advice of other persons, just as Plato himself greatly benefited in this way from the moral advice of his teacher, Socrates. Yet that acknowledgment by no means divests the individual of the responsibility for sifting through that moral advice and deciding whose advice to follow.

I am certainly also on Plato's bandwagon, as it were, when it comes to his view as to how an individual, at least ideally, should (morally ought to) aim at becoming a virtuous person through the achievement of an integrative harmony of the various aspects and inclinations of personal selfhood under the guidance of conceptual reason in its apprehension of the Good as an ultimate standard or criterion. For me, as well as for Plato, reason seems vested by its very nature with a self-directive capacity that establishes its moral authority over both active energy and desire. Nor do I disagree in general with his project of designating a moral virtue corresponding to the morally proper functioning of the various aspects of personal selfhood. If I have any hesitation here, it concerns the use of the term *courage* as the general name for the proper virtue corresponding to active energy; courage is certainly *one* element in the proper functioning of active energy, but there seem to be other elements as well—the achievement of balance in the coordination of our active propensities, and the establishment of priority relations among them, for example. At the same time, I have no substitute term to suggest for the virtue coordinated with all our active energies as human beings; but the one that occurs to me on reflection would be *moral equilibrium* or some such synonymous expression. On the other hand, I have no such hesitation about the terms *wisdom* and *temperance* (i.e., rational self-control) as designations for the virtues of reason and desire; nor do I have any criticism of construing individual personal justice as a harmony or balance in the integrated achievement of the other three virtues under the rational direction of conceptual reason.

But I do have two moderate qualms about Plato's doctrine of the virtues. The first concerns an issue that I previously raised in discussing the ethical views of Aristotle and (especially) John Dewey. Plato seems to adopt the view that active energy and desire have, somehow, a moral right to balanced and moderate expression in any life that could be characterized as morally virtuous. But is it not persons alone that can lay claim to moral rights in this sense? Are not desires and active energies properly construed rather as means of self-realization rather than as intrinsically valuable ends?

8.62) The rational direction of the self to virtue:

8.63) reason is the proper authority over active energy and desire;

8.64) but perhaps *courage* should be viewed as merely one aspect of moral equilibrium in the direction of active energy.

8.65) Critical difficulties:

8.66) Do active energy and desire have any moral right to balanced expression across the board?

	If so, then there is no compelling reason for supposing that every person morally ought to achieve balanced and moderate expression that extends across the whole range of our active energies and emotions, except so far as that achievement would, more than any alternative distribution for that individual, actualize that person's selfhood in long-range terms. It is perhaps impossible to conceive a morally virtuous life without some elements that involve the active energies and emotion; but it is possible to conceive many different patterns of self-actualization, not all of which would achieve the comprehensive and balanced totality that Plato (along with Aristotle and Dewey) envisioned. Surely such a comprehensive expression would constitute one sort of morally virtuous life—and it is the one that I recognize as appropriate for myself; but a person's life might be no less virtuous if actualized selfhood took the form of commitment to some single or limited expression of active energy and emotion, provided that the objective was itself morally worthwhile and that it aimed at achieving otherwise only that limited expression of active energy and desire that would be a minimum requirement for any morally virtuous life at all. Otherwise, a life devoted to scholarship, or art, or self-denying human service, to the neglect of any more than a minimum expression of active energies and desires, would have to be judged as being defective in moral virtue—a conclusion that appears to be morally and logically absurd. It is even plausible to suppose that Plato himself, in his commitment to contemplation and teaching, probably lived such an alternative type of life that did not, in its expression, range across the whole spectrum of active and emotional possibilities envisioned in his own moral ideal; indeed, if that were not the case, he could scarcely have achieved such a plethora of literary and pedagogical results. And if I am right about this, need Plato have been any less morally virtuous? Differently virtuous, yes; but less virtuous, no. There must therefore be a wide variety of morally good lives (at least conceivably), many of which would involve the relative neglect of aspects of active energy and desire that would be essential in some alternative pattern of moral virtue. I even venture the opinion that, in view of the uniqueness of individual persons, the pattern of the morally good life is unique for each person as well, even though there are many partial
8.67) Perhaps persons alone have moral rights;	
8.68) if so, there could be many different patterns of moral virtue with very different proportions of the realization of active energy and desire.	
8.69) Plato himself, in his devotion to philosophical reflection, may have lived one of these alternative lifestyles, which was not, for that reason, any less virtuous;	
8.70) perhaps the moral ideal is uniquely different for each individual;	

and overlapping similarities. The moral community of ethically committed persons is not a collection of individuals struck from the same mold ethically; it is rather a moral organism in which each individual is a unique expression of the moral ideal.

My other qualm, about Plato's doctrine of the virtues, concerns the question whether his list of the moral virtues does not leave out at least one essential ingredient. The whole impact of Plato's ethic, involving as it does the aim at individual self-realization or self-actualization, strongly implies the thesis that personal being possesses intrinsic moral worth in a unique and unsurpassable way: otherwise, why aim at an ideal of moral virtue at all, if not for the sake of realized selfhood or personhood? And yet Plato's ethic, while recognizing such intrinsic worth in each person for himself, includes no such other-regarding virtue as moral love—a virtue which would recognize the obligation to accept and, so far as possible, implement the moral well-being of other persons who, just as persons, are as intrinsically valuable morally as oneself. Of course, I have not even discussed Plato's social and political philosophy in which he envisions a harmoniously ordered relationship of different classes of society under the rule and direction of philosopher-kings. But even there it is no such other-regarding virtue as moral love that functions as an adhesive to bind society together; it is rather the pattern of a social and political order in which each individual, under the ruling supervision of the philosophically wise, can work at realizing his own moral selfhood. But is there not something incongruous about a moral perspective that recognizes so strongly each individual's intrinsic worth as a context for achieving his own moral virtue, but which fails, on the whole, to recognize the obligation of each such individual to accept and subserve the moral well-being of other persons for exactly the same reason—intrinsic personal worth in the moral sense?

And all this leads me to a still more comprehensive criticism of Plato's ethical idealism. For him, the ultimate ground of all being and value is the essence or absolute idea of the Good. It is true that, for Plato, the Good is not merely essence but is rather the essence of all essences and the ground of the being, intelligibility, and worth of all lesser essences. If, in this way, the Good is something more than essence and

8.71) while Plato's ethic recognizes the intrinsic worth of the individual person, he makes no reference to moral love as an other-regarding virtue;

8.72) even in his social and political ethic, no such moral love is mentioned as a basic ingredient;

8.73) this omission seems incongruous, since intrinsic moral worth is common to all persons as such.

8.74) If lesser essences depend on the Good in their being and intelligibility, this must mean that the Good is 'something more' than essence (as Plato claimed);

yet, like essence, is transcendent (independent of the realm of empirical particulars), how conceptually is this transcendent 'something more' to be construed? Since all other essences depend on the Good for their being, it would follow that essences, merely as such, are not self-subsistent, do not possess reality merely in and of themselves, even for Plato. Now, if that is the case, what could reasonably be the character of that 'something more' that the Good is, in itself, but other essences are not in themselves? Clearly it could be nothing natural, empirical, or particular (in the relevant sense intended here): for empirical particulars can only exist by instantiating essences. The only conceivable alternative would be to suppose that the 'something more' is ultimate or absolute Mind, and that essences find their locus or transcendent status as either constitutive principles or structures of that Mind or as the logically self-completed content of that Mind. Plato himself comes very close to saying something like this, except that he does not introduce the term *Mind* here; but later Christian Platonists like Augustine made that step explicit on Plato's behalf, and then went on to construe the character of that ultimate Mind in the personalistic terms of the Hebrew-Christian tradition (more of this in a later context). And if the Good *is* construed as ultimate personal Mind in this way, that would not only answer the question about the 'something more' that the Good must be, but it would alleviate an otherwise vexing problem for Plato's moral philosophy. If, as Plato seems to imply, personal being possesses intrinsic moral (and nonmoral) worth, and if the Good is itself the basis of the being and worth of all else, including finite, intrinsically valuable persons, how could the Good be anything less than personal in its ultimate character, and how could finite persons have any obligation to an impersonal Good? No doubt the Good may be (or even is) more than personal being, but surely it could not be less. And if the Good is the ground of all being, how could it be anything less than the Creative Cause of all particular existing beings and therefore of the space-time universe itself together with all its contents? If we thus construe the ultimate Good as transcendent, self-subsisting personal mind and the locus of all lesser essences in their transcendent status, then the only thing lacking to the claim that the Good, for Plato thus modified and reconstructed, is God as

8.75) it seems plausible to go beyond Plato and construe that 'something more' as transcendent personal Mind, and to view lesser essences as principles or content of that mind;

8.76) if, in this way, the Good is construed as personal, that would account for its being the ground of the being and worth of finite persons, as well as of those persons' being morally obligated to the Good.

8.77) This in turn could lead to construing the Good as the creative cause of all finite particulars, a transition that becomes explicit in the Christian Platonism of Augustine and others after him.

construed in the Hebrew-Christian tradition, would be the term (God or *ho theos*) itself. Of course, Plato himself seems explicitly to have thought of God as an intermediary (perhaps personal) world soul whose causality accounted for the existence of particular things as instantiations of the transcendent essences. But perhaps this fragmentary view can be regarded as an untidy detail in an otherwise impressive worldview. If this untidy detail is corrected or removed, it will no longer seem surprising that Augustine, uncompromising in his commitment as a Christian, also continued, like many after him, to think of himself as a Platonist until his dying day. Meanwhile, however, there are, in the tradition of ethical idealism, other perspectives to consider as alternatives to this 'baptism' of Plato into traditional orthodox Christianity.

Absolute Idealism: G.W.F. Hegel and F.H. Bradley

Like Plato, Hegel begins with a comprehensive metaphysical scheme in which he construes (quite differently from Plato) the whole of reality as a series of opposing and progressively reconciled phases in which and as which the all-inclusive Absolute Spirit both constitutes and manifests the process of its own self-actualization, in the final stage of which all oppositions are (at least ideally) reconciled in the concrete unity of that Absolute Spirit. This totality involves, for Hegel, a dialectic of triads in which every concept (notion, determinate point of view, or thesis) logically generates its own opposite and then is reconciled with it in a more determinate, explicit, and concrete concept which preserves in reconciled or transcended form both sides of the opposition. In turn, that new and more concrete concept logically generates its opposite, thus leading to a further and still more concrete reconciling concept, and so on until all oppositions are transcended and reconciled in the comprehensive unity of the Absolute Spirit. The pattern, termed the method of dialectical opposition (*Gegensatz*) and reconciliation (*Aufhebung*) constitutes the very structure and essence of being. From a logical (and ontological) point of view, the system starts with the most abstract concept of being as such, without any explicit determinateness, and culminates in the concept of the Absolute Spirit as philosophical mind in its

8.78) Hegel's dialectical metaphysic and method:
8.79) reality as an all-inclusive Absolute Spirit, constituting itself through opposition and reconciliation;

8.80) this process moves from abstract indeterminateness to complete concreteness in which all oppositions are reconciled;

8.81) while the Absolute is self-identical with all its elements, the more abstract is less explicitly true, and the more concrete more explicitly true;

8.82) thus there are no false philosophies but merely fragments of a larger totality of truth.

8.83) Hegel sometimes implies that his system, if fully worked out, would be the final reconciliation;

8.84) but he also suggests that his actual system is itself a fragment capable of being transcended.

8.85) The system, as a whole, is a general triad of:

8.86) Logic (the Absolute in itself),

8.87) Nature (the Absolute for itself),

8.88) Mind (the Absolute in and for itself).

most concrete and finally reconciled form. The Absolute itself is self-identical with every concept or notion in the entire system; and a proposition expressing that self-identity in any specific case is always true. But the more abstract a concept is the less true it is, and the more concrete, the more true. Hence, there are no intelligible propositions, concepts, or even philosophical worldviews that are explicitly false. Those that appear to be false, are so only in isolation from all the rest: in the concrete unity and finally reconciled form, all the parts are true as fragments of the larger totality. The mistake comes only in supposing that some part or fragment of the whole is itself this finally reconciled totality. In view of this all-inclusive feature of Hegel's perspective, his philosophy has often been caricatured as the omnivorous philosophy, since, metaphorically speaking, it 'gobbles up' every alternative perspective as a paragraph, fragment, or part of itself, and therefore as a genuine aspect of truth in its wholeness. The implication often hinted at by Hegel is that his own philosophy, if (contrary to fact) it were fully worked out, would be the final reconciliation of the Absolute itself in the historical process. But in other passages (as interpreted by some scholars), Hegel is supposed to have humbly acknowledged that all his own best efforts, at expressing the system, together constitute but a paragraph or fragment which, by hypothesis, would admit of its logically generated opposite and lead to still further reconciliation, and so on *ad indefinitum*. Unfortunately (for Hegel), either way of viewing the matter seems to lead to irreconcilable contradictions; but more of that in a later context.

It is important to see that the basic parts of the system as a whole (and not merely the logically successive and directly generated individual triads) also possess and actualize the complex relation of dialectical opposition and reconciliation. According to Hegel, the most general triad of this sort is the triad in which Logic (the Absolute in itself [*an sich*] as a system of necessary concepts and principles which make concrete being possible) generates as its opposite Nature (the Absolute proceeding out of itself and for itself [*für sich*] as a logically ordered series of external manifestations at physical, chemical, and biological levels), and then results in the reconciling concept of *Mind* (the Absolute in and for itself [*an und für sich*] as the reconciling and explicit self-awareness of that Absolute in individual self-consciousness, social and political relationship, and culminating in the symbolic [religion and art] and conceptual [philosophy] as fully concrete and reconciled totality). Each of these three general phases subsumes under itself, and constitutes, a series of more limited triads under which are still further triads: the last triad of Logic leads to the first under Nature, and both of these are initially and provisionally reconciled in the first triad of Mind. The Absolute *is* Logic (and vice versa), but it is more concretely and therefore more truly Nature, and most concretely and truly Mind; and since the culminating notion or concept of Absolute Mind (or Spirit-Geist) is philosophy, it would be more concretely and truly the case that the Absolute is its own self-reflection in the development and final achievement of philosophy, than that the Absolute is anything else whatever. Each successive phase of the Absolute thus transcends its previous phase, and the Absolute in its finally reconciled totality therefore transcends the mere succession of its successive limited phases. Since the space-time universe is the Absolute as Nature, and since Nature, though vast, is a limited aspect of the Absolute in its totality, clearly the Absolute as that totality transcends Nature, even though it is also true, more abstractly and less concretely, that the Absolute is Nature.

Just as reality is the Absolute in its totality, and just as truth, finally indistinguishable from reality ('the real is the rational, and the rational is the real'), is identically that same totality, so also Goodness or Value (in both moral and nonmoral senses) is again identically the Absolute as that totality. It follows that, from the standpoint of the Absolute as a Whole, all the phases in the self-development or self-diremption of the Absolute are, in the unified context of that totality, good and right (is and ought are here identical). But each fragment or aspect of the Absolute, when considered in isolation as if it were a separate and self-subsisting fragment, is, from that limited point of view, evil and wrong (is and ought are never identical here). But of course, in reality as comprehensively viewed, there simply *are* no separate fragments, no isolated acts or events, since each aspect is what it is only through its complex interrelationships with the totality. Hence, in the Absolute as a whole there is no evil in any irreconcilable sense; the

8.89) Each phase of this triad:
8.90) subsumes other triads under itself, and is truly the Absolute;

8.91) but the Absolute is most truly and concretely Mind, and especially philosophy as the culmination of Mind;

8.92) in this way the Absolute, in its totality, transcends all its less explicit and distinguishable phases.

8.93) The concept of Goodness:
8.94) In general, the Absolute, in its totality, is Goodness as such, so that:

8.95) all its phases are good and right in the totality, but they are evil and wrong from an isolated point of view;

8.96) there is no real isolation and therefore no evil in any finally irreconcilable sense;

supposition to the contrary is the product of a limited and distorted point of view which is itself transcended in the Absolute as a Whole.

8.97) morality in the specific sense (objective mind):

Morality or ethics in the more limited sense, as concerned with individual persons or agents in relation to each other in the formal and informal structures of a civilized society, is precisely composed of the notions that make up the doctrine of objective mind in contrast and opposition to subjective mind as the phenomenology or conceptual development of individual consciousness. For Hegel, the idea of moral philosophy emerges in an explicit sense only in the context of a plurality of individual persons standing in some complex of relationships among themselves in society; and in this sense morality is intrinsically social, so that individuals have no ethical duties or obligations solely in themselves as separate persons—which probably means that persons, as separate selves, have no purely self-referential duties or obligations to themselves. But as soon as those persons are considered in social relationships, the structures of morality begin to emerge clearly and explicitly, although they were always implicit, of course. The principal triad of the doctrine of objective mind begins with the idea of the individual personal self (mind) rendering explicit, in logical order, the complex of its social relationships; this process starts with the development of the concept or notion of *Law* or the *Right* (*das Recht*), which, through intervening triads, generates as its opposite the notion of *Morality* (*die Moralität*), both of which (Law and Morality) are then reconciled and taken up into unity with the concept of *Social Ethics* or, in the broadest sense, *Custom* (*die Sittlichkeit*). Each of these phases involves the idea of will as it makes the transition from individual personal will to universal social will. Law (the Right) is the individual will expressed in existence, and it involves rights and duties which accrue to human beings considered simply as particular persons rather than as elements in some social community. According to Hegel, the will thus construed first expresses itself and its personal freedom in the acquisition of possessions which are regarded as the *property* of the person and as that to the possession of which he or she has a right, while other persons have a duty to respect that right. This notion of property generates as its opposite the notion of *contract* as the

8.98) emerges in the context of social relationships;

8.99) moves through the triad of

8.100) Law or the Right,

8.101) Morality,
8.102) Social Ethics or Custom;

8.102a) involves the transition from individual personal will to universal social will.

8.103) This process begins with Law or Right as subdivided into:
8.103a) property,

8.103b) contract,

mutual agreement of individual wills through which property rights of individuals are respected and terms are recognized by means of which that property may be transferred from one individual to another through the fixing of an economic value or the honoring of a hereditary prerogative. But about these terms, disputes characteristically arise among individuals which result in the urging of conflicting titles to the same property; and since claimants regard their competitors as wrong and themselves as right, there emerges, as a reconciling concept between property and contract, the notion of *right versus wrong*. This conflict about who is right (or has the right) and who is wrong (or lacks the right) can clearly only be settled by an appeal to the idea or principle of a reasonable claim as a quasi-objective criterion or standard; and this idea results in the explicit emergence of morality as the opposite generated by the whole notion of law, since the essence of morality involves the notion of an objectively reasonable principle in which the will is self-reflected in and as the reason common to all individual personal wills.

Morality, therefore, has as its central core the idea of an implicit rational will, shared by all rational persons and functioning as the criterion for assessing the propriety or impropriety of existent individual acts of will. To decide an issue on objectively moral grounds is to decide therefore on the basis of a rational principle which is intrinsic to the nature of the moral agent himself, so that a genuinely moral choice is an act of self-determination rather than an act of submission to any sort of external authority. In such a genuinely moral choice it is the principle of my own true will as rational that binds me through its authority. But, as always with Hegel, the clear recognition of this result passes through a triad of dialectical transitions. At the outset, the individual will accepts as its own and as its responsibility only those choices and acts which are the *purpose* or aim of the agent himself; but this simple and relatively unreflected identity moves out of itself into its opposite as rational *intention* to pursue morally justifiable well-being or happiness. The justification must rest, in the end of course, on implicit rational will as the principle moral self-determination. But this determination can be incorrectly or wrongly (perhaps even reprehensibly) particularized in the case of an individual act or choice by a particular person; and that predicament

8.103c) right versus wrong;

8.104) this development produces the concept of morality as expressed in an objectively reasonable principle or implicit rational will as a criterion or standard;

8.105) this principle is intrinsic to human nature and involves a process of self-determination rather than external authority;

8.106) the triad moves from purpose to intention,

8.106a) and is reconciled in the tension between moral goodness and moral evil;

leads to the reconciling notion of the tension between moral *goodness* and moral *evil* or *wickedness*. This tension is between the individual subjective aim of the particular person, on the one hand, and the principle of universal rational will, on the other hand. Of course, universal rational will is the authentic ground of moral self-determination and therefore of moral goodness, while evil or wickedness is based on some maverick and isolated individual principle. However, according to Hegel, this tension between universal will and individual will collapses into an identity, since both are conceivable only as acts of self-determination. But individuals cannot really and actually act with isolated and rebellious particularity, since individuals are what they are only through their relations to the various wholes (of society, for example) to which they belong; their choices or acts can, at least provisionally, be construed as abstract and isolated (wrongly or incorrectly construed, of course), but they cannot actually be that way from an adequate rational point of view. Thus the apparently abstract, isolated, and wicked choice or act is assimilated or absorbed into a simple universality of rational will and thus becomes (or rather *is*) a limited aspect of the universal rational good. In a sense, this brings us back to Hegel's general idea of the Good (both moral and nonmoral) as the whole, in contrast to the evil as the isolated fragment wrongly construed. But in our particular context (the dialectical opposition between Law and Morality), we are brought more concretely, by means of the simple universality of rational will, to Social Ethics—the universal will actualized as a totality of rational necessity in the social wholes or groups to which inevitably each individual belongs.

For Hegel, these social wholes are themselves triadically related. The *family* is the initial social whole to which each individual belongs (ideally, at least) by birth; and it is there that individuals first learn the truth that their own true and individual good is most fully actualized if they subordinate their abstract individual will to the more concrete will of the group as a whole—which is really their own will as it is that of all the other members of their family. This whole becomes a kind of hub from which the individuals (and the family as a whole) branch out like spokes into the wheel whose circumference is composed of all the formal

8.107) but this tension collapses into an identity, since the isolated individual will cannot sustain itself against the universal rational will;

8.108) and this leads to the social wholes in which that will expresses itself, and hence to:

8.108a) social ethics;
8.108b) involves the triad:
8.108c) the family,

and informal wholes of *civil society*—which is therefore the dialectical opposite generated by the family. That opposition itself is taken up into the largest social whole which subsumes all the lesser wholes as facets of its own comprehensive and inclusive social totality—the *political state* as the highest and most concrete human expression of the universal rational will, in Hegel's opinion. Thus a choice becomes or is morally right, as is an act, principle, or state of character, if it expresses and subserves, more fully than any alternative, the well-being of all these logically interrelated social wholes. To be and to act rightly in the moral sense is therefore to subordinate oneself to the universal rational will, which is after all a person's own authentic will as well, so that in so acting an individual is at the same time both genuinely free in the moral sense while he or she is also bound by objective rational necessity. The human self, as an aspect of the Absolute Mind in its subjective or immediate self-affirming phase, has the capacity in principle to rethink (reconstitute in the self's own thought) the self-diremtping process of the Absolute and thus apprehend the truth through which goodness can be achieved in his or her own personal existence. If the individual fails while possessed of this capacity for rational insight, it is due to a culpable ignorance of the whole which leads the individual to affirm for himself separated and isolated existence, even though, in the end, such fragmented thinking and such isolated existence are parallel elements in a vanishing illusion.

A somewhat modified version of this Hegelian ethical panorama was developed some half a century after Hegel's death by the British philosopher, F.H. Bradley, in his volume entitled *Ethical Studies*, first published in 1876 and then reissued in revised form in 1927 after Bradley had died. Now while Bradley derives much by way of insight from Hegel, he is certainly no mere stereotype but develops the ethic of absolute idealism with his own distinctive emphasis. His basic claim is that, since morality implies an end in itself, and since that end cannot lie in the pursuit of any objective determined by subjective emotion, feeling, or desire (that would be to deny the rational objectivity of the true moral end), and since the moral end cannot be truly moral if it takes the form of any sort of external authority, it is reasonable to identify the moral end as self-realization. In fact, Bradley argues that

8.108d) civil society,

8.108e) the political state.

8.109) An act, principle, or state of character is thus morally right if it promotes the well-being of these interrelated social wholes;
8.110) moral rightness is essentially subordination to the universal rational will, which is also the individual's own authentic will;
8.111) the human self has the capacity to apprehend the truth of goodness and act accordingly;
8.112) failure is due to ignorance of the whole and isolated self-preference, which as fragments, are finally unreal.

8.113) F. H. Bradley's version of absolute idealism in ethics:

8.114) The moral end as self-realization in the context of the infinite whole;

Normative Ethical Idealism

8.115) all morally justifiable ends aim at the well-being of the self;

8.116) but it must be the true self (rather than any misconstrued false self) as a rational whole, rather than as a fragment;

8.117) this end is achievable only in union with the social wholes to which the individual belongs.

8.118) Self-realization is thus the fulfillment of the universal rational will, which is also free and autonomous because wholly self-determined;

8.119) the individual is preserved in his or her union with universal will by finding his or her place or

any ends whatever, that are pursued by an individual person, are ends that are subsumed under larger aims which find their focus in the realization of some contemplated state of the self, even though this focus need not be characteristically conscious in particular cases of decision and choice. To pursue an ideal of the good or even a limited object of desire is always to aim implicitly at implementing the well-being of the self; for any motives that stir us to choice or action, we sense ourselves asserted or affirmed or enriched in the pursuit of the objects of those motives. But here we find it necessary to distinguish between the true self that a person intrinsically and potentially is, on the one hand, and, on the other, some limited, bad, and (as it were) false self that is a wrongly identified external garb. In aiming at any inclusive end at all, the individual is aiming at a whole of some sort, and the question then becomes the one of identifying the true whole (the morally justifiable whole) that will realize the true self (the self I ought to be and implicitly am). And the answer is that the true self is the self as a rational whole, rather than some fragmentarily limited aspect of that self. Thus this whole of selfhood that persons are to realize is an infinite whole, that is, a whole that is inwardly determined or self-determined. Yet this infinite whole of selfhood cannot be realized by individuals in isolation, for persons are the admittedly unique individuals that they are only in harmonious union with the social wholes to which they belong and which constitute an inclusive moral organism of which each individual is a functioning part or aspect. Thus the moral imperative, 'Realize yourself, as an infinite whole!,' actually means, 'Realize yourself as the self-conscious member of that infinite whole which is the moral organism of society.' Hence, we come back to Hegel's concept of the universal rational will which constitutes the authentic core of all personal selfhood. And this will is not merely universal (the same end generically for all rational, moral selves); it is also free (because wholly self-determined, independent of all external influences) and autonomous (because in willing itself as universal it is a law to itself which legislates for all rational wills).

But according to Bradley, all this does not mean that the self ceases to be finite and individual, for the infinite whole that it is to become morally is the unity of the finite personal self with the universal rational will, such that the individual finds his or her true self as a unique person in organic union with that universal will. In fact, Bradley captures this unity of the moral organism in the phrase, 'My Station and Its Duties.' For him, each individual has a unique place or station in the universal rational scheme, so that the morally good and right, while generically the same for all individuals, is uniquely and specifically distinctive for each. By fulfilling the unique station that each individual has in the moral organism, persons not only find and actualize their own true moral self, but they also implement the true moral well-being of all the other members of that moral organism—and at the same time partially actualize that organism itself as the embodiment of universal rational will. Yet Bradley is not naïve about all this: he realizes that realizing oneself as an infinite whole is a distant goal never more than imperfectly actualized by the finite self; and he acknowledges that in actual moral practice individuals do not characteristically trace up their actual moral decisions and actions to such lofty universal principles—instead, so far as individuals achieve moral goodness, they bring their decisions and choices into conformity with universal rational will by a process of intuitive subsumption without conscious reflection on ultimate principles at all. Still the framework of the moral organism is always there as the sole context within which genuine moral selfhood, however incompletely it may be actualized, can be achieved at all. Thus in summary, for both Hegel and Bradley, the good (both moral and nonmoral) is transcendent in the sense in which an organic totality, in its integrative wholeness, is greater than and extends beyond the mere collection of its parts or aspects; the principle of the good is the principle of universal rational will; and the locus of the good is that same totality or whole. A personal decision or act is morally good or right if it recognizes, expresses, and implements that wholeness more fully than any identifiable alternative of decision or action; otherwise, that decision or act, considered and put forth in isolated independence from the whole, is, from that limited point of view, evil or wrong, although that limited point of view and its principle of self-isolation are, logically and in the end, elements of that selfsame totality which, as a whole, is good. More generally, each element of the totality of being, including personal agents along with their decisions and actions, is

station in the universal rational scheme;

8.120) the moral good or right is thus unique for each individual, while it also implements the well-being of the whole (the moral organism);

8.121) no actual individual perfectly actualizes the moral goal, or typically becomes aware of the principles that justify his or her actions.

8.122) Summary on the Good for Hegel and Bradley:

8.123) The Good is the rational whole;

8.124) an act is right so far as it implements the actualization of the whole;

8.125) it is wrong if it is the product of self-isolation (which is itself part of the totality as good);

8.126) each element of the totality is determined through its relations to all the other elements;

what it is necessarily through its interdependent and logical relations to all the other elements of the totality. This is pervasive metaphysical determinism, of course; but it is supposed by its proponents to make possible for each personal agent and for the Absolute itself the morally relevant and only intelligible sense of freedom. A decision or act is not, for this view, free because it has genuinely possible alternatives; it is rather the case that it is free because it is inwardly self-determined with such completeness that it excludes any and all conceivable alternatives. As Hegel maintained, the truth of freedom is necessity, and the truth of necessity is freedom. In the final analysis, the Absolute subsumes and takes up into itself all its apparently isolated, fragmentary, and evil parts as constitutive elements of the comprehensive good of the whole. The individual's responsibility is to recognize, accept, and fulfill, with clear and complete conscious commitment, his or her true position in this universal rational scheme.

    Once again, my final task here is to attempt a critical evaluation of the sort of absolute idealism in ethics that is represented by Hegel and Bradley. I cannot, of course, in a treatise on moral philosophy, attempt anything approaching a critique of absolute idealism as a total philosophical system; hence I shall concern myself only with its ethical aspects and with such other aspects as bear directly on those ethical features in some fashion. And I shall acknowledge at the outset that my positive appreciation for this perspective is relatively limited; just as I advised the reader to be wary of my relatively unbounded enthusiasm for Platonism, I advise that same reader here to be wary of my rather pervasive suspicion about absolute idealism. But nevertheless I shall make every attempt to be as rationally objective in my judgment as it is possible for me to be, while at the same time acknowledging my imperfections and limits as a human being, as well as the approximative character of my own rational insight.

    A comprehensive system like Hegel's is extremely difficult to approach from a critical standpoint. If Hegel is consistent in his view that there are no false philosophies and that all intelligible philosophical judgments form a part of the all-inclusive total truth, then Hegel's proper tactic for dealing with any criticism, however negative, is to invite it to become

Margin notes:

8.127) such a determinism involves freedom as necessary self-determination;

8.128) thus the Absolute subsumes all its isolated (and evil) parts as elements of the good of the whole.

8.129) Critical evaluation of absolute idealism in ethics:

8.130) personal approach—limited positive appreciation;

8.131) Hegel's system is difficult to criticize, since he claims there are no false philosophies; 8.132) any criticism will thus be absorbed by the system;

a qualifying paragraph in his own system of thought; and hence, by Hegel's own philosophical method, it will be logically impossible to foist upon his system any decisively destructive criticism of any feature of the system. At the same time and for the same reason, Hegel cannot, with full logical consistency, offer any decisively negative criticism of any other or alternative system of philosophy without violating his own thesis that all philosophical systems are true in varying degrees as fragments of the total truth. A purportedly alternative system can be reconciled, absorbed, or transcended (taken up into the larger totality), but it cannot be consistently eliminated either in whole or in part. And this result raises the question whether Hegel's method is adequate to the task of providing a criterial basis for choosing rationally among alternative philosophical worldviews—which would render his method voluntaristic by reducing philosophical commitments to non-rational acts of volitional choice. How, furthermore, can Hegel establish his claim that his perspective is the whole which other perspectives are invited to join? It could as easily be the other way around: perhaps some other system is the whole or totality into which Hegel's own system should be invited as a qualifying paragraph. If Hegel's philosophy can provide no consistent response to this problem, then we are left with non-rational voluntarism; but if a response to the criticism is forthcoming, it is difficult to avoid the conclusion that any viable response would contradict the claim that all philosophies are elements of the total truth.

A similar criticism confronts us in the consequences of Hegel's fundamental dialectical thesis that every determinate point of view logically generates its opposite and then is reconciled with that opposite in a more concrete concept which in turn generates its opposite, and so on. Once this thesis is granted, there seems no way even in principle (let alone practice) for deciding when the final reconciliation in the Absolute Spirit has been achieved without violating the dialectical principle itself. Consider Hegel's own complete philosophy as a determinate point of view: either it is regarded, inconsistently with the dialectical principle itself, as the final synthesis, or, as Hegel sometimes intimates, his own total view is itself susceptible, in principle and practice, of being transcended in a still more concrete

8.133) but it is also the case that Hegel can offer no decisive criticisms of alternative views without inconsistency.

8.134) Hegel's method is inadequate to provide an objective criterion for choosing among alternative worldviews, unless that criterion contradicts his claim to all-inclusiveness.

8.135) The method of dialectical opposition seems contradictory;

8.136) it provides no way of deciding when the final reconciliation has been achieved, without a denial of the method itself.

8.137) Hegel's own system would be a fragment to be transcended;

perspective, in which case his system would, by hypothesis, be only a fragment in some larger whole which forever eludes identification. Or, still more pertinently, consider the dialectical principle itself (that every determinate viewpoint generates its opposite and so on *ad indefinitum*): by its own thesis it should generate its own opposite (that there are at least some points of view that do not logically generate their opposites); but then where would that leave the dialectical method itself, and how is a reconciliation of these two opposites in a consistent whole of concrete conception even conceivable?

In turn, this result leads to the following perplexity: what is the exact nature of the logical opposition (*Gegensatz*) that is involved in Hegel's dialectical method? It would appear to be the case that the purported opposites in a given case are, if they are logically opposed at all, either contradictory or contrary in the logical sense. If the opposites are genuinely contradictory, then reconciliation is logically impossible, since contradictories by definition are so related that the truth of one logically entails the falsity of the other, and vice versa. If, on the other hand, the opposites are merely contrary (i.e., so related that they cannot both be true but might both be false), then the opposition can be resolved, but only by accepting as true propositions that jointly entail the falsity of the opposites; but in that case reconciliation is out of the question, since it can hardly be supposed that two propositions are reconciled by rejecting both as false—this is not reconciliation at all, it is joint dismissal. Consider, for example, the following contrary propositions: All philosophers are idiots; no philosophers are idiots. These propositions cannot both be true; but they can both be false if (and only if) it is the case that some philosophers are idiots, and some philosophers are not idiots. But these propositions, regarded as true, remove the original opposites, not by reconciling them, but by dismissing them as false. If, finally, the opposites in Hegel's scheme are neither contrary nor contradictory, then they are not logically opposed at all but are rather logically compatible, so that there is nothing whatever to reconcile. And what then has become of the notion of dialectical opposition? No doubt a typical post-Russellian philosopher will try to resolve all this by appealing to the concept of a metalanguage that occupies a different

---

8.138) the dialectical principle itself would generate its own opposite;

8.139) the principle of dialectical opposition cannot itself be consistently clarified;
8.140) propositions that appear to oppose each other are either contradictory, contrary, or compatible,

8.141) but for these alternatives, reconciliation is either impossible or irrelevant;

8.142) nor will any meta-linguistic thesis (à la Russell) solve these problems, since

logical level than the propositions about which it makes judgments; but however useful this device may be in other contexts (frankly, I regard it as having quite as many logical perplexities as Hegel's theory of dialectical opposition), it will be of no use to solve Hegel's problems here, since it is central and essential to his system that all true propositions are reconcilable within a single logical scheme or at a single logical level, for that is part of what the so-called final synthesis or reconciliation is all about.

> Hegel views reconciliation as falling within a single all-inclusive scheme.

Now from all the criticisms I have so far discussed (in the form of dilemmas), I conclude that Hegel's method of dialectical opposition and reconciliation has serious and (in my opinion) unresolvable logical difficulties which call into question not only the method itself but any results that depend upon that method in any decisively significant logical fashion. And since his theory, that the Good (both moral and nonmoral) is the reconciled whole or totality of being, is thus decisively dependent on the notion of dialectical opposition and reconciliation, it follows that that central ethical thesis is equally called into question from a logical point of view. For if there is no reconciliation of opposites, then there can be no unreconciled fragments with which to identify evil from a limited and inadequate point of view; and there can be no finally reconciled totality with which to identify the ultimate good. And I regard this criticism as both adequate and decisive in a logical sense. Nevertheless, I am not content to let my whole case, against the adequacy of Hegel's absolute idealism in ethics, rest merely on this general logical ground. So let us rather proceed to explicit details.

> 8.143) It is concluded that the method of opposition is critically defective, as are results dependent upon it;
>
> 8.144) the theory that the Good is the reconciled totality is dependent on this method;
>
> 8.145) hence, this central ethical thesis is called into question as well.

To begin with, it is perplexingly difficult to know what to make of Hegel's development of ethical concepts in the doctrine of objective mind. Is this analysis (which I earlier summarized) supposed to be a descriptive account of the way in which the indicated ethical concepts emerged historically? If so, it would, I think, be very hard to amass any plausible historical evidence in support of it, though I will not attempt to make any judgment one way or the other here. Or again, is the analysis alternatively supposed to be an account of the logical relations among these concepts (following, we may suppose, the intrinsic and implicit logical order of being)? If so, one is often hard-pressed to find any clear logical order of this sort. It is certainly difficult,

> 8.146) It is difficult to accept the triads of objective mind as either historical description or logical deduction, since there is no plausible evidence for the former, and no clear logical transition or order to support the latter;

for example, to understand in what sense Law and Morality are logically opposed or how they can be plausibly said to be reconciled in Social Ethics. And the same can be said of any of the internal triads: how, for instance, are Purpose and Intention logically opposed?; and how, especially, are they logically reconciled in the tension between Goodness and Wickedness? Surely one cannot reasonably suppose that these are genuine logical deductions; it is not even clear that the connections make complete sense empirically (as some alert reader may have observed in reading my earlier account of the analysis).

8.147) since Hegel's ethic collapses good and evil, right and wrong into an identity:

But all these perplexities being left aside, the upshot of Hegel's analysis is clear enough: it involves the collapse of any enduringly significant distinction between morally good and morally evil, between morally right and morally wrong. Evil and wrong can be identified only as fragments grasped from a limited and admittedly inadequate point of view, while from the point of view of the synthesized totality, evil and wrong are either themselves elements in the good of the whole (and means to the realization of that good), or else they are absorbed and vanish in the universal sublimation. How can such an ethic provide any intelligible criterion for moral judgment or any clear guidance for moral choice and decision? Any whole or totality that a finite moral agent can identify to aim at morally is inevitably a mere fragment in a larger totality that is beyond the agent's comprehending grasp, so that the agent is left to choose among evils and wrongs as defined by these incorrectly isolated fragments. And if one makes a list of the more significant moral tragedies of history, ranging from, say, the slaughter of the innocents to the Nazi holocaust, can one take seriously the insight that these and countless others are essential ingredients and even necessary conditions of the universal rational good (the final totality)? The alternative would be to say that these and other moral travesties were and are just flatly and irreconcilably evil and wrong, in which case they logically could not be ingredients in the universal rational good. And that would be the collapse of the whole general structure of Hegel's ethic.

8.148) it provides no intelligible criterion for moral judgment;

8.149) it results in the absurdity that all moral tragedies are necessary ingredients in the universal good;

8.150) it is questionable whether rationally necessary self-determination can be

A further critical problem confronts us in the question whether the notion of rationally necessary self-determination makes any finally intelligible sense from a moral point

310

of view. Is this the morally relevant sense of freedom on which a plausible notion of finite personal moral responsibility can be built? In my much earlier discussion on freedom and determinism, I have already argued extensively for the conclusion that such a view is not the morally relevant sense of freedom; and I need not rehearse my earlier arguments here. If such a notion of rationally necessary self-determination makes any sense at all, it makes sense only for the Absolute Spirit as a totality (the final reconciliation). But clearly I am not that totality in my status as a finite personal self or agent; on Hegel's ground, what I am, what I choose, and what I do are all determined by a complex of elements in the totality, most of which are quite external to myself as a finite agent. But it is precisely just the moral responsibility and accountability of such finite agents with which we are concerned in ethical reasoning. And for that, Hegel provides no reasonable or applicable explanation, in my opinion.

<blockquote>identified with the morally relevant sense of freedom for finite agents, since it implies that all an agent's choices are determined by the reconciled totality.</blockquote>

Closely associated with the previous criticism is the problem that emerges from the tendency of both Hegel and Bradley to regard the political nation-state as the largest identifiable human totality in the context of which the individual person can dependably determine, as Bradley would say, his station and its duties. But that seems to be a sort of double blind spot: first, because the entire human community, composed of the conjunction of all political nation-states, is a clearly identifiable human totality which transcends the state and within which such a moral determination would be more adequately decided on rational grounds. If the state were the finally determining criterial totality, there would then be no rationally objective ground on the basis of which to judge critically the moral quality of the state itself, or to recognize some states as more adequate morally than others; and surely such judgments must be rationally plausible on some grounds logically independent of political states themselves. The second blind spot here would be discerned by recognizing that there must be objective grounds as well for morally evaluating the total human community; certainly that community is empirically variable in the degree to which it actualizes ideal moral adequacy in the structures of social relationship. In the end, the logic of absolute idealism would have to identify the

<blockquote>8.151) It is implausible to regard the political nation-state as the final human moral community;

8.152) because there would then be no objective basis for assessing the moral quality of political states in relation to the total human community; 8.153) and that latter community itself would require moral assessment in the context of the Absolute totality;</blockquote>

Absolute Spirit itself as the all-inclusive moral community, since that finally and wholly reconciled totality would be, by definition, the only non-fragmented and complete reality. But since no finite and determinate view on the part of finite individuals can ever clearly grasp that reality, and since in any case, again by hypothesis, the Absolute in its finally reconciled state justifies morally all of its fragmented parts in the totality, we would again have no objective criterion for making moral distinctions between good and evil, right and wrong. We can again raise here, as we did with Plato, the question as to whether the relationship between finite personal agents and an impersonal totality can be moral in the relevant sense, since it is difficult to construe persons as having moral duties or obligations toward any reality that is less than personal. While the Absolute has personal elements (i.e., finite personal agents like ourselves), nevertheless, it is not, on the standard interpretation of either Hegel or Bradley, characterized in its totality by or as ultimate personal selfhood.

8.154) but the Absolute justifies all its 'evil' fragments and provides no genuine moral criterion;

8.155) and there is the question whether there can be any morally relevant relation between personal agents and a non-personal totality.

While, for all the critical reasons I have suggested (along with other possible ones I did not include), I must therefore judge absolute idealism as rationally inadequate for providing a clarification of the transcendent objectivity of the ultimately good or right, it is at the same time important not to overlook a battery of significant moral insights that we find in this philosophical context. On the one hand, for example, absolute idealism recognizes, as a criterion of philosophical assessment, the ideal of universal and objective reason (or rational objectivity), while, on one interpretation at least and on the other hand, it acknowledges that no determinate point of view or actual version of philosophical truth on the part of a finite knower can ever do more than imperfectly approximate, and therefore recognize the tentativity of, any finite attempt to actualize that ideal. Furthermore, absolute idealism attempts, perhaps with only the same sort of inevitably limited success, to apply that ideal of rational objectivity to the domain of moral or ethical judgments, so that any version of radical ethical relativism is decisively rejected or dismissed. Again, this perspective recognizes and laboriously defends the claim that the principal domain of moral worth is that of personal beings standing in reciprocal personal relationships with each other: is the notion of moral

8.156) Positive elements:

8.157) the recognition of universal and objective reason as a criterion of philosophical assessment—which, however, can only be approximated by finite knowers;

8.158) the rejection of radical ethical relativism;

8.159) personal beings and their relationships as the context of moral worth;

duty or responsibility even intelligible in any other, especially any lesser, context? For absolute idealism, therefore, intrinsic personal worth is at the core of the moral sphere; and Bradley goes on to recognize, appropriately I judge, the moral uniqueness of each individual person who, when entrenched in his or her station and duties, embodies a unique and unrepeatable focal point for the actualization of the moral ideal. So even though we find ourselves partly surrounded with conceptual problems in the framework of absolute idealism, there certainly is, even here, much that we can carry along with us on our continued journey toward the rediscovery of the highest good.

8.160) the moral uniqueness of individual persons.

The Postulational Orientation in Ethical Idealism: Immanuel Kant

The overall philosophical project of Immanuel Kant, especially in his three *Critiques* (the *Critique of Pure Reason*, the *Critique of Practical Reason*, and the *Critique of Judgment*) is arguably one of the most impressive and significant products of western (or even world) intellectual history. And even though Kant held that ethical principles possessed an authority that was autonomous and, for the most part, logically independent of other aspects of philosophical thought (especially metaphysics), it is necessary to have at least an abbreviated account of his general philosophical views in epistemology and metaphysics in order to understand his perspective about ethics and the moral law. In the first (and largest) of his *Critiques*, Kant argued that the two main epistemological traditions of western philosophical history, namely, *rationalistic apriorism* (represented, for example, by Plato, who contended that all knowledge is made up of concepts and principles that characterize the mind prior to and independently of the data of empirical experience) and *traditional empiricism* (represented, for example, by David Hume, who held that all the principles and content of knowledge were based on and therefore logically dependent upon the elements of empirical experience), were both extreme and intrinsically skeptical. As a solution to the controversy between these two epistemological standpoints, Kant proposed a conflation of the two positions which he

8.161) Kant's epistemological and metaphysical views:

8.162) Both rationalistic apriorism and traditional empiricism were regarded by Kant as extreme.

8.163) His rational empiricism combines the two views;

8.164) the faculties of the mind involve a structure of principles that characterize the mind prior to and independently of sense experience (synthetic *a priori*);

8.165) but the content of knowledge is derived from sense experience as organized by the *a priori* principles;

8.166) the legitimate use of the *a priori* forms limited to the phenomenal and the empirical for genuine knowledge (synthetic *a posteriori*);
8.167) distinction between synthetic and analytic judgments;
8.168) analytic judgments or predicates are true only by definition of the subject term;
8.169) synthetic judgments are true other than by definition:
8.170) either empirically,
8.171) or as grounded in *a priori* principles, without which analytic and empirical judgments would be impossible.

designated as *rational empiricism*: on the one hand, Kant granted to the rationalistic apriorists that genuinely objective and universal knowledge is possible only if the knowing mind possesses intellectual faculties whose structure involves rational forms and principles that are characteristic of the mind *a priori* (i.e., independently of the elements of empirical experience, and underivable from them), and that function as necessary presuppositions of the possibility and actuality of empirical experience and conceptual apprehension; on the other hand, Kant granted to the traditional empiricists that the content (as distinguished from the form or structure) of all genuine theoretical knowledge was derived from the raw data or material of sense experience—in fact, he held that the legitimate use of the *a priori* forms of sensibility and the *a priori* categories of pure understanding, was restricted to *phenomena* (things as they appear to us, rather than things as they are in themselves or *noumena*) and to actual or possible objects of sense experience. Kant termed the *a priori* forms and categories that make knowledge possible synthetic *a priori* principles or judgments, while he termed the elements of empirical experience synthetic *a posteriori* data. And thus genuine content knowledge involves the application of the synthetic *a priori* principles to the synthetic *a posteriori* data—hence, rational (the *a priori* aspect) empiricism (the *a posteriori* aspect). Kant uses the term *synthetic* here in contrast to the complementary term *analytic*. An analytic judgment or principle is one in which the predicate term in the judgment stands for a meaning that is logically derivable from the meaning of the subject term, so that the judgment or principle is true by definition in the case of an affirmative judgment or principle. By contrast, a judgment is called synthetic if the predicate term is not derivable in its meaning from that of the subject term, but must be imported from some other source. This can happen in two ways, according to Kant: first, in ordinary empirical judgments, the applicability of the predicate term to the subject term depends on the data of empirical or sense experience (synthetic *a posteriori* judgments); but second (and more importantly for Kant) a judgment can also be synthetic if its truth is a necessary presupposition of all possible intelligible thought, such as the forms of sensibility or the categories of pure understanding when expressed in propositional form (synthetic *a priori* judgments). Kant reasoned that intelligible thought would be impossible either about analytic connections or about sense objects, unless the knowing mind operated from the beginning with certain interpretive principles or concepts which were the initial basis of all understanding of meaning and of all apprehension of sense objects, so that those ultimate principles could themselves be neither analytic nor *a posteriori* (empirical) and would therefore have to be synthetic and *a priori*.

As I indicated earlier, however, Kant argued that, since we invoke these synthetic *a priori* principles as an explanation of the possibility of our attaining any knowledge of phenomena or sense objects, we can make no legitimate use of these principles outside the limits of phenomena and actual or possible sense objects; they could not, for example, be used to attain genuine knowledge about purely rational objects which are incapable of being experienced as either phenomena or sense objects. Kant further pointed out that all the principal objects of metaphysical philosophy are defined by the absence of empirical content and cannot be experienced as phenomena. In his opinion, these three principal objects are *God* (as the absolutely necessary and transcendent ground of all contingent being or existence), the *soul* (the rational self as the logically pure subject of all experience), and the *world* or *cosmos* (as the totality of all contingent beings or existences). Kant then reasoned that since, by definition as indicated, these ideas are purely rational objects and cannot be construed as either possible objects of sense experience or as phenomena, and since genuine theoretical knowledge by means of the synthetic *a priori* principles is limited to phenomena and sense objects, it follows that there can be no genuine theoretical knowledge of God, the soul, or the world. Now since every speculative metaphysical philosophy has these three concepts at the core of its consideration, it therefore follows that there can be no genuine theoretical knowledge in metaphysics, as Kant viewed the matter. This is not to say that there could not be rationally plausible beliefs about such purely rational, nonempirical objects; it is rather to say that such plausible beliefs are not genuine knowledge. Kant called such rational objects regulative ideals or principles on the ground that they could provide integrative harmony and motivation for the

8.172) Since the legitimate use of synthetic *a priori* principles, to attain knowledge, is limited to the phenomenal and the empirical, 8.173) it follows that there can be no genuine knowledge about purely rational objects, 8.174) and thus none about God, the soul, or the world as the principal concepts of metaphysics;

8.175) hence there can be no genuine speculative knowledge in metaphysics, although there may be plausible beliefs about such purely rational objects.

pursuit of the phenomena and empirical knowledge that *is* legitimately possible for finite knowers; but I need not develop that regulative role any further in this context.

The conclusion, that metaphysical knowledge is impossible in this way, has, however, a fundamentally significant bearing on Kant's moral philosophy. Kant argued, as a result, that if any genuine moral knowledge is possible for rational selves, then it cannot be based on metaphysical knowledge (as Plato, and, later, Hegel and Bradley wrongly supposed that it could), because there is no metaphysical knowledge for moral knowledge to be based on. Now Kant was confident (he would have said rationally certain) that moral knowledge (i.e., knowledge of the fundamental law of morality) is possible (and even actual) for rational selves. And this confidence left Kant with two alternatives for explaining the possibility of moral knowledge within the parameters of his own theory of knowledge: moral knowledge would have to be either empirical in its basis and principles, or (the only other alternative for Kant) rationalistically *a priori* (i.e., synthetic and *a priori*). But Kant argues extensively in his moral writings that the propositions of genuine morality or true moral judgments of a normative sort cannot possibly be empirical. We have ourselves already investigated a number of either meta-ethical or normative ethical theories (naturalistic definism and normative ethical hedonism, for example) which claim precisely what Kant denies, namely, that so-called moral principles are empirically derived. Why, then, does Kant think such a derivation of moral principles is impossible logically? Well, as he sees it, moral principles are always directive or imperative in nature; that is, they tell us what acts we ought to perform, what ends we ought to pursue, or what maxims or rules we ought to follow. There are, of course, as Kant recognized, empirically derived directives or rules; they tell us that, *if* we have certain desires or aspirations or tendencies (etc.), then we ought to act in certain ways, pursue certain objectives, follow certain rules, and so on. If you want to lose weight, then you ought to eat less and get more exercise, or, more generally, if you want to feel happy (or any other way), then you ought to carry out various procedures. Now the common characteristic of all such empirically derived directives or imperatives is that (like all empirically derived insights) they

---

8.176) If there is any genuine moral knowledge,

8.177) it cannot be based on metaphysical knowledge (since there is none);

8.178) it must therefore be either empirical or synthetic *a priori* in its basis;

8.179) moral knowledge cannot be empirical;

8.180) moral principles are always imperatives or rules;

8.181) but empirically derived imperatives or rules are always contingent or conditional, rather than necessary and unconditional.

8.182) These conditions are grounded in desires which may or may not be fulfilled;

are all contingent and conditional, never necessary and unconditional; there is always an *if* or a series of conditions that may or may not be fulfilled. I may want to lose weight and I may not; or, more generally, I may want to feel happy and I may not (for *happy* one can substitute any other generalized epithet, such as healthy, rich, successful, or comfortable). But according to Kant, all this is not morality at all; it is merely prudence or self-interest. As such it is all optional (do it or not, as you like). For morality addresses us quite otherwise: here there are no 'ifs' or conditions, no contingent whims or desires that we may or may not have; no, morality says quite or rather completely categorically, unconditionally, and necessarily: 'you ought!'—no 'ifs,' 'ands,' or 'buts' about it. You *ought* to tell the truth; you *ought* to make no promises you cannot keep; you *ought*, furthermore, to keep your promises; you *ought* not to steal, or murder, or commit adultery, etc. *This* is morality, at least in form if not in substance. Hence, any genuinely moral imperative is categorical and unconditional; empirically contingent and variable desires, aspirations, or tendencies have nothing to do with the morality of these and other such commands or imperatives, although they may provide a context for them. Thus no genuinely moral imperative or principle is empirically derivable.

Now if moral principles are therefore not empirical, and if nevertheless it is possible for rational selves to have a knowledge of the moral law, then it follows that moral principles (if they are genuinely moral and not merely prudential) are based on *a priori* reason. Principles of reason, formally or structurally considered, are precisely categorical, unconditional, non-empirical; they are, in fact, objective, universal, and necessary. And these are all the formal requirements of a genuinely moral principle or law: whatever the ultimate law of morality is, therefore, it is a synthetic *a priori* principle, one cannot demonstrate the moral law by any truths logically more basic than itself; we can only recognize that synthetic *a priori* status as the necessary ground for the possibility of there being any genuinely moral knowledge at all. Just as the synthetic *a priori* categories of substance, causation, and existence (for example) are necessary presuppositions of the possibility of any genuine empirical knowledge, so the synthetic *a priori* law of morality is

8.183) but such rules are merely prudential, not moral;

8.184) morality is categorical, unconditional, and necessary;

8.185) thus no genuinely moral principle is empirically derivable.

8.186) Moral knowledge must therefore be based on *a priori* reason;

8.187) the properties of rational principles are precisely those of moral law—which is thus synthetic and *a priori*;
8.188) as such, the moral law cannot be demonstrated, but only recognized as the necessary ground of all moral knowledge.
8.189) This is wholly parallel to the *a priori* principles that form the basis of all knowledge in general;

the necessary presupposition of the possibility of any genuine moral knowledge. It never occurred to Kant that there might not be any genuine moral knowledge, any more than it ever occurred to him that there might not be any genuine knowledge in mathematics or physics.

8.190) the *a priori* moral law is the obligation to act according to rules that can be universalized without inconsistency;

What then is the synthetic *a priori* law of morality stated as a categorical imperative? According to Kant, it is not any particular and limited moral rule (such as: 'Always tell the truth!'); it is rather the more general obligation to act according to rules which, when applied, will exhibit the formal logical properties of any synthetic *a priori* principle whatever, namely, universality, and rational self-consistency (freedom from self-contradiction). Whenever persons make a morally significant choice or perform a morally significant act, they implicitly subsume their act under a general moral rule to the effect that any moral agent, choosing or acting under the same or closely similar morally relevant circumstances, ought to choose or act in the same or a closely similar way. If, for example, I ought (morally) to tell the truth under a certain set of circumstances, then any moral agent ought to tell the truth under the same or closely similar circumstances, and so on. But a particular moral rule (or maxim, as Kant called it) can, with rational intelligibility, fulfill this condition only if, when it is universalized in the way indicated, its functioning in the status of such a universal law of reason would not generate any rational inconsistency or contradiction. Hence, the ultimate categorical imperative is: Act morally only in accordance with that rule or maxim which you could, with rational consistency, will to become a universal law; or: Act morally only in accordance with that rule or maxim which, if universalized, would generate no rational inconsistency or contradiction. Suppose, for example, that you are pondering whether it is morally permissible or right to make a promise to someone either with the intent of not keeping it or with the knowledge that, under the attending circumstances, you will assuredly not be able to keep it. The question is not whether it would be prudential or self-advantageous to make such a promise, for that is an empirical and therefore (as we have seen previously) a nonmoral issue, although Kant suggests that a person is never fully confident that, in the end, consequences will serve one's self-advantage if one does make

8.191) the universality of genuine moral rules;

8.192) the rational self-consistency of genuine moral rules;

8.193) formulations of the moral law;

8.194) illustrative application;

8.195) morality is not a question of self-advantage;

such a specious promise. No; the question is whether the act would be unconditionally (and thus independently of any question of consequences) right or permissible in the purely moral sense. Could you, then, with a rational consistency, universalize the rule that one ought or morally may so promise? To universalize the rule would be to say either that any person in the same or closely similar morally relevant circumstances would be justified in so promising; or else (more strongly) it is to say that any such person would always so act and also be morally justified in so doing. But clearly either of these universalizations would generate inconsistency or contradiction in the sense that universalizing the rule would undermine the intent of making the promise in the first place. That intent would be to get the false promise accepted as *bona fide* or genuine with whatever self-advantageous consequences might ensue. But if falsely promising became either a universally permissible or a universally actual practice, then that intention could not be fulfilled, since no one would credit promising as genuine on such terms, and doubtless also, no one would bother to make such pointless promises. Thus my original maxim or rule destroys itself (and in that sense contradicts itself) as soon as it is universalized. Now at first sight, it might appear that Kant is reintroducing a prudential consideration here, since it is self-interest that would lead a person either to make or to credit such promises. And while that is true, yet that is clearly not Kant's point; for it is the contradiction, not the prudence involved, that disqualified the rule or maxim from being a moral law. A moral law is a law of reason and, as such, cannot be self-contradictory; hence, universalized moral rules that generate contradictions cannot be moral laws as laws of universal reason. And this analysis leads to another logical result, namely, that it is possible to do what, in an objective sense, is morally right, but to do it on grounds which are subjectively prudential (and how intrinsically delighted we should all be that such is the case, since otherwise objectively right moral practice would be far less common than it is). But, as Kant sees it, one deserves no moral credit for choosing or acting with moral rightness if one does so on such nonmoral or prudential grounds. For moral duty requires, not merely that we act in accordance with moral law, but that we do so solely out of a motivation

8.196) it is a question of unconditional moral rightness, regardless of prudential consequences.

8.197) If universalization generates inconsistency, the act in question is immoral;

8.198) such acts are morally wrong, not because of their prudential consequences, but because of their inconsistency;

8.199) a moral law, as a law of reason, cannot be self-contradictory;

8.200) if persons do what is morally right on prudential grounds, they deserve no moral credit for so acting;

8.201) morality requires not only action according to moral law, but action motivated by pure respect for that law as a law of reason;

provided by pure respect for the moral law as a law of reason. Otherwise I am not fulfilling my moral duty, but merely acting out of my nonmoral self-interest. And Kant believes that we can also turn this around and affirm that if a person habitually acts out of pure respect for the moral law, that person will, in the long run, be acting in such a way as to subserve his or her own true and moral self-interest, even if such a habitual practice does not in the end subserve one's more narrowly construed prudential self-interest, although Kant does not even rule that out, as I interpret him. What is morally ruled out is acting for the sake of prudential self-interest; for if one habitually acts out of respect for the moral law, one makes one's self morally worthy of happiness in the sense of genuine human well-being—which is far more important than actually *being* happy in the more narrow prudential sense.

Now from this analysis it becomes apparent that, for Kant, the essence of immorality (or moral evil) consists in making an exception of yourself by following moral rules that cannot be universalized without generating inconsistency or contradiction. Falsely promising will only work for me if it is not a universal practice or even a morally and universally permissible practice; for my false promise will be credited only if promises are expected to be genuine in actual moral practice for the most part. Thus when persons act immorally, they make of themselves a falsely oriented end, while at the same time they make of other persons mere means or instruments of their own prudential goals. From this point of view Kant proposes a second formula for the categorical moral imperative: Act always in such a way as to treat humanity, whether in your own person or in that of another person, as an end possessed of intrinsic worth and never merely as a means to your own self-interest. This formulation seems to commit Kant to the thesis that the fundamentally intrinsic moral good or value is personal being; and in a sense this is the case. But it must always be remembered that, for Kant, respect for persons, as intrinsically valuable in the moral sense, is grounded in moral law as the law of duty for its own sake, rather than the other way around. Instead of it being the case that we are bound by moral law because it expresses the ideal of intrinsic personal worth, it is rather the case that, because persons are

8.202) if persons act out of pure respect for the moral law as a matter of habit, they will subserve their true moral self-interest, and make themselves morally worthy of happiness as genuine well-being.

8.203) Since the essence of immorality consists in making an exception of yourself for prudential ends, it also results in making other persons means to those ends;

8.204) the moral law can be thus restated as the obligation to treat human beings as ends possessing intrinsic worth, and never merely as means;
8.205) but for Kant, the worth of persons is dependent on their capacity to recognize and respect the moral law, rather than vice versa.

uniquely capable of recognizing and respecting the unconditional moral law, they are for that reason deserving of respect as themselves intrinsically valuable. This capacity of each rational being to legislate, from its own rational will, rules or maxims that have the status of universal moral law, suggests for Kant a third formulation of the categorical imperative, based on the idea that all rational beings constitute, in their obligation to universal and moral law, a kingdom of ends (or intrinsic values) which is a systematic union of rational beings through common objective laws. In such a union, ideally considered, each member rationally legislates for all the members and regards himself as bound by that same legislation. Hence, the categorical imperative can be again reformulated: Act always on those rules or maxims which, as universal moral laws of reason, could constitute the legislation through which such an ideal moral community or realm of ends would be implemented in its existence and functioning.

8.206) A third formulation of the moral law is suggested by the capacity of rational beings to legislate moral law: the obligation to act according to rules that would implement a universal kingdom of persons as ends.

Granted such a concept of the moral law as an unconditional categorical imperative expressed in these three ways (and others that Kant also suggests), under what conditions can the absolute and unconditional authority of the moral law achieve maximum rational intelligibility for rational moral beings like ourselves? Or, alternatively put, under what conditions can conformity with the absolute and unconditionally authoritative moral law be achieved in human experience? Since these questions are tantamount to asking what properties must be attached to being if morality is to be rationally intelligible and practically possible, they are clearly metaphysical questions; and since metaphysics, as genuine theoretical and speculative knowledge, is, in Kant's view, impossible, any answer that is given cannot constitute an extension of our genuine knowledge, but can be no more than a proposal for reasonable belief, which Kant designates as rational faith. The moral law of duty is itself autonomous in an objective sense, as we have seen, and does not depend for its authority on any metaphysical knowledge or even beliefs. It is rather the other way around: the reasonableness of beliefs, which for us make the moral law rationally intelligible or practically conceivable, depends on the authority of the moral law. But we have no way of knowing that the conditions of rational intelligibility and practical

8.207) The conditions of maximal rational intelligibility for unconditionally authoritative moral law:

8.208) There can be no genuine knowledge of those conditions (since they are metaphysical by definition);
8.209) at most it will be a matter of reasonable belief or rational faith;
8.209a) the moral law, as autonomous, is independent of all metaphysical basis;
8.210) it is rather the case that reasonable metaphysical beliefs

are conditions of intelligibility for the independently authoritative moral law;	possibility *for* us are also conditions of objective existence; hence, the most we can hope for here is reasonable belief, not knowledge; and Kant called such reasonable beliefs regulative principles or postulates of practical (i.e., moral) reason. At the same time, these principles or postulates are not laws of moral duty, so that no finite moral agent is morally obligated to belief in such principles; it is rather conformity to the requirement of the moral law to which we are obligated, not acceptance of the principles that, for us, make that conformity rationally intelligible (in the fullest sense) or practically possible.
8.211) such beliefs are regulative postulates of practical or moral law.	
8.212) The ideals of pure reason relevant to morality:	According to Kant, the ideas or ideals of pure reason involved in the general possibility of plausible metaphysical belief are God, the soul, and the cosmos; but the regulative principles or postulates that function as conditions of the intelligibility and practical possibility of morality are freedom, immortality, and God. Since my concern here is with moral philosophy rather than with general metaphysics, I shall confine myself to the discussion of the postulates of practical (moral) reason. The postulate of *freedom*, to begin with, is the belief that morally responsible finite agents actually possess the capacity of moral self-determination essential to aiming at conformity to the moral law as the law of duty; of course, they also possess the ability, through that same capacity of self-determination, to reject that conformity as an ideal. The possession of this capacity is precisely the morally relevant sense of freedom. In Kant's eyes, it would be rationally unintelligible for persons to be held morally responsible or obligated, if they did not possess genuine freedom in the indicated sense. And it follows, for Kant (who is thus an incompatibilist), that morally responsible choices and acts logically and morally cannot be determined by nonmoral causes (causes other than the free causality of the agent), since in that case the agent would not possess, relatively to those choices and acts, the freedom essential to that responsibility. 'I ought' or 'I morally must,' implies 'I can'; and 'I can' implies that my choice and act are both contingent. But this agent causality view poses a serious logical problem for Kant, since choices and acts, as empirical occurrences, are phenomena, and he holds that from the standpoint of genuine theoretical knowledge, all phenomena are determined by necessary and sufficient antecedent empirical causes. How
8.213) freedom: that finite moral agents have the capacity for moral self-determination;	
8.214) this freedom is a necessary condition of moral responsibility, and it implies the rejection of any notion of determinism by nonmoral causes;	
8.215) but Kant also holds that choices are, as empirical occurrences, determined by empirical causes;	

logically could one and the same choice or act be, at the same time, both empirically determined and morally free and responsible? This appears to constitute a contradiction. Kant's answer is perhaps difficult to accept for most interpreters; but it is clear enough. A choice or an act is indeed a phenomenon and, as such, it is indeed empirically determined; but the morally responsible self belongs, not to the empirical world, but to the noumenal world of things in themselves (or the 'intelligible world,' as Kant designates it). In that intelligible or noumenal world, any morally significant choice or act is free in the morally relevant sense. Kant claims, whether questionably or not, that there is not the least contradiction between a thing being causally determined as an empirical phenomenon and that same thing being independent of such determination as a noumenon or thing in itself. We do not know, of course, that we are free in this noumenal sense; but believing that we are is an essential condition of the rational intelligibility of our being bound by the moral law.

8.216) this appears to be contradictory; 8.217) but Kant holds that, since the moral self belongs to the noumenal world, one and the same choice can be both noumenally free and phenomenally determined.

Another such condition, or postulate of practical reason, is the belief that we are *immortal* as rational, moral selves. Morality requires of us that we do the morally right thing as a matter of habitual practice out of pure respect for the moral law. But we can never, in any finite period of time, be wholly and rationally confident that this pure moral motive is not commingled with varying degrees of empirical and prudential motives of a nonmoral sort. Yet we morally ought to act out of the pure motive of respect for the moral law; 'ought' in turn implies 'can' in the morally relevant sense of freedom; but since the perfection of this conformity to the moral law is clearly unachievable in any finite period of time, it follows that the moral cause of 'can' implies that we are going to exist endlessly as rational, moral selves in order to have the unlimited opportunity progressively to approximate the achievement of the highest moral ideal. If that were not the case, it would undermine the full rational intelligibility of the unconditional authority of the moral law over us and of our responsibility for complete conformity to that authority. Again, however, we do not know that we are immortal as rational, moral selves; it is simply reasonable to believe that we are, as a condition of the full rational intelligibility of the moral law itself (which we *do* know).

8.218) Immortality: that finite moral agents are immortal as a necessary condition for the fullest approximation of the fulfillment of the moral law;

Normative Ethical Idealism

8.219) God: that God exists as the supreme causal and purposive ground of nature.

8.220) The highest good consists of:

8.221) complete conformity to the moral law,

8.222) well-being proportionate to moral virtue;

8.223) either element devoid of the other would be irrational;

8.224) but since there is no intrinsic harmony between virtue and well-being, nor does it lie within the control of the finite moral agent,

8.225) it follows that the ground of this harmony is a rational will, which is the cause of nature in conformity to moral purpose—which would be the transcendent personal God of theism.

The final postulate of practical or moral reason is the belief in *God* as the supreme causal and purposive ground of nature. According to Kant, the highest good, morally construed from the standpoint of finite rational and moral agents, contains two elements: the first is simply the achievement of moral virtue as the complete conformity of the personal will to the requirement of the moral law in its unconditional authority, although no actual individual ever fully meets that moral requirement; the second element, postulated as equally necessary to the conception of the highest good (according to Kant), is a degree of happiness or overall personal well-being that is completely proportionate to the individual's moral virtue. What Kant appears to be claiming here is that an ideal and objective moral order of being could not be actualized without both elements as composing the highest conceivable good in a finite order of existence: complete personal well-being devoid of moral virtue would be rationally absurd, while morality conjoined with the universal absence of any proportionate degree of personal well-being would be equally irrational from a moral point of view. But since personal well-being depends on the harmony of the whole of nature with the moral end of finite persons, while the moral law itself is grounded on a motivation (pure respect for the moral law) that is entirely independent of nature and its harmony (or otherwise) with personal well-being, it follows that there is no intrinsic harmony between moral virtue and well-being. Nor can the morally virtuous individual bring about this harmony through his or her own efforts to the complete extent that would be required for an ideal moral order of being, since the moral individual is not the cause of nature. Hence the only possible ground for the realization of the highest good in existence would be a supreme cause of the whole of nature whose causality corresponds with this ideal or highest good in purposive intent; now such a cause would be a rational or intelligent will which itself embodies and constitutes complete moral perfection—which would be God in the transcendent, personal, and thus theistic sense. Hence the possibility of a highest derived good (well-being proportionate to moral virtue) is conceivable only by postulating God as the highest original and absolute good; and in this sense it is morally necessary to assume the existence of God.

But some further clarification is essential. First, the well-being that Kant construes here, as proportionate to moral virtue, is clearly not the nonmorally construed satisfaction derived from hedonistic gratification; it is rather the integrative and harmonious well-being that is in complete concord with the motivation provided by pure respect for the moral law. And while Kant does not provide any detailed explanation of this point (to my knowledge), perhaps what he had in mind was a balanced state of mental and physical health which found its highest fulfillment and satisfaction in moral virtue itself. The second clarification is once more to point out that the necessity of God is practical or moral in nature, not speculative and theoretical in the sense of extending our actual knowledge. It cannot be anyone's moral duty to believe in God; moral duty is limited to the pursuit of moral virtue and the furtherance of the realization of the highest good in the world at large, so far as that is possible for finite moral agents. It is just that such a highest good can be intelligibly postulated for our reason only by presupposing the existence of God as thus construed. At this point, the line between such an ethical idealism and ethical theism grows thin indeed; the difference is that, for the ethical theist, what Kant puts forward as a morally necessary postulate of practical or moral reason, the theist regards as sheer and objective metaphysical truth.

In retrospect, for Kant there is an objective, universal, and necessary law of unconditional and autonomous moral duty or obligation. It is rationally autonomous in the sense that, as a synthetic *a priori* principle of reason, it is logically prior to and independent of any metaphysical scheme whatever. Of course, Kant's analysis assumes an epistemological theory (rational empiricism); and it assumes the existence (whether possible or actual) of finite rational, moral beings who are subject to the authority of that moral law. The moral law obliges such moral beings always to act on principles that can be universalized without generating any inconsistency or contradiction; and by logical extension it also obliges them to treat humanity, whether in oneself or in other persons, always as an end and never merely as a means to one's own nonmoral prudential goals. While morality is therefore, on the whole, independent of all metaphysical basis (with the exception of the minimum just stated),

8.226) The well-being construed as proportionate to virtue is not that of hedonistic satisfaction, but rather a balanced state of being wholly proportionate to virtue itself;

8.227) nor is belief in God a moral duty, but rather a condition of the intelligibility of realizing the highest good in conformity to moral law.

8.228) Brief summary of Kant's ethical perspective

and while, for Kant, metaphysical knowledge is impossible (since it is neither phenomenal nor empirical), nevertheless plausible metaphysical beliefs can be argued on purely moral grounds: an ideal and objective moral order of being is one in which finite persons are genuinely free in the morally relevant sense, in which those persons are immortal as providing an endless opportunity for moral progress, and in which a transcendent personal God, as rational and intelligent will, brings about a total proportion between moral virtue and personal well-being. But none of this metaphysical belief is either an extension of knowledge or a matter of moral duty—that is what the autonomy of the moral law is all about.

8.229) Critique of Kant's ethical perspective:

From a critical point of view, there is, in my opinion, a great deal in Kant's philosophy, especially his moral philosophy, which seems eminently rational and plausible, and with which I can personally and conceptually identify. In fact, just as I have often been charged with, or accused of, being a Platonist, so I have also often been designated as a Kantian, although I do not regard either characterization as an insult but rather as an honor and a compliment. I even remember a cool, clear, moonlit night in Portland, Oregon, some half a century ago, when, gazing out the window from my desk at the beauty of the night with my lamp out, I had what Plato might have described as a dialectical vision, in which I saw, after prolonged study of the *Critique of Pure Reason*, both that Kant was essentially right about the marriage, as it were, of rationalistic apriorism and traditional empiricism, and at the same time that he was seriously mistaken about the restriction of genuine knowledge to objects that were either phenomenal or empirical. Although more than fifty years have transpired since that memorable night, I have never wavered from either of these insights, much less entertained any serious doubt about them; and somewhere between then and now I gradually came to accept, with a wholehearted commitment, the central core of Kant's moral philosophy as well, although here too I have some modest qualifications. As for my conclusions about Kant's epistemology, since I have written extensively about this in my earlier books and in one article, and since I am here concerned primarily with moral philosophy, I can in this context offer no more than a brief summary critique.

8.230) my personal attitude toward Kant;

To begin with, then, I find Kant's doctrine of synthetic apriorism logically and intellectually inescapable: if the mind were not characterized at the outset with an array or battery of interpretive principles of reason and rational categories which therefore belonged to it prior to, and independently of, all empirical experience, there would be no intelligible way in which the mind, as such a *tabula rasa*, could derive anything from empirical experience by way of content. To be a mind at all is to be necessarily predisposed to understand objects in certain unavoidable conceptual ways; and that is perhaps why Leibniz (of whom Kant had earlier been a historically removed disciple) offered the criticism, of all pure empiricism, that there is indeed nothing in the mind prior to sense experience, *except*, of course, the mind itself (with all its *a priori* structural principles). About this point, therefore, I regard both Leibniz and Kant as soundly correct. But with that gold medal of epistemological victory clearly in hand, Kant then wrongly proceeded, as I see it, to surrender both the silver and bronze medals to the empirical and Humean tradition by claiming that genuine theoretical knowledge was restricted in its objects to the phenomenal and the empirical, thus making any knowledge of noumenal and non-empirical objects impossible by definition. This restriction seems clearly mistaken: it certainly does not follow logically from the fact that the mind requires *a priori* principles and categories as a necessary condition of apprehending phenomenal and empirical objects, that therefore the legitimate use of these *a priori* structures is logically illegitimate beyond such limits. Kant himself claims that it is possible to have genuine theoretical knowledge of the reality and function of *a priori* principles and categories themselves, which are *defined* by the absence of any empirical basis of content; and more specifically he claims that we can have a knowledge of the wholly non-empirical moral law (or categorical imperative) as a synthetic *a priori* principle of reason. To deny this would mean the self-annihilation of Kant's entire philosophical project. There is, therefore, no clear and consistent reason to deny the mind's capacity, through its *a priori* structural principles, to achieve a knowledge in principle of non-empirical objects of thought. I cannot here deal with Kant's claim (in the doctrine of the antinomies of pure reason and in the

8.231) Kant (and Leibniz) seem clearly right about moderate rationalistic apriorism;

8.232) if the mind did not possess *a priori* interpretive principles of reason, it could derive nothing from empirical experience;

8.233) but Kant seems clearly wrong in limiting genuine knowledge to the phenomenal and the empirical.

8.234) Kant himself claims that it is possible to have genuine knowledge:
8.235) both of the *a priori* categories,
8.236) and of the *a priori* moral law;

8.237) thus there is no reason, in principle, to deny the possibility of the knowledge of non-empirical objects;

doctrine of the paralogisms of rational psychology) that the attempt to use the *a priori* categories, to attain a knowledge of non-empirical objects (God and the soul, for example), leads to insoluble logical contradictions and fallacies, which would indicate that the mind has transgressed its legitimate sphere of operation. On this point, I will merely say that I regard all these antinomies and paralogisms as themselves involving contradictions and fallacies of the very sort that Kant charges against those he criticizes here. The muddles he identifies are, if that is the case, soluble in principle and thus not insuperable objections against the claim to genuine metaphysical knowledge. Again, I have written much more about that elsewhere.

8.238) nor are Kant's arguments about antinomies and paralogisms incapable of rationally plausible solution.

What then of Kant's moral philosophy? Here again I agree with Kant that the very notion of moral duty or obligation ultimately implies that no universal moral law is logically based on empirical grounds (such as desire, inclination, or prudential self-interest), and that therefore the unconditionally authoritative and universal principle of moral duty or obligation (assuming, as I have previously argued, that there is one) must be, when logically construed, a synthetic *a priori* principle of reason. I even agree, within certain limits, that one can use the logical test of universalization without inconsistency to determine whether the maxim or rule, that one is following (or would follow) in making a moral decision, would vindicate the moral rightness of that decision. The essence of immorality, as Kant clearly saw, does consist in making a moral exception of oneself by following rules or maxims which, if universalized, would destroy their own motive and intent. And finally, Kant seems clearly right in extending this point to the reformulation of the categorical imperative as the law that we ought always to act in such a way as to both recognize and implement the intrinsic moral worth of persons. Nothing formally abstract, nothing less than personhood, can possibly possess intrinsic moral worth or value.

8.239) Positive critique of Kant's moral philosophy:
8.240) non-empirical basis of moral law, and its *a priori* status;

8.241) universalization without inconsistency as a test of moral rules;

8.242) the intrinsic worth of personal being.

But my enthusiasm for all this certainly has its limits and qualifications. First of all, the unconditional authority of the moral law as an *a priori* principle of reason, is not, I think, autonomous in Kant's sense; for the moral authority of a law depends, in the end, on the intrinsic moral worth or goodness of being. On Kant's view, the intrinsic moral

8.243) Negative critique:
8.244) The moral authority of a law depends on the intrinsic worth of personal being, not the other way around (as Kant supposed);

worth of persons is grounded in their ability to act habitually out of pure respect for the moral law as an abstract rational principle. Quite the other way around, in my opinion: the authority of the moral law as an abstract principle depends rather on the effectiveness of its application in recognizing and implementing the intrinsic moral worth of personal being. As I have earlier argued, there can be no moral duty or obligation to any formal or abstract principle in itself or as such. It is persons who, as such, are both the subjects and the objects of moral duty or obligation; such duty is always on the part of a person and in relation to a person or persons. Otherwise, abstract principles are devoid of significant direction. If I am logically and morally correct about this, then it is the second formulation of the categorical imperative that is the core of all genuine morality—respect for persons as possessing intrinsic moral worth. The universalization-without-inconsistency principle, on the other hand, is incomplete and misdirected unless it is subordinated to the principle of intrinsic personal worth. Universalized principles that have no such moral direction, toward the worth of persons, are empty and pointless indeed.

8.245) there can be no duty or obligation to abstract principle as such;

8.246) duty is always between or among persons;

8.247) the universalization principle is morally significant only in relation to personal worth;

Another, though perhaps less important, problem with the universalization-without-inconsistency principle is that it provides no method for distinguishing between moral permissibility and moral obligation. The principle works especially well, in my opinion, if a person is situated close to the line between morally wrong and morally permissible and is therefore wondering into which category a proposed act falls. Would it be morally right (permissible) under certain circumstances to indulge my inclination to take a walk, or to refuse my neighbor's request for a loan, etc.? Suppose these questions pass the universalization test; in that case, there would be nothing morally wrong about taking the walk or refusing the request. But surely no one would conclude that these acts alone were right in the circumstances and that I was therefore morally obligated either to take the walk or to refuse the loan. How then, by the universalization test alone, am I to tell the difference between acts that are morally right in the sense of being morally permissible, on the one hand, and acts that are morally right in the sense of being morally obligatory? There must be a large

8.248) the universalization principle, as such, provides no way to distinguish between the morally permissible and the morally obligatory;

class of possible acts that are supererogatory; that is, they conform to moral responsibility, but they are not required by it. By itself, Kant's universalization test provides little or no help in making this distinction. In my opinion, the recognition of personal worth as morally primary would go a long way toward solving this problem, even if it does not completely eliminate it.

8.249) Kant's claim, that acts are morally praiseworthy only if they are done out of pure respect for the moral laws, seems problematic:

In his discussion of the moral law, Kant invariably pits moral duty against inclination and/or desire. He clearly takes the position that, if a person even habitually does the morally right thing out of the motivation of psychological inclination or desire, that person deserves no moral credit for having so acted. That credit is deserved only if the individual acts out of pure respect for the moral law. This position certainly seems to entail a number of moral conundrums. For one thing, Kant himself acknowledges that no finite human agents can be rationally certain that their motivations in making any choice or performing any act of moral significance are actually motivated solely by pure respect for the moral law, since it is always logically and empirically possible that inclinations, desires, or tendencies of an empirical sort are mixed in with that motivation; and this would have the effect that no such agents could ever know that they had the morally required motivation in doing anything whatever—which seems incompatible with the unconditional requirement of the moral law always to act in the morally right way for the morally right reason. A second difficulty appears when we compare two different agents with respect to the moral worth of their motivation: one of them, we will suppose, clearly recognizes his or her objective moral duty in a particular situation but is devoid of any inclination or desire to perform that duty, although, after a fierce struggle with opposed inclinations and desires, the agent finally does his or her objective moral duty in the situation; the other agent has progressively disciplined his or her inclinations and desires over a long history of moral choice to the point where the agent is always totally and habitually inclined to do his or her moral duty as soon as the agent recognizes it rationally (the agent actually desires habitually to do the morally right thing), and therefore the agent also does that morally right thing in the particular situation. From Kant's point of view, the first agent,

8.250) on this basis no one could ever know that he or she was acting from the morally right motivation.

8.251) On Kant's view, a person who did his or her moral duty against all desire or inclination would be deserving of greater moral credit than a person who was habitually inclined to do the right thing as a result of disciplined moral choice;

by hypothesis, acted solely out of the motivation of pure respect for the moral law, since otherwise the agent would not have acted at all, his or her inclinations being entirely opposed to moral duty; the second agent acted out of a sustained self-discipline that resulted in a habitual inclination and desire to do his or her moral duty, and the agent also acted out of a vague and sublimated respect for the moral law without however being explicitly conscious of its principle or authority in the particular case. To be consistent, Kant would have to judge the first agent as subjectively the better person morally, while most moral judges would regard the second agent, acting out of disciplined character disposition, as subjectively the better person morally. It seems clearly paradoxical to regard a person who has control of his or her inclinations and desires as less deserving of moral credit than one who does not. Thus Kant appears to have been partly right and partly wrong in this matter of the relation of moral duty and moral credit to inclination and desire: right in supposing that objective moral duty could not be morally and logically grounded in empirical inclination and desire; wrong in supposing that, for that reason, a person, who is partly or entirely motivated consciously to do his or her duty out of inclination or desire, deserves less moral credit than one who does his or her moral duty without such inclination or desire. No doubt an agent who acts out of respect for the moral law deserves moral credit precisely to the extent that the agent does so without having a strenuous struggle against opposing inclinations and desires, even if in his or her respect for the moral law the agent is buttressed by positive and supporting inclinations and desires regardless of whether that support is the product of deliberate self-discipline or natural emotional endowment. A final problem, about Kant's view concerning the relationship between moral duty and inclination (and/or desire) is, that the logic of Kant's view would lead ultimately to the conclusion that the morally best person of all would be that individual who in acting out of respect for the moral law, was totally unmoved or uninfluenced by inclination or desire either by way of support or by way of opposition—a person, in other words, who had succeeded in totally disengaging his or her emotions or inclinations from any involvement whatever in moral decision and choice. That again seems

8.252) but this view seems clearly paradoxical in devaluating the discipline of inclination and desire;

8.253) thus Kant seems right in refusing to ground duty in empirical inclination, but wrong in regarding a person who is inclined to duty as morally less praiseworthy.

8.254) On Kant's view, the morally best person would be one whose emotions and inclinations were totally disengaged from his or her moral decisions; but this would leave an essential aspect of human nature unintegrated with the person's moral selfhood.

both paradoxical and counter-intuitive: how can persons be judged to be at their moral best under circumstances in which, by hypothesis, a central and essential aspect of human nature is totally out of relation to their choice and action? Would they not rather be at their best when, in moral decision and action, they integrate all aspects of their selfhood into the unity of their moral commitment?

8.255) In regard to the postulates of practical (or moral) reason:

There is finally, to be considered critically, Kant's concept of the postulates of pure practical reason (freedom, immortality, and God), which endow our commitment to the moral law with the highest conceivable rational intelligibility, but which do not extend our knowledge of reality.

8.256) the denial that these postulates constitute genuine knowledge is based on the claim that knowledge is limited to the phenomenal and the empirical; 8.257) but this claim has already been argued to be coherent; 8.258) if so, there is no reason in principle to deny the possibility of genuine metaphysical knowledge.

This whole notion is in general grounded in Kant's claim that metaphysical knowledge is impossible in principle since its central objects are neither phenomenal nor empirical and therefore do not fall into the realm of genuine theoretical knowledge. Now I have already argued (successfully, I think) that Kant's attempt to limit genuine knowledge to the phenomenal and the empirical is itself both groundless and incoherent (or inconsistent). If my argument (or any other to this effect) is essentially sound, then there is no reason to claim that metaphysical knowledge is impossible in principle, and no reason to drive a wedge between the conditions of rational intelligibility and the conditions of objective, actual existence and being. Kant claims that we simply do not know that the conditions of rational intelligibility are also the conditions of objective reality. But this claim is intrinsically skeptical and self-contradictory.

8.259) The claim, that we do not know that principles of reason are principles of being, would involve an appeal to the very principles called into question;

How does Kant know that we have no knowledge (or logically cannot have any knowledge) on this point? Either he knows this (or someone knows this) or he does not know it. If the latter is the case, the point collapses; if the former is the case, his knowledge could only be based on the use of the very principles of rational intelligibility that his point calls into question—which would be self-contradictory. I therefore conclude that neither Kant nor anyone else could, with logical consistency, deny the universal applicability of the principles of reason or rational intelligibility.

8.260) if then, the postulates of practical reason are conditions of the rational intelligibility of the moral law, it is also reasonable to conclude that they are genuine metaphysical knowledge.

And I then further conclude that if the beliefs in freedom, immortality, and God are actually conditions of the rational intelligibility of the moral law (and if, of course, there is, as I agree with Kant, an unconditionally and objectively universal law of moral duty or obligation), then the propositions properly expressing these beliefs are objectively true and therefore constitute genuine metaphysical knowledge.

That leaves the question whether, in fact, the beliefs in freedom, immortality, and God are, as Kant claimed, necessary conditions of the full rational intelligibility of the moral law as a principle of duty or obligation. I need say little more about the concept of moral freedom interpreted as agent causality; I have already exhausted all my arguments in support of this view of freedom in earlier contexts. The possession of this sort of freedom on the part of moral agents, I agree with Kant, is a necessary condition of an agent's being morally obligated to act one way rather than another; if I am not free, in this sense, to choose to act one way rather than another, it cannot be the case that I ought to act in one way rather than another, since I cannot be morally obligated to act in a way that I am in fact incapable of acting (which would be the case if any sort of rigorous determinism were true). At the same time, I agree with most critics of Kant that it is a logical contradiction to suppose that one and the same morally significant act can be at the same time both wholly determined phenomenally and wholly free (in the relevant moral sense) noumenally. But this conundrum is a function of Kant's arbitrary and restricted limitation of genuine knowledge to the phenomenal and the empirical, an issue with which I have already dealt. So I conclude that transcendental personal freedom (agent causality) is indeed a necessary condition of the full rational intelligibility of the moral law.

About the question of immortality (interpreted not merely as the personal survival of physical death, but as the endless and uninterrupted possibility for moral improvement or closer approximation to the complete and perfect fulfillment of the law of duty), I am not so confident. For the reader's information, I will say at the outset that I do believe in immortality in both of these senses; I am simply doubtful that the truth of the belief is a necessary condition of the full intelligibility of the moral law. For one thing, Kant's overall notion here seems somewhat incoherent. On the one hand, he argues that a person is obligated morally to the complete and perfect fulfillment of the moral law in act, disposition, and character; while on the other hand he

8.261) Are the postulates really such necessary conditions?

8.262) Freedom, as agent causality, clearly is such a condition of objective moral duty or obligation;

8.263) one cannot have an obligation that one is not, in principle, capable of acting upon;

8.264) yet Kant seems contradictory in his claim that one and the same act can be both phenomenally determined and noumenally free.

8.265) About immortality, I am less confident;

8.266) would immortality make possible the complete and perfect fulfillment of the moral law by any finite moral agent?

argues immortality (in the sense indicated) as the condition that would make this possible. But would it? Kant admits that no finite agent could achieve this fulfillment in any finite period of time through moral self-effort; but then immortality, viewed as unending existence, provides no more than a finite period of time, even though it extends endlessly beyond this life. It follows that, on Kant's ground, even if we *are* to be immortal, we will never achieve complete and perfect conformity to the moral law; but then it also follows that, under the conditions specified, neither are we obligated morally to do so—which is the denial of Kant's original premise. Perhaps it is therefore more reasonable to claim that our moral duty on any particular occasion is to do the morally right thing in an objective sense, supported by whatever motives are possible for us at that juncture of experience, bearing in mind that motives of whatever sort, while they may provide the occasion for moral choice and action by confronting us with genuine options, are never the decisive cause of that choice and action—a role that is reserved for the transcendentally free agents themselves. If, in some larger sense beyond the parameters of individual moral responsibility, moral agents ought nevertheless to be complete and perfect in their commitment to moral duty, the cause of that total conformity will lie outside the scope of any merely human moral effort and self-discipline. In any case, immortality is not required as a ground of the full rational intelligibility of the unconditional and universal requirement of the moral law; that moral authority is sufficiently and fully intelligible on each successive occasion in which the free personal agent is obligated to do the morally right thing, and, as such a free agent, is genuinely capable of so choosing and acting. At the same time, while immortality does not seem to be required logically as a necessary condition of moral duty and responsibility, it is nevertheless logically compatible therewith and might even provide an extended opportunity for the sort of moral growth that Kant had in mind.

Finally, is the belief in a transcendent personal God a necessary condition of the full rational intelligibility of the moral law? It seems reasonable to divide this question into two issues: first, whether Kant's argument shows this to be the case, and second, whether, even if Kant's argument

8.267) Kant admits that this goal can never be achieved in a finite period of time (which is all immortality would provide), but that fact would undermine the original obligation;

8.268) our duty seems rather to be to do the morally right thing on each successive occasion of moral choice;

8.269) complete and total moral commitment to moral duty would require a more than human cause;

8.270) while immortality would provide an opportunity for moral growth, it is not required as a ground of the full rational intelligibility of the moral law.

8.271) As for the theistic postulate:

does not meet the rigor of his own logical requirement, his conclusion is nevertheless true on some other and further ground. On the first issue, it is my opinion that Kant's argument, to the effect that God logically must exist as the sole adequate ground of the ideal moral proportion between moral virtue and well-being on the part of finite moral agents, is a highly plausible and logically probable argument for the conclusion he draws (and I enthusiastically accept his conclusion in this form), but that the argument does not meet the level of logical rigor that Kant requires of himself, since it does not show that God is a rationally necessary condition of the full intelligibility of the moral law. And it does not meet this requirement, because it does not provide any logically compelling and demonstrative reason for the claim that an ideally perfect moral order of being is necessarily one in which moral virtue and well-being are precisely proportionate. The concept of the moral perfection of God may indeed point in this direction, but there is no compelling reason for supposing that God's constitutive and absolute goodness is necessarily limited to this result in the case of finite moral agents. It could well be the case that if God exists in the theistic sense in which Kant construes him, it would be perfectly compatible with his consummate moral goodness and indeed its highest expression, if God granted to finite moral beings a state of well-being that finally exceeded the extent of their actual moral virtue, provided only that these finite agents met the condition of unconditional commitment to God himself as their true and sole ultimate Good. This would be to say that justice is perfectly compatible with God's moral character, but that his goodness in the highest sense goes beyond justice and finds its highest expression in love and gracious forgiveness. Such a notion is surely compatible, in the fullest sense of rational intelligibility, with the moral goodness of God as the ultimate transcendent locus of moral law. At least Kant has said nothing, in my opinion, that demonstrates anything to the contrary; in fact, he even says that it is perfectly appropriate for us morally to hope that this is the case and that divine grace may well supplement sheer justice without any detriment to the moral perfection of God. For all these reasons, I conclude that Kant's principal argument here is highly plausible and even

8.272) Kant's basic argument (that God is the sole adequate ground of the ideal proportion of virtue with personal well-being) is a highly plausible and logically probable argument, but it does not meet the level of logical rigor that Kant requires of himself, 8.272a) since the ideal proportion proposed is not the only conceivable character of a perfect moral order of being.

8.273) It is conceivable that God's goodness might express itself in a gracious and loving forgiveness that goes beyond sheer justice (as Kant himself elsewhere suggests).

probable in its conclusion, but that it lacks the rigor of logical necessity.

On the other hand, Kant himself suggests, in the context of the argument just analyzed, the skeletal framework of a further argument which, though not absolutely demonstrative, seems to me to have a much higher degree of logical rigor. He suggests that there logically could not be a highest derived moral good in the form of the intrinsic worth of finite persons, if there were not a highest underived, ultimate, and self-constituted good as its ground; and he identifies that good and ground with God as theistically construed. The fundamental thrust of this argument is that, if, as ethical idealism claims, there is a transcendent moral good which functions as the ultimate standard and criterion of all moral worth, then it is the final ground and basis of the intrinsic worth of finite persons; but this underived highest good (to use Kant's terminology) cannot itself be less than personal, since that would be to say that the impersonal or non-personal possessed a higher worth than the personal. Hence, the transcendent and highest Good can be reasonably construed only as the transcendent personal God of theism in his moral aspect. As such, the elements of divine moral character (holiness, righteousness, justice, and love, for example) constitute the criterion or standard of moral goodness or rightness expressed in the unconditional and universal moral law of duty or obligation. From this point of view, we can now reassert Kant's claim that the existence of a transcendent personal God, as the underived and highest Good, is indeed a logically (and metaphysically) necessary condition of the full rational intelligibility of the moral law. The moral law logically could not be unconditional, objective, and universal, if it has no such transcendent ground, which is to say therefore that it would, in that case, not be a moral law at all in Kant's sense. This argument seems to me to accomplish Kant's purpose here with considerably greater logical effectiveness, since it does not involve the difficult (but nevertheless highly plausible, in my opinion) conception of an ideal and perfect proportion between moral virtue and well-being. And if we accept this sort of argument (or some similar sort of argument to the same effect), we will find ourselves standing on the very threshold of a fully theistic ethical perspective. The only difference here between

8.274) Kant hints at a further and more rigorous argument to the effect that the intrinsic moral worth of finite persons requires a transcendent ground which cannot itself be less than personal, so that the God of personal theism is the transcendent ground of personal worth.

Kant's ethical idealism and ethical theism is that Kant regards the belief in God as merely a postulate of practical reason rather than a plausible extension of genuine metaphysical knowledge. But even that difference will fade for those who, like myself, regard Kant's restriction of genuine knowledge to the phenomenal and the empirical as both implausible and contradictory. From that standpoint it will appear that, when we plummet Kant's ethical idealism to its depths and foundations, we find ourselves, conceptually (and perhaps morally), confronted 'face to face' with the God of ethical theism.

And now we can perhaps make some general estimate of the entire upshot of ethical idealism in normative ethics. It is not so much that it seems to be mistaken at its core (as might be judged of normative ethical naturalism); it is rather, to borrow Hegel's phraseology, fragmentary, incomplete, and (relatively speaking) abstract. Its claim, that the ultimately good or right in the moral sense must be transcendent in its basis and ground, seems incontestable, if morality in an objective sense is to survive at all. But that ground will be relatively vacuous in its moral content and unclarified or incomprehensible in its reality status if we fail to pass beyond the abstract fragments to the concrete personal God of theism. It is that further and perhaps higher ground that must now be explored; and in that exploration many elements and facets of ethical idealism will surely survive, as will even some misplaced bursts of ethical light from the naturalistic ethical tradition.

8.275) Summary conclusion on normative ethical idealism: although its claim to transcendence is essentially sound, it is incomplete and abstract unless it is combined with ethical theism.

Chapter IX

Normative Ethical Theism

The General Theistic Perspective in Ethics

It is a necessary condition, of the possibility of the normative ethical view that I have designated ethical theism, that theism itself, as a metaphysical view, must in some sense be true; for if God in the theistic sense does not exist, then God cannot be the transcendently objective and ultimate Good, as ethical theism claims. For my purposes, I take metaphysical theism in general to be the view that God, as an absolutely necessary and transcendent being, characterized by personal intelligent (purposively and conceptually directive) will and constituting essential or absolute goodness (both moral and nonmoral), exists; and that God, so construed, is related to the contingent world order (the space-time universe in its entirety) as its creative ground, its continuously sustaining cause, and its providential director toward morally and spiritually significant ends. While this definition would benefit greatly by a reasonably elaborate clarification even in the present context of ethics, I have provided that clarification in my earlier books and will therefore not repeat that discussion here, even though I will assume, as a basis for further analysis, that the reader understands the definition in a reasonably explicit and clear fashion. It is

9.1a) the definition of metaphysical theism; God as:

9.1b) transcendent personal mind,
9.1c) essence of absolute goodness,

9.1d) creative ground and providential director of the universe.
9.2) The clarification and defense of theism is covered in my earlier writings;

of course one thing to define the meaning of metaphysical theism and quite another to suppose that it is true. On that subject, I have expressed myself in previous publications even more extensively than on the clarification of the definition. Believers in the metaphysic of theism are historically divided on the question whether the existence of God, theistically construed, must be presupposed as a matter of sheer volitionally grounded religious commitment (theistic voluntarism) or whether it is possible by rationally objective and empirically grounded argumentation to provide a plausible philosophical defense for the conclusion that God exists (theistic rationalism). I can only say without cavil here that I am personally a theist and that I side, on the whole, with theistic rationalism as an approach to the question of the existence of God. Beyond that it would be redundant for me to reconstruct even in the briefest summary form my earlier defense of these conclusions. Meanwhile, I will simply assume here that metaphysical theism, however grounded, is at least a live metaphysical option for a considerable cross-section of persons seriously interested in the study of philosophical ethics; if any readers do not presently fit into that cross-section, I urge them simply to presuppose its possibility for the sake of argument, in order to see with some clarity what theism can provide by way of a context for the justification of moral objectivism.

9.2a) the distinction between

9.2a1) theistic voluntarism and

9.2a2) theistic rationalism.

9.3a) It is assumed that metaphysical theism is at least a live option as a context for justifying moral objectivism;

9.3b) the scope of the theistic metaphysical tradition;

Theism, in the sense defined, is of course not limited to the Hebrew-Christian intellectual tradition of the western world. There is, for example, the massive theistic tradition of Islam. In addition, there are theistic versions of orthodox Hinduism and even (though to a lesser extent) of some elements in Mahayana Buddhism. And there are, in addition, versions of theism in the western philosophical tradition that have no essential connection with the Hebrew-Christian religious milieu—Aristotle would be a conspicuous example (although, as we have seen, he makes no use of the concept of God in his moral philosophy). But since I have already published my analysis of oriental philosophical perspectives, including their moral aspects, and since most readers who are likely to take theistic ethics seriously will have come to that interest through the Hebrew-Christian tradition, I have chosen my exemplars of ethical theism from that tradition and even limited that selection to the explicitly Christian wing of it. One of these thinkers (Thomas Aquinas) is clearly a theistic rationalist in my nomenclature; a second (Søren Kierkegaard) is, equally clearly, a theistic voluntarist who, in principle, rejects the ideal of rational objectivity across the board in philosophy; while the third (Aurelius Augustine) represents a hybrid mixture between these two methodological approaches, since he appears to begin in his earlier writings (like the *Treatise on Free Will*) with a heavy rationalistic slant with few (but some) voluntarist leanings, but then to move in a progressively more voluntaristic direction in his later writings (like the *Treatise on the Trinity* and the *City of God*). But these epistemological differences seem to have no more than a modest bearing on the overall ethical perspectives of the three thinkers, except in the case of Søren Kierkegaard, though even in his case that influence is not striking.

Aquinas, Augustine, and Kierkegaard are all centered in their ethical interest on the transcendent personal God of theism as the ultimate locus and reality of both moral and nonmoral goodness. For all three God is the only conceivable ground of objective moral goodness, so that, if God did not exist, there could be no objective morality; all three regard God, in his essential goodness, as the supreme and ultimate objective of moral commitment, while other finite persons are, in a derived sense, objects of moral commitment through causal dependence on God for their intrinsic moral worth; and finally, all three regard moral laws as grounded in the divine moral character rather than in the volitionally arbitrary legislation of God's sovereign will. Aside from certain epistemological and historically contextual contrasts, not to mention (of course) matters of stylistic expression, the principal ethically relevant differences among the three thinkers are primarily concerned with distinctions of interest and subject matter across the whole spectrum of ethical issues, with the result that the combination of the three perspectives provides a comprehensive and inclusive treatment of the whole range of ethical topics and questions of a general theoretical sort. To put it somewhat differently, their views on Christian moral philosophy, while noticeably distinct, are more complementary than they are competitive. Thomas, of course, as a medieval churchman and member of the Dominican order, regarded Augustine as a revered

9.3c) the limitation of the present discussion to Christian theism:
9.4) Aquinas
9.5) Kierkegaard
9.6) Augustine

9.7) The common ethical stance of the three thinkers:
9.7a) God as: the ultimate locus and ground of all goodness,
9.8) the only conceivable ground of objective morality, and
9.9) the ultimate object of moral commitment through the grounding of moral law in Divine moral character.

9.10) from an ethical point of view, the differences of the three thinkers are more complementary than competitive, so that their combination provides an inclusive ethical perspective.

father of the church and, for that and other reasons, often preoccupied himself with the concord that he purported to discern between his own views and those of Augustine. Kierkegaard also, as a reformed protestant, likewise claimed Augustine as both a religious and a philosophical forebear.

Augustine on Goodness, Freedom, and Evil

9.11) The background of Augustine's thought in Platonism and Neo-Platonism;
9.11a) the combination of these two perspectives made a smoother transition to Christian theology;

Among other elements of intellectual ancestry, Augustine had been what he called a Platonist before he became a Christian through his remarkable conversion under the influence of Ambrose, Bishop of Milan. And Augustine continued to refer to himself as a Platonist even after he became a Christian and later a cleric; apparently he regarded the two, with some modifications in Platonism, as in principle conceptually compatible and supplementary. But it is generally contended by historical scholars that the Platonism imbibed by Augustine was refracted through the prism of Neo-Platonism and the philosophy of Plotinus, who lived a century before Augustine. Indeed, this refraction was a benefit to Augustine in his attempt to combine central Platonic elements with Christian theology and philosophy. In the historical Plato, as we noted earlier, there was a distinction between God, as an intermediate rational being, on the one hand, and the realm of ideas or forms culminating in the absolute idea of the Good as ultimate reality, on the other. In the version of Platonism propounded by Plotinus, however, there are steps toward conflating the notions of God and the Ultimate Good or Real in the notion of the ineffable (or conceptually incomprehensible) One. This ineffable ultimate One was regarded as the source of all being and itself the absolute Reality. Whatever else is real, and to the limited extent that it is real, proceeds from the One by a metaphorically characterized emanation or overflow of the unqualified Reality of the One, as (but not really like) water flows spontaneously from a spring or light moves out spontaneously from a source of illumination. This emanation (which cannot be literally characterized) results in various levels that thus proceed from the One, though they are progressively less real than the One itself. The first of these levels, each of which has a subjective and objective aspect, is objectively the realm of absolute ideas or forms, while subjec-

9.11a1) in Plato, God and the Absolute Idea of the Good are kept distinct;

9.11a2) but in Plotinus the two notions merge in the ineffable One.
9.11a3) The One overflows into and has lesser realms of being that are co-mingled with varying degrees of darkness or non-being;

9.12) absolute ideas are the objective correlate of Pure Mind as a rational subject;

tively it is Pure Mind, as the rational subject apprehending these forms. In this way the absolute ideas are well on their way, so to speak, to being regarded as the content and structure of the Ultimate or pure Mind as an aspect of Divine Reality. As for the rest of the Neo-Platonic system (which need not concern us here), the next level includes the World Soul as the subjective correlate of the objective sensory level of particular existing things, while at the outer perimeter of being is matter or the darkness of non-being into which the light of being extends. At each level of being below the One there is a mixture of the darkness of non-being or matter with the light of true being, and the proportion of this darkness increases as the process extends toward particular existence, while at each level, in its depth of reality, all being is an aspect of the being of the One, which is therefore the only true reality.

9.13) the outer limit of being as the unpenetrated darkness of non-being which in itself is nothing.

As a Christian, of course, Augustine could not accept all this without modification and reinterpretation. But he saw clearly, through the correlation between Pure Mind and the absolute ideas, that the transcendent ideas or forms should be viewed as finding their transcendent locus of reality as the content and structure of the mind of God, while the ultimate and erstwhile ineffable One became, in Augustine's eyes, the transcendent personal God of theism, beyond whom there is no higher reality. The idea of emanation or overflow, with the resultant notion that all true reality was an aspect or manifestation of the Ultimate One itself, constituted an objectionable pantheism which Augustine likewise set aside in favor of a strong contrast between God as pure being and creative ground of all else, on the one hand, with created contingent beings that, though produced by God, were not to be viewed as parts or aspects of God, even at the depth of their being. Contingent things were not created by God out of his own substance, as it were, by any sort of emanation or overflow; instead, they were created out of nothing, so that matter itself becomes a creature of God, though only in conjunction with its assumption of form or essence. This is, of course, a traditional Christian conception; and while the notion of 'nothing' was not explicitly interpreted as a kind of outer darkness or 'something of no particular sort,' still Augustine used the concept of creation out of 'nothing' in ways that continued to show the imprint

9.14) Augustine interpreted all this in relation to Christianity;

9.14a) the One is the personal God of theism whose mind is the locus of Absolute ideas;

9.15) 'overflow' or emanation is displaced by creation out of nothing as an act of divine will, so that matter itself is a creation of God, but only in conjunction with the instantiation of form in particular things.

of Neo-Platonism on his thinking, as our subsequent analysis will indicate.

9.16) The thesis that God created the realm of contingent being, and that God is goodness as such implies that the world order is compatible with that goodness;

If God, as transcendent personal Mind, created the whole realm of contingent being out of nothing, then God did so (or does so) as an act or succession of acts of rational will with explicit purposive intent; and since God, in Augustine's view, is essential, absolute goodness as such, God could and did create the contingent world order as an expression of that goodness and in complete logical compatibility with it. In fact, this line of analysis leads to (and is partly grounded in) Plato's thesis that the ultimately Real and the ultimately Good are identical: Being is Goodness (again in Latin, *Ens est Bonum*). Now Plato had believed that particular things in the contingent world order were real only to the extent that they participated in the absolute ideas and therefore also in the absolute idea of the Good. But Plato had also believed that particular entities had a material aspect (which in itself and apart from participation in the ideas would be nothing determinate, hence non-being); matter, of course, could only be actually existent through participation in essence or form (or absolute ideas), but in another sense, matter, as in itself inert and indeterminate, provided a certain recalcitrancy or resistance to being determinate or participating in form. As a result, no particular thing was ever (or even could be ever), an ideally complete and perfect exemplification of the forms or essences it instantiated, precisely because of the resistance occasioned by its material aspect. Hence Plato could use the notion of the relative non-being of matter as an explanation of all the imperfections of evils of actual existence in the contingent world order, while at the same time maintaining that ultimate reality was essential, absolute goodness and the cause of all the genuine reality in particular things—matter, after all, was, in itself and as such, just nothing (determinate) at all; and hence it required no explanation, since non-being cannot even conceivably have a cause in any fundamental sense. But while matter itself required no explanation, it nevertheless and surprisingly provided an explanation for much else. Just as the resistance of its material keeps the form of any sculpture from being flawless, so the matter of living things could keep them from being perfectly healthy and environmentally adapted, the stuff of the universe could keep climate, weather, and

9.16a) since Plato believed that particular things had a material aspect (in itself, nothing) that embodied the actualization of the forms or ideas in things, he could use that material principle to explain the evils and imperfections of particular things, while also maintaining that ultimate reality was absolute goodness and the cause of all genuine reality in things;

geological occurrences from being ideally suited to living things, and the human body itself could pose repressive opposition to the soul in the pursuit of wisdom and moral virtue. Hence, all the natural and moral evils of existence could be explained by the non-being and recalcitrancy of matter in its relative non-being.

But Augustine, while strongly attracted by this neatly plausible philosophical package, could not, without modification, avail himself of it as a means of reconciling the essential and absolute goodness of God with the natural and moral evils of contingent existence. For him too (as for Plato), particular things were a union of form (essence) and matter; but, quite differently from the case of Plato, for Augustine matter itself was a creation of God that was produced conjunctively with the creation of particular things as the material aspect of them, so that matter also, as real in conjunction with particulars, must be good as a creation of God, who is the Ultimate and Essential Good. So the problem of reconciling the Good (as God) with the evils of existence is a presumably much stiffer and less wieldy perplexity for Augustine. The 'bite' of this difficulty was especially painful for him because, besides having been a Platonist before becoming a Christian (and remaining a qualified Platonist), Augustine had also been a Manichean (which he ceased to be either before or on becoming a Christian). The Manicheans held that there was both an ultimately good being and an ultimately evil being, since they believed the problems occasioned by natural and moral evil were otherwise insoluble: goodness in things requires an ultimately good cause, and evil in things, as incompatible with the nature of goodness, requires an ultimately evil cause. But Augustine, committed in his Christian faith to the unqualified self-existence and omnipotence of God, would have none of this unbridgeable moral and metaphysical dualism. How then was he to work out this agonizing conceptual (and, in his own past moral history, practical) perplexity?

In effect, Augustine conceptually needed a parallel 'nothing' to replace Plato's concept of the relative 'non-being' of matter as an explanation of the evils of existence, both natural and moral. It could not be as extreme a non-entity as Plato's matter or the outer darkness of Neo-Platonism; but neither could its reality, however indispensable, in any sense

9.16b) but since Augustine believed that matter had been created by God and thus rejected any version of ultimate dualism (of good and evil), he was compelled to hold that the material aspect of things was fully compatible with divine goodness.

9.16c) Still, he found a parallel to the nothingness of Plato's matter in the fact that all contingent things were created by God out of 'nothing';

parallel the self-existence and necessity of God. Augustine found what he regarded as a rationally satisfactory solution through an analysis of the concept of contingent or dependent being as having been created by God *ex nihilo*, or out of 'nothing.' The very idea of created or originated being entails, he thought, a degree of imperfection or incompleteness of being in contrast to God's perfection of self-existent, self-explanatory being. If God were to create a contingent world order at all, it would have to be less perfect in being than his own being, partly because the very notion of origination out of nothing implies imperfection of being (whatever originates is less perfect in being than that which is self-existently real and therefore unoriginated); but partly also because the idea of God producing an identical clone, another reality as perfect in being as his own being, is a self-contradictory notion. By definition, if God exists at all, his existence is necessarily unique and unparalleled, since, if there were more than one absolutely perfect being, each would pose a limit to the being of the rest and none would be absolutely perfect in being. Of course, finite things can be relatively perfect as the contingent and limited sorts of things they are, but not absolutely and unconditionally perfect. Furthermore, since finite things have been created out of nothing, they are intrinsically capable of becoming non-existent, both in the absolute sense that they could be annihilated by their Creator, and in the relative sense that they are corruptible, so that they could continue to exist but with some of their parts or functions becoming or being defective, either in a natural or in a moral sense. Thus your body is susceptible of becoming defective in health (through blindness, or tooth-decay, or any other kind of biological degeneration), and your soul or self (as a rational moral agent) is susceptible of becoming defective either in the exercise of its rational powers or in the state of its moral virtue. All this is possible because contingent things, having originated by divine creation out of 'nothing,' are in principle corruptible. If God were to create a contingent world order at all, it was a necessary condition of God's doing so that, in an absolute sense, that world order and all its contents be both imperfect and corruptible, even though it could be, in varying and different ways for different kinds of things, relatively perfect in its kind and relatively shielded from the sort of absolute corruption

9.17) the idea of created being implies relative imperfection and incompleteness of being, in comparison to God's absolute perfection;
9.18) anything God created would have to be less perfect than himself, since his being is unique;

9.19) finite things can be relatively perfect as belonging to limited classes of being, but they are also in principle corruptible as well;

that would be tantamount to sheer non-existence. Of course, to be a world of this sort as a manifestation of the creative goodness of God, it would also have to be a world in which, while the evil of corruption from the state of relative perfection was possible, it would also be possible that the relative perfection of each limited sort of thing could be realized as well, at least in principle. The relative metaphysical imperfection of finitude and contingency of being is inevitable in a created and originated world order; but in that order, while degenerative evil must be possible in the broad sense, it cannot be universally inevitable, if that created order is, in its limited way, to reflect the goodness of God by involving in general the possibility for the achievement of the limited goodness that is also an open option in the same general circumstances. Thus the conditions that are necessary as a basis for the realization of contingent finite goodness are also the conditions that make the occurrence of evil possible but by no means inevitable.

9.20) so created beings are both relatively corruptible and relatively capable of limited perfection of being: finitude makes both of these results possible.

Now as Augustine contemplates the relation of the evils of existence to the goodness of God as the Creator and Sustainer of the contingent world order, he clearly regards moral evil as a more crucial and significant issue than natural evil, even though the general explanation of both (just developed above) is the same and involves the notion of the corruption of that which was contingently good and therefore both justified in its existence and logically (as well as morally) compatible with the goodness of God. God's chief purpose in creation centers on the production and progressive development in moral righteousness of rational moral beings like ourselves. Rational existence is superior in worth and value to both non-rational living existence and inanimate existence, since the latter are incapable by nature of participating in the realization of their contingent goodness through conscious knowledge and will. Hence, the inanimate and animate but non-rational orders exist for the sake of the realization of moral goodness on the part of finite rational agents, and the limited goods and evils achievable at those levels are clearly subordinated to the achievement of moral purpose on the part of rational moral agents. It follows that the moral corruption of rational beings is a far more serious quandary for a theistic metaphysic, at least in Augustine's eyes, than the physical evils of natu-

9.21) Moral evil is, for Augustine, a much more crucial problem than natural evil, since:

9.22) God's purpose in creation centers on moral beings as capable of recognizing and realizing moral righteousness; 9.23) rational beings are superior in value to the non-rational creation;

347

ral corruption which may themselves be regarded as an appropriate environment and even (to a limited extent) a just compensation in relation to the actual moral career and destiny of rational beings.

Turning then to the problem of moral evil, it is evident that moral vice is rampant in human beings, nay more, it is universal. In state of character, decision, and action, human beings are without exception morally corrupt apart from intervening divine grace. This corruption finds its chief ground in the corruption of the moral will in such a way that it turns away from the one true Good, which is God himself, to the pursuit of lesser goods of the body and especially to the self of the individual as its chief preoccupation. Thus all moral vices in particular spring from a morally evil will. But since rational selves are creatures of God and therefore in their original state possessed of morally good will (at least in the sense of being personally innocent morally), what could conceivably be the efficient cause of the will's becoming evil? No external influence by way of desire or inclination could constitute such a cause, since these could not produce a morally evil effect on the will unless it was itself already morally evil or corrupt. God, in his essential creative goodness, could not be the cause of the evil will, since that would contradict the divine moral nature as unconditionally good and dissolve the human agent of all responsibility for moral evil, which would therefore and by definition not really be moral evil at all. The will of a finite agent can become evil in the morally responsible sense only if it is, through the possession of a freedom that is understood as agent causality, capable of corrupting itself. There cannot be an external efficient cause of the evil will; for if the will were involuntarily corrupted from without, it would simply not be evil in the moral sense. Hence, the will corrupts itself by its own choice. Yet its rational freedom of choice was bestowed upon it by God, not for the purpose of making moral corruption possible, but for the purpose of making moral goodness possible by the soul's freely choosing God as the true and ultimate Good. Now since the soul logically could not be intrinsically free, in the relevant moral sense, to choose God as the Good, unless it was, in the possession of that same freedom, capable of choosing the evil as an alternative, it follows that the individual self is, through

9.24) the ground of human moral evil is found in the moral will as it turns away from God as the true good and toward lesser goods, especially itself, so that all moral vices spring from a morally evil will.

9.25) The moral will can become evil only by a corruption initiated by the finite agent's free choice, so that there is no external efficient cause of the evil will;

9.26) but this freedom was bestowed to make finite moral goodness possible, so that the individual is responsible for the corruption of his own moral will.

its own free choice, morally responsible for the corruption of its own will, as well as for the wrongness of its own actions. It also follows, for Augustine, that there can be no objection to the goodness of God on the ground that God created souls that became morally corrupt, since the freedom with which God created them was a necessary condition of their being able, in the morally responsible sense, to choose the good. The suggestion, that God could have created only those genuinely free agents that he knew would always choose the good was viewed by Augustine as contradictory, since such agents would have been determined by God's creative choice always to choose the good and hence would not be free in the sense postulated.

But this explanation led to a further problem that was urged by Augustine's critics. Since God would be (by definition) both omnipotent and omniscient from Augustine's point of view (and from that of Christian theism generally), it follows that God foreknows (at least in the sense of logical priority) the order and the causes of all future events and that he therefore foreknows all the moral choices and acts of finite agents as following with certainty in their order and from their causes, so that the free control of those choices and actions is effectively eliminated. On the other hand, if moral choices and acts are causally attributed to the freedom of finite agents, then they cannot have been foreknown in the order of events as following from their causes. Thus divine foreknowledge involves the denial of genuine moral freedom, and genuine moral freedom involves the denial of divine foreknowledge. Augustine's answer to this challenge is basically as follows: first, the certainty of future events (including moral choices and acts) as objects of divine foreknowledge in no way determines those events as causally necessitated, since the divine foreknowledge is not a deduction from presently operative and determining causes to their future effects; second, as previously indicated, the very essence of a choice or act, that is attributable to the agent as morally responsible, implies that agents are themselves the decisive cause of the act which has therefore no external efficient and determining cause—the cause foreknown by God would thus be simply the genuinely free causality of the agent; and third, since God's infallibly certain knowledge of his own choices and acts does not destroy the

9.27) As for the claim that divine foreknowledge of the finite agent's moral choices would destroy the freedom of those choices:

9.28) the certainty of divine foreknowledge does not determine its objects as necessary, since it does not depend on deduction from presently operative causes;

9.29) free agents are themselves the cause of responsible moral choices.

9.30) Since God's knowledge of his own choices does

not destroy their voluntary character, neither does his knowledge of the future free acts of moral agents destroy their voluntary character;	free, voluntary, and self-determined character of the divine volitions, there is no reason to suppose that his infallibly certain foreknowledge of the morally relevant choices and acts of finite moral agents would destroy the free, voluntary, and self-determined character of their volitions either. Hence, for all these reasons, Augustine urges that God's foreknowledge of human volitions is in no sense of itself incompatible with their genuinely free and voluntary character in the morally relevant sense.
9.31) is it possible for an individual, thus corrupted by his own free choice, to reverse that bent of corruption by that same free choice?	So in Augustine's eyes man's morally corrupt state and guilty plight before God as the one true ultimate Good, is chargeable to the free and voluntary misuse of his moral freedom in bringing about the corruption of his will through its being turned from the one true Good (God) to lesser and transitory goods that can be lost without his voluntary consent. Is it possible for such a corrupted individual, in turn, and through that same free moral agency, to reverse that tide of corruption and move in the direction of becoming a morally virtuous individual and thus recover a morally good will which on the whole displaces the previous evil bent of that will? Anyone who reads the *Treatise on Free Will* would certainly get the impression that such
9.32) Augustine seems clearly to claim as much in the *Treatise on Free Will* by insisting that the human agent has this capacity at his free and immediate disposal, although the virtue thus achieved is that of human excellence;	is the case. Augustine clearly and repeatedly claims, in elaborating his view of freedom and moral responsibility, that any human agent who lacks a good will can restore it simply by a process of freely willing, and that every morally responsible human agent has this capacity at his free and immediate disposal, since nothing external ever efficiently determines the will to choose or the agent to act. In fact, he says that persons who genuinely wish to live rightly in the moral sense, at the expense of preferring that above all fleeting and transient goods, may attain their object (the formation of a morally good will that predominates) with perfect ease, even though they may have passed through an agonizing struggle to get to this point of moral surrender over against the evil bent of their disposition. Such persons willingly and habitually submit themselves to the authority of the eternal moral law and attain well-ordered lives as a consequence. But it is important to point out that the moral virtue thus achieved disperses itself into the excellences of moral character extolled in humanistic Greek morality—prudence, fortitude (courage), temperance (self-

control), and justice, since these are the expressions of the life of an individual whose good will habitually determines his or her conduct. In other words, Augustine is saying that, by free and sustained moral resolve, persons can progressively release themselves subjectively from the bondage of a morally corrupted evil will. But, while Augustine does not deal with the issue in the *Treatise on Free Will*, he does make it abundantly clear in his other writings that this sort of moral self-reformation can only occur in actual practice through the sustaining and supporting influence of supervening divine grace, and that the subjective achievement of the good will through the responsible use of moral freedom in no way resolves the problem of an individual's objective moral guilt before God for his or her previous moral corruption and the moral misdeeds that resulted therefrom. As for this objective guilt, Augustine regarded it as being adjudicated only by the gracious divine forgiveness provided by redemption in Christ, through which and whom alone an individual could attain a truly righteous moral standing before God. As for the claim that the good will was in practice achievable only through special divine grace, this grew out of later developments in Augustine's theology in which he developed a rigorous doctrine of inscrutable divine election of certain individuals to divine forgiveness and eternal life. An understandable consequence of this doctrine for Augustine, as he meditated on its logical relations to the earlier *Treatise on Free Will*, was to take the position that 'perfect ease,' in achieving the morally good will and its resultant virtuous qualities, was of course realistically possible only for the mysteriously elected recipients of regenerating divine grace. Augustine even claimed that the reason he did not deal explicitly with this issue in the earlier *Treatise* was that, while it was in the back of his mind, it was not relevant to his defense of moral freedom and the goodness of God against his critics at the time. Whether that is a reasonable explanation I shall not presume to decide; but it is doubtful that even a careful reader of the *Treatise* would regard any such theological positioning as relevant to Augustine's defense of the agent causality view of freedom in relation to the goodness of God. It is also clearly doubtful whether the rigorous doctrine of divine election is in any plausible sense compatible logically with either the genuineness of finite

9.33) but in later writings Augustine claims:
9.33a) that this can happen in actual practice only through enabling divine grace bestowed on the mysteriously elected;

9.33b) that such a change does not resolve the problem of objective moral guilt, which can be forgiven only through God's redemptive provision in Christ.

9.34) Augustine was aware of apparent logical difficulty here, and he tried later to deal with it with questionable success.

moral freedom or the goodness of God. But more of that later in a more critical context.

In any case, Augustine held that the highest good for humanity and its final end, involving as it does complete moral and spiritual harmony with both God (as the chief objective and absolute Good) and those of his fellow human beings who are citizens of the heavenly kingdom or the city of God, is only fully achievable by divine grace as reinforcing man's natural inclination toward God as his chief objective end or goal. From man's point of view, this good can be described in a variety of ways, the principal among which would be eternal life or peace (in its most highly conceivable sense). The peace of the city of God (human civilization under God's complete rule and authority) would be one in which all individual persons embodied a harmony of all the aspects of their humanness and their correlated goods of body and soul, in which all such persons lived in social harmony with all their fellow citizens of the heavenly city so that all achieved their entire human well-being without conflict with the others whose well-being they sought to promote equally with their own, and in which all the citizens both individually and collectively find their joy, their good, and their fulfillment in conformity to God's eternal law and in the sheer enjoyment of God in completely harmonious fellowship. Augustine's own way of encapsulating this comprehensive human moral ideal of fulfillment in God is so impressive and insightful, that I shall here depart from my usual policy of never quoting from the sources I discuss, in order to share this delightful passage with the reader:

9.35) The chief good for humanity is thus moral and spiritual harmony with God as the ultimate objective Good, and with fellow members of God's spiritual kingdom;
9.35a) this is described as eternal life and peace as ordered fulfillment of humanness, both individually and socially, through the enjoyment of God in harmonious fellowship.

9.35b) Augustine's statement of this ultimate moral ideal;

9.36) The statement cited

The peace of the body lies in the ordered equilibrium of all its parts; the peace of the irrational soul, in the adjustment of its appetites; the peace of the reasoning soul, in the harmonious correspondence of conduct and conviction; the peace of body and soul taken together, in the well-ordered life and health of the living whole. Peace between a mortal man and his Maker consists in ordered obedience, guided by faith, under God's eternal law; peace between man and man consists in regulated fellowship. The peace of a home lies in the ordered harmony of authority and obedience between the members of a family living together. The peace of the political com-

> *munity is an ordered harmony of authority and obedience between citizens. The peace of the heavenly City lies in a perfectly ordered and harmonious communion of those who find their joy in God and in one another in God. Peace, in its final sense, is the calm that comes of order. Order is an arrangement of like and unlike things whereby each of them is disposed in its proper place.*[1]

In effect, Augustine gathers up in this passage all the limited goods—mental, physical, and social—that are advocated by the most admirable of naturalistic humanisms; all the individual and social ideals of the most developed of ethical idealisms together with their transcendent moral principles; and all the highest fulfillment in and through God that is characteristic of the best formulated version of ethical theism—all these he gathers up into an ordered and integrated unity of moral vision, from which nothing truly valuable in either the moral or the nonmoral sense is excluded, and in which each intrinsically valuable person finds a place for his or her individual uniqueness as a focal point of the true good. In Augustine's eyes, persons who commit themselves to God, as the chief and highest objective Good, find, in their own subjective realization of the moral ideal embodied in that relationship, all that is truly worthwhile and valuable at every level of human existence. Even the transient goods of life, which, if they became a person's ultimate concern, would be immoral, are in principle brought to their fullness as elements in the enjoyment of God and of one's fellow human beings. Only the false, the deceptive, the illusory, and the distorted are eliminated. Nothing truly good is lost, but is brought into the redeeming embrace of God's goodness and love.

9.37) Here all genuine limited human goods are gathered up in the vision of God as the one ultimate Good;

9.37a) nothing truly valuable is excluded,

9.37b) nor is individual worth and uniqueness eliminated: even transient goods find their place in the enjoyment of God.

For Augustine, even a person who belongs to the 'earthly city' (the company of all those who have not by faith become citizens of the heavenly city) can share, in a limited way, in this peace and order. Even in the pursuit of material and temporal goods which are sought for their own sake by the citizens of the earthly city, there is and must be some order and peace required as a framework for these pursuits and for the attainment of objectives essential to relatively har-

9.37c) Citizens of the heavenly city are within their rights in making common cause with citizens of the earthly city in promoting temporal peace and order, while inviting citizens of all nations

---

[1] *City of God*, Book IX, chapter 13.

and cultures to become citizens of the heavenly city without renouncing their human diversity of law, custom, and tradition, except where these might infringe on the faith and worship of the one true God.	monious material existence. And citizens of the heavenly city, as long as they are wayfarers in this world, have every moral right to pursue temporal peace and temporal goods as well, but never as ends in themselves, rather as means to making earthly existence as good as it can be. For this reason, the heavenly citizens are perfectly within their moral rights before God to make common cause with the citizens of the earthly city in the pursuit of temporal peace and comfortable circumstances of earthly existence, even to the extent of submitting to civil laws which are concerned with promoting order in the affairs of purely human life. At the same time, the heavenly city, through its citizens, invites citizens of all earthly nations and cultures to unite in the one pilgrim band of the morally and spiritually committed to God, while taking no issue with the diversity of laws, customs, and traditions of those who respond or even of those who cooperate with the heavenly citizens in the pursuit of temporal peace, provided only that none of these interfere with the faith and worship of the one true God.
9.38) Positive critical evaluation of Augustine's ethic: 9.38a) the combination of a Christian theistic metaphysic with a modified Platonism;	What, then, are we to make of Augustine's admirable moral vision from a critical standpoint? The astute reader, guided by the accumulated criticisms of views I have previously analyzed, will be able to go a long way toward answering this question for himself. I have already expressed my enthusiasm, for example, with a version of Platonism which is modified in the theistic direction that Augustine himself took in his thinking; and so, like Augustine, I am not only a Platonist (of sorts), but a Christian theistic Platonist as well. If I had some contrasting metaphysical worldview commitment (such as naturalism or Hegelianism), it would be expected that I would preoccupy myself here with Augustine's theistic and Christian metaphysic. But since I am committed in general to Augustine's Christian theistic metaphysic, and since I have attempted to provide a critical defense of this commitment in two of my previous books, in which I further consider negative arguments from other philosophical quarters in detail, I will therefore not repeat myself by preoccupying myself with the critical assessment of the Christian theistic metaphysical base with which Augustine girds his moral philosophy. Nor will I consider again here the basis of the modified Platonism that I share with Augustine, since that has been dealt with in a previ-

ous context of this same book in which I discussed Plato's ethic. Instead, I will address the question of the critical adequacy of Augustine's ethic on his own Christian, theistic, and Platonist ground.

In this context, it should be clear that I find much that is critically sound in Augustine's moral philosophy. In an earlier section of the present work in which I discussed the freedom/determinism problem, I defended at length a modified incompatibilism (the view that any sort of rigorous scientific or metaphysical determinism is incompatible with the sort of freedom that is relevant to moral responsibility) along with the agent causality view of freedom, which I argued was the only view of freedom that would adequately undergird the full meaning and possibility of genuinely objective moral responsibility. It is my opinion that in the *Treatise on Free Will* Augustine clearly defends essentially this same combination of positions, although he does not, of course, use the same terminology (incompatibilism, agent causality). I regard his arguments in support of these views (arguments I have already discussed) as logically sound as far as they go, and I consider the additional arguments that I myself introduced earlier as providing logically compatible and further buttressing for Augustine's position on these points. On the other hand, I regard Augustine's rigorous doctrine of electionism, as developed in his later and more theological writings, as itself logically incompatible with his own views in the *Treatise*. If, as he maintains, God is himself the highest objective Good and the ultimate object of moral commitment, and if, as he also maintains, human beings are under a universal moral obligation to make that commitment, then those same responsible agents would logically have to be free, in the relevant moral sense of agent causality, to make that commitment. But if only certain inscrutably elected individuals are actually capable of making that commitment, and are in fact determined by God's choice to do so, then even the elect are not genuinely free, in the relevant moral sense, in their commitment to God as the Good, while the rest of humankind would, by hypothesis, be totally incapable of making that choice; and in either case (of both the elect and the non-elect) they could not be morally obligated to make that commitment, so that they could not be held morally responsible for the choice

9.38b) Augustine's view of freedom in the *Treatise* is substantially the same as my own view, which combines incompatibilism with the agent causality view;

9.39) but the later doctrine of rigorous electionism is incompatible with that earlier view of freedom.

they make, even on the grounds laid out by Augustine in the *Treatise*. I have no objection in principle to Augustine's general claim that, in his morally corrupt condition, man could not overcome the sinful indisposition to make a moral commitment to God without supervening divine grace as a reinforcement of his freedom of moral choice, provided only that Augustine would regard this gracious reinforcement as universally extended to all responsible human agents; but Augustine limits this grace to a select few, namely, the inscrutably elect.

I also agree in general with Augustine's view that freedom and divine foreknowledge are logically compatible, and that such divine foreknowledge does not, in itself and as such, in any way determine morally responsible human choices as causally necessary (since, as I agree with Augustine, that would be a contradiction). Here again, as in the previous case, I regard Augustine's supporting arguments as essentially sound but as capable of being supplementally reinforced with further arguments of the sort I discussed earlier. And I further agree with Augustine that the attribution of moral evil to the wrong use of freedom on the part of finite moral agents whose freedom was intended by God to be used in the choice of God as the ultimate Good and of morally right acts as an expression of that commitment, provides a rationally plausible and satisfactory reconciliation of God's essential goodness with the presence of moral evil in a world that God created for a morally good purpose. Even more I support Augustine's claim that both moral and natural corruptibility are consequences of the creation of any contingent world order that by hypothesis must be less than absolutely perfect in the highest sense, this latter sort of perfection being unique to God alone. Actual corruption, however, whether moral or natural is merely a contingent possibility in the existence of finite beings: there is no metaphysical necessity that what is in principle corruptible should become actually corrupted, as Augustine would agree. It is certainly possible, and an element of Hebrew-Christian prophetic vision, that the citizens of the heavenly city should ultimately become so pervaded by God's sanctifying power and so confirmed in their moral and spiritual commitment to God and his righteousness as to become practically incapable of moral corruption through sheer

---

9.40) There is no objection to the concept of grace reinforcing freedom, provided that grace is universally accessible (which Augustine did not hold);

9.41) freedom and divine foreknowledge are logically compatible;

9.42) that moral evil results from the wrong use of freedom (which is essential for choosing God as the Good) does reconcile God's absolute goodness with the occurrence of moral evil.

9.43) Finite existence involves both moral and natural corruptibility, but not necessarily actual corruption in practice.

9.44) This is true not merely in the present state of humanity,

strength of character, while they live in a natural environment that is ideally adapted to their confirmed moral state; here again, the fact that corruption is possible in principle does not entail its becoming actual in practice. And in this inclusive spiritual community of the redeemed, genuine freedom, in the morally relevant sense, will not be transcended but will rather find its highest finite exercise in the uninterrupted moral commitment of the soul to God as the chief and ultimate objective Good.

9.45) but also in the ultimate state of the citizens of the heavenly kingdom;

I have already quoted Augustine's provocative description of this ideal spiritual community, and I have no hesitation in sharing with him the keen insight of this lofty vision. It is an ideal whose actualization takes its starting point in the community of the heavenly citizens in their present earthly state, while at the same time it provides an ethical model for ideal personal life and social relationship in the earthly city as well, even for those who are merely members of that city alone. But the ideal finds its culmination in the eternal extension of the heavenly community in an exalted state in which all operative obstructions to justice and righteousness have been removed and in which the faith of the redeemed has been transformed into sight. No doubt many of the elements of this vision will finally be actualized in unexpected ways which even our keenest present imagination cannot begin to sketch, but those surprises, I think, will not undo the genuineness and soundness of the vision's substance. Meanwhile it is, for Augustine's view, the moral obligation of all responsible human agents (whether members of the heavenly kingdom or not) to work toward the fullest presently achievable realization of that same moral substance.

9.46) the vision of an ultimate state of ideal individual and social harmony of moral order.

Aquinas on Nature, Grace, and Moral Law

The intellectual, philosophical, and theological achievement of Thomas Aquinas was both massive and monumental: it was massive by its sheer bulk and extent—his most important work, the *Summa Theologica*, for example, would fill some forty thousand normal-sized, present-day book pages; it was monumental as attempting to provide a comprehensive systematic exposition of the substance and ground of all the truth accessible to human insight at the time (the thir-

9.47) The historical situation of Thomas Aquinas:
9.47a) the magnitude and influence of his work;

teenth century A.D.) in philosophy, theology, and even science (in the limited state of its development in that era). In terms of effectiveness, his perspective became the predominant philosophy in the West in later medieval times and eventually became the accepted and virtually official framework for the teaching of the Christian faith in all Roman Catholic institutions of learning right down to the present century, when this elevated position has become subject to considerable challenge even among Roman Catholic philosophers (although there are still many philosophical and theological thinkers who claim to be Thomists or modified Thomists even now). In a sense, the work of Aquinas is an extension and expansion of the philosophical and theological views of Augustine (who lived about nine hundred years earlier) and other medieval thinkers—certainly Thomas often preoccupied himself with showing that his complex views on significant issues were at least not inconsistent in the main with those of Augustine, even though they went far beyond him in scope, detail, and depth. But on the other hand, there is an important contextual difference between these two giants of the Christian intellectual tradition: Augustine basically employed the framework of a modified Platonism as a context for expounding and rationally defending the Christian worldview; but Thomas, while by no means severing his connections with that philosophical tradition, largely displaced it to the periphery of his thought and placed Aristotelianism at the center of his concern in expounding and defending the Christian worldview, so much so that he even referred to Aristotle as 'the philosopher' throughout much of his writing. In part, of course, this shift was due, in a considerable degree, to historical circumstances; Aristotle's writings were virtually inaccessible in western Europe at the time of Augustine, and this continued to be the case until the high middle ages, when, by the century of Aquinas, his translated writings had swept over western Europe like a great intellectual storm and had become the center of concern in all the institutions of Christian higher learning. In this setting, the preoccupation of Aquinas with Aristotle was an attempt to adjust and adapt this newly available material to the already developed Christian intellectual tradition. As Augustine had done in the case of Platonism, so Thomas, in similar fashion,

9.47b) the relation of his work to that of Augustine: Christian Aristotelianism

9.48) His modification of Aristotelianism

found it necessary to modify Aristotle's overall philosophical perspective into conformity with what he took to be a Christian metaphysic. With Aristotle, Thomas could speak of particulars as, on the whole, a union of form (essence) and matter, actuality, and potentiality; but, in agreement with Augustine, Thomas viewed forms as archetypes in the mind of God and matter as created by God *ex nihilo* (out of nothing) in conjunction with God's creation of particular entities. With Aristotle again, Aquinas could dwell on God as *actus purus* (pure actuality without matter); but unlike Aristotle, who regarded God as only the final or purposive Cause of all being—a sort of ultimate and impersonal Mind whose sole activity was self-contemplation (thought thinking thought), Thomas, while clearly emphasizing the final causality of God, extended God's causality to God's being the creative and efficient cause of the world and its sustaining, providentially directing ground.

This modification of Aristotelianism becomes even more striking in ethics and moral philosophy. As noted earlier, Aristotle made virtually no use of the concept of God in his ethical theory, aside from his general metaphysical thesis that God provided a motivating model or exemplar, in his status as Pure Form, that all types of particulars were, in a vague general way, striving to emulate in actualizing their forms or essences as fully as possible. So of course, for Aristotle, a human person, in striving to actualize his form as subjectively rational through reason's government of active energy and emotion or desire, would also be emulating God in this general way; but he need not preoccupy himself with this universal metaphysical fact, since becoming a good human being meant actualizing one's form or essence as a rational being by achieving both intellectual and moral virtue. But God was not, for Aristotle, the ultimate object of moral and spiritual commitment, nor was divine law the fundamental principle of moral obligation and duty. And certainly, for Aristotle, a right personal relationship with God, in moral harmony and intellectual understanding, was not man's chief end and final, eternal beatitude. Yet all these things that, for Aristotle, God was not, are precisely the things that, for Thomas Aquinas, God was supremely and preeminently. Thus, while, for Aristotle, a human being can achieve the highest moral fulfillment possible to

9.49) The concept of God in the ethical views of Aristotle and Aquinas: 9.49a) Aristotle's restricted use of this concept in this context stands in strong contrast to Aquinas's extensive use of the concept of God in ethics.

9.49b) For Aquinas, God is both the ultimate object of moral commitment and man's chief moral end.

him by preoccupying himself with becoming fully rational in the pursuit of knowledge and in the government of active energy and desire (emotion, appetite) and without any extended conscious preoccupation with God, except in the general, metaphysical sense already indicated (if at all); for Thomas Aquinas, by contrast, God is the ultimate object of moral commitment, the center of human moral concern, the ground and basis of all moral goodness.

In spite of this clearly evident contrast, Aquinas obviously accepts Aristotle's thesis that God is the final, purposive cause of the universe in general and of individual things in particular, considered (in a broad general sense) as agents. But instead of limiting the function of divine final causality to the status of an ultimate model or exemplar of complete actuality, as in Aristotle, Aquinas expands and enriches that final causality by holding that God both created the universe and particular things to realize his own conscious, rational purpose in a way that involves the fulfillment of the essence of each class of particular things; and that, through universal providence, God directs all things to the fulfillment of their proper end. Sub-intelligent agents, of whatever sort, do not, of course, determine that end for themselves, but it is determined for them ultimately (and often indirectly) by God's having created them with a nature that is inclined or disposed toward an end that is appropriate to that nature, while, in an intermediate and proximate sense, that end is often partly determined through the contrived purpose of some one or more finite intelligent agents (human beings, for example). Now finite intelligent agents, in turn and within the limits of their essence as rational beings created by God with that nature, consciously determine their own ends by explicit choice. In this conscious self-determination, rational beings always aim at ends which, rightly or wrongly in the case of finite agents, have for them the character of the good, at least relatively to themselves; no intelligent agent ever intends evil relative to itself, but rather good. In this sense, and in agreement with Augustine, evil is made possible in its existence only by good—the good of being as such, and the good aimed at as an end by intelligent agents. Evil, therefore, is in general not any sort of positive being, but is rather a defect of being, something that ought not to be, from the standpoint of the good. In the case of moral evil,

9.50) God is the final, purposive cause of the universe in general and of individual things in particular.

9.50a) God created the universe to realize his own purpose through the actualization of essences;

9.50b) thus God directs all things to their proper end.
9.51) Sub-intelligent agents have no control over the determination of their end;

9.52) but finite intelligent agents, within limits, consciously determine their own ends by explicit choice.
9.52a) The ends always have the character of good for the agent;

9.52b) evil is a defect of being, and moral evil is a defect of will rather than one

which is possible only for finite intelligent agents, the defect is primarily one of will as determined by the free choice of the agent, and not characteristically a defect of judgment in apprehending the thing about which the will chooses or a defect of executive power (the capacity to act), unless in a particular case these defects are themselves the effect of a prior defect of will, since otherwise misdeeds occasioned by errors of judgment or lack of capacity to act are not morally chargeable to the agent. An act is morally significant only if it is voluntary and could have been avoided by the agent—and that is clearly a matter of will.

Now since nothing tends toward an end except under the character of the good, it follows that the highest good, namely God, is, ultimately and from the highest point of view, the proper end of all things. But of course, while God is good by being and constituting goodness itself, finite things (whether intelligent or non-intelligent) are never good in themselves, but only by participating in the being and goodness of God through the essence with which God specifically and variably created them. Thus the good of each finite thing consists in the actualization of its essence as the sort of thing it is; but since no finite thing ever fully actualizes its essence, all are in this way defective in both being and goodness as compared with God, whose very act of being constitutes the highest perfection of goodness. Each finite thing is good just so far as it exists or has derived being, and each has an end that is natural to it and is determined by the essence that it exemplifies. This is, of course, also true of human beings as intelligent agents. Since human beings are, by nature or essence, uniquely rational in the subjective, conscious sense, it follows that their proper natural good or end cannot consist in the actualization of their potential for merely bodily goods and pleasures, which humans share with other living creatures; that proper good and end must consist in the actualization of their essence as rational. And this, in turn, has for Thomas, as it had for Aristotle, two aspects: the pursuit of knowledge by rational insight and contemplation, on the one hand, and the rational direction of active energies, appetites, inclinations, emotions, and desires, on the other hand. Moral virtue, in the sense in which it is a natural possibility for human beings as finite intelligent agents, does indeed consist in those habitual and developed states

of judgment or executive power.

9.52c) God, as the highest Good, is the proper end of all things;
9.53) while God is goodness itself, finite things are good only by participating in God's goodness through their distinctive essences as created by God.

9.54) Since human intelligent agents are by essence uniquely rational, their good consists in the actualization of that rationality.

9.55) This involves:
9.56) intellectual virtue in the pursuit of knowledge,

9.57) and moral virtue in the rational direction of active energy and emotion.

of character (habits of character) which voluntarily direct the agent to aim at the mean between extremes of excess and defect; and thus we get to such naturally achievable virtues as fortitude (courage), temperance (self-control), justice, and even practical wisdom. But humans are also capable by nature or essence of achieving the intellectual virtue of theoretical wisdom in the apprehension of truth. In a sense, the higher the nature of the object, the more adequate the intellectual virtue of its adequate apprehension; and since God, by his own essence and nature, is the highest possible object of knowledge, it follows that the highest human well-being (felicity, in Thomas's parlance) consists in the intellectual knowledge of the existence and nature of God. All this is, of course, quite or rather expressly Aristotelian. But it is of the utmost importance, from Aquinas's point of view, that all this relates merely to humankind's natural end as the sort of embodied intellectual agents they are. And human beings, whatever their faults (moral and nonmoral) are capable, by rationally directed free and therefore voluntary choice, of becoming progressively more virtuous both in intellectual apprehension (even of God) and in moral self-discipline through the development of appropriate habits of character in the government of active energies and desires, although, of course, this is always an incomplete and imperfect achievement, since nothing ever fully actualizes its nature or essence through its intrinsic capacities alone. It is also true that, in all of this aiming at distinctly human virtue through rationally directed free choice, human beings are sustained by the universal creative and providential power of God. For a person can exist, act, think, and decide only through the exercise of natural capacities that depend completely and continuously on this sustaining divine causality. Yet that divine causality does not displace either the natural agent's causal capacity to act, or the human and rational agent's voluntary freedom as exercised through rational self-direction. In a sense, God is the ultimate agent (even the principal agent in a universal metaphysical fashion), and the human person is the proximate, secondary, and intermediate agent. But God's ultimate agency only makes the voluntary rational choices of the human agent possible; it does not determine them as necessary and unavoidable, since that would contradict their voluntary character as morally significant events.

9.58) The highest intellectual virtue consists in the knowledge of God's existence and nature.

9.59) All this is natural virtue; the intelligent agent is capable of aiming voluntarily at the progressive realization of both intellectual and moral virtue, although this goal is never fully achieved by the agent.

9.60) This capacity depends on the universal creative and providential power of God;

9.61) but that sustaining operation in no way undermines the causal agency or freedom of the finite agent;

But all this is not, for Thomas, the complete account of man's moral status in relation to God. For even though human nature in its primordial and original state (Thomas calls it 'the pure state of nature') is capable, through free and rational direction, of achieving the moral good that is intrinsically possible for him, and even capable of loving God above all things and above himself as creatures of God, nevertheless this possibility is only a possibility in principle in the present state of humanity. For human beings, through the abuse of their freedom, are universally in a state of moral corruption by their turning away from God as the highest Good and turning toward corruptible things and their own falsely construed self-interest as the locus for achieving the good thus improperly understood. The result is not only moral corruption, but also objective moral guilt before God who, as the highest Good, claims unconditional commitment and obedience to his law from all morally responsible human beings. The eternal law of God, against which corrupted human beings stand as morally guilty, is simply the conjoined principles, grounded in the divine moral character, by which the divine reason governs the whole community of the universe. Nor are human beings totally bereft of this law, whatever their circumstances; for that law is imprinted on all things (humanity included) by their having been created with natures or essences that incline them to their proper acts and ends. But human beings, as rational agents, are not only subject to that natural law along with the whole of creation, but, as rational, they participate in the eternal reason of God and can therefore both recognize that law intrinsic to their nature and also share in the conscious, purposive direction of themselves to their proper end. In the present corrupted (sinful) state of human nature, human beings are still free to make right (and wrong) moral choices and to aim with purposive intent toward their proper moral end through the understanding of the natural law (or in varying degrees to reject further the claim of that law upon them). However, since the corruption of moral nature involves a relative indisposition or disinclination toward the true moral good in God, human moral freedom to choose the good and human ability to persist in the pursuit of it, while still possible in principle, are nevertheless restricted and limited.

9.62) since human agents have abused their freedom in turning away from God as ultimate moral Good, the result is that they are morally corrupt and in a condition of objective moral guilt before God.

9.62a) Yet they are capable in principle, and by reason, of recognizing the moral law imprinted on their nature, and consciously moving toward its fulfillment in their natural end;

9.62b) but moral corruption restricts and limits this capacity.

9.63) In a mere state of nature human beings can, by their own resources, only aim at their natural end in God as the highest object of knowledge and the true Good.

Even in a pure state of nature, human beings, through freedom and rational direction, can only aim at ends that fall within the capacity of their natural active and rational powers. That is, they can only aim at their natural end; and this remains true even in a corrupted state of human nature, except that the task is far more difficult, across the board, as the result of this defective state of moral character. In a sense, this limited natural capacity extends even to a knowledge of the existence and nature of God as both highest Good and ultimate metaphysical ground: such knowledge is an aspect of man's natural end as including an inclination to God as the true Good and the most adequate object of knowledge. But in another sense, since God transcends the contingent natural order and is therefore a *super*natural End whose essence cannot be adequately apprehended by man's sense-based knowledge, it follows that achieving a correct intellectual knowledge of God, as well as a right moral relation to God, both exceed man's natural powers. Thus, since man's true and final good consists in a beatitude or blessedness that combines moral harmony and fellowship with God, on the one hand, with a fully adequate vision or knowledge of God, on the other, it follows that the achievement of true human goodness in this final and fulfilled sense is only actually possible for human beings through supernatural divine help, which Thomas designates (along with the whole Christian tradition) as grace (unmerited favor and enablement). But it is not only because God, as the human being's highest Good and true End, exceeds our natural powers, that human beings need divine grace; we need it also for the healing of our corrupted state of nature and for the forgiveness of our objective state of moral guilt, for the adjudication of which human beings have no natural resources, from Thomas's point of view.

9.63a) As supernatural, however, God, as our End, exceeds our natural powers of knowledge and will;

9.63b) for this reason, and also because human nature has been corrupted through the abuse of human freedom, it follows that true human goodness is only possible through divine grace.

9.64) This grace is extended through the redemption that is in Jesus Christ as God incarnate;

9.65) this grace is appropriated by means of repentance and faith.

The form of the divine grace that is extended to human beings in their corrupted and guilty plight is complex indeed, and its full elaboration would take us far afield from ethics into the elucidation of elaborate theological edifices which I cannot explore here (and in any case have already explored in an earlier book, *The Reconstruction of the Christian Revelation Claim*). Suffice it to say that this grace is objectively provided through God's having become incarnate in Jesus Christ, whose death is interpreted as a vicarious sacrifice that solves the problem of objective human guilt for all those who become spiritually united to God in Christ through repentance and faith, and who are therefore morally justified before God. But this theological solution leaves to be considered the ethically more relevant question of how such justified individuals become morally regenerated through divine grace, and even the question of how they become actual candidates for justification and regeneration in the first place. The first of these questions is answered by Thomas in his claim, rooted in the New Testament, that God, as an operation of special divine grace and through his Holy Spirit, morally transforms those who become united to Christ, through repentance and faith, by infusing into them the three theological virtues of faith, hope, and love (often translated as *charity*), so that gradually and progressively, at least in this present life, they achieve and realize the capacity for finding in God the highest object of knowledge (faith), the fullest ground of confidence and expectation (hope), and the true and complete moral Good (love). Yet all this is possible even so in our earthly state of existence only by a continuously operative empowering grace that enables the morally and spiritually redeemed to persevere in the pursuit of this ever less-than-completed but nevertheless ideal goal.

9.66) Persons become morally regenerated by the Holy Spirit, who infuses into them the three supernatural virtues of faith, hope, and love;

As to the second question about how individuals actually become the recipients of redeeming grace (in contrast to other individuals who do not), Thomas follows Augustine in regarding this as entirely a matter of inscrutable divine election and predestination. Grace, as unmerited favor, would simply not be grace if, in its redemptive efficacy, it were distributed to individuals on the basis of any act or achievement that was possible to them by the sheer operation of their natural capacities; that would be merit, not grace, and there is nothing that a man can do in his corrupted state to merit any such distribution from God—not even the fullest contingently possible achievement of Aristotelian intellectual virtue would suffice for anything more than the approximation of man's purely natural moral end, and would therefore in itself be of no avail in the requisite realization of God as man's highest and supernatural End. There is therefore nothing that a man can do through his natural powers either to prepare himself for

9.67) but only those individuals become recipients of this grace who are special objects of divine election and predestination;

grace or to receive it. Human beings do in fact so prepare themselves and so receive; but that they are able to do so, and actually do so, is possible only by God's electing and supervening grace.

9.68) thus the complete human good involves God as both natural and supernatural End, so that no truly valuable element of human well-being is excluded from this moral end.

Thus, for Thomas, man's complete good, in the moral sense, does indeed involve the achievement of the intellectual and moral virtues that are possible through his natural powers and culminate in his natural end (even in God, in a limited sense). But this is not enough for the achievement of God as man's supernatural End in which moral harmony and fellowship are conjoined with the highest intellectual vision, so that together they compose final beatitude. For that noble ideal, nature must be supplemented and fulfilled by divine grace, and human possibility completed in divine condescension. As with Augustine, so with Thomas: no truly valuable element of human well-being is excluded from the moral good—it is all right there in the Aristotelian ideal of man's natural end as a rational agent; but that naturally achievable good, possible through man's natural powers as created by God, is short-circuited and incomplete, if it is not crowned with a humanly corporate unity with God as man's highest Good and supernatural End.

9.69) Critical evaluation of the ethics of Aquinas:

9.69a) The appeal of such an ethic rests on the plausibility (or otherwise) of metaphysical theism;
9.70) but the question of theism extends far beyond ethics and cannot be given detailed consideration here.

9.71) Yet an ethically relevant case is possible if moral objectivism is granted as a premise.
9.71a) Such objectivism cannot be defended on naturalistic grounds.

For many contemporary readers and critics, the chief difficulty with the moral philosophy of Thomas (as also with that of Augustine) lies in its comprehensive metaphysical theistic context, which is simply not a live option for such individuals. Such an ethical perspective as we have elaborated here stands or falls with the plausibility or otherwise of metaphysical theism. Of course, the defense of this perspective as a general metaphysical standpoint does not really belong to ethics or moral philosophy as narrowly construed. Thomas himself, however, provided perhaps the most effective apologetic philosophic support for theism, as supported by the ideal of rational objectivity, in the entire history of western philosophical thought; and his moral philosophy can only be rightly understood in the light of that achievement. Perhaps the most ethically relevant way of seeing that connection is to reason from premises provided by ethical objectivism (as against any version of radical ethical relativism). If there is a truly objective standard of moral goodness or rightness, it cannot be adequately grounded on any purely naturalistic analysis of what human beings want or desire, since such things are socially and individually relative and variable, as we have previously argued. And since any naturalistic attempt at formulating a moral criterion leads to this same dead end as far as moral objectivism is concerned, the ultimately good or right must transcend the natural order. Now while abstract essences and formal rational principles are clearly not excluded from the clarification of such a transcendent ideal, they cannot exhaust its whole nature, precisely because nothing less than personal being can constitute either the ultimate ground of the intrinsic moral worth of finite persons or the basis of moral obligation between or among persons. The transcendent good must therefore be ultimate personal mind— and that would be ultimately ethical theism. Thus ethical or moral objectivism finally leads to God, theistically construed, as its fundamental basis and ground. This is not really said in either Augustinian or Thomistic language; but it is, I think, the substantive content of what they were trying to say in defense of ethical theism from a philosophical point of view. The theological capstone of all this, in the elaboration of the concept of divine grace as meeting corrupt human beings in the grip of their moral predicament of objective guilt before the moral judgment bar of God, is simply but very importantly an attempt to show that even ethical theism itself becomes fully plausible only in the illuminating light of divine redemption and of divinely originated moral and spiritual transformation. In this vein, I can only express essential agreement here with the main thrust of the moral philosophy of Thomas Aquinas, as with that of Augustine before him. And as I was not uncomfortable with Augustine's Platonic way of putting much of this version of ethical theism, so neither am I uncomfortable with the Aristotelian language and conceptualization of Aquinas as he discourses about form and matter, about essence and existence, about God as pure actuality and the ultimate final end of all things. It is not after all the linguistic or conceptual form of philosophical expression that is decisively important here; it is rather the substance and content of what is expressed, together with the rationally plausible support provided for it. Perhaps (but only perhaps) what Thomas claims and rationally argues could be more effectively said to contemporary reflective individuals in somewhat or even

9.71b) Ethical idealism is plausible but incomplete, since nothing less than ultimate personal being can be the final ground of moral value and moral obligation.

9.71c) Yet even ethical theism is incomplete without divinely provided redemption and moral transformation.

9.72) With all this I am in essential agreement;

9.72a) while I am not uncomfortable with Aquinas's Aristotelian language, it is substance and not form that is important.

9.72b) There is here an essential content that is independent of the outer form of expression;

radically different language and through a distinctly different conceptual context. Perhaps in this very work I have been making a very small start toward that very task, as virtually countless others have done before me and still more others will attempt to do after me. All these outer shells of thought may be dispensable, but the inner core is by contrast essential and perennial.

At the same time, in my enthusiasm for the main thrust of the moral philosophy of Thomas, I am not blind to glitches and even serious critical defects in the Thomistic perspective. While in general I agree with his conception of divine grace as fulfilling and supplementing man's natural capacity (as created by God), yet I am moderately uncomfortable with the noticeably sharp contrast that Thomas draws between them. Is it not more plausible to view them as merging into one another in a variety of ways? After all, it is the same God (the numerically identical God) who is both the capstone of man's natural end, the ultimate object of human knowledge and moral commitment, who is also man's supernatural End through grace. The intellectual knowledge of God, which is possible to man through his natural cognitive powers, is also precisely a knowledge of God as identically the supernatural creative and providential ground of the contingent world order; even creation is an expression of conscious love, while man's natural powers are operative in his highest relation to God; and vice versa. On the other hand, it seems implausible to suppose that the very creation of that contingent world order was not itself an expression of God's gracious love, especially in regard to finite rational agents who are consciously capable of finding in God the true and ultimate end of their being. And surely it is, in a parallel fashion, an exercise of man's natural cognitive powers and of free capacity for rationally directed moral commitment to finally apprehend God in fulfilled vision and find in him the completion and basis of moral and spiritual fellowship. So perhaps the distinction between nature and grace should be viewed as a matter of emphasis and direction, rather than as a matter of unbridgeable qualitative contrast. From this point of view, divine grace and nature would be co-extensive in their range: grace would both undergird the divine motivation to create a contingent world order, including finite rational agents like ourselves, while

9.72c) but there are critical problems:

9.73) Perhaps Thomas draws too sharp a distinction between nature and grace;

9.73a) it seems more plausible to view them as mutually supplementary across the whole range of relationship between man and God.

9.73b) It is the same God who is both natural and supernatural, as well as the object of knowledge and beatific vision.

9.73c) Even creation is an expression of gracious love, while a human being's natural powers are operative in his or her highest relation to God.

at the same time it would wholly encompass the final beatitude of the redeemed in God. Nature, in turn, would find its justifying basis and highest fulfillment in the beatific vision of God and the moral harmony from which that vision is inseparable, while at the same time it would constitute, in the very existence of finite rational agents at its pinnacle, the existential presupposition for the recognition and reception of divinely redemptive grace and forgiveness. Thus grace and nature would be reciprocally interdependent across the whole compass of finite being as created by God.

No doubt it is an extension of this shift of emphasis, concerning the relation between nature and divine grace, to raise once again an objection to the Thomistic conception of rigorous and inscrutable divine election, just as I raised a similar objection against Augustine. Here too there seems to be a fabric of contradiction between Thomas's strong emphasis on the moral freedom of rational human agents in his analysis of natural morality, on the one hand, and the virtual (if not complete) exclusion of this free and voluntary choice as a basis for the appropriation of divine grace in redemptive forgiveness. It is a breach of the universality of human moral responsibility to maintain that human beings are morally responsible for acknowledging the divine moral claim, while at the same time insisting that free and voluntary human response forms no part of the basis on which God elects individuals to gracious forgiveness and eternal life. If grace and nature are reciprocally co-extensive and interdependent in the relation between rational human agents and God, there is no reason not to construe God's offer of gracious forgiveness as extended to all such agents on the sole condition of their positive response to the divine offer, and to regard those agents as freely and voluntarily capable of that response as supported by both nature and grace. Otherwise, what conceivable and morally plausible basis would God have for electing some and excluding others? Indeed, is the idea of a divine choice which bears no motivational relation to the character of its objects even a rationally intelligible notion? Thomas's claim, that an election based on any fact about its objects would contradict the very nature of grace, is hardly to the point. Free and voluntary response does not function as a meritorious cause of grace, but merely as an ap-

9.74) There seems to be a contradiction between Thomas's strong emphasis on free and responsible moral choice in natural morality, and its exclusion from the appropriation of divine grace in redemptive forgiveness.

9.74a) There is no reason why the free agent could not be guided by both nature and grace in the choice to respond to the divine moral claim.

9.74b) Such voluntary response is merely the appropriating cause of grace, while its meritorious cause is God's redemptive provision in Christ.

propriating cause. From a Christian point of view, I agree with Thomas that the sole meritorious cause of the extension of grace to the morally corrupted is God's own provision for redemption in Jesus Christ as God incarnate and as vicarious substitute.

Kierkegaard on Subjectivity and Purity of Heart

9.75) The epistemological and metaphysical context:

Søren Kierkegaard, whose earthly pilgrimage came fifteen hundred years after that of Augustine and even six hundred years after that of Aquinas, was not merely far removed from them in time but even more strikingly distanced from them in the attitude of mind with which he approached issues of philosophical substance and in the criteria that he employed for resolving those issues. Aquinas (certainly and unhesitatingly) and Augustine (clearly but with some hesitation) both aimed at what I will call the epistemological ideal of rational objectivity: they believed that there were objective principles of reason which functioned as criteria for assessing truth claims and which were in principle (and to some extent in practice) accessible to finite rational and human agents; and they attempted to discover these principles and use them to construct what they regarded as objectively plausible arguments for a metaphysical theism.

9.75a) Kierkegaard rejects the ideal of objectivity as espoused by Augustine and Aquinas.
9.76) The approach of these latter thinkers found its model for Kierkegaard in the System of Hegel.

But Kierkegaard seems to have solidly rejected the ideal of rational objectivity as impossible for existing finite human subjects. The immediate historical paradigm of rational objectivity against which he pitted his rejection was the so-called System of Hegel, which he refers to simply as 'the system' with scarcely any mention of Hegel by name; but it is clear that he regarded any attempted marriage between Christianity and the ideal of rational objectivity as a joke at best and a sheer perversion of Christianity and genuine religious faith at worst. In his most extensive and significant philosophical work (*Concluding Unscientific Postscript*) he encapsulated his rejection of what he called 'the objective attitude' in the claim that a logical system is possible, but an existential system is impossible. A logical system is a formal structure of principles or general propositions in which one begins with a set of purportedly and rationally self-evident axioms, postulates, and definitions, and then proceeds, in logically necessary order and by the use of logical principles

9.77) He summarized his reaction in the claim that an existential system is impossible;
9.77a) Distinction between a logical system and an existential system:

alone, to deduce all the formal logical consequences of the original starting points—perhaps Euclidean plane geometry would be the most appropriate model for the average reader. Kierkegaard viewed the construction of such a system as unobjectionably possible as an abstract and detached experiment of thought, a sort of logical game for intellectual exercise. But an existential system, by contrast, he regarded as impossible in practice for an existing human subject. Such a system would be a logical system (as previously defined) that actually provided a comprehensive explanation of existence, of the whole of reality. Kierkegaard then went on to argue the claim he made against the possibility of such a system by constructing a series of what appear to be the very sort of rationally objective arguments, with conclusions about existence, that he himself was in principle attempting to reject by the use of those same arguments; he was, one might say, attempting to beard the lion (in this case, Hegel and all other rational objectivists) in his own den. Kierkegaard argues, for example:

9.77b) The latter would have to be both logically consistent and existentially explanatory, which Kierkegaard claimed was impossible,

(1) an existential system is impossible because reality, construed as particular existence (things and events in space and time), is always changing and in process, while a logical system is by its very essence a logically self-completed totality, so that the notion of an unfinished system (the only kind that could apply to existence as changing) is a contradiction in terms;

9.78) because existence is always in process;

(2) an existential system is impossible because, constituted as a logical system through universal essences and principles, it is *ipso facto* indifferent to the particular entities of which the world order is clearly composed, and especially to the unique sort of existence actualized by persons, since particulars can neither be deduced from universal essences nor explained, in their particularity, as grounded in such essences;

9.79) because a logical system is indifferent to particular entities;

(3) an existential system is impossible because such a logical system would require an absolute, self-evident, immediately discerned, and therefore universal starting point, whereas such a starting-point is not humanly achievable, partly because the thinkers who propose such a system are themselves in-

9.80) because no existing individual could achieve the requisite absolutely self-evident starting point, since such an individual is involved in existence, so that any actual starting point would be arbitrary and inapplicable.

volved in existence as contingent, historically and culturally conditioned individuals and thus lack the objective stance required for such a discernment, partly because there is always something logically and existentially arbitrary about the principle that such thinkers adopt as such a starting point (which is therefore not objective in the required sense after all), and even if they succeeded in this goal (indeed to the very extent to which they succeeded) the principle arrived at would be so totally abstract and vacuous that it would afford no applicable starting point for concrete thought at all without the supplemental support of contingent and existential truths which by hypothesis and definition would be external to the system, and partly also because thinkers themselves, as discerning the starting point, always stand beyond it (as a condition of its objectivity) in such a way that, as object of their thought, it could not explain them as the subjects apprehending that purportedly objective content.

9.81) For Kierkegaard, truth is subjectivity;

9.82) truth is constituted through propriety of the individual's attitude in discerning it.
9.82a) The objective attitude falls on the *what* of truth, the subjective attitude falls on the *how* of the discernment of truth.
9.82b) It is passionate inwardness and urgency that are crucial;

9.82c) such truth is *faith* in the religious sense;

Since, for such reasons as these, truth as objectivity is humanly impossible (an existential system is impossible), Kierkegaard infers or concludes that the only truth possible for an existing individual is truth as subjectivity, not in such a way that its content is judged to be objectively false (that would still be the objective standpoint), but in such a way that truth is constituted for the individual through the propriety of his attitude in discerning it, an attitude of urgent concern or passionate inwardness. The objective attitude falls, as it were, on the *what* or *content* of truth, while the subjective attitude falls on the *how* or *relation* of the individual's discernment of truth. If the relation to truth involves grasping it with the passion of inwardness and a sense of anxious urgency, rather than with disinterested contemplation (the objective or spectator standpoint), then the individual is in the truth, even if what one believes or commits one's self to is, objectively considered, false. This sort of truth, which combines the recognition of objective uncertainty with the most passionate inwardness, is the highest truth possible for an existing individual. But truth as thus defined is precisely *faith* in the religious sense, according to Kierkegaard, and he therefore goes on to claim that the truth of Christianity (to which he was personally committed) exists only in this sort of subjectivity, and that, objectively considered, Christianity (or its truth) has no existence at all.

On the other hand, there must, for Kierkegaard, be some way of characterizing the truth of Christianity from the standpoint of objective discernment. In fact, there can be only one such way, and that is the way that views the ultimate truth (God incarnate in Jesus Christ) as paradox. But the paradox takes two forms: a provisional phase for which the ultimate truth is not paradoxical in itself, but only in relation to the situation of a finite, existing subject (a human rational agent, for example); and an ultimate phase in which subjectivity, as truth, posits its own subjectivity as untruth (i.e., as self-contradictory from an objective standpoint) and views the eternal, essential truth itself (rather than merely in relation to the existing subject) as sheer, essential, and logically unresolvable contradiction. It is only in this ultimate phase, conjoined as it is with the repulsion of the logically absurd, that all objective security or confidence is cut loose, and the passion of inwardness is potentiated to the highest degree. In this contrast truth or religious faith adds to the objective uncertainty the repulsion of the logically absurd, so that the paradox is complete and the *how* has, as it were, banished the *what* as objectively considered.

Yet for Kierkegaard it is precisely through this sort of subjective discernment that the individual is capable of confronting the infinite, personal God of theism as the correlate of his discernment in passionate inwardness. From his own standpoint, the individual confronts God through truth as subjectivity; but the God who thus confronts him is no self-projected aspect of his own conceptualization or imagination (if I may speak anachronistically and metaphorically, there is here not the slightest conceptual shadow of Feuerbach or Freud)—no, it is the objectively real and absolutely transcendent creative Ground of the contingent world order, and, more relevantly to our present purpose, the Infinite God making an unconditional (even the *sole* unconditional) moral claim on the individual in his particular finite existence. Here is the true and authentic Divine Objectivity standing over against the inwardness and sheer

9.83) from an objective standpoint, truth is paradoxical.

9.84) Two phases of paradox:
9.85) Provisional phase: truth paradoxical only in relation to the finite subject.
9.86) Ultimate phase: truth paradoxical in itself and thus absurd.
9.87) In this last phase passionate inwardness reaches its highest expression.

9.88) The development of a Christian theist's ethic:

9.89) through truth as subjectivity the individual confronts God as the objectively real Ground of the contingent world;

9.90) God, so construed, makes an unconditional moral claim on the individual;

subjectivity of the finite individual, for whom now there is no lingering question about God's existence to be resolved by any sort of natural theology. There is instead only the question whether individuals will respond with unconditional moral and spiritual commitment on their part. If they do not, if they blatantly refuse, then they simply exacerbate and deepen their moral perversion and guilt. But if they do respond with a commitment appropriate to the absoluteness of God's moral authority, they are morally transformed or regenerated through divine love and power. Yet they are not thereby morally perfected; standing as they now do in the absolute God-relationship, they confront the task of making the claim of the Infinite God relevant and applicable to their own particular existence and specific tasks. They are, so to speak, caught in the dialectical tension between the unconditional divine claim and the comparative triviality or insignificant detail of their human existence; a tension that Kierkegaard views as capable of resolution (though only partially in this present life) by viewing the nonmoral details of existence as a sort of diversion from one's preoccupation with the absolute God-relationship, though even this leaves the problem of deciding the occasions, the forms, and the frequency of diversion, so that the appropriate attitudinal stance is one of humble self-acceptance before God. In this present life, a person has, after all, no other possible recourse.

Yet it is possible, for Kierkegaard, to clarify the ultimate moral ideal for man's existence and contrast it with the gravity and hopelessness of his plight apart from the God-relationship. On the whole, human beings find themselves initially in the *aesthetic* state of existence in which decision is determined (even though morally free and responsible) by immediate hedonistic inclination, so that there results an indifference to all alternatives. It is a question of either/or—do this or do that, be this or be that, choose this or choose that, with the consequence being indifferent. The ultimate upshot is that the actual direction of such a morally unstructured life is determined in reality by external circumstances, just as the direction and speed of a rudderless ship is determined, not by the helmsman (Could there actually *be* a helmsman on such presuppositions?), but by the winds and the currents. Such a life is the essence of moral bondage combined with the illusion of personal freedom.

9.91) the individual responds either with unconditional commitment or willful refusal;
9.92) the committed individual is morally transformed by divine love and power.

9.92a) The task is then to connect the absolute God-relationship to the triviality of individual existence;

9.92b) this leads to humble self-acceptance before God;

9.92c) clarification of the moral ideal through the classification of the stages of life:
9.93) the aesthetic stage (immediate hedonistic inclination as the guide to decision);
9.93a) alternatives of choice are indifferent so that the result is determined by external circumstances;

If and when persons, discontent with their enslavement to aesthetic immediacy, begin to recognize that not all available alternatives stand on an equal footing and that there must therefore be a real difference, a decisive distinction, between good and evil, right and wrong, they are making the transition to the *ethical* stage in which that distinction is apprehended in relation to, and by means of, an ultimate and abstract moral principle which functions as a criterion of moral judgment. Since the aesthetically oriented persons did not really choose but only seemed to themselves to do so, persons who make the shift to the ethical stage not only leave aesthetic determination behind, but also, for the first time, make genuine choices possible for themselves. And it is not so much a question of choosing the right, although that is their moral duty, but it is a question of choosing with the whole inwardness and earnestness of their personality. In thus choosing under the guidance of objective moral principle, they have elevated their existence to a higher plane and have come into an immediate relation to the 'eternal Power,' however vaguely construed, that interpenetrates all existence and is the basis of all moral worth. Such persons cannot return to the aesthetic stage in which the absoluteness of moral distinction is removed from the field of their consciousness: for they could only do this by morally choosing the evil and thus being subject to ethical determinants—it would be immorality or sin, not mere aesthetic immediacy.

But moral obligation to an abstract moral principle, even though that principle may be transcendent in the sense indicated by ethical idealism, is still not the highest level of moral actualization, unless the recognition of that transcendent principle passes over, in the mind and conscience of the agent, to the recognition of the unconditional moral authority of God as the sole unitary Good. Here the ethical individual and his morally significant acts and choices are not *merely* subsumed under an abstract moral principle (though they are thus subsumed), but the individual, as a particular existing agent and through the absolute God-relationship, stands above all principles and is confronted with the transcendent, personal God whose moral character as absolute Goodness is the basis, substance, and ground of all such rationally discerned principles. This confrontation, together with the individual's unconditional commitment to divine

9.93b) the upshot is moral bondage and illusory freedom.
9.94) The ethical stage is the reorganization of the distinction between right and wrong in relation to moral principle;
9.94a) genuine moral choice becomes possible with inwardness and earnestness.

9.94b) This involves an immediate relation to the eternal power as the basis of all moral worth;

9.95) the religious stage is the unconditional moral authority of God as the sole unitary Good whose moral character is the ultimate ground of all conditional discerned moral principles.

9.95a) God's moral authority calls for the individual to unconditional moral commitment;

moral authority, constitutes the culminating and religious stage of human moral existence. But for Kierkegaard (as for all Christians who understand their relation to God with reasonable correctness), commitment to divine moral authority, or to the 'eternal Power' in general, is not the highest phase of the religious stage. For that, the individual must concretize his relation to God in the recognition of Jesus Christ as the God-man through whose vicarious sacrifice on the cross the individual is morally justified before God, and through whose transforming, regenerating power by the Holy Spirit the individual becomes a new moral creation, capable, through divine grace, of living his life in an increasingly explicit realization of the absolute God-relationship.

> 9.95b) but general theism is abstract without the redemption provided by Jesus Christ as God incarnate;
>
> 9.95c) thus the moral ideal becomes the achievement of integrated personal selfhood through willing the Good (i.e., God) as one thing and the ultimate End of human existence.

From the standpoint of the individual in this higher phase of the religious state, the moral ideal is the achievement of integrated personal selfhood through the resolution of his psychological and ethical tensions in willing the Good (in and as God) as 'one thing' and as the ultimate End of human existence. Apart from this absolute God-relationship, the individual has not achieved authentic human selfhood, but is in a predicament of sin and guilt before God in terms of his moral status, and in a psychological predicament of despair—either the despair of *weakness* in not willing to be himself before God and in finding his goal in some finite object or relationship, or the despair of *defiance* in willing to be himself in deliberate opposition to God's moral authority, through commitment to Whom and Which alone the individual can find the integrated personal wholeness that comes from, or rather even *is*, the willing of the Good as one thing (i.e., willing it as the sole unitary good in God).

> 9.96) The alternative to this ideal is despair and disintegration.
>
> 9.97) The meaning of willing the Good in God as one thing:
>
> 9.97a) It is the progressive realization of unified selfhood through unconditional commitment to God.

In his remarkable book-length essay entitled *Purity of Heart Is to Will One Thing*, Kierkegaard brings all this—his whole theistic moral philosophy—to its appropriate climax. Indeed, the essay was written as 'spiritual preparation for the office [that is, the religious ritual] of confession'; but it contains what confronts the reflective reader as genuine moral philosophy and provocative argumentation in support of ethical theism, whether Kierkegaard intended it in that way or not. 'Purity of heart' is of course the state of the individual who, justified before God in Christ, has been morally regenerated and is progressively achieving unified selfhood (authentic human existence) through the extended application of the unconditional moral authority of God to his moral life and practice by willing the Good in God as the sole unitary Good. Of course, the practical goal of all moral philosophy is to achieve such a unified selfhood in a progressively realized sense, to become the authentic and genuine self that I morally ought to be. But the true moral Good, if the commitment to it, or willing of it, is to result in integrated selfhood, must be absolutely unitary, devoid of all diversity, if its pursuit is to avoid the double-mindedness or even multiple-mindedness that, through plurality and divisiveness of purpose, would result in personal disintegration, rather than personal integration and wholeness both in oneself and in one's moral relation to God. Kierkegaard argues accordingly that God alone, in his transcendent moral personhood, is such a totally unitary End or Good. For any other or alternative view of goodness, the unity of the 'moral' goal is only a superficial, apparent unity which, on analysis and in moral practice, resolves itself into a self-destructive multiplicity. This is certainly true of the ordinary 'goods' of human life—pleasure, honor, riches, power, for example; but it is also true (though Kierkegaard does not argue the point in detail) of various moral ideals found in normative ethical theories that are less than fully theistic. This is especially the case with naturalistic theories—hedonism is a prime example, since pleasure as a moral goal dissolves itself virtually by definition into endless variety and multiplicity with a resultant sacrifice of unitary purpose. If this is less strikingly the case with ethical idealism, it is because every version of ethical idealism (Platonism, Hegelianism, Kantianism, for example) contains, even if unintentionally, an implicit theistic thrust in its claim that the ultimately right or good is transcendent and changeless in its moral authority; remove that implicit theistic core, and the multiplicity, divisiveness, and disintegration will break out afresh. And there is this danger even in the recognition of God as the true unitary Good (and this Kierkegaard does emphasize): for if one's commitment to the Good is for the sake of external reward, or out of the fear of punishment, or is a commitment only to certain degree (reserving for oneself an area of diverse and finite 'good'), the double-mindedness is everywhere apparent. No; to be genuine one's commitment to the unitary Good in God must be for the sake of the

9.97b) But the Good must be absolutely unitary if it is to correlate with integrated selfhood, rather than ending in disintegration.

9.98) God alone is such a unitary Good;

9.99) all other moral ideals resolve into a self-destructive multiplicity.

9.100) This is true not only of ordinary human goods, but also of alternative normative moral ideals, whether naturalistic or idealistic, unless there is an implied theistic core in the theory.

9.101) Even commitment to God can be conjoined with double-mindedness through motives of reward, fear, and limitation in commitment.

Good (for the sake of God) alone, and it must be unqualified and unconditional. At the same time, Kierkegaard suggests and implies that, in fact, if one so commits oneself to God, it is often the case that God, in his overwhelming generosity, will respond to that commitment with external rewards as means of moral realization and practice. But there must be no hypocrisy, no double-mindedness here—one's commitment must never be for the sake of that supererogatory generosity on God's part. Indeed, a life stripped of all external support, and finding its sustenance in God alone, would still be one sort of fullest and best moral life. So for Kierkegaard it is either God as sole unitary Good and the conjoined achievement of authentic human selfhood, or it is a disguised multiplicity that leads to moral disintegration and destruction, perhaps even perdition.

Again, and for one last time in this treatise, there is the task of critical evaluation. As in the case of my assessment of earlier versions of ethical theism, I cannot deal here with the question of the general plausibility or otherwise of theism as a metaphysical perspective. In the case of Kierkegaard, such an analysis would be useless in any case, since he maintains that there is no rationally objective case for theism (or any other general metaphysical perspective) or for the Christian incarnation claim (that God was incarnate in Jesus Christ), precisely on the ground that the ideal of rational objectivity itself is in serious question, so that religious-metaphysical truth can only be approached through truth construed as subjectivity and paradox, understood in Kierkegaard's particular way. Nor will I develop any detailed critique of either Kierkegaard's attack on rational objectivity or his conception of truth as subjectivity and paradox. It is quite enough to point out that Kierkegaard's own arguments against the ideal of rational objectivity are intelligible as criticisms only if they are themselves interpreted as rationally objective truth claims (which would be existentially contradictory), since otherwise they would have to be interpreted as attitudinal projections of Kierkegaard's own subjectivity as an individual and would therefore not constitute any genuine criticism of his own or anyone else's epistemological method. Perhaps Kierkegaard's rejection of rational objectivity was motivated by his having viewed the plausibility of that ideal solely through his use of Hegel's unwar-

9.102) If commitment is single-minded, God sometimes gives rewards as well;

9.103) but the pursuit of God as the sole unitary Good must never be for the sake of such rewards.

9.104) Critical evaluation of Kierkegaard's ethic, as to the relation between epistemology and metaphysics: 9.104a) Since Kierkegaard rejects the ideal of rational objectivity, any rational case for theism would be regarded by him as irrelevant or even perverse;

9.104b) but his own arguments against rational objectivity are themselves irrelevant unless they are interpreted as rationally objective truth claims.

ranted and virtually incredible rationalistic self-confidence. In any case, it is important to point out that there is no necessary logical connection between Kierkegaard's epistemological relativism and irrationalism, on the one hand, and his bold commitment to theistic metaphysics and ethics on the other. Quite the contrary, for one can urge that there is in fact a clear inconsistency between Kierkegaard's subjectivist epistemology and his equally evident objectivism in metaphysics and ethics, since in Kierkegaard's conceptual framework that latter objectivism would itself have to be viewed (consistently) as an attitudinal projection on the part of Kierkegaard. I therefore prefer to set the epistemological issue aside and raise instead the question whether, if theism is presumed to be rationally plausible in some objectivist sense (like that of Augustine or Aquinas), Kierkegaard's ethic is a critically reasonable version of ethical theism.

From that point of view, I judge Kierkegaard's ethical perspective, especially in *Purity of Heart*, as one of the most appealing and provocative available. His overall argument (which perhaps he does not think of as an argument in the philosophical sense) is a modern version of the general case already developed by Augustine and Aquinas. All ethical naturalisms (with hedonism and its aesthetic immediacy as the paradigm case) fall away by failing to provide any genuinely objective criterion of morality; all truly ethical thinking must view the Good at least as transcendent essence or principle to provide ethical objectivity; but abstract essence and principle cannot in themselves be viewed as the ultimate Good or the basis of genuine moral obligation. The Good (both moral and nonmoral) can be nothing less than personal, if true moral objectivity is to be plausibly maintained—and this is theism in ethics.

Kierkegaard's ideal of authentic and integrated personal selfhood, as the moral goal for finite moral agents, is the clear recognition of the principle of the intrinsic worth of personal being, which Kierkegaard also clearly envisions as grounded in the transcendent moral personhood of God. But above all, his penetrating argument that the ultimate Good must be unitary if authentic human selfhood is to be achieved in integrative wholeness, and that only God as the unitary Good truly meets this requirement, while lesser moral ideals fall apart in a disruptive

9.104c) There is no necessary logical connection between Kierkegaard's epistemological relativism and his metaphysical/ethical objectivism, except for the evident inconsistency between them;
9.104d) so the important issue is whether, given theism, Kierkegaard's ethic is a plausible version of an ethic so based.
9.105) Kierkegaard's argument in *Purity of Heart* is a modern version of the case for ethical theism in Augustine and Aquinas:
9.106) naturalism provides no objectivity;

9.107) idealism rests on abstract essence or principle;
9.108) only the Good as personal provides true objectivity.

9.109) Integrated personal selfhood and intrinsic personal worth have their sole adequate objective ground in God as the ultimate unitary Good, while all lesser ideals fall apart into a disintegrative multiplicity.

and disintegrative multiplicity that leads to self-destruction—that argument (or moral exhortation, if you prefer) seems telling indeed. Is that after all what is finally behind Kant's variously interpreted statement that 'I ought' implies 'thou shalt'? Either God or the self-contradictory denial of moral objectivity.

_{9.110) Kierkegaard's view is compatible with the claim that nothing truly valuable in human experience is excluded by commitment to God as the ultimate Good, while yet unique individuals present a variety of ways in which that Good can be lived out in detail.}

Finally, although Kierkegaard does not appear to emphasize the point, his ethical perspective is fully compatible with the claim, common to Augustine and Aquinas, that nothing truly valuable and worthwhile in the range of actual or possible human experience is either proscribed or excluded on moral grounds for those who aim at unconditionally committing themselves to God as the sole unitary Good. The absolute God-relationship takes up into itself all the ordinary goods of human life, and it can be brought into harmony with all the details and decisions involved in human tasks, even if, in humble self-acceptance, the human self must acknowledge before God that one's actual achievement of this wholeness and harmony is always fragmentary and sometimes unavoidably misdirected in part. At the same time, Kierkegaard clearly recognizes the uniqueness of the individual and the resultant variety of the ways in which unconditional commitment to God as the unitary Good can be lived out in the details of any given personal life. On the whole, then, I judge Kierkegaard's version of Christian theistic ethics as a highly plausible and provocative way of construing this sort of moral philosophy.

<sub>9.111) General conclusion on ethical theism:
9.111a) Moral objectivity implies the Good as transcendent personal Mind;</sub>

More generally, and with respect to the whole tradition of normative ethical theism, I find the overall transition of thought which moves beyond every ethical naturalism to the view that the ultimately good or right must be transcendent (in the sense I have explained), and which then argues that this transcendent moral ideal cannot be adequately or perhaps even intelligibly construed otherwise than as ultimate personal Mind or God in the theistic sense—this entire transition, I repeat, I find to be the most reasonable normative ethical conclusion that could be made in the elucidation of the concept of moral objectivity, so that, in consequence, I judge the sort of ethical perspective that has this general insight at its core as, in the end, more plausible than any purely naturalistic or purely idealistic normative ethical perspective. At the same time, I do not regard the case for ethical theism as any sort of formal demonstration: it is instead an accumulation of relevant considerations and arguments that make it a rationally plausible ethical perspective to believe in; and, in my opinion, the case makes it more plausible to believe in ethical theism than in any naturalistic or idealistic alternative, although I respect the epistemic rights of those who think otherwise, since moral lunacy is not the only alternative to ethical theism. Of course, in a total systematic sense, the case for ethical theism depends on the rational plausibility of theistic metaphysics in general (of which I have had much to say elsewhere). The further step to a Christian version of theism is an issue for religious apologetics and philosophy of religion (of which I have also written elsewhere). Obviously I cannot here fill out those parts of the argument in detail. I can only say that the ethical considerations I have discussed themselves compose an equally significant part of any philosophically plausible case for what I will call the truth claim of the Christian worldview itself.

9.111b) yet the case for ethical theism is not a formal demonstration: it is rather a matter of relatively higher plausibility.

9.112) The case depends on the rational plausibility of theistic metaphysics;
9.113) but this in turn finds support in ethical objectivism as already treated;

9.114) and both ethical and metaphysical theism provide a part of the case for the Christian worldview itself.

Chapter X

In Retrospective Reflection: An Epilogue

How, then, might a reasonable person weave together the threads of our extended and varied analysis? To answer this question, a person needs to be sure that one understands what the ethical theism, for which I have argued, involves and implies. It does not imply that any or all other normative ethical theories are vacuous or devoid of significant ethico-philosophical content or substance. Nor does it imply that a person could not find some alternative meta-ethical stance, to the one I have argued, to be logically conjoinable to normative ethical theism. As far as meta-ethics is concerned, one might go with a deontological approach rather than with the modified teleological position I have tried to defend; but it is hard for me to see how a person could opt for any alternative to some version of ethical intuitionism (even if it is quite different from mine), since definism and non-cognitivism seem both to entail the 'death' of any sort of moral objectivism. Since I regard radical ethical relativism as leaving us with ethical preferences without any objective ethical truths, and since I view such a relativism as internally inconsistent and incoherent, it follows that ethical or moral objectivism is 'bedrock' for me. If not, then the whole of normative ethics would be purely descriptive and contain no genuine ethical element whatever (which would be to dismiss normative ethics from any serious philosoph-

10.1) Elements of an adequate total perspective:

10.1a) the recognition of alternative outlooks as partially plausible;

10.1b) modified teleological intuitionism;

10.1c) ethical objectivism (*vs.* radical ethical relativism) is essential;

10.1d) libertarian incompatibilism;	ical consideration at all). As for the controversy between determinists and indeterminists, while I respect those who dismiss the issue as morally irrelevant, along with those who think that rigorous determinism and the morally relevant sense of freedom (whether in the sense of agent causality or not) are both true and logically compatible, I see no way to render the notion of objective moral responsibility intelligible unless those who are to be judged morally responsible are genuinely free in a sense that is logically incompatible with any such determinism.
10.1e) ethical objectivism is a starting point for normative ethics;	Since the viability of any normative ethical theory whatever, in a genuinely moral or ethical sense, hinges, as I see it, on moral objectivism, I judge all theories that imply (whether admittedly or not) radical ethical relativism as critically defective just for that reason, while I fully and freely admit that countless moral *beliefs* are doubtless individually and culturally relative. The question of normative ethics that is of central concern then becomes: Which normative ethical perspective provides the most plausible conceptual framework for ethical objectivism? In response
10.1f) ethical theism (but interpreted as subsuming many valid elements in naturalism and idealism).	to that question, I have already argued at length the claim that ethical naturalism gives way to ethical idealism, and ethical idealism in turn, to ethical theism. But in the turning, I take much that is central to naturalism and idealism along with me in my thinking. Pleasures that are compatible with individual and social moral well-being, personal and social integration as elements in the pursuit of that well-being, the achievement of authentic selfhood as the core of that well-being, the intrinsic worth of persons as the central principle and content of that well-being, the test of universalizability without inconsistency as the proximate criterion of that well-being in particular cases—all this is quite consistently subsumed (along with much else that I forbear to mention) in what it means to commit oneself to the transcendent personal God of theism as the sole ultimate and
10.2) Commitment to God as the Good assimilates into itself all that is truly worthwhile and valuable.	unitary moral Good in the objective sense. To bring all these elements together in such a moral commitment to God is the essence of the absolute God-relationship. Nothing truly worthwhile or valuable in either the moral or the non-moral sense is left behind in the commitment to God as the true moral Good. That is perhaps (even more than perhaps) what Jesus meant by saying that he came to bring abundant life

to human beings (John 10:10); and it is certainly what the apostle Paul meant when he said that, while bodily exercise is profitable to a certain extent (the goods of the body are morally important), the worship and service of God are profitable for the realization of all truly valuable ends, since they promise fulfillment in this present life as well as in the next (1 Timothy 4:8).

Amor vincit omnia!

Index

Absolute, The, 144, 306
   see also God

Absolute Idealism, 174, 281, 297–313
   Bradley's Concept of, 303–6
   Critical Response to, 306–13
   Hegel's Concept of, 297–303
   see also Ethical Absolutism; Ethical Idealism

Absolute Mind, 10, 121, 160–61, 342–43, 359
   Hegel's Concept of, 114, 174, 296–99, 303
   As Ultimate Good, 367, 380

Absolute Spirit, 121, 297–300
   Reconciliation in, 307–8, 311–12

Acceptance, Rational, 272–73

Act(s)
   Agent Causality View of, 113, 124–26, 129–36, 145–46
   Alternatives for, 110–11, 151–52, 179, 225
   Consequences of, 39, 65
   Contingent, 156–57, 163
   Deontological/Teleological Assessments of, 44–47
   Determination of, 115–22, 154, 156
   Divine Foreknowledge and, 161, 162, 349–50
   Efficiency in, 227
   Evil, 211, 302, 320, 348–49
   Free, 109–14, 128–29, 145–46, 148
   Guidance for, 63–64, 67
   Hedonism's Influences on, 182, 185–88, 195–96, 197, 198, 200, 201
   Judging, 39, 43
   Logically Necessary, 271
   Moral, 29–30, 46–54, 72, 82, 159, 210–11, 219, 292, 321–23, 334, 356, 361, 375
   Morally Relevant, 59–60, 112–13, 121–22, 156
   Moral Responsibility for, 130–34, 148
   Motives for, 4, 112, 301–2
   Rational Control of, 207
   Right/Good, 25, 26, 31–32, 104–5, 179, 209, 286–87, 303, 305–6, 319
   Rightness or Wrongness of, 10–11, 19–20, 22, 33–34, 45–46, 75–76, 89, 93–94, 164, 182, 305
   Rules Governing, 316, 318
   Utilitarian, 181–82
   Virtues *vs.* Vices of, 66, 68, 208–9, 216
   see also Choice(s), Moral

Advice, Ethical/Moral, 11, 171, 183, 190, 247, 284, 292–93

Agent Causality View of Personal Freedom, 112–13, 115, 117–18, 165

Index

Augustine's Defense of, 351–52
  Author's Support of, 123–28, 241–42
  Criticisms and Responses, 145–64
  Divine Foreknowledge and, 348–50
  Moral Freedom as, 333–35, 355, 384
  Rigorous Determinism *vs.,* 235, 322, 333, 384
  Summary of, 127–45
  see also Personal Freedom
Agents, 224, 305–6
  Advice to, 292
  Capacity to Act Otherwise, 109–12, 117–18, 120, 123, 125–26, 130–34, 151–55, 163, 227, 232, 362
  Choices by, 3, 83, 102, 136, 138–39, 159–60, 318
  Hedonism's Influence on, 185–87, 189, 192
  Intelligent, 360–61, 362
  Intrinsic Worth of, 55, 59, 229, 233, 261–62
  Knowledge of, 39, 54, 56, 137–39, 142, 219
  Moral, 135, 161, 208–9, 335
  Moral Obligations of, 258, 260, 312, 357
  Moral Responsibility of, 110–22, 126, 129, 146–47, 183, 229, 248, 271–72, 274–75, 310–11, 322
  Nature and, 174
  Personal Freedom of, 10, 53, 109, 156, 227–28, 246, 278, 349–50, 356, 361, 369
  Rational, 347, 368–69, 370, 373
  Self-Determining Causality of, 129–31, 134, 137–40, 142–44, 146, 157–60, 348
  see also Motivations/Motives
Agreement, Moral, 93–94
Altruistic Hedonism, 181–82
Analytical Ethics, 8, 9–12, 17–24, 170, 186, 265–66

Anthropos, 205–6
  see also Human Beings
Antinomies, 328
A Posteriori Principles, 286, 314–15
Appetites, Control of, 360, 361
Applied Ethics, 11, 12
Approval, 68, 79
  Ethical Terms Expressing, 63, 64, 65, 67
A Priori Principles, 192, 250, 286, 290, 314–15
Arguments
  Moral, 9, 60, 76–79, 80, 89
  Nonethical Premises for, 26–27
  Open-Question, 36–37
  Uses of Normative Terms in, 17, 20–21, 23
Aristippus, 179
Aristocrats. *See* Free Spirits, Aristocratic; Master-Morality of the Aristocrats
Aristotle, 59, 169, 193, 261, 262, 282
  Dewey Compared with, 220–23, 224
  Ethics, 190, 204–5, 212–13, 217, 219–22, 289, 293, 294
  Moral Philosophy, 170–71, 218–20, 340, 359
  Principle of Rationality, 205–6, 209–11, 214, 217, 218–20
  Realistic Humanism, 204–14
  Thomas Aquinas Compared with, 362
  View of God, 178, 203
  On Virtue, 365
Arminian View of Liberty, 156–57
Assertions. *See* Propositions
Atheism
  Nietzsche's, 249
  Sartre's, 237–38, 243–45, 249
Attitudes
  Changing, 272–73, 275, 276
  Ethical Disagreements over, 76–77, 79
  Ethical Terms Expressing, 63, 64, 65

Attitudinalism, 73–81
  Critical Response to, 77–81
  Summary of, 73–77

Aufhebung. See Reconciliation

Augustine, Saint, 370
  Critical Response to, 354–57
  Ethical Theism, 341–57, 379
  Ethics, 367
  As Follower of Plato, 297, 342–45, 354–55, 358
  Historical Background, 342–43
  Metaphysics, 354–55
  Moral Philosophy, 175, 354–55
  Thomas Aquinas Compared with, 362, 365–67, 380

Authority
  God's, 374, 375–77
  Hegel's Concept of, 301, 303
  Knowledge by, 94
  Moral, 60, 102, 171–72, 174, 203, 224, 247, 293
  Of Moral Law, 323–29, 334
  Nonrational Beliefs in, 253, 257
  Reason as, 294
  Unconditional, 96

Aversion(s), 67, 90, 239, 240, 265

Avoidability View of Personal Freedom, 110–11, 115, 117, 147–48, 152–54, 165
  see also Agents, Capacity to Act Otherwise

Axiology, 5

Ayer, Alfred Jules, 73–76, 77, 79, 98, 103

Balance, 200, 221, 226, 229, 232, 289, 293–94
  see also Moderation

Beatitude, Final, 359, 364, 366, 369

Behavior, 80, 186, 201, 247
  Guidance for, 63–64, 66, 206

Being(s)
  Contingent, 245, 346–47
  Descartes' Concept of, 263
  Determination of, 118–19
  Essence of, 297–98
  Goodness of, 10, 328–29, 344
  Intrinsic Moral Worth of, 320–21, 325
  Personal, 142–43
  Rational, 236–37, 291, 332, 347–48, 360–62
  Totality of, 305–6, 309, 315
  Truth about, 7n
  Ultimate, 160–61, 284, 289
  see also Human Beings; Non-Being; Substance

Beliefs
  Causes of, 137–39
  Ethical Disagreements over, 76–77, 79
  Logical Status of, 240, 253, 258, 262
  Metaphysical, 321–22, 326
  Non-Rational *vs.* Rational, 256–58, 261
  see also Moral Beliefs

Belief-Truth Fallacy, 99

Beneficence, 84–85

Benevolence, 70–71, 189, 199
  see also Virtue(s)

Bentham, Jeremy, 19, 26–27, 179–80, 181, 185, 188, 196–97

Beyond Good and Evil (Nietzsche), 248

Blame, Moral, 66, 68

Body, 263–64, 274–75, 287, 345–46, 352
  see also Mind/Body Identity

Bondage, Moral. *See* Emotional Bondage

Bradley, Francis Herbert
  Absolute Idealism of, 28, 114, 303–6, 316
  Critical Response to, 311–13
  Intuitive Subsumption, 46n2

Brandt, Richard B., 83

Broad, Charlie Dunbar, 36, 42

Index

Burtt, Edwin A., 281
Butler, Joseph, 126, 193

Calculus of Hedonistic Measurement, 185, 188
"Can," Implications of, 322, 323
Categorical Imperatives, 318, 320, 321, 327–29
   see also Imperatives/Imperativism
Categories, 179, 237, 243, 250, 292
   A Priori, 314, 317, 327–28
   see also Classes
Causality
   Divine, 118, 119, 120, 264, 296, 326, 359, 360, 362
   Moral, 156
   Nietzsche's View of, 258
   A Priori Categories of, 317
   Self-Determining, 157–60
Causal Universality View of Determinism, 122, 131, 134
   Agent Causality View Compared with, 113, 115–18
   Author's Support of, 123–28, 164–65
   As Principle of Reason, 130, 145–46, 159–60, 192
Character
   Corruption of, 348–49
   Formation of, 206, 209, 216
   Greek Ideals of, 350–51
   Moral, 52, 54, 82, 210–11, 229, 232–33, 336, 341, 363, 364
   States of, 208–9, 303, 361–62
   Transformation of, 276
Choice(s), Moral
   Agent Causality View of, 113, 124–26, 129–36
   Alternatives for, 49n3, 110–11, 136, 148, 151–52, 179
   Causes of, 159–60
   Consequences of, 3–4, 34–35, 102, 181, 227

Contingent, 156–57, 163
Determination of, 115–22, 154, 156, 301, 311
Divine Foreknowledge and, 162, 349–50
Free, 1, 109–14, 142, 145–46, 148, 277, 322, 348–50, 356, 361, 362–63, 369
Guidance for, 10–11, 63–64, 83, 84–85, 99, 310
Hedonism's Influences on, 182, 187, 188, 195–96, 200, 201
Individual, 237, 238–39, 245
Logically Necessary, 271
Moral Relevance of, 112–13
Rational, 207, 273, 302
Rightness of, 49–51, 83–85, 303, 305, 375
Rigorous Determinism of, 161
Situational Relativism and, 96
Uncaused, 145–46
   see also Act(s); Decision(s); Motivations/Motives
Christianity/Christians, 114, 364
   Kierkegaard on, 370, 376
   Metaphysics of, 359
   Moral Philosophy of, 243, 341–44
   Sartre on, 249
   Teachings of, 358–59
   Theism of, 349, 354–55, 373, 381
   see also Hebrew-Christian Theism
City of God, 341, 352
   see also Earthly City; Heavenly City
Classes, 204–5, 212–14, 243, 282, 295, 346, 360
   see also Categories; Essence(s)
Cognitivism, 25–61, 84
   Definist, 25–42
   Ideal Observer Theory of, 85–87
   Intuitionist, 42–61
   Language of, 23, 73–74, 77
   Logical Positivist Doctrine of, 78
   Non-Cognitivism *vs.*, 17–24, 81, 85, 87
Commands, 74, 79–80

Commendation, Ethical Terms Expressing, 63, 64

Communities
　Moral, 295, 311–12, 321
　Philosophical, 124, 169
　Social, 300

Compatibilism, 7, 8, 109, 112, 147, 150, 271
　see also Strong Compatibilism; Weak Compatibilism

Concepts, 6, 149, 299

Concluding Unscientific Postscript (Kierkegaard), 370

Conclusions, Ethical/Moral, 72, 91–92
　Disagreement over, 79
　Non-Ethical Premises for, 26–27, 38–39
　Truth or Falsity of, 67, 137
　see also "Is-Ought" Thesis

Concreteness, Hegel's Concept of, 297–99, 307–8

Conduct. *See* Behavior

Consciousness, Individual. *See* Mind; Self-Consciousness

Consequences, 44–56, 81–84
　Of Choices, 3–4, 34–35, 102, 181, 227
　Good/Right, 44–45, 48–50, 72, 83, 105, 164
　Hedonistic, 185, 186, 187, 188, 192, 196–97, 200, 201
　Individual, 225, 238–39
　Moral, 10, 23, 39, 46–47, 50–56, 65, 164, 319
　Nonmoral, 46–47, 52
　Painful, 179
　Responsibility for, 238–39
　Well-Being Related to, 223

Consistency, Rational, 7, 318–19

Constraint, Absence of, 111, 156, 227

"Contemporary Philosophy and the Analytic-Synthetic Dichotomy" (Hackett), 73n1

Contingency
　Of Acts and Choices, 156–57, 163
　Of Being, 245, 346–47
　Open-Ended, 227–28

Contra-Causal View of Personal Freedom, 109–10, 113, 124–25, 128, 129–30

Contract, Hegel's Concept of, 300–301

Contradiction, Principle of, 318–20, 323
　see also Law of Contradictions

Corruption, 346–48, 356–57, 363, 364, 367

Cosmos, 315, 322

"Could-Would" Claims, 154–55

Courage, 208, 209, 288, 293, 350, 362

Creation, 343–47, 356, 359, 360, 368–69

Critique of Judgment (Kant), 313

Critique of Practical Reason (Kant), 313

Critique of Pure Reason (Kant), 313, 326

Custom, Hegel's Concept of, 300

Cyrenaicism, School of, 179

Data
　Ethical, 8–9, 11, 29, 190
　Factual, 6, 7, 27, 65
　see also Fact(s)

Decision(s)
　Corrupt, 305, 348–49
　Deontological *vs.* Teleological Approaches to, 56–57
　Guidance for, 182, 310
　Hedonistic, 374
　Human destiny of, 1–4
　Limits on, 241–42
　Moral, 10–11, 63–64, 210, 219, 224, 231, 292, 328, 330–31
　Personal, 237, 238–39, 241, 245
　Right/Good, 304, 305–6
　see also Choice(s), Moral

Definism, 25–42, 57, 58, 89, 91, 95

Index

Definism (cont.),
 Critical Response to, 30–32, 36–42, 57, 60–61, 92, 383
 Rejection of, 81
 Summary of, 25–27, 29–30, 37–42
 see also Meta-Ethical Definism

Definist Fallacy Argument, 37–42

Deliberation, Moral, 225, 227
 see also Truth Claims

Deontology
 Intuitionism and, 51–57, 60, 104–5, 164
 Meta-Ethical Approach of, 44–47, 383

De Rerum Natura (Lucretius), 185

Descartes, René, 263

Descriptive Ethics, 8–9, 10–12

Descriptive Relativism, 65–73, 96–97, 103
 Critical Response to, 69–73
 Summary of, 65–69

Descriptive Statements, 64, 71, 88, 91

Descriptivism. *See* Empirical Description; Meta-Ethical Cognitivism

Desire(s), 233–34, 287–89, 316–17, 328
 Control of, 206–7, 209, 211, 214–18, 221–22, 232–33, 293, 360–62
 Emotional Bondage to, 265–69, 277
 Freedom of, 227
 Frustrated, 272–73, 276
 As Grounds for Moral Claims, 67, 225
 Moral, 187, 228–30, 235, 262
 Moral Duty *vs.*, 330–32
 As Motivation, 49, 53, 192–93, 304
 Realization of, 55, 223
 Rightness or Wrongness of, 48, 90–91
 Subjective, 303
 Utilitarianism of, 82–83

Despair, 376

Destiny, Human, 1–4

Determinism
 Capacity to Act and, 147, 152–55
 Critical Response to, 108, 145–65, 384
 Freedom *vs.*, 109, 122–23, 145–46, 165, 227, 249, 273, 278, 311
 Language and, 151–52
 Morally Relevant Sense of, 125–26
 Problems Concerning, 108
 Rejection of, 322
 Resolution of Problems, 123–28
 Varieties of, 114–23
 Views of, 109–14
 see also Causal Universality View of Determinism; Religious Determinism; Rigorous Determinism

Dewey, John, 90, 204, 261
 Aristotle Compared with, 220–23, 224
 Ethics, 98, 221–29, 235–36, 293–94
 Pragmatic Humanism, 220–36

Dialectical Oppositions, 297–98, 302–3, 307–9

Disagreements, 93, 97

Disapproval, 67, 68, 79

Discourse. *See* Empirical Description; Moral Discourse; Non-Normative Discourse

"Does Moral Philosophy Rest on a Mistake?" (Prichard), 47–49

Duty, 10–11, 43, 45, 49–53, 189, 300
 Aristotle on, 220
 As Virtue, 216–17
 see also Moral Duty

Earthly City, 353–54, 357

Edwards, Jonathan, 114, 161
 Compatibilism, 155–59

Ego, 142–43, 144, 275
 see also Self, The

Egoistic Hedonism, 180–83, 199, 201

Electionism, 351, 355–56, 365–66, 369

Emanations, 343

Emotional Bondage, 265–69, 270, 374–75
   Deliverance from, 271–72, 275–76, 277

Emotions, 289, 294, 331
   Active *vs.* Passive, 267–68, 287–88
   Control of, 280, 360, 361
   Positive, 277
   Subjective, 303
   see also Feelings; Passions

Emotivism, 73–81
   Critical Response to, 77–81
   Summary of, 73–77

Empirical Definism, 29
   see also Naturalistic Definism

Empirical Description
   Ethical Sentences Used in, 25, 63, 64, 77, 88
   Of Moral Causes, 116
   Testing Moral Claims with, 27, 28–30, 33–34, 43

Empirical Determination, 73–75

Empirical Ethical Theory, 223, 230

Empirical Possibility, 111

Empiricism, 6, 73, 192–93, 313–14, 325

End(s)
   Desirable, 187, 189–90
   As Means, 221–23, 229
   Moral, 227, 304
   Pleasure as, 193
   Proper, 360–61, 363–64
   Pursuit of, 289
   Supreme, 4, 365, 366, 368, 376, 377

Energy, Active, 287, 288, 293–94, 360–62

Entelechy, 205–6
   see also Human Beings, Good

Environment
   Habit and, 226
   Individual and Social, 222, 225
   Influence of, 1, 234, 241–42

Epicurus, 180, 184–85

Epistemological Necessity, 162–63

Epistemological Relativism, Kierkegaard's Concept of, 379

Epistemology
   Author's, 5–7
   Definism and, 28
   Foundationalism in, 57
   Kant's, 313–15, 325
   Plato's, 282, 285–86
   Principles of, 58, 280–81
   Rational Objectivity, Rejection of, 370, 378–79
   see also Logical Positivism; Radical Empirical Epistemology; Radical Epistemological Relativism

Equality, 55, 84, 200

Equilibrium, 156–57, 293

Essay on Free Will, An (Van Inwagen), 135

Essence(s), 174, 237, 344–45
   Abstract, 367, 379
   Actualization of, 361
   Doctrine of, 204–5
   God's, 263–64, 269–70, 272, 359, 364
   Human, 3–4, 10, 205–6, 213–14, 220, 224, 231–32, 245–46, 262
   Instantiation of, 245–46
   Plato on, 282–86
   Real, 212–13, 221
   Sartre's Rejection of, 237–38, 243, 245
   Transcendent, 289–90, 295–97
   Universal, 243–44, 290–91, 371
   see also Particulars; Universals

Essentialism, 281–97
   Critical response to, 289–97
   Summary of, 281–89

Eternal Cyclical Recurrence, Doctrine of, 249

Eternal Life. *See* Immortality

Ethical Absolutism, 96, 223–24, 225, 246

Ethical Analysis. *See* Analytical Ethics

Ethical Claims. *See* Moral Claims

Index

Ethical Emotivism, 95
Ethical Hedonism, 185–202, 316
    Consequences Defined in, 46, 200
    Critical Response to, 191–202
    Pleasure and, 178, 184–85, 188–202, 220
    Summary of, 43, 185–91
    Utilitarian, 199–200
Ethical Humanism, Sartre's Concept of, 261–62
Ethical Idealism, 104, 174, 278, 279–337, 353, 367
    Aristotle's, 218–20
    Ethical Theism and, 375, 377, 379, 384
    Metaphysical Orientation, 281–97
    Postulational Orientation, 174, 281, 313–37
    Subdivisions of, 280–81
    Summary of, 279–80
    see also Life, Morally Good; Normative Ethical Idealism; Philosophical Idealism
Ethical Naturalism, 379, 380, 384
Ethical Objectivism, 251, 261–62, 340, 367, 380–81
    Author's Support for, 383–84
    Kierkegaard's Concept of, 379
    Normative Ethics and, 10, 96–105, 117, 190, 230, 247, 270–71, 275–76, 366–67
    Radical Ethical Relativism *vs.*, 95–96, 99–101, 105, 127, 164–65, 225–27, 234–36
    Sartre's Rejection of, 246
    see also Objectivity
Ethical Relativism. *See* Radical Ethical Relativism
Ethical Statements
    Analysis of, 22–23
    Contradictory, 75–76
    Evaluative, 78, 89, 98
    Non-Cognitive Nature of, 74–75, 80–81, 98

    Non-Ethical Premises for, 26–28
    As Property Statements and, 87–89
    Propriety of, 65
    As Truth Claims, 63–64, 74, 78
    Validity of, 86–87
    see also Moral Claims; Propositions
Ethical Studies (Bradley), 303
Ethical Subjectivism, 75, 95, 261
Ethical Terms, 147–53
    Descriptive, 64–65
    Evaluative, 25, 63–65
    Logical Uses, 9, 17, 21, 26–28, 60
    Meanings, 9, 17, 26–28, 34, 43–44
    Moral Uses, 18, 43–44
    Non-Ethical Equivalents, 17, 18–19, 25, 27–29, 31–34, 36–42, 41–44, 57, 178
    Objectively Relational, 87–89
    Ordinary Language Thesis, 147–50
    Standard Usage, 32–33, 41
    Subjectively Relational, 87–89
    Unique Moral Properties, 104
    see also Normative Terms
Ethical Theism, 104, 174–75, 278, 325, 366–67, 383–84
    Ethical Idealism and, 375, 377, 379, 384
Ethics
    Aristotle's, 212–13, 217, 219–22, 289, 293, 294, 359
    Christian, 249
    Concepts and Principles, 5–8, 57–58
    Dewey's, 221–29, 235–36, 293–94
    Disagreements in, 89
    Empirical Theory of, 223, 230
    Hegel's Concept of, 300, 309–11
    In Human Nature, 221, 238
    Kant's, 313–26
    Kierkegaard's, 379
    Mathematics Contrasted with, 210
    Nietzsche's, 254, 258, 259–61
    Rational Objectivity in, 57–58, 82
    Sartre's, 240–41
    Theistic Perspectives, 339–42

Thomas Aquinas's, 366–67
see also Analytical Ethics; Applied Ethics; Descriptive Ethics; Meta-Ethics; Moral Beliefs; Normative Ethics; Philosophical Ethics

Ethics Proved in Geometrical Order (Spinoza), 262, 272

Euclidian Geometry, 371

Eudaimonia, 206
see also Happiness; Well-Being

Evaluation, 27, 64–65, 67–68, 172

Evil, 299, 309
   Augustine's Concept of, 342–57
   Goodness *vs.*, 122, 301–2, 310, 312, 375
   Hegel's Concept of, 310
   Kant's Concept of, 317, 320
   Moral, 9, 211, 270–71, 347–48, 356, 360–61
   Natural, 347–48
   Nietzsche's Concept of, 252
   Spinoza's Concept of, 265
   Ultimate, 345

Evolutionary Humanism, 204, 248–62
   Critical Response to, 254–62
   Summary of, 248–54

Evolutionary Naturalism, 173–74

Ewing, Alfred C., 42

Exhortations, 11, 74

Existence, 245–46, 332
   Aesthetic State, 374–75
   Evils of, 345, 347
   Finite, 356–57
   Human Moral, 376
   Kierkegaard's Concept of, 370–74
   A Priori Categories of, 317
   Totality of, 315

Existential Humanism, 204, 236–48
   Critical Response to, 240–48
   Summary of, 236–40

Existentialism, 101–2

Atheistic, 249
Impossibility of, 370–72
Meaning of, 236–37
Radical Subjectivity of, 237–38

Experience(s)
   Emotive, 194–95
   Empirical, 6, 30, 327
   Moral, 274–75
   Of Pain/Pleasure, 225
   Relevance of, 7
   Sense, 314

Extension, 264, 274
see also Thought/Extension Identity

Fact(s)
   Empirical, 76, 234
   Ethical Claims as, 90
   Ethical Disagreements over, 76–79
   Hume's Definition of, 69, 71–72
   Moral Judgments Based on, 91–93
   Nonmoral, 75
   Rational Discernment of, 67–69
see also Data

Faith, 321–22, 365, 372–73
see also God, Belief in

Falk, Werner David, 80

Fallacies, 37–38, 39, 40–41, 99

Falsity, 101
   Assessing, 31–34, 39–40, 43, 308
   Determination of, 73, 74, 75, 77
   Of Ethical/Moral Propositions, 22, 23, 66–67, 86–87, 97–98, 100
   Objective, 257
   Philosophical, 250, 254
   Truth *vs.*, 139–40

Families, 302–3

Fear, 50, 53, 71, 208

Feelings, 35, 96, 172, 194
   Ethical Terms Expressing, 63, 64, 65, 66–67
   As Grounds for Moral Claims, 225

Index

Feelings (cont.),
  Role in Moral Judgments, 10, 68–72, 103
  see also Emotions; Passions
Fidelity, 208, 216–17
1 Timothy 4:8, 385
Firth, Roderick, 85–87, 92
Foreknowledge, Divine, 160–63, 349–50, 356
Forgiveness, 335, 351, 364, 369–70
Formalistic Definism, 26, 28, 31, 36, 58
Formal Logic, 7, 22–26, 40–41, 63, 73–75, 77
Formal Logico-Mathematical Necessity, 276
Forms
  Absolute, 342–45
  God as Pure, 359, 367
  Plato on, 282–83, 285–86
  see also Classes; Essence(s)
Foundationalism, 6, 57
Frankena, William, 39–42, 83–85, 87, 90, 92
Freedom
  Arminian View of, 156–57
  Augustine's Concept of, 342–57
  Belief in, 174, 322
  Determinism *vs.*, 109, 122–23, 145–46, 165, 227, 249, 273, 278, 311
  Illusion of, 374–75
  Indeterminateness and, 115, 123, 124–25, 128–29, 165, 242, 246
  Kant's Concept of, 332–34
  Meanings of, 147–52
  Metaphysical, 227–28
  Moral, 227, 332–33, 351–52
  Morally Relevant Sense of, 311, 323
  Necessity and, 2, 114, 306
  see also Act(s), Free; Choice(s), Moral, Free; Personal Freedom
Freedom of Will (Edwards), 155–57

Free Spirits, Aristocratic, 248, 249, 251–52, 260
  see also Master-Morality of the Aristocrats
Free Will, 10, 135–36, 145–46, 361
  see also Volition; Will
Frustration, 272–73, 276

Gegensatz. *See* Dialectical Oppositions
Genealogy of Morals, The (Nietzsche), 248
Geneticism, 253, 254, 255–59, 261, 262
Goals
  Achievement of, 206, 221–22, 224–25
  Personal, 3–4
  Of Popular Morality, 190
  Pursuit of, 228, 233–35
  see also End(s)
God
  As Absolute, 174–75, 262–63
  Aristotle's Concept of, 178, 203, 359–62
  Belief in, 174, 257, 322, 324, 325, 334–37
  Causality of, 118, 119, 120, 264, 296, 326, 359, 360, 362
  Commands from, 26, 28, 31–32
  Commitment to, 341, 356, 357, 359–60, 363, 368, 374, 375–78, 380, 384–85
  As Creator, 343–47, 356, 359, 360, 368–69
  Essence of, 263–64, 269–70, 359, 364
  Existence of, 144, 339–40, 364, 374
  Fellowship with, 364, 366
  Foreknowledge Possessed by, 160–63, 349–50, 356
  Goodness of, 345, 347, 348–49, 351–52, 353
  In Hebrew-Christian Tradition, 296–97
  Kant's Concept of, 315, 332–33
  Knowledge of, 160–63, 328, 362, 364,

365, 368
As Locus of Essences, 243–44
Love and, 189, 268–69, 277, 353, 363, 368–69, 374
Man's Relationship with, 359, 368, 374, 375–77, 380, 384
Mill's View of, 178
As Mind, 343–44, 359, 380
Perfection of, 269, 335, 345–47, 356, 361
Personal, 10, 114, 174–75, 203, 324, 341, 343, 373
Plato's Concept of, 342–43
Power of, 362, 374, 375–76
Properties of, 85–86
Reality in, 269–70
Self-Existence of, 345–46
Spinoza's Concept of, 262–64, 266, 268–71
Thomas Aquinas's Concept of, 359–62, 367
As Ultimate Good, 335–36, 339, 345, 348, 350, 352–53, 355–57, 360–61, 363–64, 367, 375–80, 384
Will of, 123, 341
see also Atheism; City of God; Grace, Divine; Holy Spirit; Jesus Christ

Good/Goodness, 4, 10–12, 26–27, 170–75, 377
Actualization of, 302, 363
Aristotle's Concept of, 203–7, 217–18
Assessing, 30, 31–32
Augustine's Concept of, 342–57
Bradley's Concept of, 305–6
Dewey's Concept of, 224–25, 230–31, 234–35
Evil vs., 122, 301–2, 310, 312, 375
Of God, 345, 347, 348–49, 351–52, 353
Human, 205–7, 209–14, 214, 228–29, 261–62, 328–29, 364
Ideal of, 224, 365, 366
Judgments of, 195
Knowledge of, 288

Meaning of, 37, 43
Nietzsche's Concept of, 252
Objective Standard of, 366–67
Pleasure as, 19, 178–79, 201–2
Properties of, 87–88
Rightness Related to, 44–45, 49, 196
Spinoza's Concept of, 265
Transcendent, 174, 279–80, 284, 289
Truth of, 303
see also Moral Good/Goodness; Right/Rightness; Ultimate Good

"Good Reasons" Approach, 81–103
Critical Response to, 87–103
Summary of, 81–87

Grace, Divine, 335, 348, 351–52, 356, 364–68, 376
Thomas Aquinas's Concept of, 357–70

Greatest Happiness Principle, 188, 190

Guidance
In Decision-Making, 224
Ethical/Moral, 63–64, 65, 98, 230–31, 286–87, 310, 375
Intelligent, 228, 232
Of Reason, 293

Guilt, 351, 363, 364–65, 367, 376

Habit(s)
Of Character, 288, 362
Environment and, 226
Impulses and, 228, 231–33

Hackett, Stuart C., 73n1, 243

Happiness, 47, 206, 301, 316–17
Hedonistic, 188–90
see also Well-Being

Hard Determinism, 117
see also Rigorous Determinism

Hare, Richard Mervyn, 82–83, 83, 87, 90, 92

Harmony
Aristotle's Concept of, 207, 212, 220
Augustine's Concept of, 352–54

Index

Harmony (cont.),
    Dewey's Concept of, 221–23, 225–26, 228–29
    Integrative, 202–3, 230–34, 293, 315–16, 324, 380
    Moral, 359, 364, 366, 369
    Plato's Concept of, 289
    Social, 82, 207, 230, 357
    Spiritual, 352–53

Hartmann, Nicolai, 290

Heavenly City, 352, 353–54, 356–57

Hebrew-Christian Tradition, 118, 175, 296–97, 340, 356
    see also Christianity/Christians

Hedonism. *See* Egoistic Hedonism; Ethical Hedonism; Pleasure; Utilitarian Hedonism

Hedonistic Naturalism, 173, 178–202, 377, 379
    Activist, 179–80
    Arguments for, 185–91
    Meaning of, 178–79
    Psychological, 185–88, 199, 200–201
    Qualitative *vs.* Quantitative, 196–97
    Universalistic, 188, 199
    Utilitarian, 199–200, 201

Hegel, Georg Wilhelm Friedrich
    On Absolute Idealism, 281, 297–303, 337
    Critical Response to, 306–11
    Ethics, 300, 309–11
    On Freedom, 2, 114, 120–21
    Idealism, 174
    Philosophy of, 250, 254, 316, 354, 377, 378–79
    System of, 370–71

Highest Good. *See* Ultimate Good

Holy Spirit, 365, 376

Human Beings
    Actualization of, 231–33, 262, 265–66, 359–64
    Awareness States of, 194
    Duties of, 300
    Essence of, 3–4, 10, 205–6, 213–14, 220, 224, 231–32, 245–46, 262, 270
    Good, 203, 205–7, 209–14, 217–18, 261–62, 279–80, 287, 288, 328–29, 364
    Intrinsic Worth, 261–62, 295, 312–13, 320–21, 328–30, 336, 367, 384
    Moral Predicament of, 265–66, 275
    Moral Responsibility of, 125, 363, 369
    Nietzsche's Concept of, 248
    Peace among, 352–53
    Rationality of, 289
    Responses of, 10, 35, 66, 172, 231–32
    Rights of, 233, 294, 300
    Treatment of, 43, 325
    Well-Being of, 173–74, 211–15, 219–20, 223–25, 228, 230, 262, 320, 352, 362, 366
    see also Body; Mind; Personhood; Self, The; Soul

Humanism. *See* Ethical Humanism; Realistic Humanism

Humanistic Naturalism, 173, 202–62, 353
    Evolutionary Humanism, 204, 248–62
    Existential Humanism, 204, 236–48
    Pragmatic Humanism, 204, 220–36
    Realistic Humanism, 204–20
    Religious Humanism, 262–78

Hume, David, 143
    Agnosticism of, 244
    Definitions by, 69, 71–72
    Descriptive Relativism, 65–73, 103
    On Traditional Empiricism, 313, 327

Husserl, Edmund, Phenomenology of, 290

Ideal Cognitive Observer Theory, 36, 86–87

Idealism/Ideals. *See* Absolute Idealism; Ethical Idealism; Moral Ideals

Ideal Moral Observer, 81–103
    Critical Response, 87–103

Summary of, 81–87

Ideas, 5, 67, 274–75
    Absolute, 282–83, 286, 288, 295–96, 342–43

Identity, 32, 34, 68, 269, 301–2, 310
    Personal, 232, 275, 298
    Principles of, 243
    Ultimate Good, 291

Ignorance, 186, 266–69, 270, 275, 276, 280, 303

Immanental Pantheism, 269, 270–71

Immorality. *See* Evil, Moral

Immortality
    Augustine's Concept of, 351, 352
    Kant's Concept of, 174, 322, 323, 326, 332–33

Imperatives/Imperativism, 74, 79–80, 316–17
    see also Categorical Imperatives; Rules

Impulse(s), 217–18, 225, 228–30
    Control of, 206, 207, 209, 214, 216, 231–34
    Moral Beliefs Grounded in, 256, 262
    Truth Claims as, 250, 254
    Tyrannical, 248, 250, 258–59, 261

Inclinations, 156, 218, 293, 328–32, 361
    see also Motivations/Motives

Incompatibilism, 109, 120, 124, 136–37, 150, 322, 355
    see also Libertarian Incompatibilism

Inconsistency. *See* Contradictions

Indeterminateness, 109–10, 113, 114
    Abstract, 297–98
    Agent Causality View as, 117, 130
    Freedom as, 115, 123, 124–25, 128–29, 165, 242, 246

Indifference, Principle of, 2–3, 156–57

Individual, The, 225, 247, 374
    Duties of, 311, 312
    Empirical Abilities of, 241–42
    Unique Station of, 305, 311, 313
    see also Personal Freedom; Personhood; Self, The

Indulgence, 208–9, 214–15, 216–18, 233, 289
    see also Sensualistic Indulgence

Inferences, 75, 76

Infinite Regress, Argument, 52, 94, 105, 143–44, 154–55, 157–58, 171

Integration, Personal and Social, 225

Intelligence, 228, 284

Intelligibility, Rational, 321–23, 325, 332–36

Intensity, 179–80

Intentions, 35, 50–51, 54, 301–2, 310, 319
    see also Motivations/Motives

Intuitionism, 42–61, 81–82, 88
    Meta-Ethical, 44, 57–61, 90, 95, 103–4
    see also Modified Teleological Intuitionism

Intuitive Subsumption, 46n2

"Is-Ought" Thesis, 27, 38–39, 68, 71, 91–92, 95, 299

Jesus Christ, 384–85
    God Incarnated in, 364, 370, 373, 376, 378
    Redemption by, 351, 357, 364–65, 367, 370, 376

John 10:10, 385

Judgments, Ethical/Moral, 33–36, 43–45, 46n2, 48–49, 55–60
    Contradictory, 59, 75–76, 84
    Criterion for, 84–87, 182–83, 240, 310, 375
    Errors in, 50, 56, 58–59, 361
    Evaluative, 60
    Feelings' Role in, 68–72
    God's, 367

Index

Judgments(cont.),
    Hedonism's Influence on, 197, 198–201
    Moral Relevance of, 111
    Non-Ethical Premises for, 26–28, 29, 30, 32–33
    Objectivity of, 81, 83, 87, 89, 92–95, 235
    Propriety of, 103–4
    Rational Objectivity in, 193–94, 196, 288, 312
    Reason's Role in, 30, 67, 219–20
    Synthetic Apriorism, 314–15
    Truth or Falsity of, 66, 77, 316
    Uses of Normative Terms in, 9–10, 17, 20–21, 170

Justice, 199–200, 351, 357, 362
    Moral, 102, 289, 335–36
    Personal, 293
    Rational, 84–85

Justification. *See* Moral Justification

Kant, Immanuel, 169, 242, 281
    Epistemology, 313–15, 325
    Ethics, 313–26
    On Freedom, 332–34
    Idealism of, 174
    Metaphysics, 313–26
    On Moral Duty, 50, 51, 238, 329
    Moral Philosophy, 93, 187, 190, 316–17, 322, 328, 377, 380
    Nietzsche on, 251
    Postulational Orientation, 313–37
    Rational Empiricism of, 313–14
    Terminology of, 6

Kierkegaard, Søren
    Critical Evaluation of, 378–81
    Ethical Naturalism, 376–77, 379
    Ethical Theism, 175, 237, 341–42, 370–81
    Metaphysics, 379
    Summary of, 370–78

Knowledge, 56, 58, 206, 228
    Adequate, 267–69, 270, 271–73, 275, 276
    Agent's, 54, 56, 137–39, 142, 219
    By Authority, 94
    Empirical, 313–16, 332–33, 337
    Of Essences, 283–87
    Of God, 160–63, 328, 362, 364, 365, 368
    Goodness through, 347
    Metaphysical, 316–17, 326–28, 332–33, 337
    Moral, 57, 210, 316, 317–18
    Objective, 250, 326
    A Priori Principles of, 290, 313
    Pursuit of, 5–6, 214, 218–19, 272–73, 276–77, 315–16, 360–61, 361
    Of the Ultimate Good, 288, 292–93
    see also Foreknowledge, Divine

Language
    Cognitive Uses, 23, 73–74
    Ethical/Moral Uses, 29, 32–33, 35, 41–42, 80–81, 89, 103, 148–52, 253
    Forms of, 74, 81, 87
    Non-Cognitive Uses, 74–75
    see also Ethical Terms; Metalanguage; Normative Terms

Language, Truth, and Logic (Ayer), 73

Law(s)
    Of God, 352, 359, 363
    Hegel's Concept of, 300, 301, 302, 310
    Natural, 363
    Universal, 236–37
    see also Moral Law

Law of Contradictions, 6, 192, 255, 259, 308

Leibniz, Gottfried Wilhelm, 114, 327

Libertarian Incompatibilism, 110, 112, 124, 135, 384

Libertarianism, 109, 124, 130, 145, 160–61
    Edwards on, 156–58, 159

Liberty. *See* Freedom; Personal Freedom

Life
    Morally Good, 180, 202, 214–15, 218–21, 286, 288, 293–94, 352, 357, 378
    Stages of, 374–75
    see also Immortality

Logic, 5, 6, 12, 90
    Absolute Idealism and, 298–99, 311–12
    Ethical Disagreements over, 76–79
    Imperatives *vs.* Ethical Claims, 80
    Kierkegaard's, 370–72
    Laws of, 205, 277
    Moral Judgments Based on, 91–92
    Pure, 58, 277
    Statements of, 73, 170
    see also Formal Logic

Logical Necessitarianism, 120–23, 124, 135

Logical Necessity, 120, 121, 264, 266–67, 270, 272, 276, 336

Logical Positivism, 73, 78

Love, 295, 335, 336, 365
    see also God, Love and

Lucretius, 180, 184–85

Manicheans, 345

Master-Morality of the Aristocrats, 251–52, 258–59

Mathematics, 133, 210, 277, 371

Matter, 344–35, 359, 367

Mean Between Extremes, Doctrine of, 208–11, 214–16
    see also Balance

Meaning, 4, 12, 169–70, 315
    Standard Ethical Usage and, 148–52
    Subjectively Relational, 32–36

Mechanistic Determinism, 116–17, 122–23

Meta-Ethical Analysis, 17–21

Meta-Ethical Cognitivism, 22–23, 25–61
    Intuitionism and, 42–61

Meta-Ethical Definism, 29, 36, 57, 89, 91

Meta-Ethical Naturalism, 26–27, 178
    see also Naturalistic Definism

Meta-Ethical Non-Cognitivism, 22–23, 63–105
    Conclusions Regarding, 103–5
    Descriptive Relativism and, 65–73
    Meta-Ethical Emotivism and, 73–81
    Qualified Objectivist Non-Cognitivism, 81–103
    Summary of, 63–65

Meta-Ethics, 8, 9–13, 61, 383–84
    Author's Theory of, 104–5, 164–65
    Cognitivism and, 17–61
    Ethical Idealism and, 281–97
    General Conclusions, 164–65
    Non-Cognitivism and, 17–24, 63–105
    Normative Ethics Distinguished from, 169–73
    Theories of, 21–24, 29, 61, 103–5, 316

Metalanguage, 308–9
    see also Language

Metaphysical Claims, Moral Claims and, 10

Metaphysical Determinism, 109, 306, 355

Metaphysical Naturalism, 177–78

Metaphysical Necessity, 118, 162–63

Metaphysical Orientation, Ethical Idealism and, 281–97

Metaphysical Theism, 339–40, 366, 379, 381
    Kierkegaard's Concept of, 370, 378

Metaphysics
    Aristotle's, 212–13
    Augustine's, 354–55
    Author's views, 354
    Christian, 359
    Kant's, 313–26
    Kierkegaard's, 379
    Plato's, 289
    Spinoza's, 264–65, 269–70, 273, 275, 277

Index

Metaphysics (cont.),
    Theistic, 339–40, 347
    Theories of, 7–8, 127, 160–61, 173
    Worldviews Based on, 30, 173, 280–81
    see also Knowledge, Metaphysical

Methods of Ethics, The (Sidgwick), 42n1

Mill, John Stuart, 143, 169, 178, 181, 183–87, 189, 196–97, 199

Mind, 268, 327
    Essences and, 284, 285
    Faculties of, 279–80, 291–92, 313, 314, 315
    God as, 343–44, 359, 380
    Subjective, 300
    Training of, 286–87
    see also Absolute Mind; Objective Mind, Doctrine of

Mind/Body Identity, 263, 269, 270, 273–75
    see also Thought/Extension Identity

Moderate Rationalistic Apriorism, 6

Moderation, 207–11, 212, 214–18, 220, 222, 233–34, 289
    see also Balance

Modes, Finite, 263–64

Modified Teleological Intuitionism, 104–5, 164–65, 383

Moore, George Edward, 36, 42, 45, 47, 88
    Frankena's Criticisms of, 39–41

Moral Beliefs, 251, 261
    Analytic Approach, 8, 9–13
    Descriptive Approach, 8–9, 10–12
    Descriptive Relativism and, 96–97
    Individual, 165, 247, 384
    Meta-Ethical Approach, 8
    Nietzsche's, 253
    Non-Rational Factors Affecting, 97–98
    Normative Approach, 8, 11–12
    Origins of, 190, 262, 264
    Substantive Approach, 8, 11–12
    see also Beliefs

Moral Claims
    Ethical Hedonism and, 201
    Ethical Principles of, 90
    God's, 373
    Grounds for, 66–68, 178, 225
    Justification of, 52–53, 89, 91, 95–96, 170–71, 229–30
    Normative Terms for, 9–11, 18–20, 30
    Objectivity of, 81, 84, 87, 95–96, 103
    As Property Statements, 45
    Resolution of, 232–33
    Testing, 27–36, 39
    see also Truth Claims

Moral Discourse, 10, 17–21, 57, 63, 64–65, 77
    Meaning of, 16, 103, 105, 107
    Moral Distinctions in, 66–67
    Rendered Unnecessary, 27, 30, 35, 95

Moral Distinctions, 66–72, 271, 312, 375

Moral Duty, 47, 197–99, 201, 275, 334, 375
    Dewey's Concept of, 232–33
    Inclination *vs.*, 328–32
    Kant's Concept of, 328–29
    Law of, 237–38, 320–22, 336
    Moral Philosophy and, 202
    As Motivation, 53, 130, 191
    Personal Freedom and, 278
    Universal Principle of, 221, 254, 333–34
    Virtues Involving, 216–17, 325–26
    see also Duty; Moral Obligation; "Ought"

Moral Good/Goodness, 9, 43–59, 127–28, 189, 229, 270–71, 276, 336
    Of Acts and Choices, 19–20, 105, 198, 287
    see also Good/Goodness; Life, Morally Good; Ultimate Good

Moral Ideals, 187, 234, 374, 376, 377, 379
    Achievement of, 234, 313, 323
    Dewey's Concept of, 232
    Of Human Nature, 270
    Kant's Concept of, 315–16
    Nietzsche's, 248, 254

Normative, 247
Objective, 278
Plato's, 294–95
Spinoza's, 271–72
Transcendent, 380

Moral Inquiry, 1–4

Morality, 190, 316, 337
  Bradley's Concept of, 303
  God as Locus of, 341
  Greek, 350–51
  Hegel's Concept of, 300, 301, 302, 310
  Human, 92, 224
  Kant's Concept of, 317–26
  Natural, 369
  Nietzsche's Concept of, 256
  Objective Criterion of, 379
  Reason as Standard for, 220
  Self-Legislated, 237–39, 247
  Sentimental Basis for, 69–70
  Social, 82
  Subjective-Objective Balance in, 226–27
  see also Master-Morality of the Aristocrats; Slave Morality of the Masses

Moral Justification, 82, 101, 102, 231, 242, 365

Moral Law
  Authority of, 325–26
  God as Locus of, 335, 341
  Kant's Concept of, 313
  Knowledge of, 317–18, 327–28
  As Law of Reason, 318–21
  Rational Intelligibility of, 332–35
  Respect for, 320, 323–25, 329, 330–31
  Self-Legislated, 237–39, 247
  Thomas Aquinas's Concept of, 357–70
  Universal Principle of, 328, 333–34, 336
  see also Law(s)

Moral Necessity, 118, 156

Moral Objectivism. *See* Ethical Objectivism

Moral Obligation, 9–11, 48–49, 53, 59, 96, 253, 300, 379
  Agents', 260, 275, 357
  Aristotle's Concept of, 220
  Commitment to God as, 355–57
  Hedonistic Views of, 197–99, 201–2
  Interpersonal, 253, 367
  Kant's Concept of, 328–29
  Moral Permissibility *vs.*, 329–30
  Normative, 247
  Objective, 333–34
  Personal Freedom and, 271–72
  Principles of, 171–73, 189–90
  Universal Law of, 96, 183, 254, 336
  Virtues Involving, 216–17
  see also Moral Duty

Moral Philosophy, 44, 47–48, 56, 377
  Aristotle's, 210, 218–20, 340, 359
  Augustine's, 354–55
  Christian, 341–42, 343
  Concepts and Principles, 1–13, 57–58, 164, 171–73
  Hegel's, 300
  Kant's, 316–17, 322, 326, 328, 380
  Moral Duty as Element of, 202
  Naturalistic, 177–78
  Nietzsche's, 251–52
  Plato's, 289–90
  Spinoza's, 262–65
  Thomas Aquinas's, 366–68
  Western Tradition, 169
  see also Philosophy

Moral Principles, 9–11, 76, 79, 82–83, 164–65, 189–90
  Applied to Moral Choices, 59, 67
  Dewey's Concept of, 230–31
  Hedonistic Influences, 199
  Impulsive, 253–54
  Intelligibility of, 281
  Moral Claims and, 90
  Nature and, 177–78
  Objective, 247, 375
  A Priori, 317–18
  Situationally Relative, 228
  Transcendent, 353
  Ultimate, 96, 98–99
  see also Principles

Index

Moral Properties, Unique, 43–44

Moral Responsibility, 107–65, 232–33
  Agent Causality View of, 124, 130–37, 160
  Agents', 110–22, 126, 146–47, 183, 229, 248, 271–72, 274–75, 310–11, 322
  Determinism and, 114–23, 125
  Human Beings', 125, 363, 369
  Individual, 238–39, 323, 334
  Legitimacy of, 153–54
  Limitations on, 207
  Meanings of, 147–52
  Moral Goodness and, 127–28
  Morally Relevant Sense of, 135–36
  Normative, 247
  Objective, 103, 133, 164, 165
  Personal Freedom and, 109–15, 164, 242, 271–72, 278, 349–50, 355–56
  Problems of, 108
  Resolution of Problems Concerning, 123–28
  Rigorous Determinism *vs.*, 165
  see also Act(s), Moral Responsibility for; Human Beings, Moral Responsibility of

Moral Right/Rightness, 9, 10–11, 22, 40, 51, 53–54, 56, 92, 328
  Of Acts and Choices, 19–20, 29, 47–48, 51, 198, 303, 319

Moral Thinking (Hare), 83

Moral Truth(s), 9, 58, 66–67, 95, 96–98, 165, 247, 275
  see also Truth(s)

Moral Value(s), 5, 9, 52, 76
  Aristotle's Concept of, 217
  Dewey's Concept of, 226–29
  Empirical Theory of, 230
  Hedonistic View of, 179, 187
  Intrinsic, 320–21, 367
  Judgments of, 169–70
  Nature as, 177–78
  Nietzsche's Concept of, 248
  Self-Legislated, 238–39

  Subjective-Relative Relationship of, 234–35
  Ultimate Principle of, 96, 102–3, 127, 279–80

Moral Worth, 127, 170, 278
  Of Acts, 46–54, 72, 104–5
  Of Desires, 234–35
  Grounds of, 188, 280, 291
  Intrinsic, 226, 229, 232–36, 295, 312–13, 320–21, 328–30, 336, 341, 367
  Of Pleasure, 194–95
  Power as Basis of, 259–60, 375–76

Motivations/Motives, 217, 304, 315–16
  Agent Causality View of, 125–26, 129–31, 134
  Alternative, 146, 157, 160
  Duty as, 48, 129–30
  Equilibrium of, 156–57
  Hedonistic, 185–86, 191–93
  Moral, 50–51, 53–55, 66–67, 71–72, 82, 330, 334
  Moral Responsibility and, 112–13, 129–30, 134, 156, 160
  Non-Rational, 253
  Personal Freedom and, 242
  Psychological, 258
  see also Intentions

Nation-States, 311

Naturalism, 26, 173–74, 177–278, 354, 384. *see also* Ethical Naturalism; Hedonistic Naturalism; Humanistic Naturalism; Meta-Ethical Naturalism; Normative Ethical Naturalism; Religious Naturalism

Naturalistic Definism, 25–28, 32–37, 58, 104, 178, 187, 316
  see also Definism

Naturalistic Determinism, 116–17, 123, 135
  see also Determinism

404

Index

Naturalistic Fallacy, 37–38, 39

Natural Order, Doctrine of, 174, 203, 243, 279–80, 364, 367

Natural Uniformity, Doctrine of, 28

Nature, 10, 121, 278
    Absolute Proceeding Out of, 298, 299
    As Context for Principles and Values, 177–78
    God as, 263–64, 266, 268, 269, 270, 324
    Grace and, 368–39
    Knowledge of, 272
    Laws of, 116–17, 118, 123, 135–36, 147
    Perfect Order of, 174, 363–64
    Thomas Aquinas's Concept of, 357–70

Necessary Self-Determination, 113, 115, 117, 120

Necessitarianism. *See* Logic Necessitarianism

Necessity, 117, 118, 156, 162–63, 250, 302–3
    Freedom and, 2, 114, 306
    see also Logical Necessity; Moral Necessity

Neo-Platonism. *See* Plato

Neutral Criterion View, 6

Newton, Sir Isaac, Gravitational Theory, 94

Nietzsche, Friedrich
    Ethics, 254, 258, 259–61
    Evolutionary Humanism and, 204, 248–62
    Morality, 253, 256
    Sartre Compared with, 249, 254, 260–61

Nominalism, 289–90

Non-Being, 344–47

Non-Cognitivism, 63–105
    Attitudinalism and, 73–81
    Cognitivism *vs.*, 17–24, 81, 85, 87
    Critical Responses, 30–31, 383
    Descriptive Relativism and, 65–73
    Emotivism and, 73–81
    Linguistic, 74–75
    Qualified Objectivist, 81–103
    see also Meta-Ethical Non-Cognitivism

Non-Descriptivism. *See* Meta-Ethical Non-Cognitivism

Non-Existence. *See* Non-Being

Nonmoral Terms, as Equivalents of Ethical Terms, 17, 18–19, 25, 27–28, 31–34, 36–44

Non-Normative Discourse, 18, 21

Normative Content Thesis, Meta-Ethical Naturalism and, 26–27

Normative Discourse. *See* Moral Discourse

Normative Ethical Hedonism, 316
    see also Ethical Hedonism

Normative Ethical Idealism, 174, 279–337
    Absolute Idealism and, 281, 297–313
    General Aspects, 279–80
    Metaphysical Orientation, 281–97
    Postulational Orientation, 281, 313–37
    Transcendent Realm and, 279–81
    see also Ethical Idealism; Ethical Naturalism

Normative Ethical Naturalism, 177–278, 280–81, 337, 379, 380, 384
    Doctrine of Real Essences, 213
    Evolutionary Humanism and, 248–62
    Existential Humanism and, 236–48
    Hedonistic, 178–202
    Humanistic Naturalism and, 202–62
    Metaphysical Naturalism and, 177–78
    Naturalistic Definism and, 177–78
    Pragmatic Humanism and, 220–36
    Realistic Humanism and, 204–20
    Reality and, 177–78
    Religious Naturalism and, 262–78
    see also Ethical Naturalism

Normative Ethical Objectivism, 261
    see also Ethical Objectivism

Normative Ethical Relativism, 96
    see also Radical Ethical Relativism

Index

Normative Ethical Theism, 339–81
    Aquinas's Concept of, 341, 357–70
    Augustine's Concept of, 341, 342–57
    Conclusions, 380–81
    Evil and, 342–57
    Freedom and, 342–57
    Goodness and, 342–57
    Grace and, 357–70
    Hebrew-Christian Tradition, 340–41
    Kierkegaard's Concept of, 341, 370–81
    Moral Law and, 357–70
    Nature, 357–70
    Perspectives, 339–42
    Purity of Heart and, 370–81
    Subjectivity and, 370–81
    see also Ethical Theism; Theism

Normative Ethics, 8, 11–12, 26–27, 82, 90–91
    Evaluation of, 383–85
    Evolutionary Humanism, 173–74
    Hedonism, 43, 200–202
    Idealism, 174, 279–337
    Judgments, 44, 46
    Meta-Ethics Distinguished from, 169–73
    Metaphysics and, 280–81
    Plato's, 290, 295
    Spinoza's, 264, 265, 275
    Theism, 339–81
    Theories of, 29, 169–75, 190–91, 316, 377
    Ultimate Good in Terms of, 60, 284
    see also Ethical Objectivism, Normative Ethics and; Ethics

Normative Terms, 17–21, 81, 170
    see also Ethical Terms

Nothing, Notion of, 343–44, 345–47, 359

Noumena, 314, 323, 327–28, 333

Objective Approximationism, 6

Objective Mind, Doctrine of, 300, 309

Objective Property Approach, 87–89, 91

Objectivism. *See* Ethical Objectivism

Objectivitivism. *See* Radical Ethical Objectivism; Rigorous Objectivism

Objectivity, 234–35, 341, 373
    see also Rational Objectivity

Objects, 5, 163, 284–86, 315–16, 326–28

Occam's Razor, 147

Omniscience, 160–61, 163

Ontology, 5

Open-Question Arguments, 36–37

Opinions, 10, 35, 96, 103, 172, 225

Options, Live, 129, 130, 132

"Ought"
    Ethical/Moral Uses, 43, 74, 197, 238, 247, 260, 318, 322, 323, 380
    Nonmoral Uses, 18–19, 316–17
    see also "Is-Ought" Thesis

Pain, 37, 68, 195, 225
    Absence of, 26–27, 173
    Aristotle on, 211–12
    Minimizing, 25, 46, 179, 180, 181, 183, 185–87, 192, 197–98, 200–202
    see also Pleasure

Pantheism, 160–61, 343
    Spinoza's, 269, 270–71, 275
    Stoic, 118

Paralogisms, 328

Particulars, 204, 243, 245, 282–83, 344–35, 359, 360, 371
    Empirical, 289, 290–91, 296–97
    see also Essence(s); Universals

Passions, 67, 217–18, 287
    Control of, 206, 207, 209, 211, 214, 216
    Emotional Bondage to, 265–69, 277
    Frustrated, 272–73
    Knowledge of, 276

Passivistic Hedonism, 180

Past, Actual, 116–17, 123, 135–36, 147, 161

Paul (Apostle), 385

Peace, 265, 352–53, 354

Perfection
    Divine, 269, 335, 345–47, 356, 361
    Moral, 265, 270–71, 324

Perry, Ralph Barton, 29

Personal Freedom, 107–65
    Agents', 10, 53, 109, 227–28, 246, 278, 349–50, 361, 369
    Edwards on, 157–58
    Foreknowledge's Effects on, 160–61
    Illusory, 374–75
    Morally Relevant Sense of, 115, 117, 120, 122, 124–26, 135–36, 306, 326, 384
    Moral Responsibility and, 109–15, 164, 242, 271–72, 278, 350, 355–57
    Problems of, 108
    Radical, 237–42, 246, 249
    Resolution of Problems, 123–28
    Rigorous Determinism vs., 235, 273, 276, 355–56
    see also Agent Causality View of Personal Freedom; Contra-Causal View of Personal Freedom

Personhood, 3–4, 203, 279, 328
    see also Human Beings; Self, The

Phenomena, 314, 322–23, 327
    Knowledge of, 332–33, 333, 337

Philosopher-Kings, 295

Philosophers, True, 287

Philosophical Ethics, 3–4, 6–13, 340

Philosophical Idealism, 114

Philosophy, 5–8, 121, 148, 237, 358
    Central Concerns, 9–13, 171
    Hegel's, 298–99, 306–8, 377
    Kant's, 313, 377, 378–79
    Metaphysical, 315–16

    Objectivity in, 341
    Study of, 184–85
    see also Moral Philosophy

Philosophy of Religion, 381

Physicalistic Determinism, 116–17, 122–23, 124, 135

Pierce, Charles Sanders, 93

Plato, 169, 313, 326, 377
    Augustine as Follower of, 342–45, 354–55, 358
    Essentialism, 204, 281–97, 344–45
    Ethics, 290, 295
    Metaphysics, 289, 316
    Moral Philosophy, 289–90
    Rationalistic Apriorism, 291–92
    Theory of Absolute Ideas, 282–83, 286
    On Ultimate Good, 213, 220, 284–88, 291–92, 295–97, 342–43, 344
    Virtues Doctrine, 293–95

Pleasure
    Aristotle's Concept of, 211–12, 220
    Bodily, 196–97
    Emotional, 268
    Ethical Hedonism and, 179–81, 184–85, 188–202
    Experiences of, 68, 225
    Goodness and, 19, 26–27, 43, 173, 178–79, 377, 384
    Maximizing, 25, 31, 37, 46, 179, 183, 185–87, 192–93, 197–98, 200, 201–2
    Mental, 183–85, 196–97
    Qualitative vs. Quantitative, 183–88
    For Self and Others, 47, 180–83
    As Standard of Moral Judgment, 201–2
    see also Pain

Plotinus, Philosophy of, 342

Political Institutions, 286–87, 295, 303, 352–53

Positivism. See Logical Positivism

Postulational Orientation, Ethical Idealism, 174, 281, 313–37

Index

Postulational Orientation (cont.),
    Critical Response to, 326–37
    Summary of, 313–26

Power
    Of God, 374
    Principle of, 251–52, 252, 258, 259–61

Pragmatic Humanism, 204, 220–36
    Critical Response to, 228–36
    Realistic Humanism Compared to, 220–23
    Summary of, 220–28

Praise, Moral, 66, 68

Precepts-Concepts Relationship, 6

Predestination, 365–66
    see also Electionism

Preferences, 10, 35, 82–83, 172
    As Grounds for Moral Claims, 225
    Hedonistic, 188, 193
    Moral Beliefs Originating from, 101, 262
    Rightness or Wrongness of, 90–91
    Role in Moral Claims, 67–69, 72, 96, 103, 240

Price, Richard, 42

Prichard, H.A., 42, 47–49, 51, 53

Priest-Philosophers, 252

Principia Ethica (Moore), 37–38

Principles
    Abstract, 379
    Ethical, 313
    Formal Rational, 367
    Kant's, 315–16
    Objective, 238
    Obstructive, 252
    Power as Basis of, 258
    A Priori, 250
    Right/Good, 104–5, 303
    Societal, 82–83
    Ultimate, 171–73
    Universal, 236–37, 371
    see also A Priori Principles; Moral Principles

Probability, 111, 126

Problems
    Moral, 195, 224–25
    Resolution of, 123–28

Promises, Making, 216, 317–19, 320

Propensities, 217–18, 225–26, 228–30, 233–34
    Control of, 206, 207, 209, 214, 216, 231–33

Property, Hegel's Concept of, 300–301

Property Doctrine, 23, 28, 30–44, 91
    Cognitivism and, 25, 57
    Definism and, 30–31, 95
    Nonmoral-Moral Equivalencies, 37–38
    Rejection of, 42, 63

Property Statements, 22–23, 29–31, 33, 43–44, 45, 87–89

Propinquity, 180

Propositions
    Contradictory, 308
    Empirically *vs.* Logically Determinate, 77, 78, 89
    False, 254–56
    Non-Ethical Terms Replacing, 20, 27, 30
    Of Rigorous Determinism, 149
    Self-Contradictory, 100–101
    As Truth Claims, 21–23, 57, 170
    Truth or Falsity of, 66–67, 74, 77, 97–98, 137–39, 188, 193, 194, 308–9
    see also Ethical Statements

Prudence, 5, 189, 350

Psychological Hedonism, 185–88, 189, 191–94, 199, 200–201

Purity of Heart, Kierkegaard's Concept of, 370–81

Purpose, 264, 360, 377
    Intention and, 301, 310
    Moral, 324, 347, 356

Qualified Objectivist Non-Cognitivism, 81–103
    Critical Response to, 87–103
    Summary of, 81–87

Radical Empirical Epistemology, 73, 98

Radical Epistemological Relativism, 249, 254
    Nietzsche's Concept of, 260–62

Radical Ethical Objectivism, 103, 270–71

Radical Ethical Relativism, 75, 84, 172, 209–10, 261–62, 278, 366
    Criticisms of, 36, 383–84
    Ethical Objectivism *vs.*, 95–96, 99–101, 105, 127, 164–65, 225–27, 234–36
    Hedonism Compared to, 201
    Rejection of, 312
    Sartre's Concept of, 246, 247
    Spinoza's Concept of, 265

Radical Personal Freedom, 237–42, 246, 249

Radical Subjectivism, 236–40, 244, 246, 261

Rational Empiricism, 6, 325
    Kant's Concept of, 313–14

Rationalism, 306, 340, 341

Rationalistic Apriorism, 291–92, 313–14, 316, 326

Rationalistic Deductivism, 228

Rationalistic Definism, 26, 28, 31, 36, 58

Rationalistic Idealism, 174

Rationalist Thesis, 66–68

Rationality, 222–23, 262, 299
    Aristotle's Concept of, 205–6, 209–11, 214, 217, 218–20

Rational Necessity, 302–3

Rational Objectivity, 140–42, 236–40, 250, 262, 366–67
    Kierkegaard's Rejection of, 370–71, 378

Of Moral Judgments, 193–94, 196, 288, 312
    Nietzsche's rejection of, 249, 253–56
    Sartre's Concept of, 240, 242–45

Rational Plausibility, 126

Rational Universality, 84

Rawls, John, 181

Realistic Humanism, 204–223
    Critical Response to, 214–20
    Pragmatic Humanism Compared to, 220–23
    Summary of, 204–14

Reality, 5, 8, 177, 277
    Absolute as, 299
    Actualization of, 174, 312
    Determination of, 118–20
    Divine, 135, 253, 269–70, 270–71
    Kierkegaard's Concept of, 371
    Objective, 332
    Opposing Viewpoints on, 250–51
    Ultimate, 284, 291, 342–43, 344

Reason
    Agents', 210, 217
    Categories of, 277
    As Criterion for Judgments, 219–20
    Divine, 363
    Foundations of, 58
    As Framework for Self-Direction, 3
    Functions of, 206
    Hume's Definition of, 71–72
    Laws of, 318–21
    Logically Appropriate, 81–82
    Moral, 45, 66–68, 197, 220, 230–31
    Practical, 322–24, 332, 337
    Principles of, 6, 145, 159, 192, 203, 224, 243–44, 255, 286, 312, 317–18, 370
    A Priori Principle of, 287–89, 325, 327–29
    Virtue of, 293
    see also "Good Reasons" Approach

Reasonable Claim Principle, 301

Index

Reconciliation
  In Absolute Spirit, 307–9, 311–12
  Hegel's Concept of, 297–99, 302

Reconstruction of the Christian Revelation Claim, The (Hackett), 364

Redemption, 265–66, 268–69, 271, 369–70
  In Jesus Christ, 351, 357, 364–65, 367, 370, 376

Relations, Hume's Definition of, 71–72

Relationships
  Personal, 312–13
  Social, 203, 299, 300, 310–11

Relativism. *See* Descriptive Relativism; Ethical Relativism; Radical Ethical Relativism; Situational Relativism

Religion, 10, 121, 299, 381

Religious Determinism, 118–19, 121, 123, 124, 135, 161

Religious-Metaphysical Definism, 26, 28, 36

Religious Naturalism, 262–78
  Critical Response to, 269–77
  Summary of, 262–69

Republic, The (Plato), 281, 282–83

Resentment, Morality of, 252

Responses, 96, 103
  Ethical/Moral, 75, 225
  Human, 10, 35, 66, 172, 231–32
  Unified, 233–34

Restraint, 2, 8, 111, 156, 259

Resurrection of Theism (Hackett), 73, 243n3

Righteousness, 336, 347, 356–57

Right/Rightness, 44–57
  Bradley's Concept of, 305–6
  Goodness Related to, 44–45, 49, 104–5, 196
  Meaning of, 31–32, 37, 43
  Objective, 54, 366–67
  Properties of, 87–88
  Subjective, 54
  Testing, 30, 31–32
  Transcendent, 279–80
  Wrongness *vs.,* 66, 122, 196, 299, 301, 312, 329–30, 375
  see also Moral Rightness; Ultimate Right

Rigorous Determinism, 109, 115, 117–18, 333, 384
  Acts and Choices Influenced by, 156, 160
  Agent Causality View and, 127–28, 130–31, 146–47
  Dewey's Concept of, 227
  Falsity of, 131, 134–37, 139–40
  Foreknowledge's Effects on, 161, 163
  Moral Responsibility and, 114
  Nietzsche's Concept of, 249, 260–61
  Personal Freedom *vs.,* 235, 273, 276, 355–56
  Rejection of, 145, 148, 152–55, 159, 164, 165, 273
  Spinoza's Concept of, 264–65, 269–73, 275, 276–77

Rigorous Objectivism, 226–27

Roman Catholicism, 358
  see also Christianity/Christians

Ross, David, 50–51

Ross, Sir William David, 42

Rules
  Consequences of, 39
  Deontological/Teleological Assessments of, 43–47
  Empirical, 316–17
  Moral, 30, 96, 99, 224, 228, 230–31, 318
  Obstructive, 252
  Rightness or Wrongness of, 10–11, 164, 179
  Universalization of, 18, 27, 28, 32, 318–20
  Utilitarian, 181–82
  see also Imperatives/Imperativism

Russell, Bertrand, Philosophers Following, 308–9

Index

Salvation. *See* Redemption

Sartre, Jean-Paul
- Existential Humanism, 204, 236–48
- Nietzsche Compared to, 249, 254, 260–61

Satisfaction, 191, 194–95, 223, 226, 289, 325

Scheler, Max, 290

Science, 117, 145, 148, 358

Scientific Empiricism, 73

Scientific Knowledge, 228

Scientific Method, 221

Self, The
- Actualization of, 173–74, 236, 239, 246–47, 249, 293–95, 304, 312
- Aspects of, 288–89
- Corruption of, 348–49
- Integrated, 229, 376–79, 384
- Moral, 274–75, 331
- Personal, 146, 300
- *see also* Ego; Human Beings; Individual, The; Personhood

Self-Consciousness, 142–45, 219, 232, 299, 300

Self-Control, 180, 289

Self-Determination, 113–14
- As Agent Causality, 129–31, 134, 137–40, 142–44, 146, 156–60
- Moral, 301–2, 322
- Necessary, 113, 115, 117, 120
- Personal Freedom as, 112–13, 123, 125, 137, 165, 306
- Rational, 310–11, 360
- Of the Will, 304

Self-Direction, 3, 288, 362–64

Self-Discipline, 330–31, 334, 362

Self-Interest, 69, 71, 183, 186, 188, 217, 317, 319, 320, 328, 363

Self-Realization, 293, 295, 303–5

Sensibility, *A Priori* Forms of, 314

Sensualistic Indulgence, 179–80, 184, 191, 202

Sentimentalist Thesis, 66–72

Sentiments. *See* Feelings

Serenity, 180, 272, 273

Sidgwick, Henry, 42, 42n1, 59–60, 181, 189–90, 199

Sin, 375, 376

Situational Relativism, 96, 210, 228, 231

Slave Morality of the Masses, 249, 251–52, 258–59

Smart, J.J.G., 181

Social Ethics, 310
- Hegel's Concept of, 300, 302

Social Order/Society
- Harmony in, 221, 222, 384
- Moral, 82, 225
- Well-Ordered, 186, 212
- *see also* Political Institutions; Whole, The

Socrates, 292

Soft Determinism, 109

Soul, 287–89, 345
- Belief in, 322
- Corruption of, 346, 348–49
- Kant's Concept of, 315
- Knowledge of, 328
- Peace of, 352
- World, 297, 343

Space. *See* Universe, Space-Time Properties

Spinoza, Baruch (Benedict), 169, 196
- On Determinism, 120–21
- Ethics, 264, 265–66, 269, 275
- Metaphysics, 264–65, 269–70, 273, 275, 277
- Moral Philosophy, 262–65
- Religious Naturalism, 262–78
- Rigorous Determinism, 264–65, 269–73, 275, 276–77

Spirit, 160–61, 174, 287–89
- *see also* Absolute Spirit

Index

Spirit-Geist, 299
  see also Absolute Mind
Standards, 3, 6–7, 12, 90, 172–73, 180, 183, 191, 193
Stevenson, Charles Leslie, 73, 76–77, 79, 103
Strong Compatibilism, 109, 112, 114, 120, 156
  Author's View as, 123–24
Subjective Property Approach, 87, 88–89
Subjective Relativism, 226–27, 240, 244–45, 251, 254
Subjectivism
  Ethical, 75, 95, 261
  Kierkegaard's Concept of, 370–81
  Radical, 236–40, 244, 246, 261
Substance, 121, 263–64, 266, 268, 317
Substantive Ethics, 8, 11–12, 82
Summa Theologica (Thomas Aquinas), 357–58
Summum Bonum. See Ultimate Good
Superman, Nietzsche's Concept of, 248
Symbolic, The, 299
Synthetic Aposteriorism, 314–15
Synthetic Apriorism, 5, 6, 314–15, 316, 317–18, 325, 327

Teleological Determinism, 118–19, 121, 123, 124, 161
Teleology, 179, 196, 383
  Intuitionism and, 44–57, 60, 104–5, 164–65
Temperance, 208, 209, 288–89, 293, 350, 362
Theism, 10, 160–61, 324
  Christian, 349, 354–55, 373, 381
  Hebrew-Christian, 118
  Kant's Concept of, 334–37
  Kierkegaard's Concept of, 237
  See also Ethical Theism; Metaphysical Theism; Normative Ethical Theism; Pantheism
Theology, 119, 343–44, 358, 374
Thomas Aquinas, Saint, 169
  Augustine Compared with, 358–61, 362, 365–67, 380
  Critical Response to, 366–70
  Ethical Theism, 341–42, 357–70
  Historical Background, 357–59
  Moral Philosophy, 367–68
  Philosophical Tradition of, 175, 243
  Theism, 379
Thought, 240, 263–64, 274, 292
Thought/Extension Identity, 263, 269, 270, 273–74
  see also Mind; Mind/Body Identity
Time. *See* Universe, Space-Time Properties
Toulmin, Stephen E., 82–83, 87–89, 90, 181
Traditional Empiricism, 313, 326
Tranquility, 180, 267–68, 276
Transcendental Idealism, 281
Transformation, Moral, 367, 376
Treatise on Free Will (Augustine), 341, 350–51, 355, 356
Treatise on the Trinity (Augustine), 341
Triads, Dialectic of, 297–301, 309
Triangularity, 282, 285
Truth(s), 120, 170, 193
  Assessing, 5, 31–34, 36, 39–40, 43, 308
  Determination of, 74, 75, 77
  Empirical, 58, 73, 95
  Of Ethical Propositions, 22, 23, 86–87, 100
  Falsity *vs.*, 139–40
  Of Goodness, 303
  Kierkegaard's Concept of, 372–73
  Knowledge of, 193, 362
  Logical, 95

Metaphysical, 325
Nietzsche's Concept of, 252, 253–55
Objective, 7, 140–41, 236–37, 249, 257
Philosophical, 312
Subjective, 237, 378
Thomas Aquinas on, 357–58
Total, 121, 298–99, 307
Ultimate, 250, 284, 291, 373
Value of, 100
see also Moral Truth(s)

Truth Claims, 6, 21–23
Assessing, 28–32, 171, 370
Christian, 381
Ethical/Moral, 57–58, 63–64, 74, 78, 98, 164–65
Impulsive, 250
Justification of, 137
Logical Status of, 240
Moral Judgments as, 66–67
Objective, 378

Ultimate Good, 52, 60, 246
Absolute Mind as, 367
Absolute Spirit as, 299
Aristotle's Concept, 221, 222, 223
Augustine's Concept, 344, 352
Dewey's Concept, 222, 230–31
God as, 335–36, 339, 345, 348, 350–57, 360–61, 363–64, 375–80, 384
Hegel's Concept, 302, 309, 310
Humanistic Naturalism and, 203
Kant's Concept, 18, 324–25
Knowledge of, 288, 293
Natural Order Related to, 170–75, 177
Plato's Concept, 213, 220, 284–88, 291–92, 295–97, 342–43, 344
Pleasure as, 26, 179, 187, 194–95, 199, 211–12
Power as, 259–61
Spinoza's Concept, 265, 269, 271, 276, 278
Transcendence of, 380–31

see also Good/Goodness; Moral Goodness

Ultimate Right, 52, 60, 170–75, 246
Hegel's Concept of, 300
Moral Sense of, 179–80
Nature and, 177, 367
Theories Regarding, 194–95
Transcendence of, 380–81
see also Right/Rightness

Ultimate Value, 60, 90–91, 104–5, 164, 170–75, 279–80, 299

Universal Determinism, 227, 273

Universalistic Hedonism, 181–82, 199–200

Universalization Principle, 45, 66, 318–20, 328–29, 330, 332, 384
see also Principles, Universal

Universals, 282–83, 290–91
see also Essence(s)

Universe, 116–17, 118
Space-Time Properties, 177, 277, 296, 299, 339

Utilitarian Hedonism, 181–82, 189–90, 199–200, 201

Utilitarianism, 82–83, 225

Valuational Relativism, 100–101

Value(s), 4–5, 223
Aristotle's Concept of, 204–5, 220
Of Consequences, 164
Interest Theory of, 29–30
Intrinsic, 321
Judgments of, 169–70
Moral, 79, 226–27
Of Pleasure, 194–95
Power as Locus of, 251, 258
Relativistic, 172
Sartre's Concept of, 240–41
see also Moral Value(s); Ultimate Value

Van Inwagen, Peter, 135–36

Index

Vice(s), 288, 348
    Virtue(s) Distinguished from, 66, 68, 208–9, 216

Virtue(s), 12, 54, 206–12
    Acquisition of, 211, 217, 287–88, 293, 345
    Aristotle's Concept of, 365
    Of Duty, 216–17
    Intellectual, 206–7, 212, 214, 366
    Moral, 190, 206–14, 276, 289, 293, 324–25, 350–52, 361–62, 366
    Plato's Doctrine of, 293–95
    Vices Distinguished from, 66, 68, 208–9, 216
    Well-Being and, 324–26, 335, 336

Vision, Moral, 353

Volition, 67, 156–63, 280, 350
    see also Will

Voluntarism, 307, 340, 341

Weak Compatibilism, 109, 112, 227, 235

Well-Being, 384
    Hedonistic, 187, 188, 189–90, 199, 200, 201–2
    Human, 173–74, 211–15, 219–20, 222–25, 228, 230, 262, 320, 352, 362, 366
    Moral, 301
    Of Others, 59–60, 102, 181, 199, 203, 295, 303, 305
    Of Self, 52, 59, 102, 181, 304
    Virtue and, 324–26, 335, 336
    see also Happiness

Whitehead, Alfred North, 290

Whole, The, 295, 300, 304–6, 306, 310
    Hegel's Concept of, 299, 302–3
    see also Social Order/Society

Wickedness. *See* Evil

Will
    Contingency of, 227
    Corruption of, 348–51
    Of God, 326, 341, 343–44
    Good, 347, 350–51
    Individual, 300–303
    To Power, 252
    Rational, 324
    Training of, 286
    Universal, 300, 302–5
    see also Free Will; Volition

Wisdom, 210, 287, 288, 293, 295, 345, 362

Wittgenstein, Ludwig, 148–52, 289

World Order, 369–70, 371
    Contingent, 339, 344, 346–47, 356, 368, 373

Worldviews, 7
    Alternative, 307
    Christian, 358, 381
    Kant's, 315
    Metaphysical, 30, 173, 280–81
    Transcendental Religious, 118–19, 121, 135, 161

Worth, 172, 204–5
    see also Human Beings, Intrinsic Worth of; Moral Worth

Wrong/Wrongness, 10–11, 195
    Bradley's Concept of, 305
    Hegel's Concept of, 310
    Moral, 19–20, 22, 270–71
    Right/Rightness *vs.*, 66, 122, 196, 299, 301, 312, 329–30, 375

www.ingramcontent.com/pod-product-compliance
Lightning Source LLC
Chambersburg PA
CBHW071228290426
44108CB00013B/1331